Lecture Notes in Computer Science 12005

More information about this series at http://www.springer.com/series/7407

Luís Soares Barbosa · Alexandru Baltag (Eds.)

Dynamic Logic

New Trends and Applications

Second International Workshop, DaLí 2019
Porto, Portugal, October 7–11, 2019
Proceedings

Springer

Editors
Luís Soares Barbosa
University of Minho
Braga, Portugal

Alexandru Baltag
Institute for Logic, Language and Computation
University of Amsterdam
Amsterdam, Noord-Holland, The Netherlands

ISSN 0302-9743 ISSN 1611-3349 (electronic)
Lecture Notes in Computer Science
ISBN 978-3-030-38807-2 ISBN 978-3-030-38808-9 (eBook)
https://doi.org/10.1007/978-3-030-38808-9

LNCS Sublibrary: SL1 – Theoretical Computer Science and General Issues

This Springer imprint is published by the registered company Springer Nature Switzerland AG
The registered company address is: Gewerbestrasse 11, 6330 Cham, Switzerland

Preface

Building on the pioneer intuitions of Floyd-Hoare Logic, Dynamic Logic was introduced in the 70s to reason about, and verify, classic imperative programs. Since then, the original intuitions gave rise to an entire family of logics, which became increasingly popular for reasoning about a wide range of computational systems. Simultaneously, their object (i.e. the very notion of a program) evolved in unexpected ways. This leads to the emergence of a number of dynamic logics tailored to specific programming paradigms and extended to new computing domains, including probabilistic, continuous, and quantum computation.

Both its theoretical relevance and applied potential have made Dynamic Logic a topic of interest for a number of scientific venues, from wide-scope software engineering conferences to events focused more specifically on modal logics. DaLí, however, is the first international workshop series entirely devoted to this area. Its first edition, published as LNCS volume 10669, held in Brasília, Brazil, during September 23–24, 2017, colocated with TABLEAUX, FroCoS, and ITP, was praised for filling a gap, fostering synergies, and providing a forum for the dissemination of new trends and applications. With this second workshop, the series seems to have reached a stage of maturity, able to attract submissions from different groups and trends in the community.

The workshop was held in Porto, Portugal, on October 9, 2019, as part of the Formal Methods Week which hosted the Third World Congress on Formal Methods. Dexter Kozen, from Cornell University, gave the invited lecture, entitled "On Free ω -Continuous and Regular Ordered Algebras."

This volume contains the revised versions of 12 submissions, out of 26, accepted for publication as full papers, plus 2 short papers reporting on-going work from doctoral students. All submissions were blind-reviewed by three referees and subject to a careful and participated discussion within the Program Committee, afterwards. As in 2017, a special issue on the workshop theme, to appear in the Journal of Logical and Algebraic Methods in Programming, is currently under preparation.

The workshop was promoted and partially funded by DaLí (POCI-01-0145-FEDER-016692), a research project supported by the European Regional Development Fund through the Operational Programme for Competitiveness and Internationalisation, COMPETE 2020, and by the Portuguese funding agency, FCT - Fundação para a Ciência e a Tecnologia.

The editors would like to express their gratitude to the authors who submitted their work to DaLí 2019, as well as to all members of the Program Committee. The end result in your hands would not have been possible without their effort and commitment.

November 2019

Alexandru Baltag
Luís S. Barbosa

Preface

Organization

Program Committee Chairs

Alexandru Baltag	Universiteit van Amsterdam, The Netherlands
Luís S. Barbosa	Universidade do Minho, Portugal

Program Committee

Guillaume Aucher	Université de Rennes, France
Carlos Areces	Universidad Nacional de Córdoba, Argentina
Mário Benevides	Universidade federal do Rio de Janeiro, Brazil
Johan van Benthem	Stanford University, USA, and Tsinghua University, China
Patrick Blackburn	University of Roskilde, Denmark
Thomas Bolander	Technical University of Denmark, Denmark
Zoe Christoff	University of Bayreuth, Germany
Fredrik Dahlqvist	University College London, UK
Hans van Ditmarsch	Loria, France
Nina Gierasimczuk	Danish Technical University, Denmark
Valentin Goranko	University of Stockholm, Sweden
Davide Grossi	University of Groningen, The Netherlands
Reiner Hähnle	Technischen Universitäten Darmstadt, Germany
Rolf Hennicker	Ludwig-Maximilians-Universität München, Germany
Andreas Herzig	Université Paul Sabatier, France
Dexter Kozen	Cornell University, USA
Clemens Kupke	University of Strathclyde, UK
Alexandre Madeira	Universidade de Aveiro, Portugal
Manuel A. Martins	Universidade de Aveiro, Portugal
Paulo Mateus	Universidade de Lisboa, Portugal
Stefan Mitsch	Carnegie Mellon University, USA
Renato Neves	Universidade do Minho, Portugal
Valéria de Paiva	Nuance Comms, USA
Aybuke Ozgün	Universiteit van Amsterdam, The Netherlands
Fernando Velazquez-Quesada	Universiteit van Amsterdam, The Netherlands
Olivier Roy	University of Bayreuth, Germany
Lutz Schröder	Friedrich-Alexander-Universität, Germany
Alexandra Silva	University College London, UK
Sonja Smets	Universiteit van Amsterdam, The Netherlands
Rui Soares Barbosa	University of Oxford, UK
Tinko Tinchev	Sofia University, Bulgaria
Renata Wassermann	Universidade de São Paulo, Brazil

Additional Reviewers

Vitor Machado
Dominic Steinhöfel
Soroush Rafiee Rad
Jens Ulrik Hansen
Eduard Kamburjan

Contents

Regular Papers

Short Papers

Regular Papers

Mechanizing Bisimulation Theorems for Relation-Changing Logics in Coq

Raul Fervari[1,2](✉), Francisco Trucco[1], and Beta Ziliani[1,2]

[1] FaMAF, Universidad Nacional de Córdoba, Córdoba, Argentina
fervari@famaf.unc.edu.ar, franciscoctrucco@gmail.com, beta@mpi-sws.org
[2] Consejo Nacional de Investigaciones Científicas y Técnicas (CONICET), Buenos Aires, Argentina

Abstract. Over the last years, the study of logics that can modify a model while evaluating a formula has gained in interest. Motivated by many examples in practice such as hybrid logics, separation logics and dynamic epistemic logics, the ability of updating a model has been investigated from a more general point of view. In this work, we formalize and verify in the proof assistant Coq, the bisimulation theorems for a particular family of dynamic logics that can change the accessibility relation of a model. The benefits of this formalization are twofold. First, our results apply for a wide variety of dynamic logics. Second, we argue that this is the first step towards the development of a modal logic library in Coq, which allows us to mechanize many relevant results in modal logics.

1 Introduction

Historically, *modal logic* [10,11] has been understood as a logic to reason about different modes of truth. Under this perspective, it can be seen as an extension of propositional logic with *modalities*, that in certain contexts may have some particular interpretations, such as necessity, knowledge, belief, temporality, or obligation, just to name a few. Nowadays, *modal logics* is a term defining a family of logics to reason about relational structures, i.e., to reason about graphs. This is a consequence of the insights provided by the most common semantics for modal logics given in terms of the so-called Kripke structures [26]. In the wide spectrum of existing modal logics, one familiy has gained in interest over the last years: *dynamic modal logics*, i.e., logics that are able to update the model while evaluating the truth of a formula. Some well-known examples of this family are dynamic epistemic logics [37], separation logics [30,31], and hybrid logics [6].

The aforementioned examples of dynamic logics are specific instances designed with a particular goal in mind. Over the last years, there has been an increasing interest in understanding the behaviour of dynamic logics from a more general point of view (see e.g. [3,27,34]). Such perspective allows us to investigate the properties of abstract operators that are the building blocks used to construct concrete modalities, and to obtain a general perspective of the impact of including such kind of operators.

L. Soares Barbosa and A. Baltag (Eds.): DaLí 2019, LNCS 12005, pp. 3–18, 2020.
https://doi.org/10.1007/978-3-030-38808-9_1

Some examples of results about operators that can change the accesibility relation of a model are collected in [18]. In [1,2] various abstract operations are presented, in particular, modalities to delete, add and swap-around an edge (both locally at an evaluation point and globally in the whole model). These logics are called *relation-changing logics*. In such works, particular notions of bisimulation for each operation are defined. A more general approach is taken in [3], where the notion of 'updating a relation' is generalized, and some results can be proved for all the logics encompassed in this framework. Also, the complexity of model checking is studied, whereas satisfiability is investigated in [4] (see also [8,27]). All these results require proofs that are tedious and of high complexity, so it would be interesting to benefit of the use of computational tools in order to guide or verify (parts of) the proofs.

The *Coq proof assistant* [9] is an interactive tool that helps us to perform complex mathematical proofs. It provides a formal language to formalize mathematical definitions, algorithms, theorems and their proofs. One of the main advantages of the Coq assistant, is that it allows us to build mathematical proofs constructively. The underlying logic in Coq is an intuitionistic logic with dependent types, known as *the calculus of inductive constructions (CIC)*. Thanks to the Curry-Howard correspondence, propositions are interpreted as types and proofs are interpreted as programs with the type of the corresponding proposition. Thus, we can say that Coq is essentially a type verifier (see e.g. [25]).

In the last years, several mathematical problems have been solved with the help of interactive tools like Coq; problems whose pen-and-paper proofs where put to doubt due to their complexity. For instance, in [22] a problem from graph theory known as *the four colour problem* was solved with the assistance of Coq. More recently, in [23] the *Kepler conjecture*, an open problem from combinatorial geometry, was proved by using a combination of the proof assistants HOL light [33] and Isabelle [29].

Motivated by examples as those in the last paragraph, we aim to develop a library to formalize and verify formal proofs in modal logic. In particular, we extend the formalization provided in [15] in order to model a particular family of dynamic logics called *relation-changing modal logics*. We introduce a family of dynamic operators, parameterized by a *model update function* that given a relational model, it returns a modified relational model. This follows the definitions introduced in [3,18]. Then we formalize a bisimulation notion which is agnostic with respect to the model update function, and mechanize the proof of the theorem of *invariance under bisimulation*. This theorem establishes that given two models that are related by a bisimulation, they satisfy the same formulas of the corresponding language. We consider this is the first step towards the development of a library for the mechanization of proofs for a wide variety of modal and dynamic logics.

Structure. In Sect. 2 we introduce the syntax and semantics of relation-changing modal logics, in which we have modalities parameterized by a model update function. In Sect. 3 we introduce the notion of bisimulation, and enunciate the invariance theorem. Then we focus on our main contribution: in

Sect. 4 we present the formalization of these results in Coq. We conclude in Sect. 5 with some final remarks and future lines of research.

2 Basic Definitions

The syntax of the family of dynamic modal logics we call herein *relation-changing modal logics*, is a straightforward extension of the propositional logic. Let us introduce their syntax and semantics.

Definition 1 (Syntax). *Let* PROP *be a countable, infinite set of propositional symbols. The set* FORM *of formulas over* PROP *is defined as:*

$$\mathsf{FORM} ::= \bot \mid p \mid \varphi \to \psi \mid \blacklozenge_i \varphi,$$

where $p \in \mathsf{PROP}$, $\blacklozenge_i \in \mathsf{DYN}$ *a set of dynamic operators, and* $\varphi, \psi \in \mathsf{FORM}$. *Other Boolean operators are defined as usual.* $\blacksquare_i \varphi$ *is defined as* $\neg \blacklozenge_i \neg \varphi$.

For $S \subseteq \mathsf{DYN}$ *a set of dynamic operators, we call* $\mathcal{L}(S)$ *the extension of the propositional language allowing also the operators in* S. *If* S *is a singleton set* $S = \{\blacklozenge\}$, *we write* $\mathcal{L}(\blacklozenge)$ *instead of* $\mathcal{L}(\{\blacklozenge\})$.

Semantically, formulas of $\mathcal{L}(S)$ are evaluated in standard relational models.

Definition 2 (Models). *A model* $\mathcal{M}$ *is a triple* $\mathcal{M} = \langle W, R, V \rangle$, *where* W *is the* domain, *a non-empty set whose elements are called points or states;* $R \subseteq W \times W$ *is the* accessibility relation; *and* $V : \mathsf{PROP} \mapsto 2^W$ *is the* valuation.

Let w *be a state in* $\mathcal{M}$, *the pair* $(\mathcal{M}, w)$ *is called a pointed model; we usually drop parentheses and call* $\mathcal{M}, w$ *a pointed model.*

In this article, we restrict ourselves to models with only one accessibility relation (i.e., the underlying modal language has only one modal operator). A generalization to models with multiple accessibility relations is possible, but leads to further choices concerning the definition of the dynamic operators (e.g., which relation is affected by a given dynamic operator). Also, we only consider changes on the accessibility relation, but changes in the valuation would be easily incorporated in this framework.

Definition 3 (Model update functions). *Given a domain* W, *a* model update function *for* W *is a function* $f_W : W \times 2^{W^2} \to 2^{W \times 2^{W^2}}$, *that takes a state in* W *and a binary relation over* W *and returns a set of possible updates to the state of evaluation and accessibility relation.*

Let $\mathcal{C}$ *be a class of models, a* family of model update functions f *is a class of model update functions, one for each domain of a model in* $\mathcal{C}$:

$$f = \{f_W \mid \langle W, R, V \rangle \in \mathcal{C}\}.$$

$\mathcal{C}$ *is* closed under a family of model update functions f *if whenever* $\mathcal{M} = \langle W, R, V \rangle \in \mathcal{C}$, *then* $\{\langle W, R', V \rangle \mid f_W \in f, w \in W, (v, R') \in f_W(w, R)\} \subseteq \mathcal{C}$.

Clearly, the class of all pointed models is closed under any family of model update functions. In the rest of the article we only discuss the class of all models.

Notice, in the definition above, that a model update function is defined relative to a domain. We specifically require that all models with the same domain have the same model update function. This constraint limits the number of operators that can be captured in the framework, but at the same time leads to operators with a more uniform behavior. We will discuss this issue further after we introduce the formal semantics of the relation-changing operators below.

We now introduce the semantics for the general case.

Definition 4 (Semantics). *Let $\mathcal{C}$ be a class of models, $\mathcal{M} = \langle W, R, V\rangle$ be a model in $\mathcal{C}$, $w \in W$ a state, f a family of model update functions for $\mathcal{C}$ and $\blacklozenge_f$ its associated dynamic modality. Let φ be a formula in $\mathcal{L}(\blacklozenge_f)$. We say that $\mathcal{M}, w$* satisfies *φ, and write $\mathcal{M}, w \models \varphi$, when*

$$\begin{array}{lll} \mathcal{M}, w \models \bot & & \textit{never} \\ \mathcal{M}, w \models p & \textit{iff} & w \in V(p) \\ \mathcal{M}, w \models \varphi \rightarrow \psi & \textit{iff} & \mathcal{M}, w \not\models \varphi \textit{ or } \mathcal{M}, w \models \psi \\ \mathcal{M}, w \models \blacklozenge_f \varphi & \textit{iff} & \textit{for some } (v, R') \in f_W(w, R),\ \langle W, R', V\rangle, v \models \varphi. \end{array}$$

The definition extends to languages with many modal dynamic operators in the obvious manner. A formula φ is satisfiable if for some pointed model $\mathcal{M}, w$ we have $\mathcal{M}, w \models \varphi$. We write $\mathcal{M}, w \equiv_{\mathcal{L}} \mathcal{N}, v$ when both models satisfy the same $\mathcal{L}$-formulas, i.e., for all $\varphi \in \mathcal{L}$, $\mathcal{M}, w \models \varphi$ if and only if $\mathcal{N}, v \models \varphi$.

Notice, in the semantic definition, how the relation-changing modal operator $\blacklozenge_f$ potentially changes both the state of evaluation and the accessibility relation. On the other hand, the domain remains the same, and hence all $\blacklozenge_f$ operators in a formula are evaluated using the same model update function.

Examples of Relation-Changing Logics. First, notice that the classical modal diamond $\Diamond$ [10,11] is one particular instance of a dynamic operator, in which the accessibility relation remains unchanged and the evaluation state is changed by some successor via R. To simplify notation we use wv as a shorthand for $\{(w, v)\}$ or (w, v); context will always disambiguate the intended use. Let W a domain and $R \subseteq W^2$, the model update function associated to $\Diamond$ is defined as

$$f_W^{\Diamond}(w, R) = \{(v, R) \mid wv \in R\}.$$

Consider now the model update functions from [3]. Given a binary relation R, let us introduce some notation:

$$R^-_{wv} = R \backslash wv \quad R^+_{wv} = R \cup wv \quad R^*_{wv} = (R \backslash vw) \cup wv.$$

Define the following six model update functions, which give rise to natural dynamic operators: Van Benthem's sabotage operator $\blacklozenge_{\mathsf{gsb}}$ [34], and a local version $\blacklozenge_{\mathsf{sb}}$ that deletes an existing edge between the current state of evaluation and a successor state; a "bridge" operator $\blacklozenge_{\mathsf{gbr}}$ that adds an edge between two previously unconnected states, and a local version $\blacklozenge_{\mathsf{br}}$ that links the current state of evaluation and an inaccessible state; and the global and local versions ($\blacklozenge_{\mathsf{gsw}}$ and $\blacklozenge_{\mathsf{sw}}$, respectively) of an operation that swaps around edges of the model.

$$f_W^{\mathsf{sb}}(w, R) = \{(v, R^-_{wv}) \mid wv \in R\} \qquad f_W^{\mathsf{gsb}}(w, R) = \{(w, R^-_{uv}) \mid uv \in R\}$$
$$f_W^{\mathsf{br}}(w, R) = \{(v, R^+_{wv}) \mid wv \notin R\} \qquad f_W^{\mathsf{gbr}}(w, R) = \{(w, R^+_{uv}) \mid uv \notin R\}$$
$$f_W^{\mathsf{sw}}(w, R) = \{(v, R^*_{vw}) \mid wv \in R\} \qquad f_W^{\mathsf{gsw}}(w, R) = \{(w, R^*_{vu}) \mid uv \in R\}.$$

It is easy to show that the basic modal logic $\mathcal{L}(\Diamond)$ enriched with other relation-changing modalities gains in expressivity. For example, the local sabotage operator $\blacklozenge_{\mathsf{sb}}$ and the local swap operator $\blacklozenge_{\mathsf{sw}}$ are logically stronger than the diamond operator when restricted to non-dynamic predicates, as the formulas $\blacklozenge_{\mathsf{sb}}p \to \Diamond p$ and $\blacklozenge_{\mathsf{sw}}p \to \Diamond p$ are valid. These operators are very expressive as they can force non-tree models (see e.g. [3,18]). For example, the formula $\blacksquare_{\mathsf{sb}}\Box\bot$ means that any local sabotage leads to a dead-end, hence the formula $\Diamond\Diamond\top \wedge \blacksquare_{\mathsf{sb}}\Box\bot$ can only be true at a reflexive state, a property that cannot be expressed in $\mathcal{L}(\Diamond)$.

3 Bisimulations

In modal model theory, the notion of bisimulation is a crucial tool. Typically, a bisimulation is a binary relation linking elements of the domains that have the same atomic information, and preserving the relational structure of the model. Because we need to keep track of the changes on the accessibility relation that the dynamic operators may introduce, bisimulations are defined as relations that link pairs of a state together with the current accessibility relation [3,18]. Notice that the notion we introduce is parameterized with a model update function, making the results general for the relation-changing logics from Sect. 2.

Definition 5 (Bisimulations). *Let $\mathcal{M} = \langle W, R, V\rangle$, $\mathcal{M}' = \langle W', R', V'\rangle$ be two models, and f a family of model update functions. A non empty relation $Z \subseteq (W \times 2^{W^2}) \times (W' \times 2^{W'^2})$ is an $\mathcal{L}(\blacklozenge_f)$-bisimulation if it satisfies the following conditions. If $(w, S)Z(w', S')$ then*

(atomic harmony) *for all $p \in \mathsf{PROP}$, $w \in V(p)$ iff $w' \in V'(p)$;*
(f-zig) *if $(v, T) \in f_W(w, S)$, there is $(v', T') \in f_{W'}(w', S')$ s.t. $(v, T)Z(v', T')$;*
(f-zag) *if $(v', T') \in f_{W'}(w', S')$, there is $(v, T) \in f_W(w, S)$ s.t. $(v, T)Z(v', T')$.*

Given two pointed models $\mathcal{M}, w$ and $\mathcal{M}', w'$ they are $\mathcal{L}(\blacklozenge_f)$-bisimilar (notation, $\mathcal{M}, w \leftrightarroweq_{\mathcal{L}(\blacklozenge_f)} \mathcal{M}', w'$) if there is an $\mathcal{L}(\blacklozenge_f)$-bisimulation Z such that $(w, R)Z(w', R')$ where R and R' are the respective relations of $\mathcal{M}$ and $\mathcal{M}'$.

Summing up, the bisimulation notion for each logic $\mathcal{L}(\blacklozenge_f)$ includes (atomic harmony) and the particular conditions for the model update function f. For instance, according to the above definition, the (zig) and (zag) conditions for the basic modal logic $\mathcal{L}(\Diamond)$ are defined as:

(zig) if $(w,v) \in S$, there is $v' \in W'$ s.t. $(w',v') \in S'$ and $(v,S)Z(v',S')$;
(zag) if $(w',v') \in S'$, there is $v \in W$ s.t. $(w,v) \in S$ and $(v,S)Z(v',S')$.

On the other hand, instantiating f with f^{sb} we get the following conditions:

(f^{sb}-zig) If $(w,v) \in S$, there is $v' \in W'$ s.t. $(w',v') \in S'$ and $(v,S^{-}_{\overline{wv}})Z(v',S'^{-}_{\overline{w'v'}})$;
(f^{sb}-zag) If $(w',v') \in S'$, there is $v \in W$ s.t. $(w,v) \in S$ and $(v,S^{-}_{\overline{wv}})Z(v',S'^{-}_{\overline{w'v'}})$.

In the same way, we can instantiate f with any of the model update functions mentioned in Sect. 2.

Theorem 1 (Invariance). *Let f be a family of model update functions, then $\mathcal{M},w \leftrightarroweq_{\mathcal{L}(\blacklozenge_f)} \mathcal{M}',w'$ implies $\mathcal{M},w \equiv_{\mathcal{L}(\blacklozenge_f)} \mathcal{M}',w'$.*

Proof. Let $\mathcal{M} = \langle W,R,V\rangle$ and $\mathcal{M}' = \langle W',R',V'\rangle$, such that $\mathcal{M},w \leftrightarroweq_{\mathcal{L}(\blacklozenge_f)} \mathcal{M}',w'$. Then there exists Z such that $(w,R)Z(w',R')$.

We prove the theorem by structural induction. In fact, we prove a more general result. Let $S \subseteq W^2$, $S' \subseteq W'^2$ such that $(w,S)Z(w',S')$, we will show that $\langle W,S,V\rangle,w \equiv_{\mathcal{L}(\blacklozenge_f)} \langle W',S',V'\rangle,w'$. The base cases hold by (atomic harmony), and the $\to$ case is trivial.
[**$\blacklozenge_f\varphi$ case:**] Suppose $\langle W,S,V\rangle,w \models \blacklozenge_f\varphi$. Then there is $(v,T) \in f_W(w,S)$ s.t. $\langle W,T,V\rangle,v \models \varphi$. Because Z is a bisimulation, by (f-zig) we have $(v',T') \in f_{W'}(w',S')$ s.t. $(v,T)Z(v',T')$. By inductive hypothesis, $\langle W',T',V'\rangle,v' \models \varphi$ and by definition, $\langle W',S',V'\rangle,w' \models \blacklozenge_f\varphi$. For the other direction use (f-zag).

Therefore, since $(w,R)Z(w',R')$, we get $\mathcal{M},w \equiv_{\mathcal{L}(\blacklozenge_f)} \mathcal{M}',w'$. □

Clearly the result holds when we extend $\mathcal{L}$ with any set of relation-changing modal operators. It suffices to require that the bisimulation comply with the various (f-zig) and (f-zag) conditions corresponding to all operators. In the next section we will reproduce the proof of Theorem 1 in Coq.

4 Formalization in Coq

4.1 The Coq Proof Assistant in a Nutshell

A typical proof in Coq looks like the following:

```
Lemma and_intro: forall (A B : Prop), A → B → A ∧ B.
Proof.
  intros A B HA HB. split.
  - apply HA.
  - apply HB.
Qed.
```

This simple proof states that if you are given a proof of proposition `A` and another proof of proposition `B`, then you have a proof for their conjunction. In order to be able to state the lemma and prove it, Coq presents three different domain specific languages: Gallina, The Vernacular and the tactics language Ltac. Gallina is Coq's mathematical higher-level language and program specification language.

Seen as a programming language, Gallina is a dependently-typed functional language, while seen as a logical system, Gallina is a higher-order type theory. In the example, the lemma's statement (what follows the :) is written in this language.

The Vernacular allows the definition of functions or predicates, the statement of mathematical theorems and software specifications, the machine checking of proofs and the extraction of certified programs to different languages. In the example we use the following Vernacular *commands*: `Lemma` indicates the desire to state a theorem; `Proof` starts the proof; and `Qed` signals that the proof is completed, and therefore must be checked for errors and stored in the database of known facts if everything is correct. The reason for this check is to guarantee that the proof is indeed complete and that the tactics used to write the proof (see below) rightfully solved the problem.

Finally, the proof itself is written using the tactic language Ltac. In formal reasoning, a deduction rule is a link between a conclusion and a list of premises. There are two ways to understand a deduction rule. With *forward reasoning*, if we want to deduce the conclusion, we first try to deduce the list of premises and then use the deduction rule to prove the conclusion. With *backward reasoning* we go in the opposite direction: in order to prove the conclusion, we must prove the premises. Coq tactics are typically deduction rules that implement backward reasoning: when applied to a conclusion, usually called a *goal*, a tactic replaces this goal with the *subgoals* it generates, one for each premise of the rule. In the example, everything between `Proof` and `Qed` are tactic invocations. For instance, the tactic `split` replaces the goal `A` ∧ `B` with two subgoals, one for proving `A` and another for proving `B`.

Not all tactics are as simple as `split`. For instance, the tactic `tauto` implements a decision procedure for intuitionistic propositional calculus, so it is appropriate to solve many trivial statements (actually, it is capable of solving the above lemma in just one tactic invocation). Ltac also allows the definition of complex user defined tactics and decision procedures. See e.g. [9] for a more complete presentation of Coq.

4.2 Formalizing Relation-Changing Logics in Coq

In the rest of this section we will present our formalization of relation-changing modal logics in Coq, and the mechanization of the proof of the general invariance theorem (Theorem 1). The source code can be found at http://tinyurl.com/rcml-in-coq0. As we will see in the formalization below, it is easy to match the mathematical definitions from Sects. 2 and 3 with their counterpart in Coq.

Syntax. In order to formalize the syntax of relation-changing modal logics, we first need to define the countable set of propositional symbols PROP. We can accomplish this by using an inductive type definition:

```
Inductive prop : Set := p : nat → prop.
```

This creates a new type called `prop` with a type constructor `p` that given a natural number `n` constructs an inhabitant of the type `prop`, namely `p n`. It is clear that `prop` correctly formalizes the countable infinite set of propositions PROP.

Before we give the definition of the syntax we need to assume that a set of dynamic operators actually exists. This assumption is necessary because the definition of $\mathcal{L}(S)$, with $S \subseteq \mathsf{DYN}$, depends on the existence of a set of dynamic operators DYN.

```
Variable Dyn : Set.
```

Now we can give the definition of the set of formulae FORM, as in Definition 1:

```
Inductive form : Type :=
| Atom    : prop → form
| Bottom  : form
| If      : form → form → form
| DynDiam : Dyn → form → form.
```

Each line of this definition is interpreted as the members of the BNF from Definition 1. Other operators are defined as syntactic sugar. For example:

```
Definition DynBox (d : Dyn) (phi : form) : form := Not (DynDiam d (Not phi)).
```

Writing formulae with these constructors can be very tedious. Fortunately, Coq allows us to define a notation for them (we present the cases of dynamic operators; other operators are defined as expected):

```
Notation "<o> d phi" := (DynDiam d phi) (at level 65, right associativity).
```

Note that between parentheses we specify the precedence level and associativity.

Semantics. We now turn our attention to the formalization of the semantics of these logics. First, we need to formalize the concept of a relational model as those from Definition 2. In turn this requires to consider how powersets and relations are represented in Coq.

Let A be a set and `A` its correspoding formalization in Coq. In order to formalize a subset S of the power set 2^A, we can view S as a function that for each element $a \in A$ determines whether a belongs to S or not. Naively, one could think that S can be modeled with a function from `A` to `bool`. However, this is overly restrictive, as it will force us to make S decidable (Coq's functions are guaranteed to terminate). Thus, we use the constructive type `Prop` instead of `bool` and write `A → Prop` to mean "a subset of the 2^A".

Similarly, a binary relation R over A can be viewed as a function that given two elements $a, b \in A$ determines whether aRb or not. For this reason, we model R as `A → A → Prop`. Or, using Coq's standard library, simply `relation A`.

Now we are ready to introduce the formalization of the models of our logic. We can think a relational model as a triple consisting of a set `W`, a binary relation `R` defined over `W`, and a valuation function that for each element in `W` and each propositional symbol with type `prop`, decides whether that propositional symbol is valid or not in that element of `W`. In Coq we write the types of `W`, `R` and `V` as:

```
W : Set
R : relation W
V : W → prop → Prop
```

The type of the valuation function deserves an explanation. Above we define the valuation function as a function $V : \mathsf{PROP} \to 2^W$. Given a propositional symbol $p \in \mathsf{PROP}$, an element $w \in W$ and their respective formalizations `p : prop` and `w : W`, we formalize the expression $w \in V(p)$ as `V w p`.

Before we can give a definition of satisfiability we must give a formalization for the type of all model update functions. Remember that a model update function for a given domain W is a function $f_W : W \times 2^{W^2} \to 2^{W \times 2^{W^2}}$ that for each state of W and for each binary relation over W, associates a set of possible updates to the evaluation state and the accessibility relation. In Coq, we define the type of a model update function (`muf`) as:

```
Definition point (W: Set) : Type := (W * relation W).

Definition muf : Type := forall (W : Set),
  (point W) → (point W → Prop).
```

As with the mathematical definition f_W, a `muf` depends on the set W, and that is why we start with `forall (W : Set), ...` . For readability, we define a type `point W` to denote `(W * relation W)`, the Coq equivalent of $W \times 2^{W^2}$. Then, we define the `muf` as `(point W) → (point W → Prop)`. Note that the parentheses are just for readability: the function type → is right-associative.

Given that we have defined the notion of model update function and both the syntax and the models of our logic, we can now define the notion of satisfiability. It must be clear at this point that in order to define it, we need a function that assigns to each dynamic operator a model update function. We can simply assume that such function exists.

```
Variable F : Dyn → muf.

Fixpoint satisfies (W : Set) (R : relation W) (V : W → prop → Prop)
                   (w : W) (phi : form) : Prop :=
match phi with
| Atom a ⇒ V w a
| Bottom ⇒ False
| If phi1 phi2 ⇒ (satisfies W R V w phi1) → (satisfies W R V w phi2)
| DynDiam d phi ⇒
    let fw := F d W in
    exists (v : W) (R' : relation W), fw (w, R) (v, R') ∧ satisfies W R' V v phi
end.
```

Note how each case has one-to-one correspondence with Definition 4. For readability, we define the following notation:

```
Notation "# W , R , V >> w |= phi" := (satisfies W R V w phi) (at level 30).
```

Properties. With all of these definitions we can now formalize the notions of modal equivalence and bisimulation. For this part, we assume we work under the following assumptions:

```
Variables W W' : Set.
Variables (V : W → prop → Prop) (V' : W' → prop → Prop).
```

The notion of modal equivalence can be formalized unsurprisingly as:

```
Definition equivalent_at_points '(w, R) '(w', R') :=
  forall (phi:form), (# W , R , V >> w |= phi) ↔ (# W' , R' , V' >> w' |= phi).
```

(The notation '(a, b) just serves to say the definition takes a pair with components a and b.)

Before formalizing the notion of bisimulation for these logics, let us define the type of relations between models. As introduced in Definition 5, the type of relations defining bisimulations relates pairs of points and binary relations over the domains of the models:

```
Definition model_to_model_relation : Type :=
  (point W) → (point W') → Prop.
```

To formalize the notion of bisimulation, we first define each condition separately and then use them as functions in the definition of bisimulation (f_zag clause is analogous). To state these conditions, we work under the assumption that we have a relation between models Z:

```
Variable Z : model_to_model_relation.

Definition atomic_harmony : Prop :=
  forall w S w' S', Z (w, S) (w', S') → V w = V' w'.

Definition f_zig (f : muf) : Prop :=
  forall w S w' S' v T, Z (w, S) (w', S') →
    f W (w, S) (v, T) →
    (exists (v' : W') T', f W' (w', S') (v', T') ∧ Z (v, T) (v', T')).
```

Each condition shares the precondition of bisimulation (see Definition 5), namely that there is a relation Z between the models, and that the condition holds for every states w and w' and relations S and S' such that they are related according to Z.

Finally, the notion of bisimulation is defined as follows:

```
Definition bisimulation : Prop := atomic_harmony ∧
  (forall d : Dyn, (f_zig (F d))) ∧ (forall d : Dyn, (f_zag (F d))).

Definition bis_at_points (p: point W) (p': point W') : Prop :=
  bisimulation ∧ Z p p'.
```

Now we are ready to formally state the Theorem of Invariance under Bisimulation (Theorem 1):

```
Theorem InvarianceUnderBisimulation :
  forall (p: point W) (p': point W'),
  bis_at_points p p' → equivalent_at_points p p'.
```

Proof. The proof follows by structural induction on the formula phi. In order to get the right induction principle, we need to first massage the goal and the list of hypotheses a bit. The first lines of the proof are the following (we use Coq's (* comments *) to explain each line).

```
intros [w S] [w' S'].          (* name each component of the points *)
unfold bis_at_points.                        (* unfold definitions *)
unfold equivalent_at_points.
unfold bisimulation.
```

At this point, the goal looks like

```
(atomic_harmony ∧
 (forall d : Dyn, f_zig (F d)) ∧ (forall d : Dyn, f_zag (F d))) ∧
Z (w, S) (w', S') →
forall phi : form, # W, S, V >> w |= phi ↔ # W', S', V' >> w' |= phi
```

We split the different components of the first hypothesis, naming each of them again with the `intros` tactic. Then we introduce the formula `phi`.

```
intros [[HAtomicHarmony [HFZig HFZag]] HZwSw'S'].
intros phi.
```

Now our hypotheses looks like follows (the ... omits the trivial ones):

```
...
HAtomicHarmony : atomic_harmony
HFZig : forall d : Dyn, f_zig (F d)
HFZag : forall d : Dyn, f_zag (F d)
HZwSw'S' : Z (w, S) (w', S')
phi : form
```

With the goal being `# W, S, V >> w |= phi ↔ # W', S', V' >> w' |= phi`. We are almost ready to use structural induction on `phi`, but first we need to strengthen our inductive hypothesis, so we can use it on any points (i.e., on any pairs composed by a state and a binary relation). We do this by generalizing the goal:

```
generalize dependent S'. generalize dependent S.
generalize dependent w'. generalize dependent w.
```

The goal now looks like

```
forall (w : W) (w' : W') (S : relation W) (S' : relation W'),
Z (w, S) (w', S') →
# W, S, V >> w |= phi ↔ # W', S', V' >> w' |= phi
```

Now, we are ready to perform structural induction on `phi`:

```
induction phi as [p | | phi IHphi psi IHpsi | d phi IH];
```

The syntax above tells Coq how it should name the different hypothesis in the different cases. Notice that we usually end the tactics with a dot (.) but this time we ended the tactic `induction` with a semicolon (;). This tells Coq that the next tactic has to be applied to all cases in the induction. In particular we unfold the definition of `satisfies` and introduce all required variables and hypothesis.

```
simpl;                   (* This tactic unfolds definitions *)
intros w w' S S' HZwSw'S'.
```

The atomic case is `V w p ↔ V' w' p`, which is solved with a simple rewrite using Atomic Harmony and a call to the tactic `tauto` mentioned in the previous section.

```
rewrite (HAtomicHarmony w S w' S' HZwSw'S').
tauto.          (* Solves the goal "V' w' p <-> V' w' p" *)
```

For the bottom case we simply use `tauto`. Now for the if case, we split the proof into two separate directions. First we prove the left-to-right direction and then the right-to-left. This is performed using the `split` tactic. Luckily, we do not need to think about the two directions separately, since the same tactics work to prove both directions. That is why we end all tactics with a semicolon. Both directions are proved simply by assuming the two antecedents and then applying the inductive hypothesis of `psi` and `phi` and these two antecedents to the current subgoal.

```
split;
intros HIf Hsat;
apply (IHpsi w w' S S' HZwSw'S');
apply HIf;
apply (IHphi w w' S S' HZwSw'S');
apply Hsat.
```

The proof of the dynamic operator follows closely the same reasoning as the one present in Sect. 3. First, like with the if case, we use the tactic `split` to consider both directions, but this time we prove them separately. We will explain the left-to-right direction only, as the other direction is analogous. After `split` and `simpl` Coq tells us that we need to prove the following:

```
(exists (v : W) (R' : W → W → Prop),
   F d W (w, S) (v, R') ∧ # W, R', V >> v |= phi) →
exists (v : W') (R' : W' → W' → Prop),
  F d W' (w', S') (v, R') ∧ # W', R', V' >> v |= phi
```

First we give a name to the existentially quantified values of the antecedent, together with its properties:

```
intros [v [T [HfWwSvT HsatTv]]].
```

We get that `v : W`, that `T : relation W` and that they also satisfy two properties that we will name `HfWwSvT` and `HsatTv`:

```
HfWwSvT : F d W (w, S) (v, T)      (* (v,T) is a succesor via F d of (w,S) *)
HsatTv : # W, T, V >> v |= phi     (* the updated model satisfies phi *)
```

At this point we can apply the `HFZig` hypothesis in `HfWwSvT`:

```
apply (HFZig d w S w' S' v T HZwSw'S') in HfWwSvT
    as [v' [T' [HfW'w'S'v'T' HZvTv'T']]].
```

This introduces the following new hypotheses:

```
v' : W'
T' : relation W'
HfW'w'S'v'T' : F d W' (w', S') (v', T')
HZvTv'T' : Z (v, T) (v', T')
HsatTv : # W, T, V >> v |= phi
```

Remember that our goal at this point is to prove that:

```
exists (v'' : W') (R' : relation W'),
  F d W' (w', S') (v'', R') ∧ # W', R', V' >> v'' |= phi
```

The existential quantifiers are removed by providing witnesses: v' and T':

```
exists v'. exists T'.
```

Now we only need to prove that:

```
F d W' (w', S') (v', T') ∧ # W', T', V' >> v' |= phi
```

The left proposition of the conjunction is identical to one of our hypothesis (namely HfW'w'S'v'T'). The other proposition can be proved by applying the inductive hypothesis to the HsatTv hypothesis. We can prove all this using the following tactics:

```
split.
* assumption.
* eapply IH. apply HZvTv'T'. assumption.
```

The proof is ended, so we issue the closing command Qed.

5 Final Remarks

In this work we formalized in the interactive proof assistant Coq, the syntax, semantics and a notion of bisimulation for a family of dynamic logics called *relation-changing logics*. These logics contain modalities that update the accessibility relation of the model while evaluating a formula. One particularity of our formalization is that, following the definition from [3], dynamic modalities are parameterized by a *model update function*, i.e., a function that given a pointed model, returns an updated pointed model. Thus, the definitions in Coq are simple, but powerful enough to encompass a whole family of logics. With these definitions at hand, we recreated the proof of the *invariance under bisimulation theorem:* if two models are bisimilar for a determined logic, then they satisfy the same formulas. Again, given the generality of our framework, we only need to prove one theorem, which holds for any instance of model update function (e.g., sabotage logics [32,34], swap logic [2], and others such as the program-based relation-changing operations from [19–21,35], which are as expressive as *propositional dynamic logic* [24] and whose bisimulation notion is the same as for the basic modal logic [10]). Moreover, the results we introduced can be straightforwardly extended to model update functions that also update the valuation of the model (see e.g. [5,7,36]).

There exist in the literature other works exploring the mechanization of proofs for modal and non-classical logics. In [15], a formalization of the basic modal logic $\mathcal{L}(\Diamond)$ is presented, in which we based our formalization. In addition, the author formalizes the extensions of the basic modal logic $S5$ and $S5^n$ [10], together with a natural deduction system. Then, the system is used to solve some logical puzzles. Regarding non-classical logics, in [39] the authors present a formalization in Coq of *linear logic*, together with the mechanization of some theorems for such logic, such as a proof of cut-elimination. A formalization in Coq of a Sahlqvist's global correspondence theorem for the very simple Sahlqvist class is presented in [13]. From such formalization, it is possible to extract a verified Haskell program that computes correspondents of simple Sahlqvist formulas. Another approach has been taken in [38], in which a formalization and verification in Lean [14] of tableaux methods for modal logics is presented. Finally, recent works present a proof language for *differential dynamic logic* [12] for applications in cyber-physical systems, in the theorem prover KeYmaera X [28].

There are several interesting directions that we would like to explore in the future. The next step will be the mechanization of more complex results for relation-changing logics, such as the *Hennessy-Milner theorem* (i.e., the other direction of the proof presented here), and the correctness of the encodings into first-order and second-order logic [3]. Some of these results can be proved for particular instances of model updates functions, while others can be proved for the general case. Moreover, we would like to use our framework for mechanizing proofs for more concrete instances of this family, such as *dynamic epistemic logics* [37] and *modal separation logics* [16,17].

We consider that this work represents a first step towards a more serious use of an interative proof assistant for proofs in modal logic. One of the main problems in the aforementioned works, is that all the formalizations are too heterogeneous, and it makes difficult to reuse previous results. Our main goal is the development of a modal logic library that allows us the mechanization in a uniform way of a wide variety of results in modal and dynamic logics.

Ackowledgements. This work was partially supported by ANPCyT-PICTs-2017-1130 and 2016-0215, MinCyT Córdoba, SeCyT-UNC, and the Laboratoire International Associé INFINIS.

References

1. Areces, C., Fervari, R., Hoffmann, G.: Moving arrows and four model checking results. In: Ong, L., de Queiroz, R. (eds.) WoLLIC 2012. LNCS, vol. 7456, pp. 142–153. Springer, Heidelberg (2012). https://doi.org/10.1007/978-3-642-32621-9_11
2. Areces, C., Fervari, R., Hoffmann, G.: Swap logic. Log. J. IGPL **22**(2), 309–332 (2014)
3. Areces, C., Fervari, R., Hoffmann, G.: Relation-changing modal operators. Log. J. IGPL **23**(4), 601–627 (2015)
4. Areces, C., Fervari, R., Hoffmann, G., Martel, M.: Satisfiability for relation-changing logics. J. Log. Comput. **28**(7), 1443–1470 (2018)
5. Areces, C., Figueira, D., Figueira, S., Mera, S.: The expressive power of memory logics. Rev. Symb. Log. **4**(2), 290–318 (2011)
6. Areces, C., ten Cate, B.: Hybrid logics. In: Blackburn, P., Wolter, F., van Benthem, J. (eds.) Handbook of Modal Logic, pp. 821–868. Elsevier, Amsterdam (2007)
7. Aucher, G., Balbiani, P., Fariñas del Cerro, L., Herzig, A.: Global and local graph modifiers. ENTCS **231**, 293–307 (2009)

8. Aucher, G., van Benthem, J., Grossi, D.: Modal logics of sabotage revisited. JLC **28**(2), 269–303 (2018)
9. Bertot, Y., Castéran, P.: Interactive Theorem Proving and Program Development: Coq'Art The Calculus of Inductive Constructions, 1st edn. Springer, Heidelberg (2010)
10. Blackburn, P., de Rijke, M., Venema, Y.: Modal Logic. Cambridge Tracts in Theoretical Computer Science. Cambridge University Press, Cambridge (2001)
11. Blackburn, P., van Benthem, J.: Modal logic: a semantic perspective. In: Handbook of Modal Logic, pp. 1–84. Elsevier (2007)
12. Bohrer, B., Platzer, A.: Toward structured proofs for dynamic logics. CoRR, abs/1908.05535 (2019)
13. D'Abrera, C., Goré, R.: Verified synthesis of (very simple) Sahlqvist correspondents via Coq. In: AiML 2018, Short Presentations, pp. 26–30. College Publications (2018)
14. de Moura, L., Kong, S., Avigad, J., van Doorn, F., von Raumer, J.: The lean theorem prover (system description). In: Felty, A.P., Middeldorp, A. (eds.) CADE 2015. LNCS (LNAI), vol. 9195, pp. 378–388. Springer, Cham (2015). https://doi.org/10.1007/978-3-319-21401-6_26
15. de Wind, P.: Modal Logic in Coq. Vrije Universiteit, Amsterdam (2001)
16. Demri, S., Fervari, R.: On the complexity of modal separation logics. In: AiML 2018, pp. 179–198. College Publications (2018)
17. Demri, S., Fervari, R., Mansutti, A.: Axiomatising logics with separating conjunction and modalities. In: Calimeri, F., Leone, N., Manna, M. (eds.) JELIA 2019. LNCS (LNAI), vol. 11468, pp. 692–708. Springer, Cham (2019). https://doi.org/10.1007/978-3-030-19570-0_45
18. Fervari, R.: Relation-Changing Modal Logics. Ph.D. thesis, Universidad Nacional de Córdoba, Argentina (2014)
19. Fervari, R., Velázquez-Quesada, F.R.: Dynamic epistemic logics of introspection. In: Madeira, A., Benevides, M. (eds.) DALI 2017. LNCS, vol. 10669, pp. 82–97. Springer, Cham (2018). https://doi.org/10.1007/978-3-319-73579-5_6
20. Fervari, R., Velázquez-Quesada, F.R.: Introspection as an action in relational models. JLAMP **108**, 1–23 (2019)
21. Girard, P., Seligman, J., Liu, F.: General dynamic dynamic logic. In: AiML 2012, pp. 239–260. College Publications (2012)
22. Gonthier, G.: Formal proof – the four-color theorem (2008)
23. Hales, T.C., et al.: A formal proof of the kepler conjecture. Forum Math. Pi **5**, e2 (2017)
24. Harel, D.: Dynamic Logic. Foundations of Computing. The MIT Press, Cambridge (2000)
25. Howard, W.A.: The formulae-as-types notion of construction. To HB Curry: Essays Combin. Log. Lambda Calc. Formalism **44**, 479–490 (1980)
26. Kripke, S.: Semantical analysis of modal logic I. Normal propositional calculi. Z. fur Math. Log. Grundlagen der Math. **9**, 67–96 (1963)
27. Löding, C., Rohde, P.: Model checking and satisfiability for sabotage modal logic. In: Pandya, P.K., Radhakrishnan, J. (eds.) FSTTCS 2003. LNCS, vol. 2914, pp. 302–313. Springer, Heidelberg (2003). https://doi.org/10.1007/978-3-540-24597-1_26
28. Mitsch, S., Platzer, A.: The keymaera X proof IDE - concepts on usability in hybrid systems theorem proving. In: F-IDE@FM 2016. EPTCS, vol. 240, pp. 67–81 (2016)
29. Paulson, L.C. (ed.): Isabelle: A Generic Theorem Prover, vol. 828. Springer, Heidelberg (1994). https://doi.org/10.1007/BFb0030541

30. Pym, D., Spring, J., O'Hearn, P.W.: Why separation logic works. Philos. Technol. **32**(3), 483–516 (2019)
31. Reynolds, J.C.: Separation logic: a logic for shared mutable data structures. In: LICS 2002, pp. 55–74. IEEE (2002)
32. Rohde, P.: On games and logics over dynamically changing structures. Ph.D. thesis, RWTH Aachen (2006)
33. Slind, K., Norrish, M.: A brief overview of HOL4. In: Mohamed, O.A., Muñoz, C., Tahar, S. (eds.) TPHOLs 2008. LNCS, vol. 5170, pp. 28–32. Springer, Heidelberg (2008). https://doi.org/10.1007/978-3-540-71067-7_6
34. Benthem, J.: An essay on sabotage and obstruction. In: Hutter, D., Stephan, W. (eds.) Mechanizing Mathematical Reasoning. LNCS (LNAI), vol. 2605, pp. 268–276. Springer, Heidelberg (2005). https://doi.org/10.1007/978-3-540-32254-2_16
35. van Benthem, J., Liu, F.: Dynamic logic of preference upgrade. J. Appl. Non-Class. Log. **17**(2), 157–182 (2007)
36. van Ditmarsch, H., van der Hoek, W., Kooi, B.: Dynamic epistemic logic with assignment. In: AAMAS 2005, pp. 141–148. ACM (2005)
37. van Ditmarsch, H., van der Hoek, W., Kooi, B.: Dynamic Epistemic Logic. Synthese Library. Springer, Heidelberg (2007). https://doi.org/10.1007/978-1-4020-5839-4
38. Wu, M., Goré, R.: Verified decision procedures for modal logics. In: ITP 2019. LIPIcs, vol. 141, pp. 31:1–31:19. Schloss Dagstuhl - Leibniz-Zentrum für Informatik (2019)
39. Xavier, B., Olarte, C., Reis, G., Nigam, V.: Mechanizing focused linear logic in Coq. ENTCS **338**, 219–236 (2018)

Behavioural and Abstractor Specifications for a Dynamic Logic with Binders and Silent Transitions

Rolf Hennicker[1], Alexander Knapp[2], Alexandre Madeira[3,4(✉)], and Felix Mindt[1]

[1] Ludwig-Maximilians-Universität München, Munich, Germany
[2] Universität Augsburg, Augsburg, Germany
hennicker@ifi.lmu.de, knapp@pst.ifi.lmu.de, felix@mindt-online.de
[3] CIDMA, University of Aveiro, Aveiro, Portugal
madeira@ua.pt
[4] HASLab INESC TEC, University Minho, Braga, Portugal

Abstract. We extend dynamic logic with binders (for state variables) by distinguishing between observable and silent transitions. This differentiation gives rise to two kinds of observational interpretations of the logic: abstractor and behavioural specifications. Abstractor specifications relax the standard model class semantics of a specification by considering its closure under weak bisimulation. Behavioural specifications, however, rely on a behavioural satisfaction relation which relaxes the interpretation of state variables and the satisfaction of modal formulas $\langle\alpha\rangle\varphi$ and $[\alpha]\varphi$ by abstracting from silent transitions. A formal relation between abstractor and behavioural specifications is provided which shows that both coincide semantically under mild conditions. For the proof we instantiate the previously introduced concept of a behaviour-abstractor framework to the case of dynamic logic with binders and silent transitions.

1 Introduction

Observability plays an important role in software development: a system is correct if it exhibits the desired observable behaviour. Formal observability notions for abstracting from internal details have been established in the theory of algebraic specifications of data types, e.g., by distinguishing between observable and non-observable sorts, and also in concurrency theory, e.g., by Milner's notion of observational equivalence of processes. For algebraic specifications an "externalised" and an "internalised" view of observability have been pursued leading to the concepts of abstractor and behavioural specification respectively. An

A. Madeira—This work is supported by ERDF European Regional Development Fund, through the COMPETE Programme, and by National Funds through FCT - Portuguese Foundation for Science and Technology - within projects POCI-01-0145-FEDER-030947 and UID/MAT/04106/2019. This author is supported in the scope of the framework contract foreseen in the numbers 4, 5 and 6 of the article 23, of the Decree-Law 57/2016, of August 29, changed by Portuguese Law 57/2017, of July 19.

L. Soares Barbosa and A. Baltag (Eds.): DaLí 2019, LNCS 12005, pp. 19–34, 2020.
https://doi.org/10.1007/978-3-030-38808-9_2

abstractor specification **abstract** *Sp* **wrt** $\equiv$ abstracts from the standard model class of a specification *Sp* by considering its closure under an observational equivalence relation $\equiv$ between algebras [13,15,16]. A behavioural specification **behaviour** *Sp* **wrt** $\models_{\approx}$ relies on an observational equality relation $\approx$ between the elements of an algebra and a behavioural satisfaction relation $\models_{\approx}$ which interprets the equality symbol by observational rather than set-theoretic equality [4,12,14]. It has been shown that for first-order logic specifications both approaches are semantically equivalent under mild conditions [1]. This result has been transferred to higher-order logic [8], to arbitrary (concrete) institutions [11] and, more recently in the context of reactive system specifications [5], to dynamic logic $\mathcal{D}^{\downarrow}$ with binders $\downarrow x \,.\, \varphi$ for state variables. In the case of $\mathcal{D}^{\downarrow}$-logic the abstraction equivalence $\equiv$ is strong bisimulation between labelled transition systems (LTS) and behavioural satisfaction $\models_{\approx}$ interprets state variables up to (strong) bisimilarity of states. In [7] we were able to extract some general conditions under which, independently of the concrete logical framework at hand, the behaviour-abstractor relationships generally hold: (BA1) behavioural satisfaction of sentences must be invariant under abstraction equivalence and, for each semantic structure, (BA2) an observationally equivalent "black-box structure" must exist for which (BA3) behavioural satisfaction of sentences coincides with standard satisfaction. The results of [7] have been applied in [7, Sects. 3 and 4] to first-order logic and higher-order logic resp., as well as to $\mathcal{D}^{\downarrow}$-logic [7, Sect. 5] and observable Hennessy-Milner logic [7, Sect. 6].

We extend $\mathcal{D}^{\downarrow}$-logic by distinguishing between observable actions and the invisible action τ (interpreted by silent transitions). The resulting logic is denoted by $\mathcal{D}^{\downarrow}_{\tau}$. Then *weak* bisimulation between LTSs (like in observable Hennessy-Milner logic) is the adequate choice for the observational abstraction equivalence $\equiv$. For the internalised observational equality we use the greatest weak bisimulation relation $\approx_M$ between the states of an LTS M. Behavioural satisfaction $\models_{\approx}$ is now defined by interpreting state variables up to $\approx_M$ and the interpretation of the diamond operator (and thus also of the derived box operator) is relaxed as in observable modal logic [17] and [7, Sect. 6]: a sentence $\langle a \rangle \varphi$ with observable action a holds behaviourally in a state w if there exist arbitrarily many silent transitions starting in w which are followed by an a-transition and then again by arbitrarily many silent transitions such that the resulting state v satisfies behaviourally φ.

The goal of this paper is to establish also in the setting of $\mathcal{D}^{\downarrow}_{\tau}$ a relationship between abstractor specifications **abstract** *Sp* **wrt** $\equiv$ and behavioural specifications **behaviour** *Sp* **wrt** $\models_{\approx}$. For this purpose, we show that $\mathcal{D}^{\downarrow}_{\tau}$ gives rise to an instantiation of the behaviour-abstractor framework in the sense of [7] satisfying the conditions (BA1–BA3) as described above. In the context of $\mathcal{D}^{\downarrow}_{\tau}$-logic, the first condition (BA1) expresses a modal invariance property with respect to weak bisimulation between labelled transition systems and behavioural satisfaction. For (BA2), we define the black-box structure of a labelled transition system M in terms of its quotient $M/{\approx_M}$ and show that both are weakly bisimilar. For getting (BA3) we show that for quotients standard satisfaction and behavioural satisfaction of formulas is the same. Thus we get a behaviour-abstractor framework and can apply the results in [7] to $\mathcal{D}^{\downarrow}_{\tau}$-logic which show that behavioural semantics is included in abstractor semantics (of specifications) and both are the same if and only if standard semantics is included in behavioural semantics.

Our results extend both, the behaviour-abstractor relationships investigated for $\mathcal{D}^{\downarrow}$-logic in [7, Sect. 5] and the Hennessy-Milner style instantiation of the behaviour-abstractor framework in [7, Sect. 6]. In contrast to [7, Sect. 6] we do not use in formulas the special empty action ε but the invisible action τ instead. Though both are equivalent in the observational interpretations of the logic $\mathcal{D}^{\downarrow}_{\tau}$ they are not in the standard interpretation of $\mathcal{D}^{\downarrow}_{\tau}$. Compared to [7, Sect. 6] this leads to a significant simplification and generalisation since we do not need to restrict our results to weakly deterministic models.

The remainder of this paper is structured as follows: In Sect. 2 we present $\mathcal{D}^{\downarrow}_{\tau}$-logic, the basis of our approach. Then, in Sect. 3, we consider two observational interpretations of $\mathcal{D}^{\downarrow}_{\tau}$ in terms of abstractor and behavioural specifications. In Sect. 4 we recall the general concept of a behaviour-abstractor framework and we show how it can be instantiated with $\mathcal{D}^{\downarrow}_{\tau}$-logic and its observational interpretations. Thus we get the semantic relationships between abstractor and behavioural specifications for free. All investigations are accompanied by examples. Concluding remarks are given in Sect. 5.

2 A Dynamic Logic with Binders and Silent Transitions

Dynamic logic with binders, called $\mathcal{D}^{\downarrow}$-logic, has been introduced in [9] as a logic which allows to express properties of reactive systems from abstract safety and liveness properties down to concrete ones specifying the (recursive) structure of processes. Thus $\mathcal{D}^{\downarrow}$-logic supports a stepwise refinement methodology for the formal development of reactive systems. The logic combines modalities indexed by regular expressions of actions, as in Dynamic Logic [3], and state variables with binders, as in Hybrid Logic [2]. In this section we extend $\mathcal{D}^{\downarrow}$-logic by splitting atomic actions into observable actions and the invisible action τ. The new logic, denoted by $\mathcal{D}^{\downarrow}_{\tau}$, is technically only a small modification of $\mathcal{D}^{\downarrow}$ but, as we will see in the forthcoming sections, the differentiation between observable and invisible actions provides a powerful basis for observational interpretations.

Signatures and Sentences. A *$\mathcal{D}^{\downarrow}_{\tau}$-signature* is a set $A = O \cup \{\tau\}$ of *atomic actions* comprising *observable actions* O and the *invisible action* τ. The class of $\mathcal{D}^{\downarrow}_{\tau}$-signatures is denoted by $\mathbb{S}^{\mathcal{D}^{\downarrow}_{\tau}}$. The set of *composed actions* $Act(A)$ over A is given by

$$\alpha ::= a \mid \alpha;\alpha \mid \alpha + \alpha \mid \alpha^*$$

where $a \in A$ and ; represents the sequential composition of actions, + the choice between actions, and * the iteration of an action.

For any $A \in \mathbb{S}^{\mathcal{D}^{\downarrow}_{\tau}}$, the set of *A-formulas* is given by

$$\varphi ::= \mathbf{tt} \mid \neg\varphi \mid \varphi \vee \varphi \mid \langle\alpha\rangle\varphi \mid x \mid \downarrow x\,.\,\varphi \mid (@x)\varphi$$

where $\alpha \in Act(A)$ is a composed action and $x \in X$ is a variable belonging to a universal set X of state variables. We use the usual abbreviations $\mathbf{ff} = \neg\mathbf{tt}$, $\varphi \wedge \psi = \neg(\neg\varphi \vee \neg\psi)$, $[\alpha]\varphi = \neg\langle\alpha\rangle\neg\varphi$, etc. An *A-sentence* is an A-formula φ containing no free variables, where free variables are defined as usual with $\downarrow$ being the only operator binding variables. The set of A-sentences is denoted by $\mathrm{Sen}^{\mathcal{D}^{\downarrow}_{\tau}}(A)$.

The idea of the binder operator $\downarrow x\,.\,\varphi$ is to assign to variable x the current state of evaluation and then to continue with evaluating φ. The operator $(@x)\varphi$ evaluates φ in the state assigned to x. $\mathcal{D}^{\downarrow}_{\tau}$ retains from Hybrid Logic these two constructions but omits the use of nominals since we are only interested in properties of states reachable from the initial state, i.e., processes.

Structures. The semantic structures of $\mathcal{D}^{\downarrow}_{\tau}$ are reachable, labelled transition systems (LTS) with initial state. For an $A \in \mathbb{S}^{\mathcal{D}^{\downarrow}_{\tau}}$, an *A-structure* $M = (W, R, w_0)$ consists of a *set of states* W, a family of *transition relations* $R = (R_a \subseteq W \times W)_{a\in A}$, and the *initial state* $w_0 \in W$ such that, for each $w \in W$, either $w = w_0$ or there is a finite sequence of transitions $(w_{k-1}, w_k) \in R_{a_k}$, $1 \leq k \leq n$, with $a_k \in A$, such that $w_n = w$. Transitions in R_τ are called *silent transitions.* The class of A-structures is denoted by $Str^{\mathcal{D}^{\downarrow}_{\tau}}(A)$.

Satisfaction Relation. To define the satisfaction relation we extend, as usual, the interpretation of actions over a structure $M = (W, R, w_0) \in Str^{\mathcal{D}^{\downarrow}_{\tau}}(A)$ to composed actions from $Act(A)$ by $R_{\alpha;\alpha'} = R_\alpha \cdot R_{\alpha'}$, $R_{\alpha+\alpha'} = R_\alpha \cup R_{\alpha'}$ and $R_{\alpha^*} = (R_\alpha)^\star$ with the operations $\cdot$, $\cup$ and $\star$ standing for relational composition, union and reflexive-transitive closure. A *valuation* is a function $g : X \to W$. Given such a valuation g, a variable $x \in X$, and a state $w \in W$, $g\{x \mapsto w\}$ denotes the valuation with $g\{x \mapsto w\}(x) = w$ and $g\{x \mapsto w\}(y) = g(y)$ for any $y \in X \setminus \{x\}$. For any A-structure $M = (W, R, w_0) \in Str^{\mathcal{D}^{\downarrow}_{\tau}}(A)$, valuation $g : X \to W$ and state $w \in W$,

- $M, g, w \models^{\mathcal{D}^{\downarrow}_{\tau}}_{A} \mathbf{tt}$ is true;
- $M, g, w \models^{\mathcal{D}^{\downarrow}_{\tau}}_{A} \neg\varphi$ iff it is false that $M, g, w \models^{\mathcal{D}^{\downarrow}_{\tau}}_{A} \varphi$;
- $M, g, w \models^{\mathcal{D}^{\downarrow}_{\tau}}_{A} \varphi \vee \varphi'$ iff $M, g, w \models^{\mathcal{D}^{\downarrow}_{\tau}}_{A} \varphi$ or $M, g, w \models^{\mathcal{D}^{\downarrow}_{\tau}}_{A} \varphi'$;
- $M, g, w \models^{\mathcal{D}^{\downarrow}_{\tau}}_{A} \langle\alpha\rangle\varphi$ iff there is a $v \in W$ with $(w, v) \in R_\alpha$ and $M, g, v \models^{\mathcal{D}^{\downarrow}_{\tau}}_{A} \varphi$;
- $M, g, w \models^{\mathcal{D}^{\downarrow}_{\tau}}_{A} x$ iff $g(x) = w$;
- $M, g, w \models^{\mathcal{D}^{\downarrow}_{\tau}}_{A} \downarrow x\,.\,\varphi$ iff $M, g\{x \mapsto w\}, w \models^{\mathcal{D}^{\downarrow}_{\tau}}_{A} \varphi$;
- $M, g, w \models^{\mathcal{D}^{\downarrow}_{\tau}}_{A} (@x)\varphi$ iff $M, g, g(x) \models^{\mathcal{D}^{\downarrow}_{\tau}}_{A} \varphi$.

If φ is an A-sentence, then the valuation is irrelevant, i.e., $M, g, w \models^{\mathcal{D}^{\downarrow}_{\tau}}_{A} \varphi$ iff $M, w \models^{\mathcal{D}^{\downarrow}_{\tau}}_{A} \varphi$. M *satisfies* an A-sentence φ, denoted by $M \models^{\mathcal{D}^{\downarrow}_{\tau}}_{A} \varphi$, if $M, w_0 \models^{\mathcal{D}^{\downarrow}_{\tau}}_{A} \varphi$.

A specification $Sp = (A, \Phi)$ over $\mathcal{D}^{\downarrow}_{\tau}$ consists of a signature $A \in \mathbb{S}^{\mathcal{D}^{\downarrow}_{\tau}}$ and a set $\Phi \subseteq \mathrm{Sen}^{\mathcal{D}^{\downarrow}_{\tau}}(A)$ of A-sentences, also called *axioms*, specifying required properties.

The semantics of Sp is given by its *model class* $\mathrm{Mod}^{\mathcal{D}^{\downarrow}_{\tau}}(Sp)$, which is the class of all A-structures satisfying the axioms of Sp, i.e.,

$$\mathrm{Mod}^{\mathcal{D}^{\downarrow}_{\tau}}(Sp) = \{M \in Str^{\mathcal{D}^{\downarrow}_{\tau}}(A) \mid \forall \varphi \in \Phi \, . \, M \models^{\mathcal{D}^{\downarrow}_{\tau}}_{A} \varphi\} \; .$$

3 Abstractor and Behavioural Specifications over $\mathcal{D}^{\downarrow}_{\tau}$

3.1 Motivation and Example

Though $\mathcal{D}^{\downarrow}_{\tau}$ extends $\mathcal{D}^{\downarrow}$ with its distinction between observable and invisible actions, its satisfaction relation does not take this difference into account. It interprets the invisible action τ in the same way as observable actions: $M, g, w \models^{\mathcal{D}^{\downarrow}_{\tau}}_{A} \langle\tau\rangle\varphi$ iff there is a $v \in W$ with $(w, v) \in R_{\tau}$ and $M, g, v \models^{\mathcal{D}^{\downarrow}_{\tau}}_{A} \varphi$. A proper integration of the invisible action τ should make clear that this action is in fact not observable: performing or not performing just τ actions should be equivalent from the observational point of view. The following example motivates the need for observational interpretations in the presence of silent transitions.

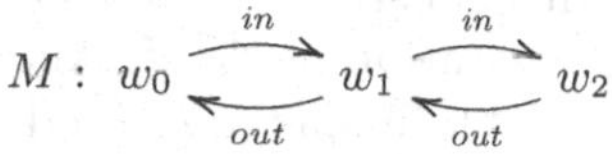

Fig. 1. A model of *2Buf*

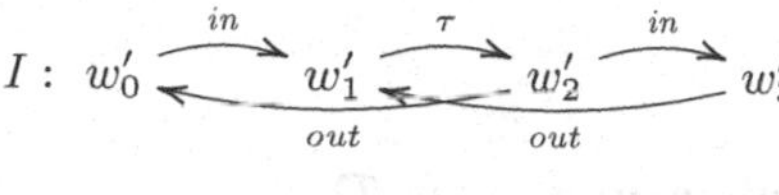

Fig. 2. LTS of two composed one element buffers

Example 1. We consider a specification *2Buf* for buffers of size 2. There are two observable actions *in* and *out*. For simplicity, we do not specify the nature of the elements inserted by *in* or removed by *out* from the buffer. It is assumed that the specification *2Buf* has the following sentence φ as an axiom[1]:

$$\varphi = \downarrow x_0 \, . \, \langle in\rangle \downarrow x_1 \, . \, (\langle out\rangle x_0 \wedge \langle in\rangle \downarrow x_2 \, . \, \langle out\rangle x_1)$$

Obviously, the LTS M shown in Fig. 1 satisfies φ and hence $M \in \mathrm{Mod}(\mathit{2Buf})$.

Now we want to construct an implementation of a two element buffer by composing two one element buffers. The composition should be achieved in a

[1] In general there could be other axioms as well specifying, e.g., disallowed behaviours.

way such that the first (one element) buffer inputs an element from the outside, then it synchronises its output with the input of the second (one element) buffer and thus transmits the received element to the second buffer. Then either the first buffer can input another element or the second buffer outputs its element to the outside, etc. Figure 2 shows an LTS I which models the (behaviour of the) synchronous composition of two one element buffers. Shifting an element from the first to the second buffer is invisible to the outside and thus modelled by a silent τ-transition.

Note that the LTS I does not satisfy the axiom φ since after an *in*-action an *out* is not possible (and also another *in* is not possible). Hence $I \notin \mathrm{Mod}(\mathit{2Buf})$. Nevertheless I should be regarded as a correct implementation of *2Buf*. It has the expected observable behaviour of a two element buffer since the shift of elements is not visible. Hence we are faced with the question: How can we formally justify the correctness of the implementation I? There are, in principle, two possible solutions.

First, we notice that I is weakly bisimilar (for the formal definition see below) to the model M of *2Buf*. A weak bisimulation relation between the states of M and I is given by the set $B = \{(w_0, w'_0), (w_1, w'_1), (w_1, w'_2), (w_2, w'_3)\}$. Thus, by constructing the closure of the model class of *2Buf* under weak bisimulation the LTS I will be an element of this "abstracted" model class and therefore can be considered as a correct implementation of *2Buf*. Another possibility is to relax the satisfaction relation for modal formulas $\langle\alpha\rangle\varphi$ (and hence $[\alpha]\varphi$) by abstracting from silent transitions (for the formal definition of behavioural satisfaction see below). Then the LTS I does behaviourally satisfy the axiom φ and therefore I can be considered again as a correct implementation of *2Buf*. □

In the sequel we will formalise the two approaches to observational interpretations of $\mathcal{D}^{\downarrow}_{\tau}$ illustrated in Example 1 and we will study relationships between them.

3.2 Abstractor Specifications over $\mathcal{D}^{\downarrow}_{\tau}$

Abstractor specifications are based on weak bisimulation equivalence. For its definition (cf. [10]), we first define the τ-closure of transition relations with observable actions. For $A = O \cup \{\tau\} \in \mathbb{S}^{\mathcal{D}^{\downarrow}_{\tau}}$, let $M = (W, R, w_0)$ be an A-structure with transition relations $R = (R_a \subseteq W \times W)_{a \in A}$. For each $o \in O$, the τ-closure of R_o is the relation $\widehat{R}_o \subseteq W \times W$ such that $(w, v) \in \widehat{R}_a$ if and only if there is a finite sequence of transitions in R from w to v containing exactly one transition labelled with observable action a surrounded by arbitrarily many τ-transitions. The relation $\widehat{R}_\tau \subseteq W \times W$ contains all pairs (w, v) such that there is a finite, possibly empty, sequence of τ-transitions from w to v, i.e., either $w = v$ or there are $(w_k, w_{k+1}) \in R_\tau$ for $1 \leq k \leq n$ with $n \geq 1$, such that $w_1 = w$ and $w_{n+1} = v$. The τ-closure for atomic actions extends to composed actions by $\widehat{R}_{\alpha;\alpha'} = \widehat{R}_\alpha \cdot \widehat{R}_{\alpha'}$, $\widehat{R}_{\alpha+\alpha'} = \widehat{R}_\alpha \cup \widehat{R}_{\alpha'}$, and $\widehat{R}_{\alpha^*} = (\widehat{R}_\alpha)^\star$.

Definition 1 (Weak bisimulation). *Let* $M = (W, R, w_0)$ *and* $M' = (W', R', w'_0)$ *be two A-structures. A* weak bisimulation relation *between* M *and* M' *is a relation* $B \subseteq W \times W'$ *that contains* (w_0, w'_0) *and satisfies*

(weak-zig) *for any* $a \in A$, $w, v \in W$, $w' \in W'$ *such that* $(w, w') \in B$: *if* $(w, v) \in R_a$, *then there is a* $v' \in W'$ *such that* $(w', v') \in \widehat{R}'_a$ *and* $(v, v') \in B$;
(weak-zag) *for any* $a \in A$, $w \in W$, $w', v' \in W'$ *such that* $(w, w') \in B$: *if* $(w', v') \in R'_a$, *then there is a* $v \in W$ *such that* $(w, v) \in \widehat{R}_a$ *and* $(v, v') \in B$.

Two A-structures $M, M' \in Str^{\mathcal{D}^{\downarrow}_{\tau}}(A)$ *are* weakly bisimulation equivalent, *denoted by* $M \equiv_A^{\mathcal{D}^{\downarrow}_{\tau}} M'$, *if there exists a weak bisimulation relation between* M *and* M'.

Weak bisimulation relations extend to composed actions and their τ-closures:

Lemma 1. *Let* M *and* M' *be two A-structures and* $B \subseteq W \times W'$ *be a weak bisimulation. Then the following holds:*

(weak-zig*) *for any* $\alpha \in Act(A)$, $w, v \in W$, $w' \in W'$ *such that* $(w, w') \in B$: *if* $(w, v) \in \widehat{R}_\alpha$, *then there is a* $v' \in W'$ *such that* $(w', v') \in \widehat{R}'_\alpha$ *and* $(v, v') \in B$;
(weak-zag*) *for any* $\alpha \in Act(A)$, $w \in W$, $w', v' \in W'$ *such that* $(w, w') \in B$: *if* $(w', v') \in \widehat{R}'_\alpha$, *then there is a* $v \in W$ *such that* $(w, v) \in \widehat{R}_\alpha$ *and* $(v, v') \in B$.

It is well known that, for any $A \in \mathbb{S}^{\mathcal{D}^{\downarrow}_{\tau}}$, weak bisimulation equivalence $\equiv_A^{\mathcal{D}^{\downarrow}_{\tau}}$ is an equivalence relation on the class of A-structures. An *abstractor specification* (over $\mathcal{D}^{\downarrow}_{\tau}$) is an expression **abstract** *Sp* **wrt** $\equiv_A^{\mathcal{D}^{\downarrow}_{\tau}}$ where $Sp = (A, \Phi)$ is a specification over $\mathcal{D}^{\downarrow}_{\tau}$. The semantics of an abstractor specification is given by the closure of the model class of *Sp* under weak bisimulation, i.e.,

$$\mathrm{Mod}^{\mathcal{D}^{\downarrow}_{\tau}}(\textbf{abstract } Sp \textbf{ wrt } \equiv_A^{\mathcal{D}^{\downarrow}_{\tau}}) = \{M \in Str^{\mathcal{D}^{\downarrow}_{\tau}}(A) \mid \exists N \in \mathrm{Mod}^{\mathcal{D}^{\downarrow}_{\tau}}(Sp) \,.\, M \equiv_A^{\mathcal{D}^{\downarrow}_{\tau}} N\} \,.$$

Example 2. Let I be the LTS in Fig. 2. Then, as discussed in Example 1, $I \in \mathrm{Mod}^{\mathcal{D}^{\downarrow}_{\tau}}(\textbf{abstract } \mathit{2Buf} \textbf{ wrt } \equiv_A^{\mathcal{D}^{\downarrow}_{\tau}})$. □

3.3 Behavioural Specifications over $\mathcal{D}^{\downarrow}_{\tau}$

Behavioural specifications rely on a behavioural satisfaction relation. The crucial idea of behavioural satisfaction in the context of $\mathcal{D}^{\downarrow}_{\tau}$ is twofold: first, we relax the satisfaction of the diamond modality (and hence of the derived box operator) by abstracting from invisible τ-transitions as done for observable modal logic in [17]. Secondly, we interpret state variables x by states which are not necessarily identical but only observationally equal to the current value of x. For the latter purpose, we recall that for any A-structure $M = (W, R, w_0)$ there exists a greatest weak bisimulation relation between the states of M. We denote this relation by $\approx_M \subseteq W \times W$ and call it *observational equality.* Note that $\approx_M$ is an equivalence relation.

Definition 2 (Behavioural satisfaction). *Let* $M = (W, R, w_0)$ *be an* A*-structure,* $g : X \to W$ *a valuation and* $w \in W$*. The* behavioural satisfaction *of an* A*-formula* φ *w.r.t. valuation* g *in state* w*, denoted by* $M, g, w \models^{\mathcal{D}^{\downarrow}_{\tau}}_{\approx A} \varphi$*, is defined analogously to the satisfaction relation for* $\mathcal{D}^{\downarrow}$ *(see Sect. 2) with the exception of diamond and state variable formulas:*

- $M, g, w \models^{\mathcal{D}^{\downarrow}_{\tau}}_{\approx A} \langle \alpha \rangle \varphi$ *iff there is a* $v \in W$ *with* $(w, v) \in \widehat{R}_{\alpha}$ *and* $M, g, v \models^{\mathcal{D}^{\downarrow}_{\tau}}_{\approx A} \varphi$*;*
- $M, g, w \models^{\mathcal{D}^{\downarrow}_{\tau}}_{\approx A} x$ *iff* $g(x) \approx_M w$*.*

For an A*-sentence* $\varphi \in \mathrm{Sen}^{\mathcal{D}^{\downarrow}_{\tau}}(A)$*, the valuation is irrelevant and* M satisfies behaviourally φ*, denoted by* $M \models^{\mathcal{D}^{\downarrow}_{\tau}}_{\approx A} \varphi$*, iff* $M, w_0 \models^{\mathcal{D}^{\downarrow}_{\tau}}_{\approx A} \varphi$*.*

A *behavioural specification* (over $\mathcal{D}^{\downarrow}_{\tau}$) is an expression **behaviour** Sp **wrt** $\models^{\mathcal{D}^{\downarrow}_{\tau}}_{\approx A}$ where $Sp = (A, \Phi)$ is a specification over $\mathcal{D}^{\downarrow}_{\tau}$. The semantics of a behavioural specification is given by the class of all A-structures which satisfy behaviourally the axioms of the specification, i.e.,

$$\mathrm{Mod}^{\mathcal{D}^{\downarrow}_{\tau}}(\textbf{behaviour } Sp \textbf{ wrt } \models^{\mathcal{D}^{\downarrow}_{\tau}}_{\approx A}) = \{M \in Str^{\mathcal{D}^{\downarrow}_{\tau}}(A) \mid \forall \varphi \in \Phi \,.\, M \models^{\mathcal{D}^{\downarrow}_{\tau}}_{\approx A} \varphi\} \,.$$

Example 3. Let I be the LTS in Fig. 2. Then I behaviourally satisfies the specification *2Buf*, i.e., $I \in \mathrm{Mod}^{\mathcal{D}^{\downarrow}_{\tau}}(\textbf{behaviour } \mathit{2Buf} \textbf{ wrt } \models^{\mathcal{D}^{\downarrow}_{\tau}}_{\approx A})$. For instance, after an *in*-action an *out*-action preceded by a silent transition and also an *in*-action preceded by a silent transition is possible. □

In the remainder of this section we show that under certain conditions behavioural satisfaction and standard satisfaction coincide. The first condition is full abstraction; it expresses that observational equality and set-theoretic equality of elements are the same.

Definition 3 (Full abstraction). *An* A*-structure* $M = (W, R, w_0)$ *is* fully abstract *if for all* $w, w' \in W$ *it holds that* $w \approx_M w'$ *if and only if* $w = w'$*.*

The second condition is observational saturation; it expresses that all elements which are related by the τ-closure of an action a are already related by the action a itself. While the idea of full abstraction is well-known, we are not aware of a notion related to observational saturation.

Definition 4 (Observational saturation). *An* A*-structure* $M = (W, R, w_0)$ *is* observationally saturated *if for all* $a \in A$ *it holds that* $\widehat{R}_a = R_a$*.*

Obviously, observational saturation extends to composed actions $\alpha \in Act(A)$ (which can be shown by structural induction on the form of α).

Lemma 2. *Let* $M = (W, R, w_0)$ *be an observationally saturated* A*-structure. Then for all* $\alpha \in Act(A)$ *it holds that* $\widehat{R}_{\alpha} = R_{\alpha}$*.*

The following lemma is used to show that for fully abstract and observationally saturated structures there is no difference between behavioural and standard satisfaction.

Lemma 3. *Let* $M = (W, R, w_0) \in Str^{\mathcal{D}^{\downarrow}_{\tau}}(A)$ *be a fully abstract and observationally saturated A-structure. Then for any* $w \in W$*, valuation* $g : X \to W$ *and for any A-formula* φ*, we have*

$$M, g, w \models^{\mathcal{D}^{\downarrow}_{\tau}}_{\approx A} \varphi \iff M, g, w \models^{\mathcal{D}^{\downarrow}_{\tau}}_{A} \varphi \,.$$

Proof. The proof is performed by structural induction over the form of the formula φ. The only interesting cases are diamond and state variable formulas.
Case $\varphi = \langle\alpha\rangle\psi$: $M, g, w \models^{\mathcal{D}^{\downarrow}_{\tau}}_{\approx A} \langle\alpha\rangle\psi$ iff there is a $v \in W$ with $(w, v) \in \widehat{R}_\alpha$ and $M, g, v \models^{\mathcal{D}^{\downarrow}_{\tau}}_{\approx A} \psi$. Since M is observationally saturated, this is, by Lem. 2, equivalent to $(w, v) \in R_\alpha$ and $M, g, v \models^{\mathcal{D}^{\downarrow}_{\tau}}_{\approx A} \psi$. By induction hypothesis this is equivalent to $(w, v) \in R_\alpha$ and $M, g, v \models^{\mathcal{D}^{\downarrow}_{\tau}}_{A} \psi$ which is in turn equivalent to $M, g, w \models^{\mathcal{D}^{\downarrow}_{\tau}}_{A} \langle\alpha\rangle\psi$.
Case $\varphi = x$: $M, g, w \models^{\mathcal{D}^{\downarrow}_{\tau}}_{\approx A} x$ iff $g(x) \approx_M w$. Since M is fully abstract this is equivalent to $g(x) = w$ which is in turn equivalent to $M, g, w \models^{\mathcal{D}^{\downarrow}_{\tau}}_{A} x$. □

As a direct consequence of Lemma 3 we obtain the following theorem.

Theorem 1. *Let* $M = (W, R, w_0) \in Str^{\mathcal{D}^{\downarrow}_{\tau}}(A)$ *be a fully abstract and observationally saturated A-structure. Then, for all* $\varphi \in \mathrm{Sen}^{\mathcal{D}^{\downarrow}_{\tau}}(A)$*, we have that*

$$M \models^{\mathcal{D}^{\downarrow}_{\tau}}_{\approx A} \varphi \iff M \models^{\mathcal{D}^{\downarrow}_{\tau}}_{A} \varphi \,.$$

4 Behaviour-Abstractor Framework for $\mathcal{D}^{\downarrow}_{\tau}$-logic

Having defined abstractor and behavioural specifications over $\mathcal{D}^{\downarrow}_{\tau}$ an obvious question is whether their semantics can be related. For this purpose we will show that $\mathcal{D}^{\downarrow}_{\tau}$-logic and its observational interpretations give rise to an instantiation of the behaviour-abstractor framework introduced in [7].

4.1 Behaviour-Abstractor Framework

The concept of a behaviour-abstractor framework identifies a small but significant set of abstract requirements which are enough to define behavioural and abstractor specifications independently of a concrete logic and to study relationships between their semantics.

Definition 5 ([7]). *A* behaviour-abstractor framework $\text{BA} = (\mathbb{S}, \mathit{Str}, \text{Sen}, \models, \equiv, \models\!\approx, \mathcal{BB})$ *consists of*

- *a class* $\mathbb{S}$ *of* signatures,
- *a family* $\mathit{Str} = (\mathit{Str}(\Sigma))_{\Sigma\in\mathbb{S}}$ *of classes* $\mathit{Str}(\Sigma)$ *of* Σ-structures,
- *a family* $\text{Sen} = (\text{Sen}(\Sigma))_{\Sigma\in\mathbb{S}}$ *of sets* $\text{Sen}(\Sigma)$ *of* Σ-sentences,
- *a family* $\models\, = (\models_\Sigma)_{\Sigma\in\mathbb{S}}$ *of* satisfaction relations $\models_\Sigma\, \subseteq \mathit{Str}(\Sigma) \times \text{Sen}(\Sigma)$,
- *a family* $\equiv\, = (\equiv_\Sigma)_{\Sigma\in\mathbb{S}}$ *of* abstraction equivalences $\equiv_\Sigma\, \subseteq \mathit{Str}(\Sigma) \times \mathit{Str}(\Sigma)$,
- *a family* $\models\!\approx\, = (\models\!\approx_\Sigma)_{\Sigma\in\mathbb{S}}$ *of* behavioural satisfaction relations $\models\!\approx_\Sigma\, \subseteq \mathit{Str}(\Sigma) \times \text{Sen}(\Sigma)$, *and*
- *a family* $\mathcal{BB} = (\mathcal{BB}_\Sigma)_{\Sigma\in\mathbb{S}}$ *of* black-box *functions* $\mathcal{BB}_\Sigma : \mathit{Str}(\Sigma) \to \mathit{Str}(\Sigma)$,

such that the following conditions (BA1–BA3) are satisfied for each signature $\Sigma \in \mathbb{S}$ *and for all* Σ*-structures* $M, M' \in \mathit{Str}(\Sigma)$*:*

(BA1) if $M \equiv_\Sigma M'$*, then* $M \models\!\approx_\Sigma \varphi \iff M' \models\!\approx_\Sigma \varphi$ *for all* $\varphi \in \text{Sen}(\Sigma)$*;*
(BA2) $M \equiv_\Sigma \mathcal{BB}_\Sigma(M)$*;*
(BA3) $\mathcal{BB}_\Sigma(M) \models\!\approx_\Sigma \varphi \iff \mathcal{BB}_\Sigma(M) \models_\Sigma \varphi$ *for all* $\varphi \in \text{Sen}(\Sigma)$.

The idea of an abstraction equivalence is to relate structures which show the same observable behaviour. The idea of behavioural satisfaction is to relax the (ordinary) satisfaction relation such that it is sufficient if properties are satisfied from the observational point of view and not necessarily literally. Condition (BA1) relates abstraction equivalence and behavioural satisfaction by requiring that abstraction equivalence preserves behavioural satisfaction of sentences. This means that behavioural satisfaction of sentences is invariant under abstraction equivalence. The black-box function constructs, for each Σ-structure M, a so-called *black-box view* of M. The intuitive idea is that $\mathcal{BB}_\Sigma(M)$ shows the observable behaviour of M abstracting away implementation details which are not visible for the user of a system. Of course, the black-box view of M should be equivalent to M according to the abstraction equivalence, and this is expressed by condition (BA2). Condition (BA3) formalises an intrinsic property of black-box views, for which behavioural satisfaction of sentences should be the same as ordinary satisfaction.

Given a behaviour-abstractor framework BA, a specification $\mathit{Sp} = (\Sigma, \Phi)$ over BA consists of a signature $\Sigma \in \mathbb{S}$ and a set $\Phi \subseteq \text{Sen}(\Sigma)$ of Σ-sentences. The (ordinary) semantics of Sp is given by $\text{Mod}(\mathit{Sp}) = \{M \in \mathit{Str}(\Sigma) \mid \forall\varphi \in \Phi \,.\, M \models_\Sigma \varphi\}$. On top of Sp an abstractor specification **abstract** Sp **wrt** $\equiv$ and a behavioural specification **behaviour** Sp **wrt** $\models\!\approx$ can be constructed with their model classes defined as follows:

$$\text{Mod}(\textbf{abstract } \mathit{Sp} \textbf{ wrt } \equiv) = \{M \in \mathit{Str}(\Sigma) \mid \exists N \in \text{Mod}(\mathit{Sp}) \,.\, M \equiv_\Sigma N\}\ ,$$
$$\text{Mod}(\textbf{behaviour } \mathit{Sp} \textbf{ wrt } \models\!\approx) = \{M \in \mathit{Str}(\Sigma) \mid \forall\varphi \in \Phi \,.\, M \models\!\approx_\Sigma \varphi\}\ .$$

The purpose of the behaviour-abstractor framework is to identify the crucial concepts needed to relate (the semantics of) behavioural and abstractor specifications such that one gets for free the results of the following theorem whenever a concrete formalism is a behaviour-abstractor framework. The first part of the theorem shows that behavioural semantics is always included in abstractor semantics; the second part shows that behavioural and abstractor semantics coincide if all ordinary models of a specification *Sp* satisfy also behaviourally the axioms of *Sp*[2].

Theorem 2 (**[7]**). *Let* $\mathrm{BA} = (\mathbb{S}, \mathit{Str}, \mathrm{Sen}, \models, \equiv, \approx\!\!\!\models, \mathcal{BB})$ *be a behaviour-abstractor framework and Sp a specification over* BA.

1. $\mathrm{Mod}(\textbf{behaviour } Sp \textbf{ wrt } \approx\!\!\!\models) \subseteq \mathrm{Mod}(\textbf{abstract } Sp \textbf{ wrt } \equiv)$.
2. $\mathrm{Mod}(Sp) \subseteq \mathrm{Mod}(\textbf{behaviour } Sp \textbf{ wrt } \approx\!\!\!\models) \iff$
   $\mathrm{Mod}(\textbf{behaviour } Sp \textbf{ wrt } \approx\!\!\!\models) = \mathrm{Mod}(\textbf{abstract } Sp \textbf{ wrt } \equiv)$.

4.2 Instantiation of the Behaviour-Abstractor Framework with $\mathcal{D}^{\downarrow}_{\tau}$

We can instantiate the behaviour-abstractor framework with the notions of $\mathcal{D}^{\downarrow}_{\tau}$-logic as follows. Signatures, structures, sentences and the (ordinary) satisfaction relation of $\mathcal{D}^{\downarrow}_{\tau}$ have been defined in Sect. 2; black-box functions are discussed below. As abstraction equivalences we use weak bisimulation (Definition 1) and the behavioural satisfaction relation is the one of Definition 2.

In the context of $\mathcal{D}^{\downarrow}_{\tau}$-logic, condition (BA1) of a behaviour-abstractor framework (cf. Definition 5) expresses modal invariance of A-sentences w.r.t. weak bisimulation equivalence and behavioural satisfaction. The proof of this modal invariance property relies on the following lemma which can be shown by structural induction over formulas (using Lemmma 1 for the case of diamond formulas).

Lemma 4. *Let* $M = (W, R, w_0)$ *and* $M' = (W', R', w_0')$ *be two A-structures and* $B \subseteq W \times W'$ *a weak bisimulation. Then for any* $w \in W, w' \in W'$ *with* $(w, w') \in B$*, for any valuations* $g : X \to W$, $g' : X \to W'$ *with* $(g(x), g'(x)) \in B$ *for all* $x \in X$*, and for any A-formula* φ*, we have*

$$M, g, w \approx\!\!\!\models_A^{\mathcal{D}^{\downarrow}_{\tau}} \varphi \iff M', g', w' \approx\!\!\!\models_A^{\mathcal{D}^{\downarrow}_{\tau}} \varphi \,.$$

As a direct consequence of Lem. 4 we obtain the following theorem that verifies the first condition of a behaviour-abstractor framework.

Theorem 3. *For any* $A \in \mathbb{S}^{\mathcal{D}^{\downarrow}_{\tau}}$ *and for all* $M, M' \in \mathit{Str}^{\mathcal{D}^{\downarrow}_{\tau}}(A)$,

$$(\mathrm{BA1}^{\mathcal{D}^{\downarrow}_{\tau}}) \text{ if } M \equiv_A^{\mathcal{D}^{\downarrow}_{\tau}} M, \text{ then } \forall \varphi \in \mathrm{Sen}^{\mathcal{D}^{\downarrow}_{\tau}}(A)\,.\, M \approx\!\!\!\models_A^{\mathcal{D}^{\downarrow}_{\tau}} \varphi \iff M' \approx\!\!\!\models_A^{\mathcal{D}^{\downarrow}_{\tau}} \varphi \,.$$

[2] It may sound strange that ordinary satisfaction does not always imply behavioural satisfaction but there are indeed some cases where this can happen; see Example 6.

Black-Box Function. To define the black-box view of an A-structure M we use the following quotient construction. It identifies observationally equal states and relates equivalence classes $[w]_{\approx_M}$ and $[v]_{\approx_M}$ by an action a if there are elements w' in $[w]_{\approx_M}$ and v' in $[v]_{\approx_M}$ which are related by the τ-closure of a (w.r.t. the transitions of M).

Definition 6 (Quotient structure). *Let* $M = (W, R, w_0) \in Str^{\mathcal{D}^{\downarrow}_{\tau}}(A)$ *be an* A*-structure. The quotient of* M *w.r.t.* $\approx_M$ *is the* A*-structure* $M/{\approx_M} = (W/{\approx_M}, R/{\approx_M}, [w_0]_{\approx_M})$, *where*

- $W/{\approx_M} = \{[w]_{\approx_M} \mid w \in W\}$ *with* $[w]_{\approx_M} = \{w' \mid w' \approx_M w\}$;
- $R/{\approx_M} = ((R/{\approx_M})_a)_{a \in A}$ *with*

$$(R/{\approx_M})_a = \{([w]_{\approx_M}, [v]_{\approx_M}) \mid \exists w' \in [w]_{\approx_M}, v' \in [v]_{\approx_M} . (w', v') \in \hat{R}_a\}$$

for any $a \in A$.

Since $\approx_M$ is an equivalence relation, $M/{\approx_M}$ is well-defined and any state $[w]$ is reachable from the initial one. For any $M \in Str^{\mathcal{D}^{\downarrow}_{\tau}}(A)$, the *black-box view* of M is defined by $\mathcal{BB}_A^{\mathcal{D}^{\downarrow}_{\tau}}(M) =_{\text{def}} M/{\approx_M}$.

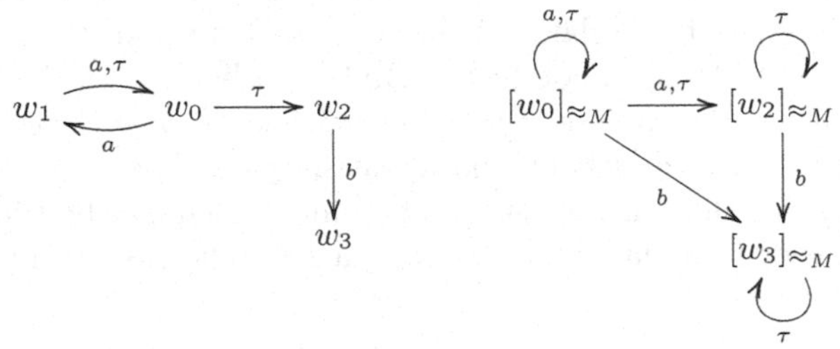

Fig. 3. A structure M and its quotient $M/{\approx_M}$

Example 4. Figure 3 shows an LTS M and its quotient $M/{\approx_M}$. By definition of quotients there is a τ-loop for each state $[w]_{\approx_M} \in M/{\approx_M}$. The states w_0 and w_2 of M are not observationally equivalent since the silent τ-transition from w_0 to w_2 removes the possibility to execute a. Hence the τ-transition remains in the quotient, now between the different states $[w_0]_{\approx_M}$ and $[w_2]_{\approx_M}$. □

The next theorem verifies the second condition of a behaviour-abstractor framework.

Theorem 4. *For any* A*-structure* $M \in Str^{\mathcal{D}^{\downarrow}_{\tau}}(A)$, *it holds*

$$(\text{BA2}^{\mathcal{D}^{\downarrow}_{\tau}}) \;\; M \equiv_A^{\mathcal{D}^{\downarrow}_{\tau}} \mathcal{BB}_A^{\mathcal{D}^{\downarrow}_{\tau}}(M) .$$

Proof. It is straightforward, though somewhat technical, to show that the relation $B \subseteq W \times W/{\approx_M}$ with $B = \{(w, [w]_{\approx_M}) \mid w \in W\}$ is a weak bisimulation relation between M and $M/{\approx_M}$, and hence between M and $\mathcal{BB}_A^{\mathcal{D}_\tau^\downarrow}(M)$. □

Let us now consider the third condition of a behaviour-abstractor framework requiring that behavioural and standard satisfaction coincide for black-box structures in $\mathcal{D}_\tau^\downarrow$. For the proof we use the next two lemmas. The first one says that quotient structures, and hence black-box structures, are fully abstract.

Lemma 5. *For any $M = (W, R, w_0) \in \mathit{Str}^{\mathcal{D}_\tau^\downarrow}(A)$, $\mathcal{BB}_A^{\mathcal{D}_\tau^\downarrow}(M)$ is fully abstract, i.e., for all $w, w' \in W$ it holds that $[w]_{\approx_M} \approx_{\mathcal{BB}_A^{\mathcal{D}_\tau^\downarrow}(M)} [w']_{\approx_M}$ iff $[w]_{\approx_M} = [w']_{\approx_M}$.*

Proof. Only the direction "⇒" is not trivial. It is straightforward, but technical, to show that the relation $B \subseteq W \times W$ with

$$B = \{(w, w') \mid [w]_{\approx_M} \approx_{\mathcal{BB}_A^{\mathcal{D}_\tau^\downarrow}(M)} [w']_{\approx_M}\}$$

is a weak bisimulation relation between the states of M. Now, let $w, w' \in W$ such that $[w]_{\approx_M} \approx_{\mathcal{BB}_A^{\mathcal{D}_\tau^\downarrow}(M)} [w']_{\approx_M}$ holds. Then $(w, w') \in B$. Since $\approx_M$ is the greatest weak bisimulation relation on M we have $w \approx_M w'$ and therefore $[w]_{\approx_M} = [w']_{\approx_M}$. □

The second lemma says that quotient structures, and hence black-box structures, are observationally saturated.

Lemma 6. *For any $M = (W, R, w_0) \in \mathit{Str}^{\mathcal{D}_\tau^\downarrow}(A)$, $\mathcal{BB}_A^{\mathcal{D}_\tau^\downarrow}(M)$ is observationally saturated, i.e., for each $a \in A$,*

$$(\widehat{R/{\approx_M}})_a = (R/{\approx_M})_a.$$

Proof. Let us write $\widetilde{R}$ for $R/{\approx_M}$; $\widehat{\widetilde{R}}$ for $\widehat{R/{\approx_M}}$; and $\widetilde{w}$ for $[w]_{\approx_M}$. The claim then reads $\widehat{\widetilde{R}} = \widetilde{R}$. $\widetilde{R} \subseteq \widehat{\widetilde{R}}$ is obvious. For the converse inclusion, we first show for every $a \in A = O \cup \{\tau\}$

(∗) if $(\widetilde{w}_1, \widetilde{w}_2) \in \widetilde{R}_\tau$ and $(\widetilde{w}_2, \widetilde{w}_3) \in \widetilde{R}_a$, then $(\widetilde{w}_1, \widetilde{w}_3) \in \widetilde{R}_a$;
(∗∗) if $(\widetilde{w}_1, \widetilde{w}_2) \in \widetilde{R}_a$ and $(\widetilde{w}_2, \widetilde{w}_3) \in \widetilde{R}_\tau$, then $(\widetilde{w}_1, \widetilde{w}_3) \in \widetilde{R}_a$.

Indeed, for (*), $(\widetilde{w}_1, \widetilde{w}_2) \in \widetilde{R}_\tau$ and $(\widetilde{w}_2, \widetilde{w}_3) \in \widetilde{R}_a$ imply that there are $v_1 \in \widetilde{w}_1$, $v_2, v_2' \in \widetilde{w}_2$, and $v_3' \in \widetilde{w}_3$ with $(v_1, v_2) \in \widehat{R}_\tau$ and $(v_2', v_3') \in \widehat{R}_a$. Since $v_2, v_2' \in \widetilde{w}_2$, we have $v_2 \approx_M v_2'$, and thus, by applying (weak-zig*) of Lem. 1 to $(v_2', v_3') \in \widehat{R}_a$, there is a $v_3 \in W$ with $(v_2, v_3) \in \widehat{R}_a$ and $v_3' \approx_M v_3$. Now $(v_1, v_2) \in \widehat{R}_\tau$ and $(v_2, v_3) \in \widehat{R}_a$ and hence $(v_1, v_3) \in \widehat{R}_a$. By $v_3 \approx_M v_3' \in \widetilde{w}_3$ we obtain $v_3 \in \widetilde{w}_3$ and thus $(\widetilde{w}_1, \widetilde{w}_3) \in \widetilde{R}_a$. The proof for (**) is symmetric.

With these auxiliary facts we obtain, for $o \in O$ and writing the relation in infix notation,

$$\begin{aligned}\widetilde{w}_1 \,\widehat{\widetilde{R}}_o\, \widetilde{w}_2 &\Longrightarrow \widetilde{w}_1 \,\widetilde{R}_\tau \cdot \ldots \cdot \widetilde{R}_\tau \cdot \widetilde{R}_o \cdot \widetilde{R}_\tau \cdot \ldots \cdot \widetilde{R}_\tau\, \widetilde{w}_2 \\ &\overset{(*)}{\Longrightarrow} \widetilde{w}_1 \,\widetilde{R}_o \cdot \widetilde{R}_\tau \cdot \ldots \cdot \widetilde{R}_\tau\, \widetilde{w}_2 \overset{(**)}{\Longrightarrow} \widetilde{w}_1 \,\widetilde{R}_o\, \widetilde{w}_2 \,.\end{aligned}$$

For $\widetilde{w}_1 \,\widehat{\widetilde{R}}_\tau\, \widetilde{w}_2$ either $\widetilde{w}_1 = \widetilde{w}_2$ or there is a non-empty sequence $\widetilde{w}_1 \,\widetilde{R}_\tau \cdot \ldots \cdot \widetilde{R}_\tau\, \widetilde{w}_2$. In the first case, we note that $w_1 \hat{R}_\tau w_1$ and hence, by definition of quotients, $\widetilde{w}_1 \,\widetilde{R}_\tau\, \widetilde{w}_1$. Since $\widetilde{w}_1 = \widetilde{w}_2$ we have $\widetilde{w}_1 \,\widetilde{R}_\tau\, \widetilde{w}_2$. In the second case, either the sequence has length one and we are done or

$$\widetilde{w}_1 \,\widehat{\widetilde{R}}_\tau\, \widetilde{w}_2 \Longrightarrow \widetilde{w}_1 \,\widetilde{R}_\tau \cdot \ldots \cdot \widetilde{R}_\tau\, \widetilde{w}_2 \overset{(*)}{\Longrightarrow} \widetilde{w}_1 \,\widetilde{R}_\tau\, \widetilde{w}_2 \,.$$

□

Since $\mathcal{BB}_A^{\mathcal{D}^{\downarrow}_{\tau}}(M)$ is fully abstract and observationally saturated we can apply Theorem 1 such that we obtain the third condition of a behaviour-abstractor framework in the context of $\mathcal{D}^{\downarrow}_{\tau}$.

Theorem 5. *Let $M \in Str^{\mathcal{D}^{\downarrow}_{\tau}}(A)$. Then, for all $\varphi \in \mathrm{Sen}^{\mathcal{D}^{\downarrow}_{\tau}}(A)$, we have that*

$$(\mathrm{BA3}^{\mathcal{D}^{\downarrow}_{\tau}})\ \mathcal{BB}_A^{\mathcal{D}^{\downarrow}_{\tau}}(M) \approx\!\!\!\!\models_A^{\mathcal{D}^{\downarrow}_{\tau}} \varphi \iff \mathcal{BB}_A^{\mathcal{D}^{\downarrow}_{\tau}}(M) \models_A^{\mathcal{D}^{\downarrow}_{\tau}} \varphi \,.$$

Corollary 1. $\mathrm{BA}^{\mathcal{D}^{\downarrow}_{\tau}} = (\mathbb{S}^{\mathcal{D}^{\downarrow}_{\tau}}, \mathrm{Sen}^{\mathcal{D}^{\downarrow}_{\tau}}, Str^{\mathcal{D}^{\downarrow}_{\tau}}, \models^{\mathcal{D}^{\downarrow}_{\tau}}, \equiv^{\mathcal{D}^{\downarrow}_{\tau}}, \approx\!\!\!\!\models^{\mathcal{D}^{\downarrow}_{\tau}}, \mathcal{BB}^{\mathcal{D}^{\downarrow}_{\tau}})$ *is a behaviour-abstractor framework.*

We thus can instantiate Theorem 2 and get the respective relationships between behavioural and abstractor specifications in the context of $\mathcal{D}^{\downarrow}_{\tau}$-logic.

Corollary 2. *Let Sp be a specification over $\mathcal{D}^{\downarrow}_{\tau}$.*

1. $\mathrm{Mod}^{\mathcal{D}^{\downarrow}_{\tau}}(\textbf{behaviour}\ Sp\ \textbf{wrt}\ \approx\!\!\!\!\models_A^{\mathcal{D}^{\downarrow}_{\tau}}) \subseteq \mathrm{Mod}^{\mathcal{D}^{\downarrow}_{\tau}}(\textbf{abstract}\ Sp\ \textbf{wrt}\ \equiv_A^{\mathcal{D}^{\downarrow}_{\tau}})$
2. $\mathrm{Mod}^{\mathcal{D}^{\downarrow}_{\tau}}(Sp) \subseteq \mathrm{Mod}^{\mathcal{D}^{\downarrow}_{\tau}}(\textbf{behaviour}\ Sp\ \textbf{wrt}\ \approx\!\!\!\!\models_A^{\mathcal{D}^{\downarrow}_{\tau}}) \iff$
   $\mathrm{Mod}^{\mathcal{D}^{\downarrow}_{\tau}}(\textbf{behaviour}\ Sp\ \textbf{wrt}\ \approx\!\!\!\!\models_A^{\mathcal{D}^{\downarrow}_{\tau}}) = \mathrm{Mod}^{\mathcal{D}^{\downarrow}_{\tau}}(\textbf{abstract}\ Sp\ \textbf{wrt}\ \equiv_A^{\mathcal{D}^{\downarrow}_{\tau}})$

Example 5. We consider the specification *2Buf* of Example 1 with axiom φ. Since φ is a positive formula (not containing negation), for all A-structures N, $N \models_A^{\mathcal{D}^{\downarrow}_{\tau}} \varphi$ implies $N \approx\!\!\!\!\models_A^{\mathcal{D}^{\downarrow}_{\tau}} \varphi$. Hence, $\mathrm{Mod}^{\mathcal{D}^{\downarrow}_{\tau}}(\mathit{2Buf}) \subseteq \mathrm{Mod}^{\mathcal{D}^{\downarrow}_{\tau}}(\textbf{behaviour}\ \mathit{2Buf}\ \textbf{wrt}\ \approx\!\!\!\!\models_A^{\mathcal{D}^{\downarrow}_{\tau}})$. Therefore, by Cor. 2(2),

$$\begin{aligned}&\mathrm{Mod}^{\mathcal{D}^{\downarrow}_{\tau}}(\textbf{behaviour}\ \mathit{2Buf}\ \textbf{wrt}\ \approx\!\!\!\!\models_A^{\mathcal{D}^{\downarrow}_{\tau}}) = \\ &\qquad\qquad \mathrm{Mod}^{\mathcal{D}^{\downarrow}_{\tau}}(\textbf{abstract}\ \mathit{2Buf}\ \textbf{wrt}\ \equiv_A^{\mathcal{D}^{\downarrow}_{\tau}}) \,.\end{aligned}$$

□

Let us still point out that the condition $\mathrm{Mod}^{\mathcal{D}^{\downarrow}_{\tau}}(Sp) \subseteq \mathrm{Mod}^{\mathcal{D}^{\downarrow}_{\tau}}$ (**behaviour** Sp **wrt** $\mathrel{|\!\approx}^{\mathcal{D}^{\downarrow}_{\tau}}_{A}$) in Cor. 2(2) does not always hold.

Example 6. (i) Consider the signature of *2Buf* and the sentence $\varphi' = \langle in\rangle\neg\langle in\rangle\mathbf{tt}$. Then, for the structure I in Fig. 2, we have $I \models^{\mathcal{D}^{\downarrow}_{\tau}}_{A} \varphi'$ but $I \not\mathrel{|\!\approx}^{\mathcal{D}^{\downarrow}_{\tau}}_{A} \varphi'$.

(ii) The $\{a\}$-structure M in Fig. 4 gives another example where standard satisfaction does not imply behavioural satisfaction. The reason is that w_0 and w_1 are different but observationally equal states.

□

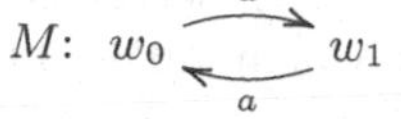

Fig. 4. $M \models^{\mathcal{D}^{\downarrow}_{\tau}}_{A} \downarrow x\,.\,\langle a\rangle\neg x$ but $M \not\mathrel{|\!\approx}^{\mathcal{D}^{\downarrow}_{\tau}}_{A} \downarrow x\,.\,\langle a\rangle\neg x$

5 Concluding Remarks

We have studied two observational interpretations of $\mathcal{D}^{\downarrow}_{\tau}$-logic, a dynamic logic with binders and silent transitions. The two approaches, behavioural and abstractor specifications, follow the lines of an intensive study of behavioural and abstractor semantics in the area of algebraic specifications which has been taken up for reactive systems in [5]. The major result is that behavioural semantics, based on a behavioural satisfaction relation, and abstractor semantics, based on observational abstraction of model classes by weak bisimulation, coincide if and only if any standard model of a specification is a behavioural model as well. To establish this result we have shown that our logic instantiates the general, logic-independent requirements of a behaviour-abstractor framework proposed in [7]. As a side-effect we get that behavioural satisfaction of $\mathcal{D}^{\downarrow}_{\tau}$-sentences is modally invariant under weak bisimulation.

There are several interesting research questions for future work. We want to integrate $\mathcal{D}^{\downarrow}_{\tau}$-logic and its observational interpretations in the development methodology for reactive systems suggested in [9]. This would involve explicit implementation constructors, e.g., for information hiding and parallel composition. Larger case studies and tools for validating the observational interpretations of $\mathcal{D}^{\downarrow}_{\tau}$-logic would be another issue. This would include the investigation of proof methods for deriving observational consequences from specifications. As an extension of our work we would like to integrate data states following the ideas of [6]. Moreover it would be interesting to see what would happen if we replace weak bisimulation by other equivalence notions like, e.g., branching bisimulation.

Acknowledgement. We would like to thank the anonymous reviewers of this work for valuable suggestions.

References

1. Bidoit, M., Hennicker, R., Wirsing, M.: Behavioural and abstractor specifications. Sci. Comput. Program. **25**(2–3), 149–186 (1995)
2. Braüner, T.: Hybrid Logic and its Proof-Theory. Applied Logic Series. Springer, Heidelberg (2010). https://doi.org/10.1007/978-94-007-0002-4
3. Harel, D., Kozen, D., Tiuryn, J.: Dynamic Logic. MIT Press, Cambridge (2000)
4. Hennicker, R.: Context induction: a proof principle for behavioural abstractions and algebraic implementations. Formal Asp. Comput. **3**(4), 326–345 (1991)
5. Hennicker, R., Madeira, A.: Observational semantics for dynamic logic with binders. In: James, P., Roggenbach, M. (eds.) WADT 2016. LNCS, vol. 10644, pp. 135–152. Springer, Cham (2017). https://doi.org/10.1007/978-3-319-72044-9_10
6. Hennicker, R., Madeira, A., Knapp, A.: A hybrid dynamic logic for event/data-based systems. In: Hähnle, R., van der Aalst, W. (eds.) FASE 2019. LNCS, vol. 11424, pp. 79–97. Springer, Cham (2019). https://doi.org/10.1007/978-3-030-16722-6_5
7. Hennicker, R., Madeira, A., Wirsing, M.: Behavioural and abstractor specifications revisited. Theor. Comput. Sci. **741**, 32–43 (2018)
8. Hofmann, M., Sannella, D.: On behavioural abstraction and behavioural satisfaction in higher-order logic. Theor. Comput. Sci. **167**(1&2), 3–45 (1996)
9. Madeira, A., Barbosa, L.S., Hennicker, R., Martins, M.A.: Dynamic logic with binders and its application to the development of reactive systems. In: Sampaio, A., Wang, F. (eds.) ICTAC 2016. LNCS, vol. 9965, pp. 422–440. Springer, Cham (2016). https://doi.org/10.1007/978-3-319-46750-4_24
10. Milner, R.: Communication and Concurrency. Prentice Hall, Upper Saddle River (1989)
11. Misiak, M.: Behavioural semantics of algebraic specifications in arbitrary logical systems. In: Fiadeiro, J.L., Mosses, P.D., Orejas, F. (eds.) WADT 2004. LNCS, vol. 3423, pp. 144–161. Springer, Heidelberg (2005). https://doi.org/10.1007/978-3-540-31959-7_9
12. Nivela, M.P., Orejas, F.: Initial behaviour semantics for algebraic specifications. In: Sannella, D., Tarlecki, A. (eds.) ADT 1987. LNCS, vol. 332, pp. 184–207. Springer, Heidelberg (1988). https://doi.org/10.1007/3-540-50325-0_10
13. Reichel, H.: Behavioural equivalence – a unifying concept for initial and final specifications. In: Arato, M., Varga, L. (eds.) In: Proceedings of the 3rd Hungarian Computer Science Conference, pp. 27–39. Akademiai Kiado (1981)
14. Reichel, H.: Behavioural validity of conditional equations in abstract data types. In: Proceedings of the 3rd Vienna Conference Contributions to General Algebra, pp. 301–324. B.G. Teubner (1985)
15. Sannella, D., Tarlecki, A.: On observational equivalence and algebraic specification. J. Comput. Syst. Sci. **34**(2–3), 150–178 (1987)
16. Sannella, D., Wirsing, M.: A kernel language for algebraic specification and implementation extended abstract. In: Karpinski, M. (ed.) FCT 1983. LNCS, vol. 158, pp. 413–427. Springer, Heidelberg (1983). https://doi.org/10.1007/3-540-12689-9_122
17. Stirling, C.: Modal and Temporal Properties of Processes. Springer, New York (2001)

The Logic of AGM Learning from Partial Observations

Alexandru Baltag[1], Aybüke Özgün[1,2], and Ana Lucia Vargas-Sandoval[1](✉)

[1] ILLC, University of Amsterdam, Amsterdam, The Netherlands
ana.varsa@gmail.com
[2] Arché, University of St. Andrews, St Andrews, UK

Abstract. We present a dynamic logic for inductive learning from partial observations by a "rational" learner, that obeys AGM postulates for belief revision. We apply our logic to an example, showing how various concrete properties can be learnt with certainty or inductively by such an AGM learner. We present a sound and complete axiomatization, based on a combination of relational and neighbourhood version of the canonical model method.

1 Introduction

In this paper, we extend our previous work [3], presented at DaLi 2017, in which we introduced a dynamic logic for learning theory, building on our past work [4,5] (that bridged Formal Learning Theory and Dynamic Epistemic Logic in a topological setting): a learner forms conjectures based on a continuous stream of observations, with the goal of inductively converging to a true conjecture. To reason about this framework, we added to Subset Space Logics [12,16] dynamic *observation modalities* $[o]\varphi$, as well as a *learning operator* $L(\vec{o})$, which encodes the learner's *conjecture* after observing a finite sequence of data $\vec{o}$. In [3], we completely axiomatized this logic, and used it to characterize various epistemological and learning-theoretic notions.

However, the learner in [3] was assumed to satisfy only very few rationality constraints (essentially, only consistency of conjectures, and the Success postulate requiring that the conjectures fit the evidence). In contrast, in this paper we focus on fully rational learners, whose conjectures obey all the AGM postulates for belief revision [1]. Semantically, such an "AGM learner" comes with a family of nested Grove spheres (encoding the agent's defaults and her belief-revision policy), or equivalently with a total plausibility (pre)order on the set of possible worlds. After observing some evidence, the learner forms a conjecture by applying "AGM conditioning": essentially, her conjecture encompasses the most plausible worlds that fit the evidence. This belief dynamics is non-monotonic, but only minimally so: it respects the principle of Rational Monotonicity (equivalent to some of the AGM postulates in [1]), requiring that the dynamics is just monotonic logical updating (the so-called "expansion", putting together the old

L. Soares Barbosa and A. Baltag (Eds.): DaLí 2019, LNCS 12005, pp. 35–52, 2020.
https://doi.org/10.1007/978-3-030-38808-9_3

conjecture with the new evidence) whenever the old conjecture is consistent with the new evidence.

Our aim is to realize the same program for such AGM learners as the one we achieved in [3]. There are many reasons to focus on AGM learners: first, AGM postulates seem inherently plausible, or at least strongly desirable as constraints on rational learners' belief dynamics. Second, imposing such constraints does not lead to any loss in learning power: as shown in [4], AGM conditioning is a "universal learning method": any questions that can be inductively solved (or solved with certainty) by some learner can also be solved by an AGM learner. Third, the additional constraints posed by the AGM postulates make the logic of inductive AGM learning more interesting, and its completeness more challenging, than the logic of unconstrained learners.

And indeed, as it turns out, forming conjectures *only based on a sequence of direct, complete observations* (as is standard in Learning Theory, and as we also assumed in [3]) does not seem to be enough to allow us to characterize AGM learning! In order to obtain our completeness result, we had to extend the domain of our learning functions to *partial observations*: incomplete reports of a full-fledged observation, equivalent to finite disjunctions of observations. Technically, we had to move from the framework of *intersection spaces* adopted in [3] (in which the observable properties were closed under finite intersections, to capture the effect of successive observations) to the one of *lattice spaces* (in which closure under finite unions is also required, to capture the effect of partial observations). At the syntactic level, this lead us to replace simple observations by *observational events*: like PDL programs, these are built from simple observations $!o$, using sequential composition $e; e'$ (to represent successive observations) and epistemic non-determinism $e \sqcup e'$ (to capture the receipt of partial information, after which the agent is not sure which of the two observations e, e' has been made). After an observational event e, the learner forms a conjecture $L(e)$, obtained by applying AGM conditioning (with respect to her plausibility order $\leq$) to the event's informational content $pre(e)$ (its "precondition", defined recursively by taking conjunctions of the preconditions in a sequential composition $e; e'$, and disjunctions of the preconditions in a epistemic non-determinism $e \sqcup e'$).

As in Subset Space Logics [12,16], our language features an S5-type *'infallible knowledge' modality*, capturing the learner's *hard information*, as well as the so-called *'effort' modality*, which we interpret as 'stable truth' (i.e., truth that will resist further observations). As in [3], we add *dynamic modalities* $[e]\varphi$, this time capturing *updates after observational events* ("φ becomes true after event e"), similarly to the role of dynamic modalities in Propositional Dynamic Logic (PDL) and especially in Dynamic Epistemic Logic (DEL).[1] Finally, we have an *AGM learning operator* $L(e)$, which encodes the AGM learner's conjecture (her "strongest belief") given an observational event e. As in [3], these can be used to give natural definitions of *belief, stable (undefeated) belief, inductive*

[1] Indeed, our observational events can be seen as corresponding to a special type of (single-agent) epistemic events in the so-called BMS style.

knowledge and *inductive learnability.* We begin the study of the expressivity of this language, and we apply it to an example, showing how these notions work on specific AGM learners.

Though our completeness proof uses some standard techniques in non-monotonic and conditional logics, there are some important differences. First, since we don't allow conditioning on arbitrary formulas, but only on those corresponding to (preconditions of) observational events, the proof is more subtle. In particular, it shows that AGM has no need for conditioning on negated formulas. Second, the completeness proof uses a mixture of relational and neighbourhood versions of the standard canonical model construction, with further complications due to the presence of the "effort" modality. As in [3], its connection with dynamic updates is embodied by our Effort Axiom and Effort Rule, which together say that a proposition φ is "stably true" iff its truth is preserved by every correct observational event. The presence of fresh observational variables as "witnesses" of stability of φ in the Effort Rule requires the restriction of the canonical model to "witnessed" theories (rather than all maximally consistent ones).

Due to space limitations, proofs are omitted from the main body and presented in the Appendix of the longer version, available online at https://analuciavargassan.com/page/.

2 Syntax and Semantics

Let Prop $= \{p, q, \ldots\}$ be a countable set of *propositional variables*, denoting arbitrary 'ontic' (i.e., non-epistemic) facts and $\text{Prop}_{\mathcal{O}} = \{o, u, v, \ldots\}$ a countable set of *observational variables*, denoting 'observable facts'.

Observational Events. We consider *observational events* e (or, in short, *observations*) by which the agent acquires some evidence about the world. We denote the set of all observational events by Π_{Ob} and define it by the following recursive clauses:

$$e := !\top \mid !o \mid e;e \mid e \sqcup e$$

where $o \in \text{Prop}_{\mathcal{O}}$. Intuitively: for every observational variable o, we have a primitive observational event, denoted by $!o$, corresponding to *the event of observing variable* o. We also denote by $!\top$ the *null event* (in which *no new observation has taken place yet*). Observational events are naturally closed under regular operations on programs, of which we consider only two: $e; e'$ represents *sequential composition* of observational events (first observation e is made then observation e' is made); while $e \sqcup e'$ captures *epistemic non-determinism*: one of the two observational events e or e' happens, but the observing agent is uncertain which of the two. The last construct can be used to represent *partial observations*, including indirect evidence obtained from other agents' reports: the agent observes (or is told) only some feature of the evidence, so her information is compatible with multiple fully-determined events.

The Language of AGM Learning. The dynamic language $\mathcal{L}$ of AGM learning from partial observations is defined recursively as

$$\varphi := p \mid o \mid \neg\varphi \mid \varphi \wedge \varphi \mid L(e) \mid K\varphi \mid [e]\varphi \mid \Box\varphi$$

where $p \in \text{Prop}$, $o \in \text{Prop}_{\mathcal{O}}$, and $e \in \Pi_{Ob}$. We employ the usual abbreviations for propositional connectives $\top, \bot, \vee, \rightarrow, \leftrightarrow$, and $\langle K\rangle\varphi$, $\langle e\rangle\varphi$ and $\Diamond\varphi$ denote $\neg K\neg\varphi$, $\neg[e]\neg\varphi$, and $\neg\Box\neg\varphi$, respectively. Given a formula $\varphi \in \mathcal{L}$, we denote by O_φ and O_e the set of all observational variables occurring in φ and e, respectively.

Intuitively, $L(e)$ denotes the learner's *conjecture* given observation e; i.e., her "strongest belief" after having performed observational event e. We read $K\varphi$ as 'the learner *knows* φ (with absolute certainty)'. The operator $[e]\varphi$ is similar to the update operator in Public Announcement Logic: we read $[e]\varphi$ as 'after event e is observed, φ holds'. Finally, $\Box$ is the so-called 'effort modality' from Subset Space Logic [12,16]; we read $\Box\varphi$ as 'φ is *stably true*' (i.e. it is true and will stay true under any further observations).

We interpret $\mathcal{L}$ on *plausibility learning models* in the style of subset space semantics, as given in turn.

Definition 1 (Plausibility Learning Frame/Model). *A* plausibility learning frame *is a triple* $(X, \mathcal{O}, \leq)$*, where:* X *is a non-empty set of* possible worlds *(or 'ontic states');* $\mathcal{O} \subseteq \mathcal{P}(X)$ *is a non-empty set of subsets, called* information states *(or 'partial observations', or 'evidence'), which is assumed to be* closed under finite intersections and finite unions*: if* $\mathcal{F} \subseteq \mathcal{O}$ *is finite then* $\bigcap \mathcal{F} \in \mathcal{O}$ *and* $\bigcup \mathcal{F} \in \mathcal{O}$*; and* $\leq$ *is a total preorder*[2] *on* X*, called* plausibility order *and satisfying the observational version of Lewis' 'Limit Condition':* every non-empty information state O has maximal elements. *More precisely, if for any evidence* $O \in \mathcal{O}$*, we put*[3]

$$Max_{\leq}(O) := \{x \in O : y \leq x \text{ for all } y \in O\}$$

for the set of maximal ("most plausible") worlds compatible with the evidence, then the Limit Condition requires that $Max_{\leq}(O) \neq \emptyset$ *whenever* $O \neq \emptyset$*. The pair* $(X, \mathcal{O})$ *is known in the literature as a "lattice frame"* [12,16]*, while* $x \leq y$ *is read as 'world* y *is at least as plausible as world* x*'.*

A plausibility learning model $M = (X, \mathcal{O}, \leq, \|\cdot\|)$ *consists of a plausibility learning frame* $(X, \mathcal{O}, \leq)$*, together with a valuation map* $\|\cdot\| : \text{Prop} \cup \text{Prop}_{\mathcal{O}} \rightarrow \mathcal{P}(X)$ *that maps propositional variables* p *into arbitrary sets* $\|p\| \subseteq X$ *and observational variables* o *into information states* $\|o\| \in \mathcal{O}$*.*

A *learner* $\mathbb{L}_{\leq} : \mathcal{O} \rightarrow \mathcal{P}(X)$ on a plausibility lattice frame $(X, \mathcal{O}, \leq)$ is a function that maps to every information state $O \in \mathcal{O}$ some 'conjecture' $\mathbb{L}_{\leq}(O) \subseteq X$. An *AGM-learner* is a learner who, upon having observed $O \in \mathcal{O}$, always

[2] A total preorder $\leq$ on X is a reflexive and transitive binary relation such that every two points are comparable: for all $x, y \in X$, either $x \leq y$ or $y \leq x$ (or both).

[3] Since $\leq$ is a *total* preorder, this definition coincides with the standard definition of maximal elements as $Max_{\leq}(O) := \{x \in O : \forall y \in O(x \leq y \text{ implies } x \leq y)\}$.

conjectures the set of most plausible O-states. That is, $\mathbb{L}_{\leq} : \mathcal{O} \to \mathcal{P}(X)$ is an AGM-learner on $(X, \mathcal{O}, \leq)$ if $\mathbb{L}_{\leq}(O) = Max_{\leq}(O)$ for all $O \in \mathcal{O}$. By the observational Limit Condition given in Definition 1, it is then guaranteed that $\mathbb{L}_{\leq}(O) \neq \emptyset$ for all $O \in \mathcal{O}$ with $O \neq \emptyset$. This means that an AGM-learner makes consistent conjectures whenever her information state is consistent.

Epistemic Scenarios. As in Subset Space Semantics, the formulas of our logic are interpreted *not* at possible worlds, but at so-called *epistemic scenarios*: pairs (x, U) of an ontic state $x \in X$ and an information state $U \in \mathcal{O}$ such that $x \in U$. Therefore, only the *truthful* observations about the actual state play a role in the evaluation of formulas. Intuitively, x represents the *actual state* of the world, while U represents the *agent's current evidence* (based on her previous observations). We denote by $ES(M) := \{(x, U) \mid x \in U \in \mathcal{O}\}$ the set of all epistemic scenarios of model M.

Dynamics: Observational Updates. Each observational event $e \in \Pi_{Ob}$ induces a dynamic "update" of the agent's information state. This is encoded in an *update function* (also denoted by) $e : \mathcal{O} \to \mathcal{O}$, that maps any information state $U \in \mathcal{O}$ to an updated information state $e(U) \in \mathcal{O}$. The map is given by recursion:

$$!\top(U) = U, \qquad !o(U) = U \cap \|o\|,$$
$$(e; e')(U) = e'(e(U)), \quad (e \sqcup e')(U) = e(U) \cup e'(U).$$

The meaning of these clauses should be obvious: the null event $!\top$ does not change the agent's information state; the single observation of variable o simply adds $\|o\|$ to the current evidence U (so that the agent will know the world is in $U \cap \|o\|$); the information state after a sequential composition $e; e'$ is the same as the one obtained by updating first with e then with e'; while the information state produced by a partial observation $e \sqcup e'$ is the disjunction of the information states produced by the two events (since the agent doesn't know which of the two happened).

It is easy to see that the update map is appropriately defined:

Lemma 1. *Let $M = (X, \mathcal{O}, \leq, \|\cdot\|)$ be a plausibility learning model and $U \in \mathcal{O}$ be an information state. Then, for all $e \in \Pi_{Ob}$ we have $e(U) \in \mathcal{O}$.*

Proof. The proof follows easily by induction on the structure of e. For the base cases $!\top$ and $!o$, we have $!\top(U) = U \in \mathcal{O}$ and $!o(U) = \|o\| \cap U \in \mathcal{O}$ by the closure of $\mathcal{O}$ under finite intersections. In the inductive case $e; e'$, we apply the inductive hypothesis to e and U, yielding that $e(U) \in \mathcal{O}$, then we obtain that $(e; e')(U) = e'(e(U))$ (by applying again the inductive hypothesis to e' and $e(U)$). Finally, in the inductive case $e \sqcup e'$, we use the inductive hypothesis for e and U, as well as for e' and U, together with the closure of $\mathcal{O}$ under finite unions, to conclude that $(e \sqcup e')(U) = e(U) \cup e'(U) \in \mathcal{O}$.

Definition 2 (Semantics). Given a plausibility learning model $M = (X, \mathcal{O}, \leq, \|\cdot\|)$ and an epistemic scenario (x, U), the semantics of the language $\mathcal{L}$ is given by a binary relation $(x, U) \models_M \varphi$ between epistemic scenario and formulas, called the *satisfaction relation*, as well as a *truth set* (interpretation) $[\![\varphi]\!]_M^U := \{x \in U \mid (x, U) \models_M \varphi\}$, for all formulas $\varphi \in \mathcal{L}$. We typically omit the subscript, simply writing $(x, U) \models \varphi$ and $[\![\varphi]\!]^U$, whenever the model M is understood. The satisfaction relation is defined by the following recursive clauses:

$$
\begin{array}{lll}
(x,U) \models p & \text{iff} & x \in \|p\| \\
(x,U) \models o & \text{iff} & x \in \|o\| \\
(x,U) \models \neg\varphi & \text{iff} & (x,U) \not\models \varphi \\
(x,U) \models \varphi \wedge \psi & \text{iff} & (x,U) \models \varphi \text{ and } (x,U) \models \psi \\
(x,U) \models L(e) & \text{iff} & x \in Max_{\leq}\, e(U) \\
(x,U) \models K\varphi & \text{iff} & (\forall y \in U)\,((y,U) \models \varphi) \\
(x,U) \models [e]\varphi & \text{iff} & x \in e(U) \text{ implies } (x, e(U)) \models \varphi \\
(x,U) \models \Box\varphi & \text{iff} & (\forall O \in \mathcal{O})\,(x \in O \subseteq U \text{ implies } (x,O) \models \varphi) \\
 & \text{i.e.} & (\forall O \in \mathcal{O})\,(x \in O \text{ implies } (x, U \cap O) \models \varphi)
\end{array}
$$

where $p \in \text{Prop}$, $o \in \text{Prop}_{\mathcal{O}}$, and $e \in \Pi_{Ob}$.

We say that a formula φ is *valid in a plausibility learning model* M, and write $M \models \varphi$, if $(x, U) \models_M \varphi$ for all epistemic scenarios $(x, U) \in ES(M)$. We say φ is *valid*, and write $\models \varphi$, if it is valid in *all* plausibility learning models.

Precondition (Informational Content). To each observational event $e \in \Pi_{Ob}$, we can associate a formula $pre(e) \in \mathcal{L}$, called the *precondition* of event e. The definition is by recursion: $pre(!\top) = \top$, $pre(!o) = o$, $pre(e; e') = pre(e) \wedge pre(e')$, and $pre(e \sqcup e') = pre(e) \vee pre(e')$. The precondition formula $pre(e)$ captures the "condition of possibility" of the event e (i.e. e can happen in a world x iff $pre(e)$ is true at (x, U), for any $U \in \mathcal{O}$ with $x \in U$), as well as its *informational content* (the learner's new information after e). Both these interpretations are justified by the following result:

Lemma 2. *Let $M = (X, \mathcal{O}, \leq, \|\cdot\|)$ be a plausibility learning model and $U \in \mathcal{O}$ be an information state. Then, for all $e \in \Pi_{Ob}$ we have:*

$$[\![pre(e)]\!]^U = e(U) = [\![\langle e\rangle\top]\!]^U.$$

2.1 Expressive Power of $\mathcal{L}$ and Its Fragments

In this brief subsection, we compare the expressive power of $\mathcal{L}$ to those of its fragments of interest. Let $\mathcal{L}_{KL\Box}$ denote the fragment of $\mathcal{L}$ obtained by removing only the operators $[e]\varphi$. The fragment obtained by further removing the effort modality $\Box\varphi$ is called the *static fragment* and denoted by $\mathcal{L}_{KL}$. Finally, we denote the epistemic fragment having only the knowledge modality K by $\mathcal{L}_K$.

Theorem 1 (Expressivity). *$\mathcal{L}$ is equally expressive as $\mathcal{L}_{KL\Box}$, and they are strictly more expressive than the static fragment $\mathcal{L}_{KL}$ with respect to plausibility learning models. Moreover, $\mathcal{L}_{KL}$ is strictly more expressive than the epistemic fragment $\mathcal{L}_K$.*

Proof. $\mathcal{L}$ is equally expressive as $\mathcal{L}_{KL\Box}$: use step-by-step the reduction axioms in Table 1 as a rewriting process and prove termination by defining a strict partial order on $\mathcal{L}$ that satisfies similar properties as in [3, Lemma 11].[4] For the second claim, consider the following two-state models $M_1 = (X, \mathcal{O}_1, \leq, \|\cdot\|)$ and $M_2 = (X, \mathcal{O}_2, \leq, \|\cdot\|)$ where $X = \{x, y\}$, $\leq = \{(x,x), (y,y), (x,y)\}$ and the valuation $\|p\| = \{y\}$. And, take $\mathcal{O}_1 = \{X, \emptyset\}$ (the trivial topology on X) and $\mathcal{O}_2 = \mathcal{P}(X)$ (the discrete topology on X). It is then easy to see that $M_1, (x, \{x,y\})$ and $M_2, (x, \{x,y\})$ are modally equivalent with respect to the language $\mathcal{L}_{KL}$. However, $M_2, (x, \{x,y\}) \models \Diamond K\neg p$ (since $\{x\}$ is an open set of M_2) whereas $M_1, (x, \{x,y\}) \not\models \Diamond K\neg p$, since the only open including x is $\{x,y\}$ and $x \notin \|p\| = \{y\}$. To prove that $\mathcal{L}_{KL}$ is strictly more expressive than the epistemic fragment $\mathcal{L}_K$, consider the models $M_1' = (X, \mathcal{O}_1, \leq_1, \|\cdot\|)$ and $M_2' = (X, \mathcal{O}_2, \leq_2, \|\cdot\|)$, where $X, \mathcal{O}_1$, and $\mathcal{O}_2$ are as above but $\leq_1 = \leq$ and $\leq_2 = \{(x,x), (y,y), (y,x)\}$. It is then easy to see that $M_1', (x, \{x,y\})$ and $M_2', (x, \{x,y\})$ are modally equivalent with respect to the language $\mathcal{L}_K$ whereas $M_1', (x, \{x,y\}) \not\models L(!\top)$ (since $x \notin Max_{\leq_1}(!\top(\{x,y\})) = \{y\}$) but $M_2', (x, \{x,y\}) \models L(!\top)$ (since $x \in Max_{\leq_2}(!\top(\{x,y\})) = \{x\}$).

3 Expressing Belief and Notions of Learnability

Having presented the Dynamic Logic of AGM Learning, we now explore how various notions of belief and learnability can be expressed within this framework. We first recall the definitions of these notions given in [3].

Certain (Infallible) Knowledge and Learnability with Certainty. The notion of infallible knowledge is in our logic directly represented by the modality K, whose semantic clause mimics the following definition. The AGM learner is said to *infallibly know* a proposition $P \subseteq X$ in an information state $U \in \mathcal{O}$ if her information state U entails P, i.e, $U \subseteq P$. The possibility of learning a proposition with such certainty in a possible world $x \in X$ by a learner $\mathbb{L}_{\leq}$ if given enough evidence (true at x) is called *learnability with certainty.*[5] In other words, P is learnable with certainty at world x if there exists some truthful information state $O \in \mathcal{O}$ (i.e., $x \in O$) such that the learner infallibly knows P in information state O. As anticipated in [16], the notion of learnability with certainty is syntactically characterised in our language by $\Diamond Kp$, as shown in the following proposition.

Proposition 1. *Given a plausibility learning model* $M = (X, \mathcal{O}, \leq, \|\cdot\|)$ *and* $(x, U) \in ES(M)$, $(x, U) \models \Diamond Kp$ *iff* $\|p\|$ *is learnable with certainty at* x.

---

[4] This is a standard method in Dynamic Epistemic Logic and we refer the reader to [18, Chap. 7.4] for further details.

[5] When we quantify over learners, learnability with certainty (by *some* learners) matches the standard concept of "finite identifiability" from Formal Learning Theory.

Belief, Inductive Knowledge, and Inductive Learnability. The notion of infallible knowledge is obviously very strong: we know very few things with such certainty (maybe some logical or mathematical truths that require only hard thinking and no empirical evidence). One needs weaker notions of knowledge if one desires to model the type of knowledge we can acquire from experimental evidence that is typically partial and incomplete. This type of knowledge is taken to be fallible, yet resistant to truthful evidence gain and stronger than plain belief. In this learning theoretical context, it is captured by an evidence-based notion of *inductive knowledge* defined as *true undefeated belief.*

In an information state U, we say that the AGM learner *believes* a proposition $P \subseteq X$ if her conjecture given U entails P, that is, $\mathbb{L}_{\leq}(U) \subseteq P$. This gives us the standard interpretation of belief on plausibility models (see, e.g., [9,10,17]):

$$(x, U) \models B\varphi \text{ iff } Max_{\leq}\, e(U) \subseteq [\![\varphi]\!]^U.$$

In our formal language, belief is not a primitive notion, but can be defined as an abbreviation:

$$B\varphi := K(L(!\top) \to \varphi).$$

Indeed, it is easy to check that this defined notion satisfies the semantic clause above.

We say that, in information state U and ontic state x, the AGM learner *has undefeated belief* in a proposition $P \subseteq X$ if she believes P and will continue to believe P no matter what new true observations will be made; i.e. iff $(x, O) \models BP$ for every $O \in \mathcal{O}$ with $x \in O$. We then say, in an information state U, the AGM learner *inductively knows* P at world x if P is true and the learner has undefeated belief in P. Finally, P is *inductively learnable* by the AGM learner $\mathbb{L}_{\leq}$ at world x if there exists some truthful information state $O \in \mathcal{O}$ (i.e., $x \in O$) such that $\mathbb{L}_{\leq}$ inductively knows P in information state O at x.[6] The following proposition shows that the Dynamic Logic of AGM Learning can capture these notions:

Proposition 2. *Given a plausibility learning model* $M = (X, \mathcal{O}, \leq, \|\cdot\|)$ *and* $(x, U) \in ES(M)$,

1. $(x, U) \models \Box Bp$ *iff the learner* $\mathbb{L}_{\leq}$ *has undefeated belief in* $\|p\|$ *(at world* x *in information state* U*).*
2. $(x, U) \models p \wedge \Box Bp$ *iff the learner* $\mathbb{L}_{\leq}$ *inductively knows* $\|p\|$ *(at world* x *in information state* U*).*
3. $(x, U) \models p \wedge \Diamond\Box Bp$ *iff* $\|p\|$ *is inductively knowable by* $\mathbb{L}_{\leq}$ *(at world* x *in information state* U*).*

Example: The alcohol inspector. An alcohol inspector needs to randomly check cars that pass through a security point in a perimetrical highway of

[6] When we quantify over learners, inductive learnability (by *some* learners) matches the standard concept of "identifiability in the limit" from Formal Learning Theory, see e.g. [13].

Munich during the October fest to check the driver's alcohol levels. The maximum alcoholic-level allowed is 30 points (which corresponds to two small beers). His alcohol-measuring tool, known as *breathalyser*, has an accuracy of ± 20. At some point, a young woman gets the stop sign in order to get inspected. The breathalyser outputs a reading of 40 points. Given the accuracy of the tool, this first measurement can be represented by the interval $(20, 60) \subseteq \mathbb{R}$. At this point, the inspector cannot know for sure that the driver has drunk more beers than allowed. The inspector then borrows a more advanced and accurate breathalyser from one of his colleagues, with an accuracy of ± 5. The more accurate breathalyser outputs a reading of 35 points. So the measurement of the second breathalyser can be represented by the interval $(30, 40)$. Therefore, after the reading of the second device, the inspector can know with certainty that the woman has exceeded the levels of alcohol, so she needs to wait for a couple of hours before driving again and to pay a costly fine. Moreover, let us assume that inspector obeys the legal principle of "*believing in innocence until proven guilty* beyond doubt": so, whenever he is in doubt (because his measurements do not prove either case), he believes the driver is *not drunk*.

This situation can be represented in a plausibility learning frame[7] $(X, \mathcal{O}, \preceq)$, where $(X, \mathcal{O})$ is a lattice frame with $X = [0, \infty) \subseteq \mathbb{R}$ is the set of "possible worlds" (=possible alcohol levels), while the family of partial observations $\mathcal{O}$ is the closure under finite intersections and finite unions of the family of breathalyser measurements (=single-step total observations) $\mathcal{B} = \{[0, b) \subseteq \mathbb{R} : 0 < b \in \mathbb{Q}\} \cup \{(a, b) \subseteq \mathbb{R} : 0 < a, b \in \mathbb{Q}\}$. The sets in $\mathcal{B}$ represent all possible readings of arbitrarily accurate breathalysers, while the sets in $\mathcal{O}$ represent all possible information states of the inspector, based on iterated (and possibly) partial reports of such readings. Finally, the policy of believing in "innocence until proven guilty" is captured by assuming that (in the absence of any evidence) the inspector considers all non-drunk states to be a priori *more plausible* than all drunk states: i.e. $x \preceq y$ for $x > 30$ and $y \leq 30$. This policy is not enough to fully determine the plausibility relation; to make it precise, let us assume for now that the inspector has *no other strong belief on the matter*, i.e. he considers all the *drunk states to be equally plausible* (and similarly for the non-drunk states). So the relation is given by putting: $x \preceq y$ iff either $y \leq 30$ or else $30 < x, y$. It is easy to check that $\preceq$ is indeed a total preorder.

Consider the propositions *drunk* $D = (30, \infty)$ and *not drunk* $ND = [0, 30]$ in the context of this example. We can then ask if the inspector knows with certainty that the woman is outside the permitted alcohol levels, namely if the inspector knows proposition D. After the second reading, the inspector knows with certainty that the woman has drunk more than allowed. Thus, given enough more accurate measurements, the inspector can infallibly know D (whenever D is actually the case); i.e. D is always learnable with certainty. However proposition ND is *not* always learnable with certainty: if the real level of alcohol happens to be exactly 30, then the driver is not drunk (ND) but the inspector will never

[7] We use $\preceq$ to denote the plausibility order in this frame, to distinguish it from the natural order on $X \subseteq R$.

come to infallibly know ND. (This is simply because any interval containing 30 has non-empty intersection with D.) Still, ND is "falsifiable" with certainty (since its negation is learnable with certainty whenever true). A property that is *neither learnable with certainty nor falsifiable with certainty* is having alcohol level *barely-above-permitted* $BAP = (30, 31]$.

Inductive learnability is of course a weaker, more general form of knowledge: *both* properties *drunk* $D := (30, \infty)$ and *not-drunk* $ND := [0, 30]$ are inductively learnable by the inspector, if endowed with the above plausibility order $\preceq$. Indeed, if the true alcohol level is some $w \in ND = [0, 30]$, then the inspector (in the absence of any evidence), starts by believing ND (since $L(X) = Max_{\preceq}X = [0, 30]$); and no matter what further direct evidence (a, b) she gets, with $a < w < b$, she will still believe ND (since in this case $L(a, b) = Max_{\preceq}(a, b) \subseteq [0, 30]$). So in this case the inspector inductively knows ND from the start! While if $w \in D = (30, \infty)$, then after doing an accurate enough measurement, the inspector will obtain some evidence (a, b), with $30 < a < w < b$. For any further refinement $(a', b') \subseteq (a, b)$ of this evidence, we will have $(a', b') \subseteq (a, b) \subseteq (30, \infty) = D$, hence $L(a', b') = Max_{\preceq}(a', b') = (a', b') \subseteq D$. Which means that, after reading (a, b), the inspector achieves inductive knowledge of D: he will believe D no matter what further observations might be made.

What about the property $BAP = (30, 31]$ of having a *barely-above-permitted* alcohol level? This property is in principle also inductively learnable (by *some* learners), but *not* by the above AGM learner! To design an AGM learner who can inductively learn it, we need to change the plausibility relation, using a different refinement of the general "innocent until proven guilty" policy. The inspector still believes *all the non-drunk states to be more plausible than all the drunk ones*; but now, within the drunk-world zone, he has a similarly generous attitude: "if guilty then barely guilty". In other words, he considers *the barely-above-permitted levels in* $BAP = (30, 31]$ *to be more plausible than the way-above-permitted ones in* $WAV = (31, \infty)$; and in the rest, he is indifferent, as before. This amounts to adopting a plausibility order $\ll$, given by putting $x \ll y$ iff: either we have $y \leq 30$, or else we have both $30 < x$ and $y \leq 31$, or otherwise we have $31 < x, y < \infty$. It is easy to check that $\ll$ is a linear pre-order, and moreover that properties D, ND, BAP, $NBAP = X - BAP = (0, 30] \cup (31, \infty)$, $WAV = (31, \infty)$ and $NWAV = [0, 31]$ are all inductively learnable by an inspector endowed with this plausibility order.

4 A Complete Proof System

In this section, we present a sound and complete proof system for our logic.

4.1 Axiomatization

Table 1 presents the axioms and inference rules of the Logic of AGM Learning (**L**).

Table 1. The axiom schemas for the Dynamic Logic of AGM Learning (**L**)

Basic axioms:		
(P)	All instantiations of propositional tautologies	
(K_K)	$K(\varphi \to \psi) \to (K\varphi \to K\psi)$	
(T_K)	$K\varphi \to \varphi$	
(4_K)	$K\varphi \to KK\varphi$	
(5_K)	$\neg K\varphi \to K\neg K\varphi$	
($K_{[e]}$)	$[e](\psi \to \chi) \to ([e]\psi \to [e]\chi)$	
Basic rules:		
(MP)	From $\vdash \varphi$ and $\vdash \varphi \to \psi$, infer $\vdash \psi$	
(Nec_K)	From $\vdash \varphi$, infer $\vdash K\varphi$	
($Nec_{[e]}$)	From $\vdash \varphi$, infer $\vdash [e]\varphi$	
Learning axioms:		
(CC)	$pre(e) \to \langle K\rangle L(e)$	Consistency of Conjecture
(EC)	$K(pre(e) \leftrightarrow pre(e')) \to (L(e) \leftrightarrow L(e'))$	Extensionality of Conjecture
(SP)	$L(e) \to pre(e)$	Success Postulate
(Inc)	$(pre(e) \wedge L(e')) \to L(e;e')$	Inclusion
(RMon)	$\langle K\rangle(L(e') \wedge pre(e)) \to (L(e;e') \to (pre(e) \wedge L(e')))$	Rational Monotonicity
Reduction axioms:		
(R_p)	$[e]p \leftrightarrow (pre(e) \to p)$	
(R_o)	$[e]o \leftrightarrow (pre(e) \to o)$	
(R_L)	$[e]L(e') \leftrightarrow (pre(e) \to L(e;e'))$	
($R_\neg$)	$[e]\neg\psi \leftrightarrow (pre(e) \to \neg[e]\psi)$	
(R_K)	$[e]K\psi \leftrightarrow (pre(e) \to K[e]\psi)$	
(R_e)	$[e][e']\psi \leftrightarrow [e;e']\psi$	
($R_\Box$)	$[e]\Box\psi \leftrightarrow \Box[e]\psi$	
Effort axiom and rule:		
($\Box$Ax)	$\Box\varphi \to [e]\varphi$, for $e \in \Pi_{Ob}$	
($\Box$Ru)	From $\vdash \psi \to [e;!o]\varphi$, infer $\vdash \psi \to [e]\Box\varphi$, where $o \notin O_\psi \cup O_e \cup O_\varphi$	

Proposition 3. *The following formulas are derivable in* **L** *for all* $\varphi \in \mathcal{L}$ *and* $e \in \Pi_{Ob}$*:*

1. $\langle K\rangle(L(e') \wedge pre(e)) \to (L(e;e') \leftrightarrow (pre(e) \wedge L(e')))$
2. $[e](\varphi \wedge \psi) \leftrightarrow ([e]\varphi \wedge [e]\psi)$
3. $\langle e\rangle\psi \leftrightarrow (pre(e) \wedge [e]\psi)$
4. *from* $\vdash \varphi \leftrightarrow \psi$*, infer* $\vdash [e]\varphi \leftrightarrow [e]\psi$
5. $\langle e\rangle pre(e') \leftrightarrow pre(e;e')$
6. *from* $\vdash pre(e) \leftrightarrow pre(e')$*, infer* $\vdash [e]\varphi \leftrightarrow [e']\varphi$
7. $[!\top]\varphi \leftrightarrow \varphi$ *(we denote it* $R[\top]$*)*
8. *from* $\vdash \psi \to [!o]\varphi$ *infer* $\vdash \psi \to \Box\varphi$ *(where* $o \notin O_\psi \cup O_\varphi$*)*

Intuitive Reading of the Axioms and Rules. The axiomatization of the Dynamic Logic of AGM Learning, roughly speaking, extends that of Dynamic

Logic for Learning Theory (DLLT) presented in [3] with axioms capturing AGM-type learning from partial observations. Group Basic Axioms and rules are quite standard: $S5$ axioms and rules for K says that the notion of knowledge with absolute certainty we study in this paper is factive and fully (both positively and negatively) introspective. ($K_{[e]}$) and ($Nec_{[e]}$) together show that dynamic modalities $[e]\varphi$ behave like normal modal operators. The reduction axioms are as in Epistemic Action Logic (EAL) [6,8] (a.k.a., Action Model Logic [18]), where the precondition of an observational event e is captured by $pre(e)$, that is, the informational content of the event e being true. The first three learning axioms - in slightly different forms - are also part of DLLT. To recap, (CC) states that the learner conjectures consistent propositions upon having received truthful information; (EC) says that the form of the observational event (primitive, sequential, or non-deteministic) is irrelevant for learning, what is important is the informational content of the observation: observing informationally equivalent events gives rise to equivalent conjectures. Moreover, (SP) states that what the learner conjectures fits what is observed, that is, the learner conjectures propositions that support what she has observed. The last two learning axioms (Inc) and (RMon) are novel to the current system and corresponds to the AGM postulates Inclusion and Rational Monotonicity in [1], respectively. These are better understood in terms of belief. (Inc) states that the agent believes a proposition P after having observed e only if she initially believes that e entails P. (RMon) on the other hand says that the agent revises her beliefs in a monotonic way as long as the newly observed event is consistent with her previous conjecture. Finally, we have the Effort rule ($\Box$Ru) and axiom ($\Box$Ax) which together explain the dynamic behavior of the effort modality. While the former expresses that if φ is stably true then it holds after any observational event has taken place, the latter states that if φ holds after any more informative event has taken place ($[e;o]$), φ is stably true after e has taken place.

4.2 Soundness and Completeness

The soundness of the axiomatization **L** is not entirely straightforward due to the non-standard inference rule $\Box$Ru. We present validity proofs for $\Box$Ax and $\Box$Ru and the completeness proof in full detail in the longer online version of this paper. We here provide sketches of the aforementioned proofs by listing the crucial lemmas.

The following lemma plays an important role in the soundness of $\Box$Ru.

Lemma 3. *Let* $M = (X, \mathcal{O}, \leq, \|\cdot\|)$ *and* $M' = (X, \mathcal{O}, \leq, \|\cdot\|')$ *be two plausibility learning models and* $\varphi \in \mathcal{L}$ *such that* M *and* M' *differ only in the valuation of some* $o \notin O_\varphi$. *Then, for all* $U \in \mathcal{O}$, *we have* $[\![\varphi]\!]^U_M = [\![\varphi]\!]^U_{M'}$.

Theorem 2. *The system* **L** *in Table 1 is sound wrt the class of plausibility learning models.*

Canonical Model Construction. The standard notion of maximally consistent theory is *not* very useful for our logic, since such theories do not 'internalize' the Effort rule $\Box$Ru. To do this, we need instead to consider *'witnessed' (maximally consistent) theories*, in which every occurrence of a $\Diamond\varphi$ in any 'existential context' is 'witnessed' by some $\langle !o\rangle\varphi$ (with o observational variable). The appropriate notion of 'existential contexts' is represented by *possibility forms*, as in e.g., [2,3,7], given in Definition 3.

Definition 3 ('Pseudo-modalities': Necessity and Possibility Forms). *The* set of necessity-form expressions *of our language is given by* $NF_{\mathcal{L}} := (\{\varphi \rightarrow \mid \varphi \in \mathcal{L}\} \cup \{K\} \cup \{e : e \in \Pi_{Ob}\})^*$. *For any finite string* $s \in NF_{\mathcal{L}}$, *we define pseudo-modalities* $[s]$ *(called* necessity form*) and* $\langle s\rangle$ *(called* possibility form*) that generalize our dynamic modalities* $[e]$ *and* $\langle e\rangle$. *These pseudo-modalities are functions mapping any formula* $\varphi \in \mathcal{L}$ *to another formula* $[s]\varphi \in \mathcal{L}$, *and respectively* $\langle s\rangle\varphi \in \mathcal{L}$. *Necessity forms are defined recursively, by putting:* $[\epsilon]\varphi := \varphi$ *(where* ϵ *is the empty string),* $[s, \varphi \rightarrow]\varphi := [s](\varphi \rightarrow \varphi)$, $[s, K]\varphi := [s]K\varphi$, $[s, e]\varphi := [s][e]\varphi$. *As for possibility forms, we put* $\langle s\rangle\varphi := \neg[s]\neg\varphi$.

Lemma 4. *For every necessity form* $[s]$, *there exist an observational event* $e \in \Pi_{Ob}$ *and a formula* $\psi \in \mathcal{L}$, *with* $O_\psi \cup O_e \subseteq O_s$, *such that for all* $\varphi \in \mathcal{L}$, *we have*

$$\vdash [s]\varphi \text{ iff } \vdash \psi \rightarrow [e]\varphi.$$

Lemma 5. *The following rule is admissible in* **L***:*

$$\text{if } \vdash [s][!o]\varphi \text{ then } \vdash [s]\Box\varphi, \text{ where } o \notin O_s \cup O_\varphi.$$

Proof. Suppose $\vdash [s][!o]\varphi$ where $o \notin O_s \cup O_\varphi$. Then, by Lemma 4, there exist $e \in \Pi_{Ob}$ and $\psi \in \mathcal{L}$ with $O_\psi \cup O_e \subseteq O_s$ such that $\vdash \psi \rightarrow [e][!o]\varphi$. Thus we get $\vdash \psi \rightarrow [e; !o]\varphi$ by an instance of R_e. Therefore, by the Effort rule ($\Box$Ru) we have $\vdash \psi \rightarrow [e]\Box\varphi$. Then, again by Lemma 4, we obtain $\vdash [s]\Box\varphi$.

Definition 4. *For every countable set* O, *let* $\mathcal{L}^{\mathrm{O}}$ *be the language of the logic* $\mathbf{L}^{\mathrm{O}}$ *based only on the observational variables in* O *(i.e., having as set of observational variables* $\mathrm{Prop}_{\mathcal{O}} := \mathrm{O}$*). Let* $NF^{\mathrm{O}}_{\mathcal{L}}$ *denote the set of necessity-form expressions of* $\mathcal{L}^{\mathrm{O}}$ *(i.e., necessity forms involving only observational variables in* O*). An* O-theory *is a* consistent *set of formulas in* $\mathcal{L}^{\mathrm{O}}$. *Here, 'consistent' means consistent with respect to the axiomatization* **L** *formulated for* $\mathcal{L}^{\mathrm{O}}$. *A* maximal O-theory *is an* O*-theory* Γ *that is maximal with respect to* $\subseteq$ *among all* O*-theories; in other words,* Γ *cannot be extended to another* O*-theory. An* O-witnessed theory *is an* O*-theory* Γ *such that, for every* $s \in NF^{\mathrm{O}}_{\mathcal{L}}$ *and* $\varphi \in \mathcal{L}^{\mathrm{O}}$, *if* $\langle s\rangle\Diamond\varphi$ *is consistent with* Γ *then there is* $o \in \mathrm{O}$ *such that* $\langle s\rangle\langle !o\rangle\varphi$ *is consistent with* Γ. *A* maximal O-witnessed theory Γ *is an* O*-witnessed theory that is not a proper subset of any* O*-witnessed theory.*

The proofs of the following lemmas are exactly as in the corresponding proofs in [3], taking into account that (maximaly) O-(witnessed) theories here are defined using primitive observational events $(!o)$ (rather than observational variables o).

Lemma 6. *For every maximal* O*-witnessed theory* Γ*, and any* $\varphi, \psi \in \mathcal{L}^{\mathrm{O}}$*,*

1. *either* $\varphi \in \Gamma$ *or* $\neg\varphi \in \Gamma$*,*
2. $\varphi \wedge \psi \in \Gamma$ *iff* $\varphi \in \Gamma$ *and* $\psi \in \Gamma$*,*
3. $\varphi \in \Gamma$ *and* $\varphi \to \psi \in \Gamma$ *implies* $\psi \in \Gamma$*.*

Lemma 7 (Lindenbaum's Lemma). *Every* O*-witnessed theory* Γ *can be extended to a maximal* O*-witnessed theory* T_Γ*.*

Lemma 8 (Extension Lemma). *Let* O *be a set of observational variables and* O′ *be a countable set of* fresh *observational variables, i.e.,* $\mathrm{O} \cap \mathrm{O}' = \emptyset$*. Let* $\widetilde{\mathrm{O}} = \mathrm{O} \cup \mathrm{O}'$*. Then, every* O*-theory* Γ *can be extended to an* $\widetilde{\mathrm{O}}$*-witnessed theory* $\widetilde{\Gamma} \supseteq \Gamma$*, and hence to a maximal* $\widetilde{\mathrm{O}}$*-witnessed theory* $T_\Gamma \supseteq \Gamma$*.*

Canonical Model for T_0**.** For any consistent set of formulas Φ, consider a maximally consistent O-witnessed extension $T_0 \supseteq \Phi$. As our canonical set of worlds, we take the set $X^c := \{T : T$ maximally consistent O-witnessed theory with $T \sim_K T_0\}$, where we put

$$T \sim_K T' \text{ iff } \forall \varphi \in \mathcal{L}^{\mathrm{O}}\,(K\varphi \in T \text{ implies } \varphi \in T').$$

It is easy to see (given the $S5$ axioms for K) that $\sim_K$ is an equivalence relation. For any formula φ, we use the notation $\widehat{\varphi} := \{T \in X^c : \varphi \in T\}$. As the canonical set of information states, we take $\mathcal{O}^c := \{\widehat{pre(e)} : e \in \Pi^{\mathrm{O}}_{Ob}\}$. Toward defining the canonical plausibility relation $\leq^c$, let

$$S_e = \bigcup\{\widehat{L(e')} : \widehat{pre(e)} \subseteq \widehat{pre(e')} \text{ and } e' \in \Pi^{\mathrm{O}}_{Ob}\},$$

and $\$ = \{S_e : e \in \Pi^{\mathrm{O}}_{Ob}\} \cup \{X^c\}$. The canonical plausibility order $\leq^c$ on X^c is given by, for any $T, T' \in X^c$:

$$T \leq^c T' \text{ iff } \forall S \in \$ \; (T \in S \text{ implies } T' \in S).$$

The definition of $\leq^c$ is inspired by the construction of the so-called *order models* from *sphere* and *selection* models presented in [14]. Roughly speaking, while $\widehat{L(e')}$ plays the role of a selection function that picks out a set of maximally consistent O-witnessed theories given e' (see, e.g., [11,14] for selection models), the collection of sets \$ forms a sphere system (see, e.g., [15] for sphere models).

The canonical valuation $\|\cdot\|_c$ is given as $\|p\|_c = \widehat{p}$ and $\|o\|_c = \widehat{o}$. The tuple $M^c = (X^c, \mathcal{O}^c, \leq^c, \|\cdot\|_c)$ is called the *canonical model.*

Theorem 3. $M^c = (X^c, \mathcal{O}^c, \leq^c, \|\cdot\|_c)$ *is a plausibility learning model.*

The following lemmas will be useful for proving the Truth Lemma.

Lemma 9. *For all* $e \in \Pi^{\mathrm{O}}_{Ob}$*,* $Max_{\leq^c}(\widehat{pre(e)}) = \widehat{L(e)}$*.*

Lemma 10. *For every maximal* O*-witnessed theory* T*, the set* $\{\theta : K\theta \in T\}$ *is* O*-witnessed.*

Lemma 11. *Let* $T \in X^c$*. Then,* $K\varphi \in T$ *iff* $\varphi \in T'$ *for all* $T' \in X^c$*.*

Lemma 12. *Let* $T \in X^c$*. Then,* $\Box\varphi \in T$ *iff* $[e]\varphi \in T$ *for all* $e \in \Pi^{\mathrm{O}}_{Ob}$*.*

Proof. The direction from left-to-right follows by the axiom ($\Box$Ax). For the direction from right-to-left, suppose, toward a contradiction, that for all $e \in \Pi^{\mathrm{O}}_{Ob}$, $[e]\varphi \in T$ and $\Box\varphi \notin T$. Then, since T is a maximally consistent theory, $\Diamond\neg\varphi \in T$. Since T is an O-witnessed theory, there is $o \in \mathrm{O}$ such that $\langle !o\rangle\neg\varphi$ is consistent with T. Since T is also maximally consistent, we obtain that $\langle !o\rangle\neg\varphi \in T$, i.e., that $\neg[!o]\varphi \in T$, contradicting our initial assumption.

Lemma 13 (Truth Lemma). *Let* $M^c = (X^c, \mathcal{O}^c, \leq^c, \|\cdot\|_c)$ *be the canonical model for some* T_0*. For all formulas* $\varphi \in \mathcal{L}^{\mathrm{O}}$*, all* $T \in X^c$ *and all* $e \in \Pi^{\mathrm{O}}_{Ob}$*, we have:*

$$\langle e\rangle\varphi \in T \;\text{ iff }\; (T, \widehat{pre(e)}) \models_{M^c} \varphi.$$

Proof. The proof is by induction on the structure of φ and uses the following *induction hypothesis* (**IH**): for all ψ subformula of φ, and $e \in \Pi^{\mathrm{O}}_{Ob}$, $\langle e\rangle\psi \in T$ iff $(T, \widehat{pre(e)}) \models_{M^c} \psi$. The base case for propositional and observational variables, as well as Boolean formulas are straightforward. We only verify the remaining inductive cases.

Observe that at this point of the proof we have that: $\forall e, e' \in \Pi^{\mathrm{O}}_{Ob}$, $\widehat{\langle e\rangle pre(e')} = [\![pre(e')]\!]^{\widehat{pre(e)}}_{M^c}$ since $pre(e)$ is a Boolean formula.

- Case $\varphi := L(e')$. We have the following sequence of equivalencies: $\langle e\rangle L(e') \in T$ iff $(pre(e) \wedge [e]L(e')) \in T$ (by Proposition 3.3) iff $(pre(e) \wedge L(e;e')) \in T$ (by R_L and CPL) iff $pre(e) \in T \wedge L(e;e') \in T$ iff $T \in \widehat{pre(e)} \wedge T \in \widehat{L(e;e')}$ (by Def. of $\widehat{\varphi}$) iff $T \in \widehat{pre(e)} \wedge T \in Max_{\leq^c}(\widehat{pre(e;e')})$ (by Lemma 9) iff $T \in \widehat{pre(e)} \wedge T \in Max_{\leq^c}(\widehat{\langle e\rangle pre(e')})$ (by Proposition 3.5) iff $T \in \widehat{pre(e)} \wedge T \in Max_{\leq^c}([\![pre(e')]\!]^{\widehat{pre(e)}}_{M^c})$ (by the above observation) iff $(T, \widehat{pre(e)}) \models_{M^c} L(e')$ (by the semantics).
- Case $\varphi := K\psi$. We have the sequence of equivalencies: $\langle e\rangle K\psi \in T$ iff $(pre(e) \wedge K[e]\psi) \in T$ (by Proposition 3.3 and R_K) iff $pre(e) \in T \wedge K[e]\psi \in T$ iff $pre(e) \in T \wedge (\forall T' \sim_K T)([e]\psi \in T')$ (by Lemma 11) iff $pre(e) \in T \wedge (\forall T' \sim_K T \text{ s.t. } pre(e) \in T')(\langle e\rangle\psi \in T')$ (by Proposition 3.3) iff $T \in \widehat{pre(e)} \wedge (\forall T' \in \widehat{pre(e)})(T', \widehat{pre(e)}) \models_{M^c} \psi)$ (by I.H.) iff $(T, \widehat{pre(e)}) \models_{M^c} K\psi$ (by the semantics).
- Case $\varphi := \langle e'\rangle\psi$. We have the sequence of equivalencies: $\langle e\rangle\langle e'\rangle\psi \in T$ iff $\langle e;e'\rangle\psi \in T$ (by R_e) iff $pre(e;e') \wedge \langle e;e'\rangle\psi \in T$ (by Proposition 3.3) iff $pre(e;e') \in T \wedge \langle e;e'\rangle\psi \in T$ iff $T \in \widehat{pre(e)} \cap \widehat{pre(e')} \wedge T \in \widehat{\langle e;e'\rangle\psi}$ iff $(T, \widehat{pre(e)} \cap \widehat{pre(e')}) \models_{M^c} \psi$ (by I.H.) iff $(T, \widehat{pre(e)}) \models_{M^c} \langle e'\rangle\psi$ (by the semantics).

- Case $\varphi := \Box\psi$. First observe the following: $\langle e\rangle\Box\psi \in T$ iff $e \wedge [e]\Box\psi \in T$ (by Proposition 3.3) iff $pre(e) \in T$ and $\Box[e]\psi \in T$ (by $R_\Box$) iff $pre(e) \in T$ and $[e'][e]\psi \in T, \forall e' \in \Pi^{\mathrm{O}}_{Ob}$ (by Lemma 12) iff $pre(e) \in T$ and $[e';e]\psi \in T, \forall e' \in \Pi^{\mathrm{O}}_{Ob}$ (by R_e) iff $pre(e) \in T$ and $[e;e']\psi \in T, \forall e' \in \Pi^{\mathrm{O}}_{Ob}$ (by Proposition 3.6).

  ($\Rightarrow$) Suppose $\langle e\rangle\Box\psi \in T$. Now let $U \in \mathscr{O}^c$ such that $T \in U$. By the definition of $\mathscr{O}^c$ we know that $U = \widehat{pre(e'')}$ for some $e'' \in \Pi^{\mathrm{O}}_{Ob}$. Since $T \in \widehat{pre(e'')}$ and by the observation above we obtain, $pre(e;e'') \in T$ and $[e;e'']\psi \in T$. Thus, $T \in \widehat{pre(e;e'')}$ and $T \in \widehat{[e;e'']\psi}$. By Proposition 3.3 we have $T \in \widehat{pre(e;e'')}$ and $T \in \widehat{\langle e;e''\rangle\psi}$. Since $\widehat{pre(e;e'')} = \widehat{pre(e)} \cap \widehat{pre(e'')}$ and $\langle e;e''\rangle\psi \in T$, by I.H. we get $(T, \widehat{pre(e)} \cap \widehat{pre(e'')}) \models_{M^c} \psi$. Since $\widehat{pre(e'')} = U$ was taken arbitrarily in $\mathscr{O}^c$, by the semantics, we obtain $(T, \widehat{pre(e)}) \models_{M^c} \Box\psi$.

  ($\Leftarrow$) Suppose $(T, \widehat{pre(e)}) \models_{M^c} \Box\psi$. By the semantics of $\Box$ and the definition of $\mathscr{O}^c$, we have that for all $e' \in \Pi^{\mathrm{O}}_{Ob}$, if $T \in \widehat{pre(e)} \cap \widehat{pre(e')}$ then $(T, \widehat{pre(e)} \cap \widehat{pre(e')}) \models_{M^c} \psi$. Let $e'' \in \Pi^{\mathrm{O}}_{Ob}$ such that $T \in \widehat{pre(e'')}$, therefore $T \in \widehat{pre(e)} \cap \widehat{pre(e'')}$. Since $\widehat{pre(e)} \cap \widehat{pre(e'')} \in \mathscr{O}^c$, we obtain, by the assumption, that $(T, \widehat{pre(e)} \cap \widehat{pre(e'')}) \models_{M^c} \psi$. Thus, by I.H., we have $pre(e;e'') \in T$ and $\langle e;e''\rangle\psi \in T$. By Propositions 3.3 and 3.6, $[e'';e]\psi \in T$. By (R_e) we have $[e''][e]\psi \in T$. Since e'' was taken arbitrarily, by Lemma 12, we have $\Box[e]\psi \in T$. Then, by ($R_\Box$), we obtain $[e]\Box\psi \in T$. Since $pre(e) \in T$ and $[e]\Box\psi \in T$, we have $\langle e\rangle\Box\psi \in T$ by Proposition 3.3.

Theorem 4. **L** *is complete with respect to the class of plausibility learning models.*

Proof. Let φ be an **L**-consistent formula, i.e., it is an O_φ-theory. Then, by Lemma 8, it can be extended to some maximal O-witnessed theory T. Then, we have $\langle !\top\rangle\varphi \in T$ i.e., $T \in \widehat{\langle !\top\rangle\varphi}$ (by Proposition 3.7). Then, by Truth Lemma (Lemma 13), we obtain that $(T, \widehat{pre(!\top)}) \models_{M^c} \varphi$, where $M^c = (X^c, \mathscr{O}^c, \leq^c, \|\cdot\|_c)$ is the canonical model for T. This proves completeness.

5 Conclusions and Open Questions

In this paper, we enriched the dynamic logic for learning theory (DLLT) from [3] with additional structure in order to model learners whose conjectures satisfy standard rationality constraints (namely, the AGM postulates for belief revision). The standard model for such learners is provided by "AGM conditioning": learners are endowed with a total preorder, describing their prior plausibility relation, and at each step they believe the set of most plausible states compatible with all the previous observations. To axiomatize the DLLT logic of AGM conditioning, we were lead to assume that the learner has access to a wider range of potential information than in [3]: not only sequences of full observations, but also *partial* observations (finite unions of observations). Semantically, this required a technical shift from intersection spaces to lattice spaces, while on the syntactic side we needed to extended our dynamic modalities from simple observations to more complex PDL-like "observational events". This leads to a rich evidential setting, with a more interesting logic and an elegant axiomatization.

Note that our move to partial observations and observational events still requires *less* information than the classical axiomatizations of AGM conditioning in the literature (which assumed full Boolean closure of the set of "conditions", i.e. the observable sets formed a Boolean algebra). Still, while this move to partial observations seems general enough, as well as natural and desirable in itself, it does require a much wider access to information than the setting in [3]. So it is fair to ask the question: is there a way to axiomatize AGM learners *without* requiring them to access partial information? In other words, is AGM conditioning over intersection spaces axiomatizable in a simple, elegant way (similar to our axiomatization)? This problem is still open, though we conjecture that the answer is *no*. If we are right, this would be an argument for a deeper philosophical point: it may be that AGM postulates are best suited to "rich" evidential settings, in which both total and partial observations are available.

References

1. Alchourrón, C.E., Gärdenfors, P., Makinson, D.: On the logic of theory change: partial meet contraction and revision functions. J. Symb. Log. **50**, 510–530 (1985)
2. Balbiani, P., Baltag, A., van Ditmarsch, H., Herzig, A., Hoshi, T., de Lima, T.: 'Knowable' as 'known after an announcement'. Rev. Symb. Log. **1**, 305–334 (2008)
3. Baltag, A., Gierasimczuk, N., Özgün, A., Vargas Sandoval, A.L., Smets, S.: A dynamic logic for learning theory. In: Madeira, A., Benevides, M. (eds.) DALI 2017. LNCS, vol. 10669, pp. 35–54. Springer, Cham (2018). https://doi.org/10.1007/978-3-319-73579-5_3
4. Baltag, A., Gierasimczuk, N., Smets, S.: Belief revision as a truth-tracking process. In: Proceedings of the 13th Conference on Theoretical Aspects of Rationality and Knowledge, pp. 187–190. ACM (2011)
5. Baltag, A., Gierasimczuk, N., Smets, S.: On the solvability of inductive problems: a study in epistemic topology. In: Ramanujam, R. (ed.) Proceedings of the 15th Conference TARK, also Available as a Technical Report in ILLC Prepublication Series PP-2015-13 (2015)
6. Baltag, A., Moss, L.S., Solecki, S.: The logic of public announcements, common knowledge, and private suspicions. In: Proceedings of the 7th Conference TARK, pp. 43–56. Morgan Kaufmann Publishers Inc. (1998)
7. Baltag, A., Özgün, A., Vargas Sandoval, A.L.: Topo-logic as a dynamic-epistemic logic. In: Baltag, A., Seligman, J., Yamada, T. (eds.) LORI 2017. LNCS, vol. 10455, pp. 330–346. Springer, Heidelberg (2017). https://doi.org/10.1007/978-3-662-55665-8_23
8. Baltag, A., Renne, B.: Dynamic epistemic logic. In: Zalta, E.N. (ed.) The Stanford Encyclopedia of Philosophy. Metaphysics Research Lab, Stanford University, Winter 2016 edn. (2016)

9. Baltag, A., Smets, S.: A qualitative theory of dynamic interactive belief revision. Texts Log. Games **3**, 9–58 (2008)
10. Board, O.: Dynamic interactive epistemology. Games Econ. Behav. **49**, 49–80 (2004)
11. Chellas, B.F.: Basic conditional logic. J. Philos. Log. **4**, 133–153 (1975)
12. Dabrowski, A., Moss, L.S., Parikh, R.: Topological reasoning and the logic of knowledge. Ann. Pure Appl. Log. **78**, 73–110 (1996)
13. Gold, E.M.: Language identification in the limit. Inf. Control **10**, 447–474 (1967)
14. Grahne, G.: Updates and counterfactuals. J. Log. Comput. **8**, 87–117 (1998)
15. Lewis, D.K.: Counterfactuals. Blackwell, Oxford (1973)
16. Moss, L.S., Parikh, R.: Topological reasoning and the logic of knowledge. In: Proceedings of the 4th TARK, pp. 95–105. Morgan Kaufmann (1992)
17. van Benthem, J.: Dynamic logic for belief revision. J. Appl. Non-Class. Log. **14**, 2004 (2004)
18. van Ditmarsch, H., van der Hoek, W., Kooi, B.: Dynamic Epistemic Logic, 1st edn. Springer, Heidelberg (2007). https://doi.org/10.1007/978-1-4020-5839-4

A Dynamic Epistemic Logic Analysis of the Equality Negation Task

Éric Goubault[1], Marijana Lazić[2], Jérémy Ledent[4(✉)], and Sergio Rajsbaum[3]

[1] LIX, CNRS, École Polytechnique, Institut Polytechnique de Paris, Palaiseau, France
[2] TU München, Munich, Germany
[3] Instituto de Matemáticas, UNAM, Mexico City, Mexico
[4] University of Strathclyde, Glasgow, UK
jeremy.ledent@strath.ac.uk

Abstract. In this paper we study the solvability of the *equality negation* task in a simple wait-free model where processes communicate by reading and writing shared variables or exchanging messages. In this task, two processes start with a private input value in the set $\{0, 1, 2\}$, and after communicating, each one must decide a binary output value, so that the outputs of the processes are the same if and only if the input values of the processes are different. This task is already known to be unsolvable; our goal here is to prove this result using the dynamic epistemic logic (DEL) approach introduced by Goubault, Ledent and Rajsbaum in GandALF 2018. We show that in fact, there is no epistemic logic formula that explains why the task is unsolvable. We fix this issue by extending the language of our DEL framework, which allows us to construct such a formula, and discuss its utility.

Keywords: Dynamic epistemic logic · Distributed computing · Equality negation

1 Introduction

Background. Computable functions are the basic objects of study in computability theory. A function is computable if there exists a Turing machine which, given an input of the function domain, returns the corresponding output. If instead of one Turing machine, we have many, and each one gets only one part of the input, and should compute one part of the output, we are in the setting of *distributed computability*, e.g. [1,20]. The sequential machines are called *processes*, and are allowed to be infinite state machines, to concentrate on the interaction aspects of computability, disregarding sequential computability issues. The notion corresponding to a function is a *task*, roughly, the domain is a set of input vectors, the range is a set of output vectors, and the task specification Δ is an input/output relation between them. An input vector I specifies in its i-th entry the (private) input to the i-th process, and an output vector

L. Soares Barbosa and A. Baltag (Eds.): DaLí 2019, LNCS 12005, pp. 53–70, 2020.
https://doi.org/10.1007/978-3-030-38808-9_4

$O \in \Delta(I)$ states that it is valid for each process i to produce as output the i-th entry of O, whenever the input vector is I. An important example of a task is *consensus*, where each process is given an input from a set of possible input values, and the participating processes have to agree on one of their inputs.

A *distributed computing model* has to specify various details related to how the processes communicate with each other and what type of failures may occur. It turns out that different models may have different power, i.e., solve different sets of tasks. In this paper we consider the *layered message-passing model* [12], both because of its relevance to real systems, and because it is the basis to study task computability. This simple, wait-free round-based model where messages can be lost, is described in Sect. 2.

The theory of distributed computability has been well-developed since the early 1990's [15], with origins even before [4,7], and overviewed in a book [12]. It was discovered that the reason for why a task may or may not be computable is of a topological nature. The input and output sets of vectors are best described as *simplicial complexes*, and a task can be specified by a relation Δ from the input complex $\mathcal{I}$ to the output complex $\mathcal{O}$. The main result is that a task is solvable in the layered message-passing model if and only if there is a certain subdivision of the input complex $\mathcal{I}$ and a certain simplicial map δ to the output complex $\mathcal{O}$, that respects the specification Δ. This is why the layered message-passing model is fundamental; models that can solve more tasks than the layered message-passing model preserve the topology of the input complex less precisely (they introduce "holes").

Motivation. We are interested in understanding distributed computability from the epistemic point of view. What is the knowledge that the processes should gain, to be able to solve a task? This question began to be addressed in [11], using dynamic epistemic logic (DEL). Here is a brief overview of the approach taken in [11]. A new *simplicial complex model* for a multi-agent system was introduced, instead of the usual Kripke epistemic $S5$ model based on graphs. Then, the initial knowledge of the processes is represented by a simplicial model, denoted as $\mathcal{I}$, based on the input complex of the task to be solved. The distributed computing model is represented by an action model $\mathcal{A}$, and the knowledge at the end of the executions of a protocol is represented by the product update $\mathcal{I}[\mathcal{A}]$, another simplicial model. Remarkably, the task specification is also represented by an action model $\mathcal{T}$, and the product update gives a simplicial complex model $\mathcal{I}[\mathcal{T}]$ representing the knowledge that should be acquired, by a protocol solving the task. The task $\mathcal{T}$ is *solvable* in $\mathcal{A}$ whenever there exists a morphism $\delta : \mathcal{I}[\mathcal{A}] \to \mathcal{I}[\mathcal{T}]$ such that the diagram of simplicial complexes below commutes.

Thus, to prove that a task is unsolvable, one needs to show that no such δ exists. But one would want to produce a specific formula, that concretely represents knowledge that exists in $\mathcal{I}[\mathcal{T}]$, but has not been acquired after running the protocol, namely in $\mathcal{I}[\mathcal{A}]$. Indeed, it was shown in [11] that two of the main impossibilities in distributed computability, consen-

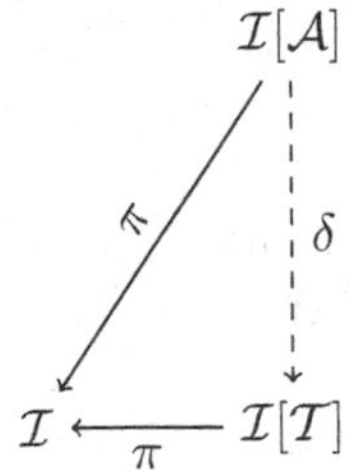

sus [7,19] and approximate agreement [12], can be expressed by such a formula. However, for other unsolvable tasks (e.g. set agreement), no such formula has been found, despite the fact that no morphism δ exists.

Contributions. In this paper we show that actually, there are unsolvable tasks, for which no such formula exists, namely, the *equality negation* task, defined by Lo and Hadzilacos [18]. This task was introduced as the central idea to prove that the consensus hierarchy [13,16] is not robust.

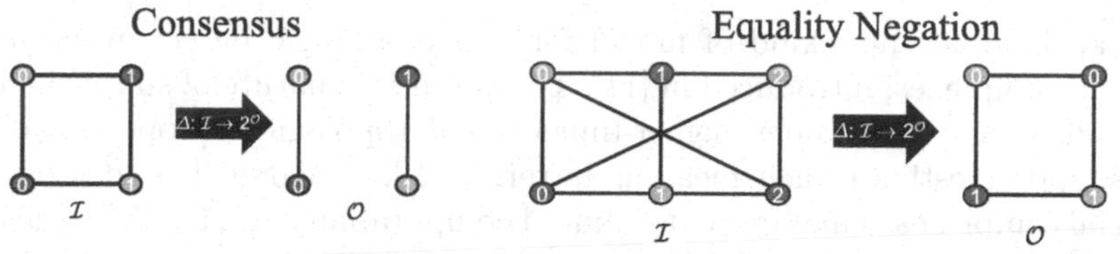

Consider two processes P_0 and P_1, each of which has a private input value, drawn from the set of possible input values $I = \{0, 1, 2\}$. After communicating, each process must irrevocably decide a binary output value, either 0 or 1, so that the outputs of the processes are the same if and only if the input values of the processes are different.

It is interesting to study the solvability of the equality negation task from the epistemic point of view. It is well known that there is no wait-free consensus algorithm in our model [5,19]. The same is true for equality negation, as shown in [10,18]. This is intriguing because there is a formula that shows the impossibility of consensus (essentially reaching common knowledge on input values) [11], while, as we show here, there is no such formula for equality negation. In more detail, it is well known that consensus is intimately related to connectivity, and hence to common knowledge, while its specification requires deciding unto disconnected components of the output complex. The equality negation task is unsolvable for a different reason, since its output complex is connected. Moreover, equality negation is strictly weaker than consensus: consensus can implement equality negation, but not viceversa (the latter is actually a difficult proof in [18]). So it is interesting to understand the difference between the knowledge required to solve each of these tasks.

Our second contribution is to propose an extended version of our DEL framework, for which there is such a formula. Intuitively, the reason why we cannot find a formula witnessing the unsolvability of the task is because our logical language is too weak to express the knowledge required to solve the task. So, our solution is to enrich the language by adding new atomic propositions, allowing us to express the required formula.

Organization. Section 2 recalls the DEL framework introduced in [11], and defines the layered message-passing model in this context. In Sect. 3 we study the equality negation task using DEL. First we explain why the impossibility proof does not work in the standard setting, then we propose an extension allowing us to make the proof go through. The long version of this paper [9] includes all proofs, as well as a detailed treatment of the equality negation task following the combinatorial topology approach, for completeness, but also for comparison with the DEL approach.

2 Preliminaries

2.1 Topological Models for Dynamic Epistemic Logic (DEL)

We recap here the new kind of model for epistemic logic based on chromatic simplicial complexes, introduced in [11]. The geometric nature of simplicial complexes allows us to consider higher-dimensional topological properties of our models, and investigate their meaning in terms of knowledge. The idea of using simplicial complexes comes from distributed computability [12,17]. After describing simplicial models, we explain how to use them in DEL.

Syntax. Let At be a countable set of atomic propositions and Ag a finite set of agents. The language $\mathcal{L}_K$ is generated by the following BNF grammar:

$$\varphi ::= p \mid \neg\varphi \mid (\varphi \wedge \varphi) \mid K_a\varphi \qquad p \in \mathrm{At},\ a \in \mathrm{Ag}$$

In the following, we work with $n+1$ agents, and write $\mathrm{Ag} = \{a_0, \ldots, a_n\}$.

Semantics. The usual semantics for multi-agent epistemic logic is based on Kripke frames. The notion of model that we use here, which is based on simplicial complexes, is merely a reformulation of the usual Kripke models using a different formalism. The benefits of this reformulation is that it makes explicit the topological information of Kripke frames. The precise relationship between the usual Kripke models and our simplicial models is studied thoroughly in [11].

Definition 1 (Simplicial complex [17]). *A* simplicial complex $\langle V, M\rangle$ *is given by a set* V *of* vertices *and a family* M *of non-empty finite subsets of* V *called* simplices, *such that for all* $X \in M$, $Y \subseteq X$ *implies* $Y \in M$. *We say that* Y *is a* face *of* X.

Usually, the set of vertices is implicit and we simply refer to a simplicial complex as M. We write $\mathcal{V}(M)$ for the set of vertices of M. A vertex $v \in \mathcal{V}(M)$ is identified with the singleton $\{v\} \in M$. Elements of M are called *simplices*, and those which are maximal w.r.t. inclusion are *facets* (or *worlds*), the set of which is denoted by $\mathcal{F}(M)$. The *dimension* of a simplex $X \in M$ is $|X|-1$. A simplicial complex M is *pure* if all its facets are of the same dimension n. In this case, we say M is of dimension n. Given a finite set Ag of agents (that we will represent as colors), a *chromatic simplicial complex* $\langle M, \chi\rangle$ consists of a simplicial complex M and a coloring map $\chi : \mathcal{V}(M) \to \mathrm{Ag}$, such that for all $X \in M$, all the vertices of X have distinct colors.

Definition 2 (Simplicial map). *Let C and D be two simplicial complexes. A* simplicial map $f : C \to D$ *maps the vertices of C to vertices of D, such that if X is a simplex of C, $f(X)$ is a simplex of D. A* chromatic simplicial map *between two chromatic simplicial complexes is a simplicial map that preserves colors.*

For technical reasons, we restrict to models where all the atomic propositions are saying something about some local value held by one particular agent. All the examples that we are interested in will fit in that framework. Let *Val* be some countable set of values, and $\mathrm{At} = \{p_{a,x} \mid a \in \mathrm{Ag}, x \in Val\}$ be the set of *atomic propositions.* Intuitively, $p_{a,x}$ is true if agent a holds the value x. We write At_a for the atomic propositions concerning agent a.

A *simplicial model* $\mathcal{M} = \langle C, \chi, \ell \rangle$ consists of a pure chromatic simplicial complex $\langle C, \chi \rangle$ of dimension n, and a labeling $\ell : \mathcal{V}(C) \to \mathscr{P}(\mathrm{At})$ that associates with each vertex $v \in \mathcal{V}(C)$ a set of atomic propositions concerning agent $\chi(v)$, i.e., such that $\ell(v) \subseteq \mathrm{At}_{\chi(v)}$. Given a facet $X = \{v_0, \ldots, v_n\} \in C$, we write $\ell(X) = \bigcup_{i=0}^{n} \ell(v_i)$. A *morphism* of simplicial models $f : \mathcal{M} \to \mathcal{M}'$ is a chromatic simplicial map that preserves the labeling: $\ell'(f(v)) = \ell(v)$ (and χ).

Definition 3. *We define the truth of a formula φ in some epistemic state $(\mathcal{M}, X)$ with $\mathcal{M} = \langle C, \chi, \ell \rangle$ a simplicial model, $X \in \mathcal{F}(C)$ a facet of C and $\varphi \in \mathcal{L}_K(\mathrm{Ag}, \mathrm{At})$. The satisfaction relation, determining when a formula is true in an epistemic state, is defined as:*

$$
\begin{array}{ll}
\mathcal{M}, X \models p & \textit{if } p \in \ell(X) \\
\mathcal{M}, X \models \neg\varphi & \textit{if } \mathcal{M}, X \not\models \varphi \\
\mathcal{M}, X \models \varphi \wedge \psi & \textit{if } \mathcal{M}, X \models \varphi \textit{ and } \mathcal{M}, X \models \psi \\
\mathcal{M}, X \models K_a\varphi & \textit{if for all } Y \in \mathcal{F}(C), a \in \chi(X \cap Y) \textit{ implies } \mathcal{M}, Y \models \varphi
\end{array}
$$

It is not hard to see that this definition of truth agrees with the usual one on Kripke models (see [11]).

DEL and Its Topological Semantics. DEL is the study of modal logics of model change [3,6]. A modal logic studied in DEL is obtained by using action models [2], which are relational structures that can be used to describe a variety of communication actions.

Syntax. We extend the syntax of epistemic logic with one more construction:

$$\varphi ::= p \mid \neg\varphi \mid (\varphi \wedge \varphi) \mid K_a\varphi \mid [\alpha]\varphi \qquad p \in \mathrm{At},\ a \in \mathrm{Ag}$$

Intuitively, $[\alpha]\varphi$ means that φ is true after some *action* α has occurred. An action can be thought of as an announcement made by the environment, which is not necessarily public, in the sense that not all agents receive these announcements. The semantics of this new operator should be understood as follows:

$$\mathcal{M}, X \models [\alpha]\varphi \quad \text{if} \quad \mathcal{M}[\alpha], X[\alpha] \models \varphi$$

i.e., the formula $[\alpha]\varphi$ is true in some world X of $\mathcal{M}$ whenever φ is true in some new model $\mathcal{M}[\alpha]$, where the knowledge of each agent has been modified according to the action α. To define formally what an action is, we first need to introduce the notion of *action model*. An action model describes all the possible actions that might happen, as well as how they affect the different agents.

A Simplicial Complex Version of DEL. An *action model* is a structure $\mathcal{A} = \langle T, \sim, \mathsf{pre}\rangle$, where T is a domain of *actions*, such that for each $a \in \mathrm{Ag}$, $\sim_a$ is an equivalence relation on T, and $\mathsf{pre} : T \to \mathcal{L}_K$ is a function that assigns a *precondition* formula $\mathsf{pre}(t)$ to each $t \in T$. An action model is *proper* if for any two different actions $t, t' \in T$, there is an agent $a \in \mathrm{Ag}$ who can distinguish between them, i.e., $t \not\sim_a t'$.

Given a simplicial model $\mathcal{M} = \langle C, \chi, \ell\rangle$ and an action model $\mathcal{A} = \langle T, \sim, \mathsf{pre}\rangle$, we define the *product update simplicial model* $\mathcal{M}[\mathcal{A}] = \langle C[\mathcal{A}], \chi[\mathcal{A}], \ell[\mathcal{A}]\rangle$ as follows. Intuitively, the facets of $C[\mathcal{A}]$ should correspond to pairs (X, t) where $X \in C$ is a world of $\mathcal{M}$ and $t \in T$ is an action of $\mathcal{A}$, such that $\mathcal{M}, X \models \mathsf{pre}(t)$. Moreover, two such facets (X, t) and (Y, t') should be glued along their a-colored vertex whenever $a \in \chi(X \cap Y)$ and $t \sim_a t'$. Formally, the vertices of $C[\mathcal{A}]$ are pairs (v, E) where $v \in \mathcal{V}(C)$ is a vertex of C; E is an equivalence class of $\sim_{\chi(v)}$; and v belongs to some facet $X \in C$ such that there exists $t \in E$ such that $\mathcal{M}, X \models \mathsf{pre}(t)$. Such a vertex keeps the color and labeling of its first component: $\chi[\mathcal{A}](v, E) = \chi(v)$ and $\ell[\mathcal{A}](v, E) = \ell(v)$.

Given a product update simplicial model $\mathcal{M}[\mathcal{A}] = \langle C[\mathcal{A}], \chi[\mathcal{A}], \ell[\mathcal{A}]\rangle$ as above, one can naturally enrich it by extending the set of atomic propositions in order to capture the equivalence class of $\sim_{\chi(v)}$ on each vertex v. The extended set of atomic propositions would then be $\widehat{\mathrm{At}} = \mathrm{At} \cup \{p_E \mid E \in T/\sim_a,\ a \in \mathrm{Ag}\}$, where $T/\sim_a$ denotes the set of all equivalence classes of $\sim_a$. In that case, the *extended product update model* is $\widehat{\mathcal{M}[\mathcal{A}]} = \langle C[\mathcal{A}], \chi[\mathcal{A}], \widehat{\ell}[\mathcal{A}]\rangle$, that differs from $\mathcal{M}$ only in labeling. Namely, the enriched labeling $\widehat{\ell}[\mathcal{A}]$ maps each vertex $(v, E) \in C[\mathcal{A}]$ into the set of atomic propositions $\widehat{\ell}[\mathcal{A}]((v, E)) = \ell(v) \cup \{p_E\}$. On this extended model $\widehat{\mathcal{M}[\mathcal{A}]}$, we can interpret formulas saying something not only about the atomic propositions of $\mathcal{M}$, but also about the actions that may have occurred.

In the next section, we describe a particular action model of interest, the one corresponding to the layered message-passing model described in Sect. 2.2.

2.2 The Layered Message-Passing Action Model

This section starts with an overview of the *layered message-passing model* for two agents, or *processes* as they are called in distributed computing. More details about this model can be found in [12]. This model is known to be equivalent to the well-studied *read/write wait-free model*, in the sense that it solves the same set of tasks. When there are only two processes involved in the computation, which is what we want to study in this article, the layered message-passing model is easier to understand. Here, we formalize this model as an action model; a more usual presentation can be found in the long version of the paper [9], along with a proof of equivalence between the two.

The Layered Message-Passing Model. Let the processes be B, W, to draw them in the pictures with colors black and white. In the *layered message-passing* model, computation is synchronous: B and W take steps at the same time. We will call each such step a *layer*. In each layer, B and W both send a message to each other, where at most one message may fail to arrive, implying that either one or two messages will be received. This is a *full information* model, in the sense that each time a process sends a message, the message consists of its local state (i.e., all the information currently known to the process), and each time it receives a message, it appends it to its own local state (remembers everything). A protocol is defined by the number N of layers the processes execute. Then, each process should produce an output value based on its state at the end of the last layer. A decision function δ specifies the output value of each process at the end of the last layer.

Given an initial state, an execution can be specified by a sequence of N symbols over the alphabet $\{\bot, B, W\}$, meaning that, if the i-th symbol in the sequence is $\bot$ then in the i-th layer both messages arrived, and if the i-th symbol is B (resp. W) then only B's message failed to arrive (resp. W) in the i-th layer. As an example, $\bot BW$ corresponds to an execution in which both processes have received each others message at layer one, then B received the message from W but W did not receive the message from B at layer two, and finally at layer three, W received the message from B but B did not receive the message from W.

For example, there are three 1-layer executions, namely $\bot$, B and W, but from the point of view of process B, there are two distinguished cases: (i) either it did not receive a message, in which case it knows for sure that the execution that occurred was W, or (ii) it did receive a message from W, in which case the execution could have been either B or $\bot$. Thus, for the black process executions B and $\bot$ are indistinguishable.

The Layered Message-Passing Model as an Action Model. Consider the situation where the agents $\text{Ag} = \{B, W\}$ each start in an initial global state, defined by input values given to each agent. The values are local, in the sense that each agent knows its own initial value, but not necessarily the values given to other agents. The agents communicate to each other via the layered message-passing model described above. The layered message-passing action model described next is equivalent to the immediate snapshot action model of [11] in the case of two processes.

Let V^{in} be an arbitrary domain of *input values*, and take the following set of atomic propositions $\text{At} = \{\mathsf{input}_a^x \mid a \in \text{Ag}, x \in V^{in}\}$. Consider a simplicial model $\mathcal{I} = \langle I, \chi, \ell \rangle$ called the *input simplicial model*. Moreover, we assume that for each vertex $v \in \mathcal{V}(I)$, corresponding to some agent $a = \chi(v)$, the labeling $\ell(v) \subseteq \text{At}_a$ is a singleton, assigning to the agent a its private input value. A facet $X \in \mathcal{F}(I)$ represents a possible initial configuration, where each agent has been given an input value.

The action model $\mathcal{MP}_N = \langle T, \sim, \mathsf{pre} \rangle$ corresponding to N layers is defined as follows. Let L_N be the set of all sequences of N symbols over the alphabet

$\{\bot, B, W\}$. Then, we take $T = L_N \times \mathcal{F}(I)$. An action (α, X), where $\alpha \in L_N$ and $X \in \mathcal{F}(I)$ represents a possible execution starting in the initial configuration X. We write X_a for the input value assigned to agent a in the input simplex X. Then, $\mathsf{pre} : T \to \mathcal{L}_\mathcal{K}$ assigns to each $(\alpha, X) \in T$ a precondition formula $\mathsf{pre}(\alpha, X)$ which holds exactly in X (formally, we take $\mathsf{pre}(\alpha, X) = \bigwedge_{a \in \mathsf{Ag}} \mathsf{input}_a^{X_a}$). To define the indistinguishability relation $\sim_a$, we proceed by induction on N. For $N = 0$, we define $(\varnothing, X) \sim_a (\varnothing, Y)$ when $X_a = Y_a$, since process a only sees its own local state. Now assume that the indistinguishability relation of $\mathcal{MP}_N$ has been defined, we define $\sim_a$ on $\mathcal{MP}_{N+1}$ as follows. Let $\alpha, \beta \in L_N$ and $p, q \in \{\bot, B, W\}$. We define $(\alpha \cdot p, X) \sim_B (\beta \cdot q, Y)$ if either:

(i) $p = q = W$ and $(\alpha, X) \sim_B (\beta, Y)$, or
(ii) $p, q \in \{\bot, B\}$ and $X = Y$ and $\alpha = \beta$,

and similarly for $\sim_W$, with the role of B and W reversed. Intuitively, either (i) no message was received, and the uncertainty from the previous layers remain; or (ii) a message was received, and the process B can see the whole history, except that it does not know whether the last layer was B or $\bot$.

To see what the effect of this action model is, let us start with an input model $\mathcal{I}$ with only one input configuration X (input values have been omitted).

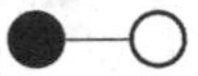

After one layer of the message passing model, we get the following model $\mathcal{I}[\mathcal{MP}_1]$:

After a second layer, we get $\mathcal{I}[\mathcal{MP}_2]$:

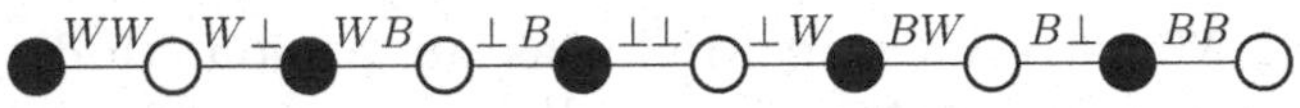

The remarkable property of this action model, is that it preserves the topology of the input model. This is a well-known fact in distributed computing [12], reformulated here in terms of DEL.

Theorem 1. *Let* $\mathcal{I} = \langle I, \chi, \ell \rangle$ *be an input model, and* $\mathcal{MP}_N = \langle T, \sim, \mathsf{pre} \rangle$ *be the* N*-layer action model. Then, the product update simplicial model* $\mathcal{I}[\mathcal{MP}_N]$ *is a subdivision of* $\mathcal{I}$*, where each edge is subdivided into* 3^N *edges.*

2.3 Outline of Impossibility Proofs

We now describe how the set up of [11] is used to prove impossibility results in distributed computing. It is closely related to the usual topological approach to distributed computability [12], except that the input complex, output complex and protocol complex are now viewed as simplicial models for epistemic logic. By interpreting epistemic logic formulas on those structures, we can understand the epistemic content of the abstract topological arguments for unsolvability. For example, when the usual topological proof would claim that consensus is not solvable because the protocol complex is connected, our DEL framework allows us to say that the reason for impossibility is that the processes did not reach common knowledge of the set of input values. This particular example, among others, is treated in depth in [11].

As in the previous section, we fix an input simplicial model $\mathcal{I} = \langle I, \chi, \ell \rangle$. A *task* for $\mathcal{I}$ is an action model $\mathcal{T} = \langle T, \sim, \mathsf{pre} \rangle$ for agents Ag, where each action $t \in T$ consists of a function $t : \mathrm{Ag} \to V^{out}$, where V^{out} is an arbitrary domain of *output values.* Such an action is interpreted as an assignment of an output value for each agent. Each such t has a precondition that is true in one or more facets of $\mathcal{I}$, interpreted as "if the input configuration is a facet in which $\mathsf{pre}(t)$ holds, and every agent $a \in \mathrm{Ag}$ decides the value $t(a)$, then this is a valid execution". The indistinguishability relation is defined as $t \sim_a t'$ when $t(a) = t'(a)$.

Definition 4. *The task $\mathcal{T}$ is solvable in the N-layer message-passing model if there exists a morphism $\delta : \mathcal{I}[\mathcal{MP}_N] \to \mathcal{I}[\mathcal{T}]$ such that $\pi \circ \delta = \pi$, i.e., the diagram of simplicial complexes below commutes.*

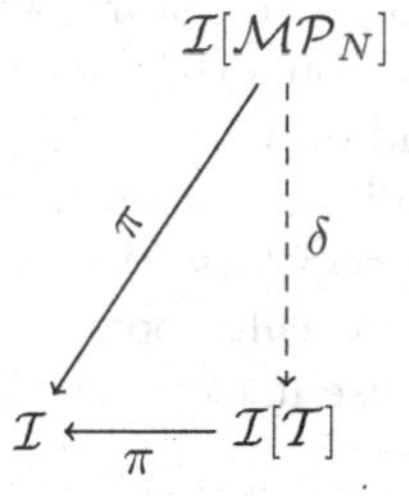

In the above definition, the two maps denoted as $\pi : \mathcal{I}[\mathcal{MP}_N] \to \mathcal{I}$ and $\pi : \mathcal{I}[\mathcal{T}] \to \mathcal{I}$ are simply projections on the first component. The intuition behind this definition is the following. A facet X in $\mathcal{I}[\mathcal{MP}_N]$ corresponds to a pair (i, act), where $i \in \mathcal{F}(\mathcal{I})$ represents input value assignments to all agents, and $act \in \mathcal{MP}_N$ represents an action, codifying the communication exchanges that took place. The morphism δ takes X to a facet $\delta(X) = (i, t)$ of $\mathcal{I}[\mathcal{T}]$, where $t \in \mathcal{T}$ is assignment of decision values that the agents will choose in the situation X.

Moreover, $\mathsf{pre}(t)$ holds in i, meaning that t corresponds to valid decision values for input i. The commutativity of the diagram expresses the fact that both X and $\delta(X)$ correspond to the same input assignment i. Now, consider a single vertex $v \in X$ with $\chi(v) = a \in \mathrm{Ag}$. Then, agent a decides its value solely according to its knowledge in $\mathcal{I}[\mathcal{MP}_N]$: if another facet X' contains v, then $\delta(v) \in \delta(X) \cap \delta(X')$, meaning that a has to decide the same value in both situations.

To prove impossibility results, our goal is thus to show that no such map δ can exist. To do so, we rely on the following lemma, which is a reformulation in the simplicial setting of a classic result of modal logics.

Lemma 1 ([11]). *Consider simplicial models $\mathcal{M} = \langle C, \chi, \ell \rangle$ and $\mathcal{M}' = \langle C', \chi', \ell' \rangle$, and a morphism $f : \mathcal{M} \to \mathcal{M}'$. Let $X \in \mathcal{F}(C)$ be a facet of $\mathcal{M}$, a an agent, and φ a formula which does not contain negations except, possibly, in front of atomic propositions. Then, $\mathcal{M}', f(X) \models \varphi$ implies $\mathcal{M}, X \models \varphi$.*

To prove that a task $\mathcal{T}$ is not solvable in $\mathcal{MP}_N$, our usual proof method goes like this. Assume $\delta : \mathcal{I}[\mathcal{MP}_N] \to \mathcal{I}[\mathcal{T}]$ exists, then:

1. Pick a well-chosen positive epistemic logic formula φ,
2. Show that φ is true in every world of $\mathcal{I}[\mathcal{T}]$,
3. Show that there exists a world X of $\mathcal{I}[\mathcal{MP}_N]$ where φ is false,
4. By Lemma 1, since φ is true in $\delta(X)$ then it must also be true in X, which is a contradiction with the previous point.

This kind of proof is interesting because it explains the reason why the task is not solvable. The formula φ represents some amount of knowledge which the processes must acquire in order to solve the task. If φ is given, the difficult part of the proof is usually the third point: finding a world X in the protocol complex where the processes did not manage to obtain the required amount of knowledge. The existence of this world can be proved using theorems of combinatorial topology, such as Sperner's Lemma; see [11] for such examples.

3 Equality Negation Task for Two Processes

The equality negation task has been introduced in [18], and further studied in [10]. In this section, we will be interested only in the case of two processes. Each process starts with an input value in the set $\{0, 1, 2\}$, and has to irrevocably decide on a value 0 or 1, such that the decisions of the two processes are the same if and only if their input values are different. In [18], it has been proved that the equality negation task is unsolvable for two processes in a wait-free model using only registers. We reproduce this proof in the long version [9], as well as a more topological proof. In this section we analyze this task using our DEL framework and use it to prove the unsolvability of the equality negation task.

3.1 DEL Analysis of the Task

Let $\text{Ag} = \{B, W\}$ be the two agents (or processes). In the pictures, process B will be associated to black vertices, and process W with white vertices. The atomic propositions are of the form input_p^i, for $p \in \text{Ag}$ and $i \in \{0, 1, 2\}$, meaning that process p has input value i. The input model is $\mathcal{I} = \langle I, \chi, \ell \rangle$ where:

- I is the simplicial complex whose set of vertices is $\mathcal{V}(I) = \text{Ag} \times \{0, 1, 2\}$, and whose facets are of the form $\{(B, i), (W, j)\}$ for all i, j.
- The coloring $\chi : \mathcal{V}(I) \to \text{Ag}$ is the first projection $\chi(p, i) = p$.
- $\ell(p, i) = \{\mathsf{input}_p^i\}$.

The input model $\mathcal{I}$ is represented below. In the picture, a vertex $(p, i) \in \mathcal{V}(I)$ is represented as a vertex of color p with value i.

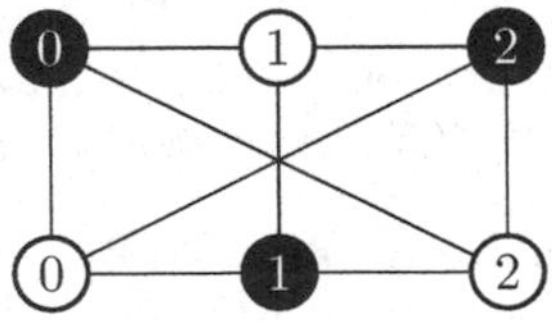

We now define the action model $\mathcal{T} = \langle T, \sim, \mathsf{pre}\rangle$ that specifies the task. Since the only possible outputs are 0 and 1, there are four possible actions: $T = \{0,1\}^2$, where by convention the first component is the decision of B, and the second component is the decision of W. Thus, two actions $(d_B, d_W) \sim_B (d'_B, d'_W)$ in T are indistinguishable by B when $d_B = d'_B$, and similarly for W. Finally, the precondition $\mathsf{pre}(d_B, d_W)$ specifies the task as expected: if $d_B = d_W$ then $\mathsf{pre}(d_B, d_W)$ is true exactly in the simplices of $\mathcal{I}$ which have different input values, and otherwise in all the simplices which have identical inputs.

The *output model* is obtained as the product update model $\mathcal{O} = \mathcal{I}[\mathcal{T}] = \langle O, \chi_\mathcal{O}, \ell_\mathcal{O}\rangle$. By definition, the vertices of O are of the form (p, i, E), where $(p, i) \in \mathcal{V}(I)$ is a vertex of $\mathcal{I}$, and E is an equivalence class of $\sim_p$. But note that $\sim_p$ has only two equivalence classes, depending on the decision value (0 or 1) of process p. So a vertex of O can be written as (p, i, d), meaning intuitively that process p started with input i and decided value d. The facets of O are of the form $\{(B, i, d_B), (W, j, d_W)\}$ where either $i = j$ and $d_B \neq d_W$, or $i \neq j$ and $d_B = d_W$. The coloring $\chi_\mathcal{O}$ and labeling $\ell_\mathcal{O}$ behave the same as in $\mathcal{I}$.

The output model for the equality negation task is depicted below. Decision values do not appear explicitly on the picture, but notice how the vertices are arranged as a rectangular cuboid: the vertices on the front face have decision value 0, and those on the rear face decide 1.

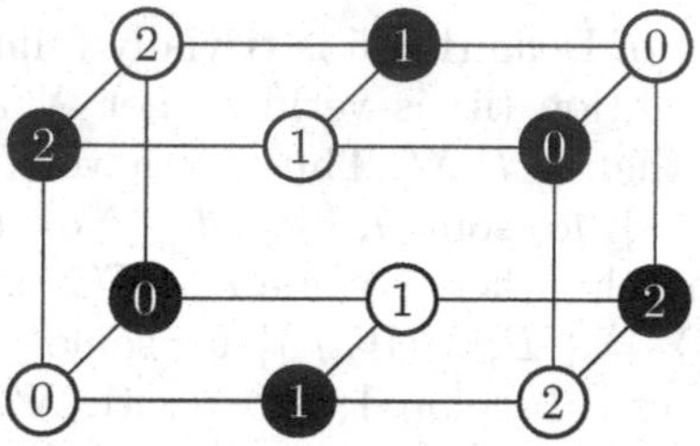

We want to prove that this task is not solvable when the processes communicate through N layers of our message passing model, no matter how large N is selected. Thus, we need to show that there is no morphism $\delta : \mathcal{I}[\mathcal{MP}_N] \to \mathcal{O}$ that makes the diagram of Definition 4 commute. In Sect. 3.2, we will show that the general proof method described in Sect. 2.3 actually fails. In Sect. 3.3, we extend the expressivity of our logic in order to obtain an epistemic proof that δ does not exist.

3.2 Bisimulation and Limits of the DEL Framework

We would like to use the proof method described in Sect. 2.3 to find a logical obstruction showing that the morphism δ cannot exist, through a formula φ. To show that, in fact, there is no such suitable formula φ, we first need to define bisimulations for simplicial models.

Definition 5 (Bisimulation). *Let $\mathcal{M} = \langle M, \chi, \ell\rangle$ and $\mathcal{M}' = \langle M', \chi', \ell'\rangle$ be two simplicial models. A relation $R \subseteq \mathcal{F}(M) \times \mathcal{F}(M')$ is a* bisimulation *between $\mathcal{M}$ and $\mathcal{M}'$ if the following conditions hold:*

(i) If $X \; R \; X'$ then $\ell(X) = \ell'(X')$.
(ii) For all $a \in \mathrm{Ag}$, if $X \; R \; X'$ and $a \in \chi(X \cap Y)$, then there exists $Y' \in \mathcal{F}(M')$ such that $Y \; R \; Y'$ and $a \in \chi'(X' \cap Y')$.
(iii) For all $a \in \mathrm{Ag}$, if $X \; R \; X'$ and $a \in \chi'(X' \cap Y')$, then there exists $Y \in \mathcal{F}(M)$ such that $Y \; R \; Y'$ and $a \in \chi(X \cap Y)$.

When R is a bisimulation and $X \; R \; X'$, we say that X and X' are bisimilar.

The next lemma states that two bisimilar worlds satisfy exactly the same formulae. This is a well-known fact in the context of Kripke models. The same results holds for bisimulations between simplicial models.

Lemma 2. *Let R be a bisimulation between $\mathcal{M}$ and $\mathcal{M}'$. Then for all facets X, X' such that $X \; R \; X'$, and for every epistemic logic formula φ,*

$$\mathcal{M}, X \models \varphi \quad \text{iff} \quad \mathcal{M}', X' \models \varphi$$

We now come back to the equality negation task for two processes. As it turns out, there is a bisimulation between the input and output models.

Lemma 3. *Let $\mathcal{I}$ and $\mathcal{O}$ be the input and output models of the equality negation task, respectively, and let π be the projection map $\pi : \mathcal{O} \to \mathcal{I}$. The relation $R = \{(\pi(X), X) \mid X \in \mathcal{F}(\mathcal{O})\} \subseteq \mathcal{I} \times \mathcal{O}$ is a bisimulation between $\mathcal{I}$ and $\mathcal{O}$.*

Proof. The first condition of Definition 5 is trivially fulfilled.

Let us check that condition (ii) is verified. Let X and X' be facets of $\mathcal{I}$ and $\mathcal{O}$ respectively, such that $X \; R \; X'$. Thus, we have $X = \{(B,i),(W,j)\}$ and $X' = \{(B,i,d_B),(W,j,d_W)\}$, for some i, j, d_B, d_W. Now let $a \in \mathrm{Ag}$ (w.l.o.g., let us pick $a = B$), and assume that there is some $Y \in \mathcal{F}(\mathcal{I})$ such that $B \in \chi(X \cap Y)$. So, Y can be written as $Y = \{(B,i),(W,j')\}$ for some j'. We now need to find a facet Y' of $\mathcal{O}$ that shares a B-colored vertex with X', and whose projection $\pi(Y')$ is Y. Thus, Y' should be of the form $Y' = \{(B,i,d_B),(W,j',d'_W)\}$, for some d'_W, such that $i = j' \iff d_B \neq d'_W$. But whatever the values of i, j', d_B are, we can always choose a suitable d'_W. This concludes the proof.

The third condition (iii) is checked similarly. □

We can finally use Lemma 2 to show that no formula φ will allow us to prove the unsolvability of the equality negation task.

Lemma 4. *For the equality negation task, let X be a facet of $\mathcal{I}[\mathcal{MP}_N]$ and let Y be a facet of $\mathcal{O}$ such that $\pi(X) = \pi(Y)$. Then for every positive formula φ we have the following: if $\mathcal{O}, Y \models \varphi$ then $\mathcal{I}[\mathcal{MP}_N], X \models \varphi$.*

Proof. Let φ be a positive formula and assume $\mathcal{O}, Y \models \varphi$. Since we have shown in Lemma 3 that $\pi(Y)$ and Y are bisimilar, by Lemma 2, we have $\mathcal{I}, \pi(Y) \models \varphi$. Since $\pi(Y) = \pi(X)$, by Lemma 1 we obtain $\mathcal{I}[\mathcal{MP}_N], X \models \varphi$. □

In the above lemma, the world Y should be thought of as a candidate for $\delta(X)$. The condition $\pi(X) = \pi(Y)$ comes from the commutative diagram of Definition 4. Thus, Lemma 4 says that we will never find a formula φ which is true in $\delta(X)$ but false in X.

Remark. As previously discussed, Lemma 4 does not apply to consensus, since we know that there exists a formula proving its unsolvability. The reason is that the projection mapping $\pi : \mathcal{O} \to \mathcal{I}$ in consensus does not induce a bisimulation. Here we show that condition (ii) of Definition 5 does not hold. Namely, if $X = \{(B,0),(W,1)\}$ and $X' = \{(B,0,1),(W,1,1)\}$ and $Y = \{(B,0),(W,0)\}$, then by definition of consensus there cannot exist a facet Y' with $Y \; R \; Y'$ and $B \in \chi'(X' \cap Y')$. Such a facet would have the form $Y' = \{(B,0,1),(W,0,d)\}$, for a $d \in \{0,1\}$, which is not a valid world in the output model of consensus for any decision d.

3.3 Extended DEL

In Sect. 3.2, we have shown that no epistemic logic formula is able to express the reason why the equality negation task is not solvable. This seems to indicate that our logic is too weak: indeed, because of the product update model construction that we use, we are only allowed to write formulas about the inputs and what the processes know about each other's inputs. But the specification of the task is very much about the outputs too! If we allow ourselves to use atomic propositions of the form decide_p^d, with the intended meaning that process p decides value d, a good candidate for the formula φ seems to be:

$$\varphi = \bigwedge_{p,i,d} \mathsf{input}_p^i \wedge \mathsf{decide}_p^d \implies \Big((\mathsf{input}_{\bar{p}}^i \wedge \mathsf{decide}_{\bar{p}}^{\bar{d}}) \vee (\mathsf{input}_{\bar{p}}^{\bar{i}} \wedge \mathsf{decide}_{\bar{p}}^{d}) \Big)$$

where $\bar{p}$, $\bar{i}$, $\bar{d}$ denote values different from p, i, d, respectively. Note that $\bar{p}$ and $\bar{d}$ are uniquely defined (since there are only two processes and two decision values), but for $\bar{i}$, there are two possible inputs different from i. So, for example, $\mathsf{input}_p^{\bar{0}}$ is actually a shortcut for $\mathsf{input}_p^1 \vee \mathsf{input}_p^2$.

This formula simply expresses the specification of the task: if process p has input i and decides d, then the other process should either have the same input and decide differently, or have a different input and decide the same. Then hopefully φ would be true in every world of the output complex, but would fail somewhere in the protocol complex $\mathcal{I}[\mathcal{MP}_N]$, meaning that the N-layer message-passing model is not powerful enough to obtain this knowledge.

To be able to express such a formula, we first need to enrich our models by saying in which worlds the atomic propositions decide_p^d are true or false. Let $\widehat{\mathrm{At}} = \mathrm{At} \cup \{\mathsf{decide}_p^d \mid p \in \mathrm{Ag}, d \in \{0,1\}\}$ be the new set of atomic propositions. The definition of the *extended product update model* $\widehat{\mathcal{I}[\mathcal{T}]} = \widehat{\mathcal{O}}$ is straightforward:

- Its vertices are of the form (p,i,d) with $p \in \mathrm{Ag}$, $i \in \{0,1,2\}$ and $d \in \{0,1\}$. The facets are $\{(B,i,d_B),(W,j,d_W)\}$ where $i = j \iff d_B \neq d_W$.
- The coloring map is $\chi_{\widehat{\mathcal{O}}}(p,i,d) = p$.
- The atomic propositions labeling is $\ell_{\widehat{\mathcal{O}}}(p,i,d) = \{\mathsf{input}_p^i, \mathsf{decide}_p^d\}$.

Thus, this is almost the same model as the one of Sect. 3.1, but we have added some annotations to say where the decide_p^d atomic propositions are true. It is easily checked that the formula φ is true in every world of $\widehat{\mathcal{O}}$.

Now, we would also like the formula φ to make sense in the protocol complex $\mathcal{I}[\mathcal{MP}_N]$, but it does not seem to have any information about decision values. It only describes the input values, and which execution has occurred. But it is precisely the role of the simplicial map $\delta : \mathcal{I}[\mathcal{MP}_N] \to \mathcal{O}$ to assign decision values to each world of $\mathcal{I}[\mathcal{MP}_N]$. Thus, given such a map δ, we can lift it to a map $\widehat{\delta} : \widehat{\mathcal{I}[\mathcal{MP}_N]} \to \widehat{\mathcal{O}}$ as the following lemma states.

Lemma 5. *Let $\mathcal{M} = \langle M, \chi, \ell \rangle$ be a simplicial model over the set of agents* Ag *and atomic propositions* At, *and let $\delta : \mathcal{M} \to \mathcal{O}$ be a morphism of simplicial models. Then there is a unique model $\widehat{\mathcal{M}} = \langle M, \chi, \widehat{\ell} \rangle$ over $\widehat{\text{At}}$, where $\widehat{\ell}$ agrees with ℓ on* At, *such that $\widehat{\delta} : \widehat{\mathcal{M}} \to \widehat{\mathcal{O}}$ is still a morphism of simplicial models.*

Proof. All we have to do is label the worlds of $\mathcal{M}$ with the decide_p^d atomic propositions, such that δ is a morphism of simplicial models. Thus, we define $\widehat{\ell} : M \to \mathscr{P}(\widehat{\text{At}})$ as $\widehat{\ell}(m) = \ell(m) \cup \{\mathsf{decide}_p^d\}$, where $\delta(m) = (p, i, d) \in O$. Then δ is still a chromatic simplicial map (since we did not change the underlying complexes nor their colors), and moreover we have $\widehat{\ell}(m) = \ell_{\widehat{\mathcal{O}}}(\delta(m))$ for all m. The model $\widehat{\mathcal{M}}$ is unique since any other choice of $\widehat{\ell}(m)$ would have broken this last condition, so δ would not be a morphism of simplicial models. □

We can finally prove that the equality negation task is not solvable:

Theorem 2. *The equality negation task for two processes is not solvable in the N-layer message-passing model.*

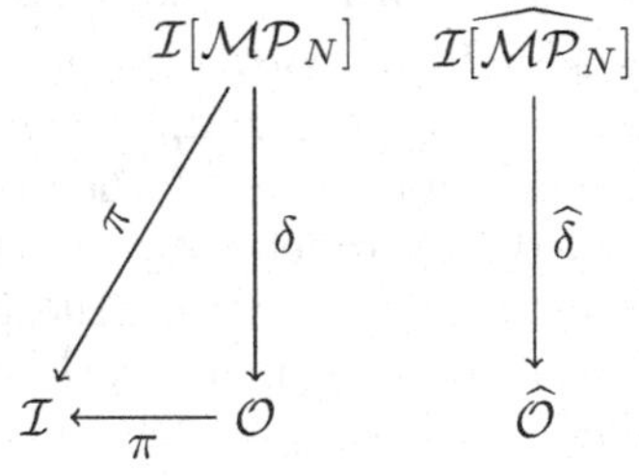

Proof. Let us assume by contradiction that the task is solvable, i.e., by Definition 4, there exists a morphism of simplicial models $\delta : \mathcal{I}[\mathcal{MP}_N] \to \mathcal{O}$ that makes the diagram commute. By Lemma 5, we can lift δ to a morphism $\widehat{\delta} : \widehat{\mathcal{I}[\mathcal{MP}_N]} \to \widehat{\mathcal{O}}$ between the extended models. As we remarked earlier, the formula φ is true in every world of $\widehat{\mathcal{O}}$. Therefore, it also has to be true in every world of $\widehat{\mathcal{I}[\mathcal{MP}_N]}$. Indeed, for any world w, since $\widehat{\mathcal{O}}, \delta(w) \models \varphi$, and δ is a morphism, by Lemma 1, we must have $\widehat{\mathcal{I}[\mathcal{MP}_N]}, w \models \varphi$. We will now derive a contradiction from this fact.

Recall that the protocol complex $\mathcal{I}[\mathcal{MP}_N]$ is just a subdivision of the input complex $\mathcal{I}$, as depicted below. (For simplicity, some input values have been omitted in the vertices on a subdivided edge; it is the same input as the extremity of the edge which has the same color. Also, the picture shows only one subdivision, but our reasoning is unrestricted and it applies to any number of layers N).

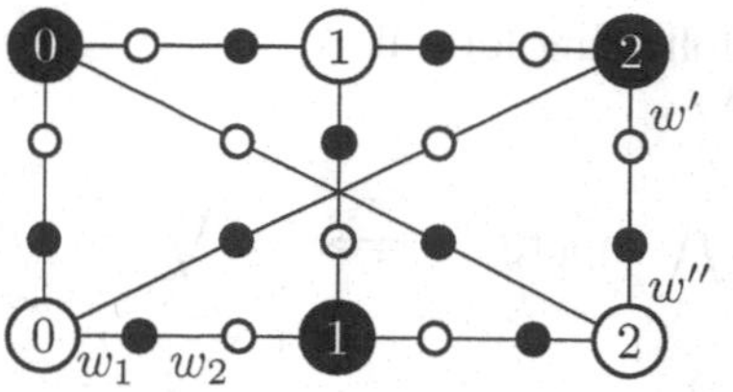

Let us start in some world w_1 on the $(W, 0) - (B, 1)$ edge. In the world w_1, the two processes have different inputs. Since in $\mathcal{I}[\widehat{\mathcal{MP}_N}]$, the formula φ is true in w_1, the decision values have to be the same. Without loss of generality, let us assume that in w_1, both processes decide 0.

We then look at the next world w_2, which shares a black vertex with w_1. Since the inputs are still 0 and 1, and φ is true, and we assumed that process B decides 0, then the white vertex of w_2 also has to decide 0.

We iterate this reasoning along the $(W, 0) - (B, 1)$ edge, then along the $(B, 1) - (W, 2)$ edge, and along the $(W, 0) - (B, 2)$ edge: all the vertices on these edges must have the same decision value 0. Thus, on the picture, the top right $(B, 2)$ corner has to decide 0, as well as the bottom right $(W, 2)$ corner.

Now in the world w', the two input values are equal, so the processes should decide differently. Since the black vertex decides 0, the white vertex must have decision value 1. If we keep going along the rightmost edge, the decision values must alternate: all the black vertices must decide 0, and the white ones decide 1. Finally, we reach the world w'', where both decision values are 0, whereas the inputs are both 2. So the formula φ is false in w'', which is a contradiction. □

It is interesting to compare the epistemic formula φ that we used in this paper to prove the unsolvability of equality negation, with the one (let us call it ψ) that was used in [11] to prove the impossibility of solving consensus. In the case of consensus, we did not need the "Extended DEL" framework. The formula ψ was simply saying that the processes have common knowledge of the input values. This formula is quite informative: it tells us that the main goal of the consensus task is to achieve common knowledge. On the other hand, the formula φ is less informative: it is simply stating the specification of the equality negation task. It does not even seem to be talking about knowledge, since there are no K or C operators in the formula. In fact, the epistemic content of φ is hidden in the decide_p^d atomic propositions. Indeed, their semantics in $\mathcal{I}[\widehat{\mathcal{MP}_N}]$ is referring to the decision map δ, which assigns a decision value d to each vertex of $\mathcal{I}[\mathcal{MP}_N]$. The fact that we assign decisions to vertices means that each process must decide its output *solely according to its knowledge.*

Despite the fact that it produces less informative formulas, the "Extended DEL" proof method has two major benefits. First, it seems to be able to prove *any* impossibility result. Indeed, let $\mathcal{T} = \langle T, \sim, \mathsf{pre} \rangle$ be a task action model, on the input model $\mathcal{I}$, and let $\mathcal{P}$ be a protocol action model. Remember that the elements of T are functions $t : \mathrm{Ag} \to V^{out}$ assigning a decision value to each agent. Let φ denote the following formula:

$$\varphi = \bigwedge_{X \in \mathcal{F}(\mathcal{I})} \left(\bigwedge_{p \in \mathrm{Ag}} \mathsf{input}_p^{X(p)} \implies \bigvee_{\substack{t \in T \\ \mathcal{I}, X \models \mathsf{pre}(t)}} \bigwedge_{p \in \mathrm{Ag}} \mathsf{decide}_p^{t(p)} \right) \tag{1}$$

where $X(p)$ denotes the input value of process p in the input simplex X. Then we get the following Theorem (whose proof is in the long version [9]).

Theorem 3. *The task $\mathcal{T}$ is solvable in the protocol $\mathcal{P}$ if and only if there exists an extension $\widehat{\mathcal{I}[\mathcal{P}]}$ of $\mathcal{I}[\mathcal{P}]$ (assigning a single decision value to each vertex of $\mathcal{I}[\mathcal{P}]$) such that φ from (1) is true in every world of $\widehat{\mathcal{I}[\mathcal{P}]}$.*

This theorem implies that the situation of Sect. 3.2 cannot happen with the "Extended DEL" approach: if the task is not solvable, there necessarily exists a world X of $\widehat{\mathcal{I}[\mathcal{P}]}$ where the formula fails. Of course, finding such a world is usually the hard part of an impossibility proof, but at least we know it exists. In fact, in the particular case of read/write protocols (or, equivalently, layered message-passing), the solvability of tasks is known to be undecidable when there are more than three processes [8, 14]. Thus, according to our Theorem, given a formula φ, the problem of deciding whether there exists a number of layers N and an extension of $\mathcal{I}[\mathcal{MP}_N]$ which validates the formula, is also undecidable.

The second benefit of the "Extended DEL" framework is that it gives us a way of using epistemic logic as a specification language for tasks. Notice that in Theorem 3, we characterized the solvability of a task without referring to $\mathcal{T}$ itself: the formula φ contains all the information of $\mathcal{T}$. Thus, instead of relying on the commutative diagram of Definition 4, we can specify a task directly as a logical formula. One could decide to pick a more informative formula, with an interesting epistemic content, and study the solvability of this "task".

4 Conclusion

The equality negation task is known to be unsolvable in the wait-free read/write model. In this paper, we gave a new proof of this result, using the simplicial complex semantics of DEL that we proposed in [11]. There are two purposes of doing this. First, the logical formula witnessing the unsolvability of a task usually helps us understand the epistemic content of this task. Unfortunately, as it turns out, the logical formula that we obtained in the end is less informative than we hoped. Secondly, this is a nice case study to test the limits of our DEL framework. Indeed, we proved in Sect. 3.2 that the basic language of DEL, where formulas are only allowed to talk about input values, is too weak to express the reason why the task is not solvable. To fix this issue, we introduced a way to extend our logical language in order to have more expressive formulas.

Acknowledgements. The authors were supported by DGA project "Validation of Autonomous Drones and Swarms of Drones" and the academic chair "Complex Systems Engineering" of Ecole Polytechnique-ENSTA-Télécom-Thalès-Dassault-Naval Group-DGA-FX-FDO-Fondation ParisTech, by the UNAM-PAPIIT project IN109917 and IN106520, by the France-Mexico Binational SEP-CONACYT-ANUIES-ECOS grant M12M01, by the European Research Council (ERC) under the European Union's Horizon 2020 research and innovation programme under grant agreement No 787367 (PaVeS), as well as by the Austrian Science Fund (FWF) through Doctoral College LogiCS (W1255-N23).

References

1. Attiya, H., Welch, J.: Distributed Computing: Fundamentals, Simulations and Advanced Topics. Wiley, New York (2004)
2. Baltag, A., Moss, L., Solecki, S.: The logic of common knowledge, public announcements, and private suspicions. In: TARK VII, pp. 43–56 (1998). https://doi.org/10.1007/978-3-319-20451-2_38
3. Baltag, A., Renne, B.: Dynamic epistemic logic. In: The Stanford Encyclopedia of Philosophy. Metaphysics Research Lab, Stanford University (2016). https://plato.stanford.edu/archives/win2016/entries/dynamic-epistemic/
4. Biran, O., Moran, S., Zaks, S.: A combinatorial characterization of the distributed 1-solvable tasks. J. Algorithms **11**(3), 420–440 (1990). https://doi.org/10.1016/0196-6774(90)90020-F
5. Chor, B., Israeli, A., Li, M.: On processor coordination using asynchronous hardware. In: Proceedings of the Sixth Annual ACM Symposium on Principles of Distributed Computing, PODC 1987, pp. 86–97. ACM, New York (1987). https://doi.org/10.1145/41840.41848
6. Ditmarsch, H.V., van der Hoek, W., Kooi, B.: Dynamic Epistemic Logic. Springer, Heidelberg (2007). https://doi.org/10.1007/978-1-4020-5839-4
7. Fischer, M.J., Lynch, N.A., Paterson, M.: Impossibility of distributed consensus with one faulty process. J. ACM **32**(2), 374–382 (1985). https://doi.org/10.1145/3149.214121
8. Gafni, E., Koutsoupias, E.: Three-processor tasks are undecidable. SIAM J. Comput. **28**(3), 970–983 (1999)
9. Goubault, E., Lazić, M., Ledent, J., Rajsbaum, S.: A dynamic epistemic logic analysis of the equality negation task. CoRR abs/1909.03263 (2019). http://arxiv.org/abs/1909.03263
10. Goubault, E., Lazić, M., Ledent, J., Rajsbaum, S.: Wait-free solvability of equality negation tasks. In: 33rd International Symposium on Distributed Computing, DISC 2019, 14–18 October 2019, Budapest, Hungary (2019). https://drops.dagstuhl.de/opus/volltexte/2019/11328/
11. Goubault, É., Ledent, J., Rajsbaum, S.: A simplicial complex model for dynamic epistemic logic to study distributed task computability. In: Proceedings Ninth International Symposium on Games, Automata, Logics, and Formal Verification, GandALF 2018, Saarbrücken, Germany, 26–28th September 2018, pp. 73–87 (2018). https://doi.org/10.4204/EPTCS.277.6
12. Herlihy, M., Kozlov, D., Rajsbaum, S.: Distributed Computing Through Combinatorial Topology. Elsevier-Morgan Kaufmann, Amsterdam (2013). https://doi.org/10.1016/C2011-0-07032-1

13. Herlihy, M.: Wait-free synchronization. ACM Trans. Program. Lang. Syst. **13**(1), 124–149 (1991). https://doi.org/10.1145/114005.102808
14. Herlihy, M., Rajsbaum, S.: The decidability of distributed decision tasks (extended abstract). In: Proceedings of the Twenty-Ninth Annual ACM Symposium on the Theory of Computing (STOC), El Paso, Texas, USA, 4–6 May 1997, pp. 589–598 (1997). https://doi.org/10.1145/258533.258652
15. Herlihy, M., Shavit, N.: The topological structure of asynchronous computability. J. ACM **46**(6), 858–923 (1999). https://doi.org/10.1145/331524.331529
16. Jayanti, P.: On the robustness of herlihy's hierarchy. In: Proceedings of the Twelfth Annual ACM Symposium on Principles of Distributed Computing, PODC 1993, pp. 145–157. ACM, New York (1993). https://doi.org/10.1145/164051.164070
17. Kozlov, D.: Combinatorial Algebraic Topology. Springer, Heidelberg (2007). https://doi.org/10.1007/978-3-540-71962-5
18. Lo, W., Hadzilacos, V.: All of us are smarter than any of us: nondeterministic wait-free hierarchies are not robust. SIAM J. Comput. **30**(3), 689–728 (2000). https://doi.org/10.1137/S0097539798335766
19. Loui, M.C., Abu-Amara, H.H.: Memory requirements for agreement among unreliable asynchronous processes. In: Advances in Computing research, pp. 163–183. JAI Press, Greenwich (1987)
20. Lynch, N.A.: Distributed Algorithms. Morgan Kaufmann Publishers Inc., San Francisco (1996)

A Logical Analysis of the Interplay Between Social Influence and Friendship Selection

Sonja Smets and Fernando R. Velázquez-Quesada(✉)

Institute for Logic, Language and Computation, Universiteit van Amsterdam, Amsterdam, The Netherlands
{S.J.L.Smets,F.R.VelazquezQuesada}@uva.nl

Abstract. This paper is part of a series of proposals for using logic to analyse social networks. It studies the intertwining of two forms of information dynamics: *social influence*, through which an agent's behaviour, opinions or features are affected by those of her social connections, and *friendship selection*, through which an agent chooses her social connections based on their common behaviour, opinions or features. The text provides a logical analysis of the two forms of dynamics (the main ingredients in the phenomenon known as *homophily*) as well as of their interaction, discussing also some of their variations.

1 Introduction

The tools of Dynamic Epistemic Logics (DEL) [1–3] have been designed to study the flow of information in complex multi-agent systems. The main feature of these Logics is the way they model the dynamics of information: an update mechanism describing how a given event acts on a given (input) system. Examples include the way agents update their epistemic or doxastic state, either as a result of an act of public or private communication, or else as the result of an intervention on the given state of affairs. This allows logicians to compute the triggered changes in truth-values of both the basic propositions and of the modal propositions used to describe a given multi-agent scenario. Going beyond the computations of epistemic and doxastic states, DEL is also well-equipped to treat scenarios that exhibit a social structure between the involved agents. This leads us to the recent development of using logic to model information flow in social networks. The line of work in this direction includes the studies by [4] on social influence, by [5] on peer pressure, by [6] on informational cascades, by [7] on belief change in social networks, by [8] on reflective social influence, by [9] on threshold diffusion and prediction update, by [10] on priority-based peer influence as well as by Smets and Velázquez-Quesada in their work [11–14] on social network formation.

In the above mentioned proposals for using logic to analyse social networks, we can distinguish two main forms of information dynamics. The first deals with changes in the local information states of agents, i.e. changes on their individual

L. Soares Barbosa and A. Baltag (Eds.): DaLí 2019, LNCS 12005, pp. 71–87, 2020.
https://doi.org/10.1007/978-3-030-38808-9_5

features, behavior, likes, opinions, etc. This first type of information flow can express aspects of "social influence" when the trigger of information change is the behavior, likes or opinions of the agent's neighbours in the network. The second deals with changes in the network-structure of agents. This second type of change can express aspects of what is called "friendship selection", with agents choosing their friends based on common features, interests or beliefs, among others. We follow [15] in adopting a broad notion of "selection", including agents *actively* selecting as their friends those who share common features as well as agents who are *implicitly* guided by their social environment to find friends who are similar to them. Building on the observations in [15], these two types of information dynamics can be seen as dual to each other. Friendship selection builds social links based on the agent's individual features, and social influence changes the agent's individual features based on the present social links. The mentioned acts of friendship selection and social influence as well as their interplay are actively studied within both the social sciences and network theory in the context of "homophily": the property observed in networks which states that agents tend to be similar to their friends. If we compare your friends to a random selected set of agents from the population, we typically observe a big difference in levels of homogeneity. The idea of similarity-based relationships, the core of homophily, has a long history which traces back to the work of Plato and Aristotle and received more and more attention in the social sciences from the 1920s and 1930s on.[1]

In this paper we focus on the interplay between friendship selection and social influence. While both of these forms of dynamics have been studied separately by logicians in various papers (see e.g. [9] for social influence and [14] for friendship selection), they have not yet been put together into a unified logical setting. In this paper we address exactly this issue. While doing so, we go beyond the single-network settings in [9] and [14], allowing our agents to be part of a variety of different networks, each one of them describing a different topic of interest (e.g., films, music), and on which each agent might hold a set of 'positions' (an agent might like alternative music and jazz, while another might like jazz and pop music). Further, these agents can change their mind about what they like and can select friends on the basis of common likes. We use the dynamic logic mechanism of DEL to model the actions of social influence and friendship selection, providing a setting in which both can be studied simultaneously. Via our logical analysis we hope to gain a better understanding of these main social mechanisms and their interaction.

The paper is organised as follows. Section 2 introduces the basics of our social network*s* models. Then, Sect. 3 focusses on the social network dynamics, providing a logical analysis of *(i)* social influence (Subsect. 3.1), *(ii)* friendship selection (Subsect. 3.2) as well as *(iii)* their interaction (Subsect. 3.3). Section 4 discusses

[1] For an overview on the topic we refer to [16] (see also [17,18]), where the authors discuss the main developments in the literature and indicate that homophily exists on a wide array of sociodemographic and behavioral and value-based dimensions.

variations and extensions of the framework, and Sect. 5 ends the proposal with concluding remarks.

2 Social Network Models

The structure that will be used for representing agents and their social connections is called *social networks model*: a relational 'Kripke' model in which the domain is interpreted as the set of agents [4,19]. However, as in [11,14,20], agents here will be 'discussing' multiple topics, on which they might adopt different positions. Even more: each topic defines a different social network.

Through this text, let $\mathcal{A} \neq \varnothing$ be a finite set of agents. Let $\mathfrak{T} \neq \varnothing$ (with $\mathcal{A} \cap \mathfrak{T} = \varnothing$) be a finite set of topics, with $\{\mathfrak{R}_T\}_{T \in \mathfrak{T}}$ a pairwise disjoint collection providing a finite non-empty set $\mathfrak{R}_T$ of positions for each $T \in \mathfrak{T}$; define $\mathfrak{R} := \bigcup_{T \in \mathfrak{T}} \mathfrak{R}_T$.

Definition 2.1 (Social Networks Model). A *social networks model (SNM)* for $\mathcal{A}$, $\mathfrak{T}$ and $\{\mathfrak{R}_T\}_{T \in \mathfrak{T}}$ is a tuple $\langle \mathrm{N}, \mathrm{V} \rangle$ where

- $\mathrm{N} : \mathfrak{T} \to \wp(\mathcal{A} \times \mathcal{A})$ is the *social network function*, with each $\mathrm{N}_T \subseteq (\mathcal{A} \times \mathcal{A})$ the social network of each topic $T \in \mathfrak{T}$, and with $\mathrm{N}_T\, \mathtt{ij}$ indicating that agent $\mathtt{i} \in \mathcal{A}$ is socially connected to agent $\mathtt{j} \in \mathcal{A}$ on topic $T \in \mathfrak{T}$;
- $\mathrm{V} : \mathfrak{T} \times \mathfrak{R} \to \wp(\mathcal{A})$ is a *valuation function*, with each $\mathrm{V}_T(r) \subseteq \mathcal{A}$ (defined only for $r \in \mathfrak{R}_T$) indicating the set of agents adopting position $r \in \mathfrak{R}_T$ on topic $T \in \mathfrak{T}$.[2] ◄

Different from other settings (e.g., [7,8,19]), the social networks N_T are not required to satisfy any property (in particular, they need to be neither irreflexive nor symmetric).

Here is an example of what a SNM looks like.

Example 1. Let the set of agents be $\mathcal{A} = \{\mathsf{a}, \mathsf{b}, \mathsf{c}, \mathsf{d}\}$. Take the topics to be *F*ilms, *M*usic and *S*ports (so $\mathfrak{T} = \{F, M, S\}$), with their ranges being

$$\mathfrak{R}_F = \{\underline{c}omedy, \underline{d}ocumentary, \underline{h}orror, \underline{t}hriller\}, \quad \mathfrak{R}_S = \{\underline{b}asketball, \underline{f}ootball, \underline{h}iking, \underline{v}olleyball\}.$$
$$\mathfrak{R}_M = \{\underline{a}lternative, \underline{c}lassic, \underline{j}azz, \underline{p}op\},$$

Consider a SNM $M = \langle \mathrm{N}, \mathrm{V} \rangle$ in which

$$\begin{array}{llll} \Lambda_F(\mathsf{a}) = \{d, h, t\}, & \Lambda_F(\mathsf{b}) = \{d\}, & \Lambda_F(\mathsf{c}) = \{c, h, t\}, & \Lambda_F(\mathsf{d}) = \{h, t\}, \\ \Lambda_M(\mathsf{a}) = \{a\}, & \Lambda_M(\mathsf{b}) = \{c, j\}, & \Lambda_M(\mathsf{c}) = \{p\}, & \Lambda_M(\mathsf{d}) = \{a, c, j\}, \\ \Lambda_S(\mathsf{a}) = \{b, f, h, v\} & \Lambda_S(\mathsf{b}) = \{h\}, & \Lambda_S(\mathsf{c}) = \{b, v\}, & \Lambda_S(\mathsf{d}) = \{b, f\}. \end{array}$$

Thus, agent a likes documentary, horror and thriller films, only alternative music, and all sports. Still, b likes only documentaries, only classic and jazz

[2] It will be useful to consider the 'dual' function $\Lambda : \mathfrak{T} \times \mathcal{A} \to \wp(\mathfrak{R})$, returning the set of positions $\Lambda_T(\mathtt{i}) \subseteq \mathfrak{R}_T$ each agent $\mathtt{i} \in \mathcal{A}$ holds on topic $T \in \mathfrak{T}$, and defined as $\Lambda_T(\mathtt{i}) := \{r \in \mathfrak{R}_T \mid \mathtt{i} \in \mathrm{V}_T(r)\}$.

music, and only hiking. Agent c prefers comedies, horror films and thrillers, she likes only pop music, and only hand-based sports. Finally, d likes horror and thriller films, everything but pop music, and both basketball and football.

With respect to the social networks, and for the sake of further *dynamic* examples, assume that the social relation on each topic has only reflexive edges (that is, $\mathrm{N}_F = \mathrm{N}_M = \mathrm{N}_S = \{(\mathtt{i}, \mathtt{i}) \mid \mathtt{i} \in \mathcal{A}\}$). The full model is displayed below.

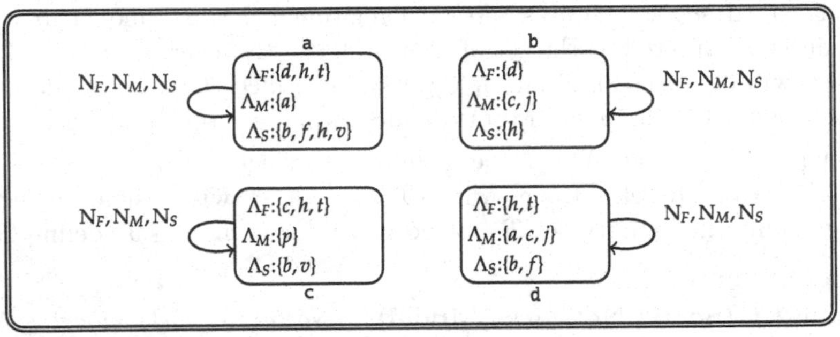

◀

Following [11,19], a SNM is described by a *propositional* language that uses special atoms indicating whether a given agent has a given position, and whether two agents are socially related on a given topic.

Definition 2.2 (Language $\mathcal{L}$). Formulas in $\mathcal{L}$ are given by

$$\varphi, \psi ::= \mathtt{i}_r^T \mid \mathtt{i} \rhd^T \mathtt{j} \mid \neg\varphi \mid \varphi \wedge \psi$$

with $\mathtt{i}, \mathtt{j} \in \mathcal{A}$, $T \in \mathfrak{T}$ and $r \in \mathfrak{R}_T$. Formulas of the form $\mathtt{i}_r^T$ are read as *"agent* i *has adopted position r on topic T"*, and those of the form $\mathtt{i} \rhd^T \mathtt{j}$ are read as *"agent* i *is socially connected to agent* j *on topic T"*. Other Boolean operators ($\vee, \rightarrow, \leftrightarrow, \underline{\vee}$, the latter representing the exclusive disjunction) are defined as usual.

Given a SNM $M = \langle \mathrm{N}, \mathrm{V} \rangle$, formulas in $\mathcal{L}$ are semantically interpreted in the following way.

$$\begin{array}{llll} M \Vdash \mathtt{i}_r^T & \text{iff}_{\text{def}} \ \mathtt{i} \in \mathrm{V}_T(r), & M \Vdash \neg\varphi & \text{iff}_{\text{def}} \ M \nVdash \varphi, \\ M \Vdash \mathtt{i} \rhd^T \mathtt{j} & \text{iff}_{\text{def}} \ \mathrm{N}_T \, \mathtt{ij}, & M \Vdash \varphi \wedge \psi & \text{iff}_{\text{def}} \ M \Vdash \varphi \text{ and } M \Vdash \psi. \end{array}$$

A formula $\varphi \in \mathcal{L}$ is valid (notation: $\Vdash \varphi$) when $M \Vdash \varphi$ holds for every SNM M. ◀

There are no special requirements on the social network function, and neither on the valuation function. Thus, any axiom system of classical propositional logic is fit to characterize syntactically the validities of $\mathcal{L}$ over the class of SNMs.

3 Social Networks Dynamics

3.1 Social Environment Influencing Agents

Agents might be influenced by their social environment in several different ways (e.g., [4–8,10,21–23] and other aforementioned references). The idea behind the specific form of social influence discussed here is that an agent will adopt certain stance/feature/behaviour when the proportion of her social connections having it is greater than or equal to a certain *threshold* [24].

Definition 3.1 (Social influence). Let τ be a real number in $[0,1]$. Let $M = \langle \mathrm{N}, \mathrm{V} \rangle$ be a SNM and, for $\mathtt{i} \in \mathcal{A}$, define

$$\mathrm{N}_T[\mathtt{i}] := \{\mathtt{j} \in \mathcal{A} \mid \mathrm{N}_T\,\mathtt{i}\,\mathtt{j}\},$$

so $\mathrm{N}_T[\mathtt{i}]$ is the set of agents socially connected to agent $\mathtt{i}$ on topic T.

The *social influence* operation, describing the way each agent is influenced by her social environment, produces the SNM $M^{\dagger(\tau)} = \langle \mathrm{N}, \mathrm{V}' \rangle$. In this new model, an agent $\mathtt{i}$ has adopted position r on topic T if and only if, within her T-social environment ($\mathrm{N}_T[\mathtt{i}]$), the proportion of agents who already held the position ($\mathrm{N}_T[\mathtt{i}] \cap \mathrm{V}_T(r)$) was larger or equal than the threshold $\tau \in [0,1]$. Formally, for any $\mathtt{i} \in \mathcal{A}$, any $T \in \mathfrak{T}$ and any $r \in \mathfrak{R}_T$, the new valuation function is given by

$$\mathtt{i} \in \mathrm{V}'_T(r) \qquad \text{iff}_{\text{def}} \qquad \begin{cases} \frac{|\mathrm{N}_T[\mathtt{i}] \cap \mathrm{V}_T(r)|}{|\mathrm{N}_T[\mathtt{i}]|} \geqslant \tau & \text{if } \mathrm{N}_T[\mathtt{i}] \neq \varnothing \\ \mathtt{i} \in \mathrm{V}_T(r) & \text{otherwise} \end{cases}$$

Note how, in particular, agents with an empty T-social environment are not affected by social influence. ◀

There are some details of this definition that are worthwhile to emphasise. First, note that the points of view of all agents on all topics are all updated simultaneously. However, the agents that influence the position of agent $\mathtt{i}$ on topic T are only those in her T-network, $\mathrm{N}_T[\mathtt{i}]$.[3] Second, note how, different from [19], the operation is not accumulative by design: the set of agents having position r on topic T at the current stage, $\mathrm{V}_T(r)$, does not need to be a subset of the set of agents having that position on that topic at the *next* stage, $\mathrm{V}'_T(r)$. In other words, agents might drop a position they held before. Finally, the operation is not idempotent. Indeed, the new stance of an agent depends on the stances of her neighbours, which can be affected by the operation itself (everybody's points of view are updated simultaneously); hence, applying the operation a second time might produce a different model and thus, in general, $(M^{\dagger(\tau)})^{\dagger(\tau)} \neq M^{\dagger(\tau)}$.

On the syntactic side, the language $\mathcal{L}$ is extended with *dynamic* modalities $\langle \dagger_\tau \rangle$, which allow us to describe the effects of the social influence operation.

Definition 3.2. The modality $\langle \dagger_\tau \rangle$ (for $\tau \in [0,1]$) is semantically interpreted as

$$M \Vdash \langle \dagger_\tau \rangle \varphi \quad \text{iff}_{\text{def}} \quad M^{\dagger(\tau)} \Vdash \varphi$$

Formulas as $\langle \dagger_\tau \rangle \varphi$ are read as *"after an act of social τ-influence, φ is the case"*. ◀

[3] Definition 4.3 presents an alternative in which an agent's new stance on topic T depends on the stances of all the agents to which she is socially connected, regardless of whether it is on topic T or on another.

Axiom System. The axiom system for the new modality is built using the *DEL* technique of *recursion axioms*: valid formulas and validity preserving rules that define a truth-preserving translation from the language with the dynamic modality to the language without it. In particular, the axiom describing the way an agent's position changes is a variation of the one presented in [19] that uses the abbreviations below ($\mathtt{i} \in \mathcal{A}$; $\mathfrak{B}, \mathfrak{B}' \subseteq \mathcal{A}$; $T \in \mathfrak{T}$).

- $\mathtt{i} \rhd^T \mathfrak{B} := \bigwedge_{\mathtt{j} \in \mathfrak{B}} \mathtt{i} \rhd^T \mathtt{j} \wedge \bigwedge_{\mathtt{j} \in \mathcal{A} \setminus \mathfrak{B}} \neg(\mathtt{i} \rhd^T \mathtt{j})$ (so $M \Vdash \mathtt{i} \rhd^T \mathfrak{B}$ iff $\mathrm{N}_T[\mathtt{i}] = \mathfrak{B}$)
- $sst_r^T(\mathfrak{B}', \mathfrak{B}) := \bigwedge_{\mathtt{j} \in \mathfrak{B}'} \mathtt{j}_r^T \wedge \bigwedge_{\mathtt{j} \in \mathfrak{B} \setminus \mathfrak{B}'} \neg \mathtt{j}_r^T$ $\left(\text{so } M \Vdash sst_r^T(\mathfrak{B}', \mathfrak{B}) \text{ iff } \begin{cases} \mathfrak{B}' \subseteq \mathrm{V}_T(r), \text{ and} \\ (\mathfrak{B} \setminus \mathfrak{B}') \subseteq \overline{\mathrm{V}_T(r)} \end{cases} \right)$

Table 1. Recursion axioms for $\langle \dagger_\tau \rangle$ w.r.t. SNMs.

$(\dagger_{\mathtt{i}_r^T})$	$\vdash \langle \dagger_\tau \rangle \mathtt{i}_r^T \leftrightarrow \Big((\mathtt{i} \rhd^T \varnothing \wedge \mathtt{i}_r^T) \vee \Big(\neg(\mathtt{i} \rhd^T \varnothing) \wedge \bigvee_{\mathfrak{B} \subseteq \mathcal{A}} \Big(\mathtt{i} \rhd^T \mathfrak{B} \wedge \bigvee_{\{\mathfrak{B}' \subseteq \mathfrak{B} : \frac{\lvert \mathfrak{B}' \rvert}{\lvert \mathfrak{B} \rvert} \geqslant \tau\}} sst_r^T(\mathfrak{B}', \mathfrak{B}) \Big) \Big) \Big)$
$(\dagger_{\mathtt{i} \rhd^T \mathtt{j}})$	$\vdash \langle \dagger_\tau \rangle \mathtt{i} \rhd^T \mathtt{j} \leftrightarrow \mathtt{i} \rhd^T \mathtt{j}$
$(\dagger_\neg)$	$\vdash \langle \dagger_\tau \rangle \neg \varphi \leftrightarrow \neg \langle \dagger_\tau \rangle \varphi$
$(\dagger_\wedge)$	$\vdash \langle \dagger_\tau \rangle (\varphi \wedge \psi) \leftrightarrow (\langle \dagger_\tau \rangle \varphi \wedge \langle \dagger_\tau \rangle \psi)$
$(\dagger_{SPE})$	From $\vdash \psi_1 \leftrightarrow \psi_2$ infer $\vdash \varphi \leftrightarrow \varphi[\psi_2/\psi_1]$, with $\varphi[\psi_2/\psi_1]$ any formula obtained by replacing one or more occurrences of ψ_1 in φ with ψ_2.

Observe the latter abbreviation, $sst_r^T(\mathfrak{B}', \mathfrak{B})$. If a further $\mathfrak{B}' \subseteq \mathfrak{B}$ is imposed, then $M \Vdash sst_r^T(\mathfrak{B}', \mathfrak{B})$ holds if and only if $\mathfrak{B}' = \mathfrak{B} \cap \mathrm{V}_T(r)$. Indeed, ***(i)*** $\mathfrak{B}' \subseteq (\mathfrak{B} \cap \mathrm{V}_T(r))$ follows directly from $\mathfrak{B}' \subseteq \mathrm{V}_T(r)$ and $\mathfrak{B}' \subseteq \mathfrak{B}$, and ***(ii)*** $(\mathfrak{B} \cap \mathrm{V}_T(r)) \subseteq \mathfrak{B}'$ follows from $(\mathfrak{B} \setminus \mathfrak{B}') \subseteq \overline{\mathrm{V}_T(r)}$, equivalent to $(\mathfrak{B} \cap \overline{\mathfrak{B}'}) \subseteq \overline{\mathrm{V}_T(r)}$ and thus also to $\mathfrak{B} \cap \overline{\mathfrak{B}'} \cap \mathrm{V}_T(r) = \varnothing$.

Theorem 3.1. The recursion axioms and the rules in Table 1 provide, together with a propositional axiom system schema, a sound and strongly complete axiom system characterising the validities of the language $\mathcal{L} + \langle \dagger_\tau \rangle$ in SNMs.

Proof. Soundness follows from the validity and validity-preserving properties of the axioms and rule. In particular, axiom $\dagger_{\mathtt{i}_r^T}$ spells out the definition of the new valuation (Definition 3.1), with $\mathfrak{B}$ playing the role of $\mathrm{N}_T[\mathtt{i}]$ (so the additional $\mathfrak{B}' \subseteq \mathfrak{B}$ implies $\mathfrak{B}' = \mathrm{N}_T[\mathtt{i}] \cap \mathrm{V}_T(r)$); then, axiom $\dagger_{\mathtt{i} \rhd^T \mathtt{j}}$ expresses that social networks are not affected by the operation. Axioms $\dagger_\neg$ and $\dagger_\wedge$ are standard for dynamic modalities semantically interpreted over functional model operations without precondition, as $\langle \dagger_\tau \rangle$ is (Definition 3.2). Completeness follows from the completeness of the propositional system, as the axioms and rule define a validity-preserving translation from $\mathcal{L} + \langle \dagger_\tau \rangle$ to $\mathcal{L}$, with the rule $\dagger_{SPE}$

(*substitution of provably equivalents*) taking care of formulas with more than one occurrence of $\langle \dagger_\tau \rangle$ (work with the deepest occurrence and, once it is eliminated, proceed with the following). More details on using the method of rewrite rules to eliminate occurrences of the dynamic modality can be found in [2, Chapter 7] and [25]. ∎

3.2 Agents Creating Their Social Environment

As in the social influence case, agents might update their social connections in several different ways [26]. This proposal follows [11] in the use of the threshold strategy [24], here implemented following a *similarity-based* policy [13].

Definition 3.3 (Friendship selection). Let θ be a real number in $[0, 1]$. Let $M = \langle \mathrm{N}, \mathrm{V} \rangle$ be a SNM and, for $\mathtt{i}, \mathtt{j} \in \mathcal{A}$, define

$$\mathrm{sim}_T(\mathtt{i}, \mathtt{j}) := \{r \in \mathcal{R}_T \mid r \in \Lambda_T(\mathtt{i}) \text{ iff } r \in \Lambda_T(\mathtt{j})\},$$

so $\mathrm{sim}_T(\mathtt{i}, \mathtt{j})$ is the set of positions on topic T on which agents $\mathtt{i}$ and $\mathtt{j}$ coincide.

The *friendship selection* operation, describing the way each social environment is defined by the agents, produces the SNM $M^{\sharp(\theta)} = \langle \mathrm{N}', \mathrm{V} \rangle$. In this new model, an agent $\mathtt{i}$ is socially connected to agent $\mathtt{j}$ on topic T if and only if the proportion of positions on topic T on which they coincide ($\mathrm{sim}_T(\mathtt{i}, \mathtt{j})$) was larger or equal than the threshold $\theta \in [0, 1]$. Formally, for any $\mathtt{i}, \mathtt{j} \in \mathcal{A}$ and any $T \in \mathcal{T}$, the new social network function is given by

$$\mathrm{N}'_T\, \mathtt{i}\mathtt{j} \qquad \text{iff}_{\text{def}} \qquad \frac{|\mathrm{sim}_T(\mathtt{i}, \mathtt{j})|}{|\mathcal{R}_T|} \geqslant \theta.$$

◀

Just as with the social influence case, there are some details of the friendship selection operation that are worthwhile to emphasise. First, all networks are updated simultaneously, and every agent is candidate for becoming socially connected to any given one.[4] Second: as the social influence case, the operation is not accumulative by design: the set of agents T-socially connected with some given $\mathtt{i}$, $\mathrm{N}_T[\mathtt{i}]$, might shrink. In other words, agents might leave social groups. Third: the function sim_T satisfies ***(i)*** $\mathrm{sim}_T(\mathtt{i}, \mathtt{i}) = \mathcal{R}_T$ and ***(ii)*** $\mathrm{sim}_T(\mathtt{i}, \mathtt{j}) = \mathrm{sim}_T(\mathtt{j}, \mathtt{i})$; hence, the operation produces reflexive and symmetric social relations (cf. [11,13]). Finally, different from the social influence case, the friendship selection operation is idempotent: the new social connections depend only on the stances of the agents (the function V), which are not modified by the operation. Hence, $(M^{\sharp(\theta)})^{\sharp(\theta)} = M^{\sharp(\theta)}$ for every model M.

On the syntactic side, the language $\mathcal{L}$ is extended with *dynamic* modalities $\langle \sharp_\theta \rangle$, which allow us to describe the effects of the friendship selection operation.

---

[4] For contrast, [11] proposes an operation through which two agents become socially connected if and only if they are similar enough *and* some agent can act as the *middleman*. See Definition 4.4 for an alternative that restricts the pool of candidates for friendship.

Definition 3.4. The modality $\langle \sharp_\theta \rangle$ (for $\theta \in [0,1]$) is semantically interpreted as

$$M \Vdash \langle \sharp_\theta \rangle \varphi \quad \text{iff}_{\text{def}} \quad M^{\sharp(\theta)} \Vdash \varphi$$

Formulas of the form $\langle \sharp_\theta \rangle \varphi$ are read as *"after an act of friendship θ-selection group creation, φ is the case".* ◀

Axiom System. The axiom system for the new modality is also built using the *DEL* technique of *recursion axioms.* The key axiom, describing the way social connections change (cf. [11,13]), uses the following abbreviation ($\mathtt{i}, \mathtt{j} \in \mathcal{A}$; $T \in \mathfrak{T}$; $\mathcal{S} \subseteq \mathcal{R}_T$) in which, recall, $\veebar$ is the exclusive disjunction.

$$sim^T(\mathtt{i}, \mathcal{S}, \mathtt{j}) := \bigwedge_{r \in \mathcal{S}} (\mathtt{i}_r^T \leftrightarrow \mathtt{j}_r^T) \land \bigwedge_{r \in \mathcal{R}_T \setminus \mathcal{S}} (\mathtt{i}_r^T \veebar \mathtt{j}_r^T),$$

so $M \Vdash sim^T(\mathtt{i}, \mathcal{S}, \mathtt{j})$ if and only if $\mathcal{S} = \text{sim}_T(\mathtt{i}, \mathtt{j})$.

Table 2. Recursion axioms for $\langle \sharp_\theta \rangle$ w.r.t. SNMs.

$(\sharp_{\mathtt{i}_r^T})$	$\vdash \langle \sharp_\theta \rangle \mathtt{i}_r^T \leftrightarrow \mathtt{i}_r^T$
$(\sharp_{\mathtt{i} \rhd^T \mathtt{j}})$	$\vdash \langle \sharp_\theta \rangle \mathtt{i} \rhd^T \mathtt{j} \leftrightarrow \bigvee_{\{\mathcal{S} \subseteq \mathcal{R}_T : \frac{\lvert \mathcal{S} \rvert}{\lvert \mathcal{R}_T \rvert} \geqslant \theta\}} sim^T(\mathtt{i}, \mathcal{S}, \mathtt{j})$
$(\sharp_\neg)$	$\vdash \langle \sharp_\theta \rangle \neg\varphi \leftrightarrow \neg \langle \sharp_\theta \rangle \varphi$
$(\sharp_\land)$	$\vdash \langle \sharp_\theta \rangle (\varphi \land \psi) \leftrightarrow (\langle \sharp_\theta \rangle \varphi \land \langle \sharp_\theta \rangle \psi)$
$(\sharp_{SPE})$	From $\vdash \psi_1 \leftrightarrow \psi_2$ infer $\vdash \varphi \leftrightarrow \varphi[\psi_2/\psi_1]$, with $\varphi[\psi_2/\psi_1]$ any formula obtained by replacing one or more occurrences of ψ_1 in φ with ψ_2.

Theorem 3.2. The recursion axioms and the rules in Table 2 provide, together with a propositional axiom system schema, a sound and strongly complete axiom system characterising the validities of the language $\mathcal{L}+\langle \sharp_\theta \rangle$ in SNMs.

Proof. Soundness is as before, with axiom $\sharp_{\mathtt{i}_r^T}$ indicating that the operation does not affect the agents, and axiom $\sharp_{\mathtt{i} \rhd^T \mathtt{j}}$ rewriting the definition of the new social networks (Definition 3.3). Completeness is by translation, as in Theorem 3.1. ■

3.3 Intertwining Dynamics

Example 2. Recall the SNM M of Example 1.

(i) A friendship selection operation with $\theta = \frac{1}{2}$ produces the SNM $M^{\sharp(1/2)}$ below, with each social network displayed separately, and with the new connections indicated with bold squiggly edges.

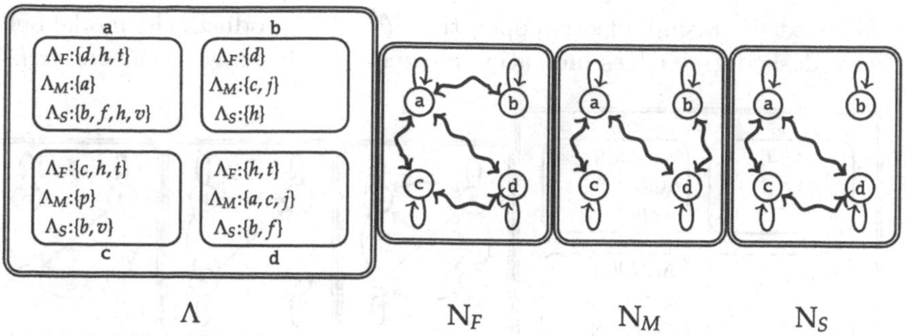

(ii) Then, a social influence operation ($\tau = 1/2$) produces the SNM $(M^{\sharp(1/2)})^{\dagger(1/2)}$ below, with ⋆ indicating topics in which actual changes have occurred.[5]

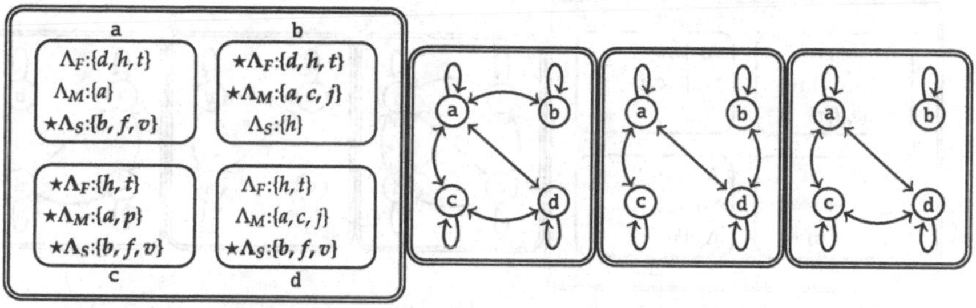

(iii) A further friendship selection ($\theta = 1/2$) yields $((M^{\sharp(1/2)})^{\dagger(1/2)})^{\sharp(1/2)}$.

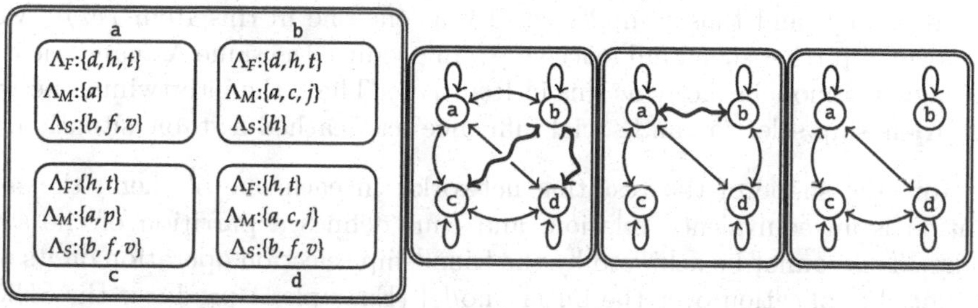

(iv) The process continues with another social influence operation ($\tau = 1/2$).

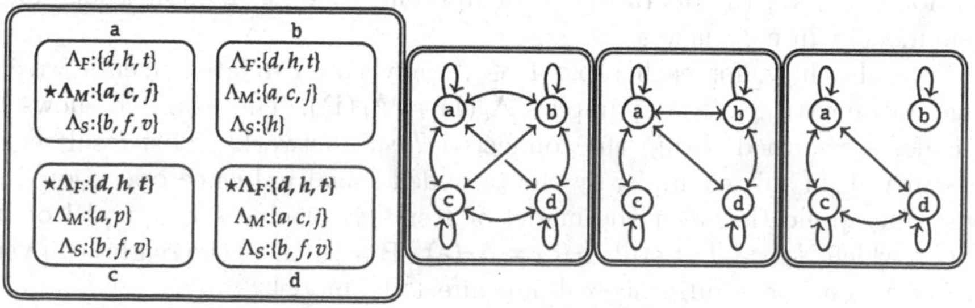

[5] The labels of the diagrams are as in Item *(i)* through the whole Example.

(v) The next friendship selection operation ($\theta = 1/2$) produces the model below, with dashed grey edges indicating connections that have been *dropped.*

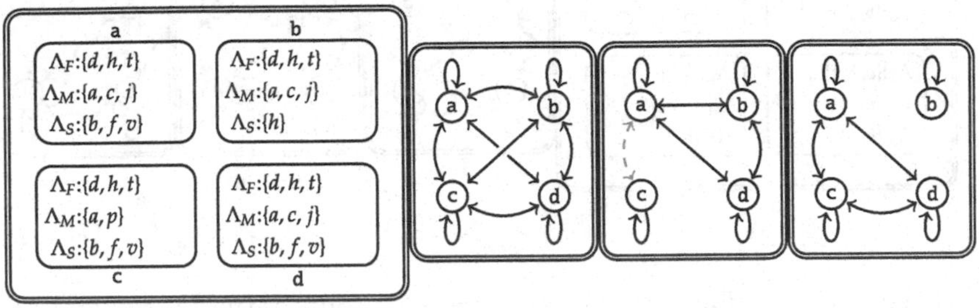

(vi) After a further social influence operation ($\tau = 1/2$), we get

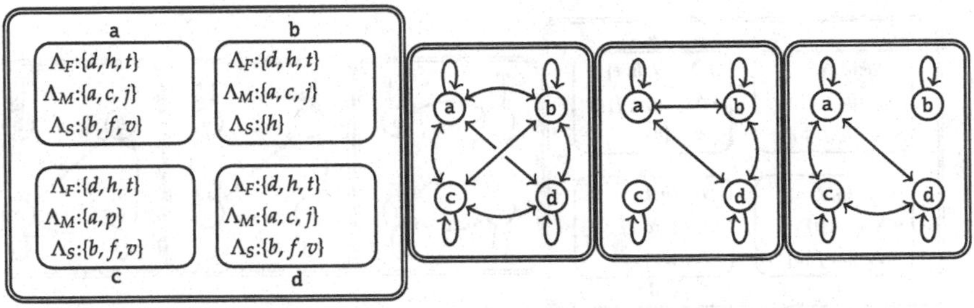

In terms of the agents' positions (Λ), this model is exactly as the one on Item *(iv)*; thus, a further friendship selection will produce networks as in Item *(v)* (and thus a model exactly as the one in this Item *(vi)*). Moreover, a further social influence step will produce the same Λ again (yielding, again, a model exactly as this in Item *(vi)*. Then, the intertwining between friendship selection and social influence has reached a stable situation.

Note the shape of the resulting networks: in each one of them, the social relation is an equivalence relation, and thus defines a partition of the set of agents. This cannot be achieved by the friendship selection operation on its own. An initial application over the initial model (Example 1) produces the SNM of Item *(i)*, in which N_F ca and N_F ab holds, but still N_F cb fails. But then, as mentioned before, the operation is idempotent, so further applications on the same model will not make a difference.

Note also how, for each topic $T \in \mathfrak{T}$, any two T-related agents have the same T-stances (i.e., N_T ij implies $\Lambda_F(\mathtt{i}) = \Lambda_F(\mathtt{i})$). The example shows how cascades are formed within the connected T-sub-networks. This result cannot be achieved, in this example, by the provided social influence operation on its own. One application over the model of Item *(i)* produces the model of Item *(ii)*, in which N_F ca, but still $\Lambda_F(\mathtt{c}) \neq \Lambda_F(\mathtt{a})$. But then, as the reader can verify, further acts of social influence will not affect the model. ◀

While the above example shows how the tandem of the two social information dynamics creates a social network that is based on a social equivalence relation, this is not a general phenomena. The induced social relation are reflexive and symmetric, but not necessarily transitive, not even in the long term.

Example 3. Take $\mathcal{A} = \{\mathsf{a}, \mathsf{b}, \mathsf{c}, \mathsf{d}, \mathsf{e}\}$, $\mathcal{T} = \{T\}$, $\mathcal{R}_T = \{p, q\}$. Consider the SNM below on the left, from which friendship selection ($\theta = 1/2$) produces the one on the right.

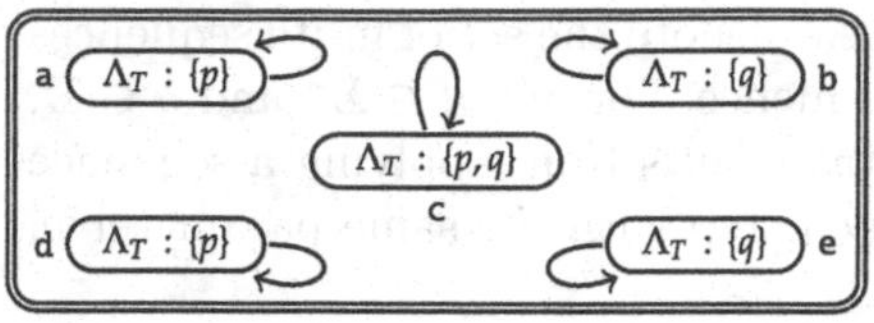

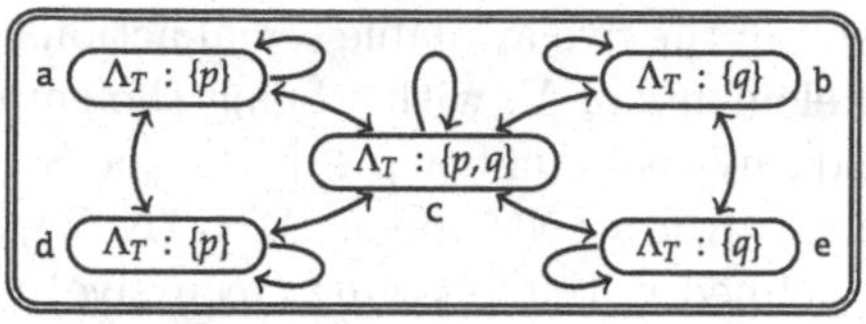

Social influence ($\tau = 1/2$) will not change the agents' stances, and thus the intertwining has stabilized without reaching transitive social relations. ◀

The previous example also shows how, even when the sequence of models stabilizes, the process does not necessarily end up in a cascade in which all agents reach a consensus with their friends on a given topic. Even more: if one allows changes in the thresholds, there are examples that do not stabilise at all.[6]

Remark. The dynamic modalities $\langle \dagger_\tau \rangle$ and $\langle \sharp_\theta \rangle$ allow us to describe the individual effects of the operations for social influence and friendship selection. Both operations always return a SNM, so these modalities can be put together in a language $\mathcal{L} + \langle \dagger_\tau \rangle + \langle \sharp_\theta \rangle$ to build formulas describing the effect of nesting their respective actions (e.g., $\neg \mathsf{a}^T_\tau \wedge \mathsf{a} \rhd^T \varnothing \wedge \langle \sharp_\theta \rangle (\mathsf{a} \rhd^T \mathsf{b} \wedge \langle \dagger_\tau \rangle\, \mathsf{a}^T_\tau))$.[7] Note how no additional axioms are required to axiomatise the new language. Indeed, given their respective recursion axioms, one can repeatedly follow the inside-out approach outlined in Theorem 3.1 to 'eliminate', at each time, the deepest occurrence of any of the modalities. The final outcome is a semantically equivalent formula in the base language $\mathcal{L}$, for which the propositional system is complete.

4 Variations

This section explores briefly a more general setting for intertwining social influence and friendship selection dynamics, while also discussing variations of the individual operations.

Protocols for Social Interaction. As Example 2 shows, the interaction between the discussed social dynamics might produce interesting results. Of course, the output depends on the order in which the two actions occur: doing two social influence steps might allow some opinions to be spread, and thus it will likely change the final situation. More generally, one would like to study the

[6] Consider a one-topic case with positions $\{p, q\}$ and agents $\{\mathsf{a}, \mathsf{b}, \mathsf{c}\}$, their initial positions being $\Lambda(\mathsf{a}) = \{p\}$, $\Lambda(\mathsf{b}) = \{\ \}$, $\Lambda(\mathsf{c}) = \{q\}$ and the initial network being just reflexive edges. The repetition of *(i)* social influence with $\tau = 1$ (no effect), *(ii)* friendship selection with $\theta = 1/2$ (adding only symmetric edges between b and both a and c), *(iii)* social influence now with $\tau = 1/2$ (no effect) and *(iv)* friendship selection now with $\theta = 1$ (removing the just added edges) does not stabilise.

[7] For contrast, a *parallel* composition, affecting both agents and social networks at once, would require a new modality.

behaviour of sequences of actions; the following definitions will be helpful in that sense.

Definition 4.1 (Sequences of social actions). Take the set $\Sigma = \{\dagger, \sharp\}$, containing the two available social actions. Let Σ^* denote the set of finite sequences of elements of Σ, with ϵ being the empty sequence. For any $\sigma \in \Sigma^*$ and $a \in \Sigma$, and any real number $\rho \in [0, 1]$, the SNM that results from applying a sequence in Σ^* over a SNM model $M = \langle \mathrm{N}, \mathrm{V} \rangle$, at each step with the same parameter ρ, is defined in the following (recursive) way:

$$M^{\epsilon(\rho)} := M, \qquad\qquad M^{\sigma a(\rho)} := (M^{\sigma(\rho)})^{a(\rho)}.$$

◀

An interesting subject of study is the way different sequences in Σ^* are related. Here is a concept that might be interesting.

Definition 4.2. Let $\sigma_1, \sigma_2 \in \Sigma^*$ be two sequences; take $\rho \in [0, 1]$. It is said that σ_1 and σ_2 are *ρ-equivalent* (notation: $\sigma_1 \sim_\rho \sigma_2$) if and only if $M^{\sigma_1(\rho)} = M^{\sigma_2(\rho)}$. ◀

Note: "$\sim_\rho$" requires for the related sequences to produce exactly the same model. In cases involving formal languages, the natural request would be rather for the resulting models to be *indistinguishable* from the perspective of the language used for describing them (i.e., for the models to satisfy exactly the same formulas).[8] However, our language $\mathcal{L}$ has a global perspective; this, together with the finiteness of the domain and the fact that every agent has a name, suggests that here identity is a reasonable requirement.

Then, this is an example of the kind of results one could be interested in.

Proposition 1. Take $\sharp^0 := \epsilon$ and, for $n \in \mathbb{N}$, $\sharp^{n+1} := \sharp^n\sharp$. Define

$$E^{\times\sharp}(\sigma) := \{\sigma' \in \Sigma^* \mid \sigma' \text{ is the result of substituting some subsequence } \sharp^n \text{ in } \sigma \text{ for some sequence } \sharp^m, \text{ with } n, m \geqslant 1\}$$

Then, for any $\sigma' \in E^{\times\sharp}(\sigma)$ and any $\rho \in [0, 1]$, we have $\sigma \sim_\rho \sigma'$.

Proof. An act of friendship selection is idempotent. Hence, any non-empty sequence of friendship selection can be replaced by any other non-empty sequence, and the result will be exactly the same. ■

Variations: Extended Social Influence. As mentioned, under the social influence operation of Definition 3.1, the only agents that can influence the positions of agent i on topic T are those agents in a's T-network, $\mathrm{N}_T[\mathrm{i}]$. However, the advantage of being part of different social networks is that an agent can hear opinions from people other than those in the topic's social environment.

---

[8] In modal languages cases, one could work directly with a semantic characterisation of the language's expressivity, i.e., with some form of *bisimulation* [27, Section 2.2].

Definition 4.3 (Extended social influence). Let τ be a real number in $[0, 1]$. Let $M = \langle \mathrm{N}, \mathrm{V} \rangle$ be a SNM and, for $\mathtt{i} \in \mathcal{A}$, define

$$\mathrm{N}_{\mathfrak{T}} := \bigcup_{T \in \mathfrak{T}} \mathrm{N}_T \qquad \text{and then} \qquad \mathrm{N}_{\mathfrak{T}}[\mathtt{i}] := \{\mathtt{j} \in \mathcal{A} \mid \mathrm{N}_{\mathfrak{T}}\,\mathtt{i}\,\mathtt{j}\},$$

so $\mathrm{N}_{\mathfrak{T}}[\mathtt{i}]$ is the set of agents socially connected to agent $\mathtt{i}$ on some topic.

The *extended social influence* operation, describing the way each agent is influenced by her social connections, produces the SNM $M^{\dagger^*(\tau)} = \langle \mathrm{N}, \mathrm{V}' \rangle$. In this new model, an agent $\mathtt{i}$ has adopted position r on topic T if and only if, among the agents that are socially connected to her on some topic ($\mathrm{N}_{\mathfrak{T}}[\mathtt{i}]$), the proportion of them who already held the position ($\mathrm{N}_{\mathfrak{T}}[\mathtt{i}] \cap \mathrm{V}_T(r)$) was larger or equal than the threshold $\tau \in [0, 1]$. Formally, for any $\mathtt{i} \in \mathcal{A}$, any $T \in \mathfrak{T}$ and any $r \in \mathfrak{R}_T$, the new valuation function is given by

$$\mathtt{i} \in \mathrm{V}'_T(r) \qquad \text{iff}_{\text{def}} \qquad \frac{|\mathrm{N}_{\mathfrak{T}}[\mathtt{i}] \cap \mathrm{V}_T(r)|}{|\mathrm{N}_{\mathfrak{T}}[\mathtt{i}]|} \geqslant \tau.$$

◀

Under extended social influence, each agent's stance on a topic T is influenced by any other agent with whom she is socially related, regardless of the topic of connection. The difference in the set of influential agents changes the result of the actions' interaction, as Example 4 below shows.

Example 4. Recall the SNM M of Example 1. Consider an intertwined sequence of actions: friendship selection as before, and now extended social influence.

(i) Friendship selection ($\theta = 1/2$) produces the SNM model in Example 2 *(i)*.
(ii) Then, extended social influence ($\tau = 1/2$) yields the model below. Recall: $\star$ indicates topics in which changes have occurred; moreover, ♠ indicates stances that are different from what the social influence of before obtains.

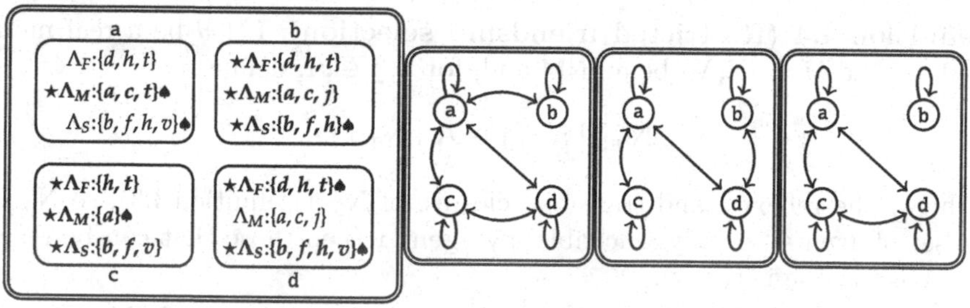

Λ $\qquad$ N_F $\qquad$ N_M $\qquad$ N_S

(iii) Further friendship selection ($\theta = 1/2$) yields the model below.[9]

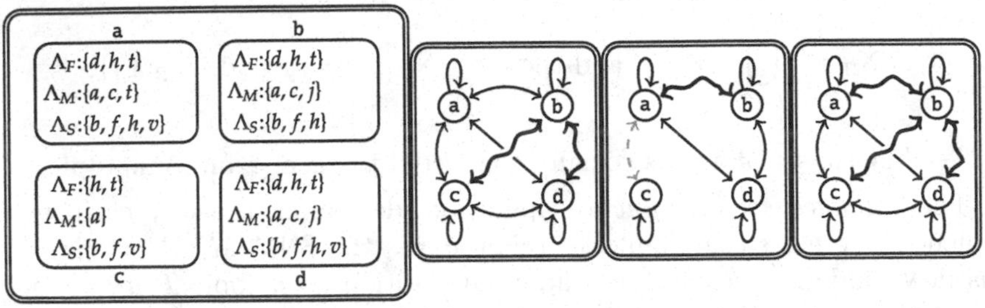

(iv) Another extended social influence operation ($\tau = 1/2$) produces a valuation function in which all agents having exactly the same stances on every topic.

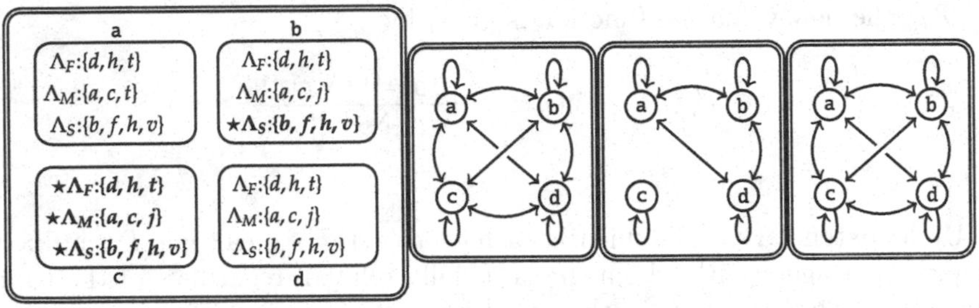

(v) Since the previous step produced a model in which all agents have exactly the same stances on every topic, a further friendship selection operation will produce, for each topic, a fully connected relation. From then on, no further change will occur. ◀

Variations: Restricted Friendship Selection. Under the discussed friendship selection operation (Definition 3.3), any similar-enough agent will become part of the social network of a given one. However, a more realistic scenario can be depicted when the candidates are only those the agent has 'heard of'.

Definition 4.4 (Restricted friendship selection). Let θ be a real number in $[0, 1]$. Let $M = \langle \mathrm{N}, \mathrm{V} \rangle$ be a SNM and, for $\mathtt{i}, \mathtt{j} \in \mathcal{A}$, define

$$\mathrm{N}^*_{\mathcal{T}}[\mathtt{i}] := \{\mathtt{j} \in \mathcal{A} \mid \mathrm{N}^*_{\mathcal{T}}\mathtt{ij}\},$$

with $\mathrm{N}^*_{\mathcal{T}}$ the reflexive and transitive closure of $\mathrm{N}_{\mathcal{T}}$ (Definition 3.3), so $\mathrm{N}^*_{\mathcal{T}}[\mathtt{i}]$ is the set of agents 'socially reachable' by agent $\mathtt{i}$ (i.e., those that can be reached by a path in the network).

The *restricted friendship selection* operation yields the SNM $M^{\natural-(\theta)} = \langle \mathrm{N}', \mathrm{V} \rangle$. In this new model, an agent $\mathtt{i}$ is socially connected to agent $\mathtt{j}$ on topic T if and only if the proportion of positions on topic T on which they coincide ($\mathrm{sim}_T(\mathtt{i}, \mathtt{j})$) was larger or equal than the threshold $\theta \in [0, 1]$, *and* $\mathtt{j}$ is within the

[9] Again, although not shown, the labels of the diagrams are as in Item *(ii)* through the whole Example.

reach of i. Formally, for any $\mathtt{i}, \mathtt{j} \in \mathcal{A}$ and any $T \in \mathfrak{T}$, the new social network function is given by

$$N'_T \mathtt{ij} \quad \text{iff}_{\text{def}} \quad \frac{|\text{sim}_T(\mathtt{i}, \mathtt{j})|}{|\mathfrak{R}_T|} \geqslant \theta \text{ and } \mathtt{j} \in N^*_{\mathfrak{T}}[\mathtt{i}].$$

◀

The restricted friendship selection operation can be applied to the example we introduced above. Among the many operations that we can consider, it is of particular interest as it will allow us to further study specific effects of social influence by taking into account the path over which information passes from one subgroup in a network to another group. This ties in with the study of information passing over a local bridge in network theory, see e.g. [15].

5 Conclusions

In this paper we have given the initial steps towards a unified logical setting to study the interplay of two main informational actions: social influence and friendship selection. We have introduced the sound and complete axiomatizations for the logic of social influence (following known results in [9]) and for the logic of friendship selection (following the results in [11]). While the mentioned papers in the literature deal with single networks and one single type of action, we introduced the formal logics to handle multiple networks and different types of acts into a combined logic. We studied the alternating one-step dynamics of the introduced social dynamic processes and indicated that further constraints need to be imposed to guarantee that the stable model in the end is a network in which connected groups of friends have reached full consensus. The study of these constraints is left for future work but can build further on results in [6] and [9] on (informational) cascades. Finally we introduced a number of interesting variations in this paper that can be further studied, including defining social influence on agents from other networks and restricting the pool of candidates for friendship.

The proposal assumes that agents know (in some implicit sense) who their friends are and what features they have; yet, in future work we plan on making the epistemic information states of agents explicit, encoding the explicit knowledge about the features of an agent before he/she can become a friend or before he/she can social influence you. To model a full epistemic setting we will build further on the epistemic framework for social influence in [9] and on the role of epistemics on friendship formation in [11]. Further extensions can allow agents to adopt new topics of interest or to develop new positions on old topics. And while we allow our agents to like (or adopt) a position with respect to a topic, one can imagine a more complex setting of agents having a preference order on positions and topics.

References

1. Baltag, A., Moss, L.S., Solecki, S.: The logic of public announcements, common knowledge, and private suspicions. In: Gilboa, I. (ed.) Proceedings of TARK 1998, pp. 43–56 (1998)
2. van Ditmarsch, H., van der Hoek, W., Kooi, B.: Dynamic Epistemic Logic. Synthese Library Series, vol. 337. Springer, Dordrecht (2008). https://doi.org/10.1007/978-1-4020-5839-4
3. van Benthem, J.: Logical Dynamics of Information and Interaction. Cambridge University Press, Cambridge (2011)
4. Seligman, J., Liu, F., Girard, P.: Logic in the community. In: Banerjee, M., Seth, A. (eds.) ICLA 2011. LNCS (LNAI), vol. 6521, pp. 178–188. Springer, Heidelberg (2011). https://doi.org/10.1007/978-3-642-18026-2_15
5. Zhen, L., Seligman, J.: A logical model of the dynamics of peer pressure. Electron. Notes Theor. Comput. Sci. **278**, 275–288 (2011)
6. Baltag, A., Christoff, Z., Hansen, J.U., Smets, S.: Logical models of informational cascades. In: van Benthem, J., Liu, F. (eds.) Proceedings of the Tsinghua Logic Conference, Logic Across the University: Foundations and Applications, Beijing of Studies in Logic, London, vol. 47, pp. 405–432. College Publications (2013)
7. Liu, F., Seligman, J., Girard, P.: Logical dynamics of belief change in the community. Synthese **191**(11), 2403–2431 (2014)
8. Christoff, Z., Hansen, J.U., Proietti, C.: Reflecting on social influence in networks. J. Logic Lang. Inform. **25**(3–4), 299–333 (2016)
9. Baltag, A., Christoff, Z., Rendsvig, R.K., Smets, S.: Dynamic epistemic logics of diffusion and prediction in social networks (extended abstract). In: Bonanno, G., van der Hoek, W., Perea, A. (eds.) Proceedings of LOFT 2016 (2016)
10. Velázquez-Quesada, F.R.: Reliability-based preference dynamics: lexicographic upgrade. J. Log. Comput. **27**(8), 2341–2381 (2017)
11. Smets, S., Velázquez-Quesada, F.R.: How to make friends: a logical approach to social group creation. In: Baltag, A., Seligman, J., Yamada, T. (eds.) LORI 2017. LNCS, vol. 10455, pp. 377–390. Springer, Heidelberg (2017). https://doi.org/10.1007/978-3-662-55665-8_26
12. Smets, S., Velázquez-Quesada, F.R.: The creation and change of social networks: a logical study based on group size. In: Madeira, A., Benevides, M. (eds.) DALI 2017. LNCS, vol. 10669, pp. 171–184. Springer, Cham (2018). https://doi.org/10.1007/978-3-319-73579-5_11
13. Smets, S., Velázquez-Quesada, F.R.: A closeness- and priority-based logical study of social network creation. Under submission (2018)
14. Smets, S., Velázquez-Quesada, F.R.: A logical study of group-size based social network creation. J. Log. Algebr. Methods Program. **106**, 117–140 (2019)
15. Easley, D., Kleinberg, J.: Networks, Crowds and Markets: Reasoning about a Highly Connected World. Cambridge University Press, New York (2010)
16. McPherson, M., Smith-Lovin, L., Cook, J.M.: Birds of a feather: homophily in social networks. Annu. Rev. Sociol. **27**, 415–444 (2001)
17. Bramoullé, Y., Currarini, S., Jackson, M.O., Pin, P., Rogers, B.W.: Homophily and long-run integration in social networks. J. Econ. Theory **147**(5), 1754–1786 (2012)
18. Kim, K., Altmann, J.: Effect of homophily on network formation. Commun. Nonlinear Sci. Numer. Simul. **44**, 482–494 (2017)

19. Baltag, A., Christoff, Z., Rendsvig, R.K., Smets, S.: Dynamic epistemic logics of diffusion and prediction in social networks. Stud. Logica **107**, 489–531 (2019)
20. Christoff, Z., Hansen, J.U.: A logic for diffusion in social networks. J. Appl. Log. **13**(1), 48–77 (2015)
21. DeGroot, M.H.: Reaching a consensus. J. Am. Stat. Assoc. **69**(345), 118–121 (1974)
22. Holliday, W.H.: Dynamic testimonial logic. In: He, X., Horty, J., Pacuit, E. (eds.) LORI 2009. LNCS (LNAI), vol. 5834, pp. 161–179. Springer, Heidelberg (2009). https://doi.org/10.1007/978-3-642-04893-7_13
23. Seligman, J., Liu, F., Girard, P.: Facebook and the epistemic logic of friendship. In: Schipper, B.C. (ed.) Proceedings of the 14th Conference on Theoretical Aspects of Rationality and Knowledge (TARK 2013), Chennai, India, 7–9 January 2013 (2013)
24. Granovetter, M.: Threshold models of collective behavior. Am. J. Sociol. **83**(6), 1420–1443 (1978)
25. Wang, Y., Cao, Q.: On axiomatizations of public announcement logic. Synthese **190**(Suppl.-1), 103–134 (2013)
26. Smets, S., Velázquez-Quesada, F.R.: A logical perspective on social group creation. In: Arazim, P., Lávička, T. (eds.) The Logica Yearbook 2017, pp. 271–288. College Publications, London (2018a)
27. Blackburn, P., de Rijke, M., Venema, Y.: Modal logic. Number 53 in Cambridge Tracts in Theoretical Computer Science. Cambridge University Press, Cambridge (2001)

A Four-Valued Hybrid Logic with Non-dual Modal Operators

Diana Costa[1(✉)] and Manuel A. Martins[2]

[1] Department of Computer Science, University College London, London, England
d.costa@ucl.ac.uk
[2] CIDMA – Department of Mathematics, University of Aveiro, Aveiro, Portugal
martins@ua.pt

Abstract. Hybrid logics are an extension of modal logics where it is possible to refer to a specific state, thus allowing the description of what happens at specific states, equalities and transitions between them. This makes hybrid logics very desirable to work with relational structures.

However, as the amount of information grows, it becomes increasingly more common to find inconsistencies. Information collected about a particular hybrid structure is not an exception. Rather than discarding all the data congregated, working with a paraconsistent type of logic allows us to keep it and still make sensible inferences.

In this paper we introduce a four-valued semantics for hybrid logic, where contradictions are allowed both at the level of propositional variables and accessibility relations. A distinguishing feature of this new logic is the fact that the classical equivalence between modal operators will be broken. A sound and complete tableau system is also presented.

1 Introduction

Four-valued logics have been extensively studied in the context of computer science and artificial intelligence. They have been applied for example in the areas of symbolic model checking [7], semantics of logic programs [9] and inconsistency-tolerant systems. The basic four-valued logic was introduced by Belnap [2], and the algebraic structure underneath it is composed of four elements $\{\mathrm{t}, \mathrm{f}, \top, \bot\}$. Intuitively, t and f represent the notions of "true" and "false", while $\top$ and $\bot$ represent inconsistent and incomplete information, respectively. Thus Belnap's logic is not only paraconsistent, it is also paracomplete. Moreover, these four values may be arranged according to two partial orders: the first one, $\leq_{\mathrm{t}}$, reflects the "*quality*" of the information, whereas the second, $\leq_{\mathrm{k}}$, reflects the "*quantity*" of information. The two lattice structures are represented in Fig. 1.

Still in the field of computer science, relational structures have been widely used in computer programs. They provide a formalism to abstractly depict connections between states, which is the idea behind the appearance of modal logics. The notion of satisfiability in modal logic is a local one and we are not able to switch our attention from the world where we are evaluating a given formula to

L. Soares Barbosa and A. Baltag (Eds.): DaLí 2019, LNCS 12005, pp. 88–103, 2020.
https://doi.org/10.1007/978-3-030-38808-9_6

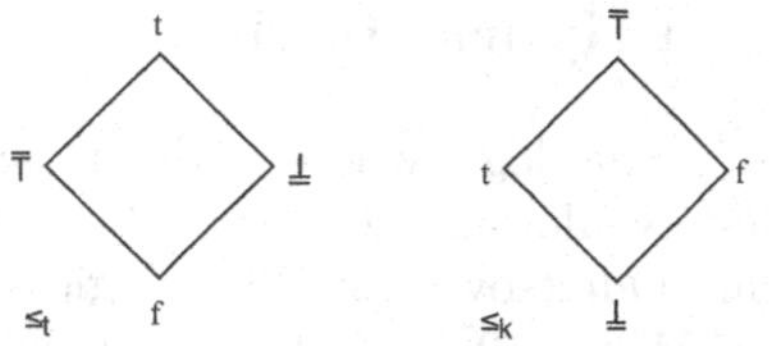

Fig. 1. The two orderings of the Belnap bilattice.

another one. In order to overcome this limitation, hybrid logics were introduced. Classical hybrid logic, [4], is obtained by adding to classical modal logic further expressive power in the form of a new class of atomic formulas, called nominals, which are true at exactly one state, together a satisfaction operator @. Equipped with this new machinery we are now able to refer to a specific state, and thus describe what happens there (the formula $@_i\varphi$ holds in a structure if and only if φ is true at the state named by i) – in particular we are also able to specify the equalities and the transitions between states.

Traditionally, the consensus among the computer science community is that inconsistency is undesirable and many people believe that databases, knowledge-bases, and software specifications should be completely free of inconsistencies and thus try to eradicate them by any means possible. However, this approach fails to use the benefits of inconsistency: if contradictory information is the norm rather than the exception in the real world, it should be formalized and used, and one should embrace it. Contradictory information does not always mean *wrong* information, in fact it may be part of a fraudulent operation, therefore detecting it may be our goal, and resolving it would result in the loss of valuable information.

Comparing heterogeneous sources often involves comparing conflicts and there are numerous examples of our daily life where we apply a paraconsistent reasoning: suppose we are dealing with a group of clinicians advising on some patient, a group of witnesses of some incident, or a set of newspaper reports covering some event: when different agents are involved, we already expect divergences, which formally translate to inconsistencies. Therefore inconsistencies are no longer seen purely as anomalies and paraconsistent logics are viewed as flexible logical systems able to handle heterogeneous and complex data as they accommodate inconsistency in a sensible manner that treats inconsistent information as informative.

The present paper introduces a new four-valued hybrid logic, where the duality between modal operators is broken. We argue that in a paraconsistent kind of logic saying that it is not possible that φ happens, formally represented by $\neg\Diamond\varphi$, should not be the same as saying that the negation of φ is mandatory, $\Box\neg\varphi$.

Another section introduces a tableau system to check if a formula is a consequence of a set of formulas under this new environment. The tableau construction algorithm is terminating, the system is sound and complete.

Due to space constrains, proofs were omitted, but included in an appendix.

2 Double-Belnapian Hybrid Logic

Paraconsistent versions of modal logic where both the accessibility relation and the propositional variables are allowed a four-valued behaviour are not a novelty. The works of Wansing and Odintsov with BK^{FS} logic and Rivieccio and Jung with modal bilattice logic MBL, [12] and [13] respectively are some examples. For a version of many-valued modal logic check Fitting's work [10].

Some combinations of hybrid logic with paraconsistency have also already been studied, for example in [5] and [8]. Nonetheless, the work on many-valued hybrid logic by Hansen et al. [11] seems to be the only version where the accessibility relation is also deemed possibly inconsistent. However, the latter does not capture the idea behind the double-belnapian hybrid logic about to be introduced. Nor does an extension with nominals and the satisfaction operator of either of the four-valued modal versions cited.

The difference between double-belnapian hybrid logic and those logics goes beyond the fact that the others do not consider disjunctive syllogism; we believe that when we are working within a paraconsistent environment it is rather suspicious to keep considering the classical equivalence between modal operators, $\langle\pi\rangle\varphi \equiv \neg[\pi]\neg\varphi$. It seems as though negation concerns only the non-modal part of the formula, and not the modal operator itself. We propose a paraconsistent version of hybrid logic where both $@_i\langle\pi\rangle j$, meaning that there is information about the presence of a transition via a modality π from i to j, and $@_i\neg\langle\pi\rangle j$ meaning that there is information about the absence of a transition via a modality π from i to j might be satisfiable; the interpretation for $@_i\neg\langle\pi\rangle j$ will be distinguished from that of $@_i[\pi]\neg j$, which will mean that whenever there is information about the presence of a transition via a modality π from i to a certain world, that world must not be named by j. This approach focuses on the relation rather than the world that is reached.

The structures underlying this system will incorporate two valuations in order to deal with inconsistencies at the level of propositional variables, V^+ and V^-, and will, analogously, consider two families of accessibility relations, $(R_\pi^+)_{\pi\in\text{Mod}}$ and $(R_\pi^-)_{\pi\in\text{Mod}}$, to deal with inconsistencies at the level of the accessibility relations.

We will take a standard semantics for nominals, such that the classical assumption that a nominal *names* a unique state is preserved. Notwithstanding, the topic of paraconsistency at the level of nominals should be addressed in the future. This seemingly easy feature carries a lot of implications and requires a lot of care in many ways. Let us not forget that we cannot simply assign one of four values to a nominal, otherwise nothing would distinguish them from ordinary propositional variables.

2.1 Syntax for Double-Belnapian Hybrid Logic

Let $\mathfrak{L}_\pi = \langle \text{Prop}, \text{Nom}, \text{Mod}\rangle$ be a *hybrid (multimodal) similarity type* where Prop is a countable set of *propositional variables*, Nom is a countable set disjoint from Prop and Mod is a countable set of *modality labels*. We use p, q, r, etc. to refer to the elements in Prop. The elements in Nom are called *nominals* and we typically write them as i, j, k, etc. Modalities are usually represented by π, π', etc.

Definition 1. *The well-formed formulas over* $\mathcal{L}_\pi$, $\mathrm{Form}_{@,\supset}(\mathcal{L}_\pi)$, *are defined by the following recursive definition:*

$$\varphi, \psi := i \mid p \mid \bot \mid \top \mid \neg\varphi \mid \varphi \supset \psi \mid \varphi \vee \psi \mid \varphi \wedge \psi \mid \langle\pi\rangle\varphi \mid [\pi]\varphi \mid @_i\varphi$$

where $i \in \mathrm{Nom}, p \in \mathrm{Prop}, \pi \in \mathrm{Mod}$.

For any nominal i and any formula φ, $@_i\varphi$ is called a *satisfaction statement.* Both @ and $@_i$, where $i \in \mathrm{Nom}$, will be referred to as *satisfaction operators.*

2.2 Semantics for Double-Belnapian Hybrid Logic

A hybrid multistructure is defined as a Kripke frame. There will be considered two valuations and two families of accessibility relations such that the interpretation of propositional variables and the interpretation of their negations is independent, as well as the interpretation of the presence and absence of a connection between two worlds. In this way, inconsistencies at the level of propositional variables and accessibility relations will be allowed without the trivialization of the whole system.

Definition 2. *A* hybrid multistructure, $\mathcal{G}$, *is a tuple* $(W, (R^+_\pi)_{\pi\in\mathrm{Mod}}, (R^-_\pi)_{\pi\in\mathrm{Mod}}, N, V^+, V^-)$, *where:*

- W *is a non-empty* domain *whose elements are called* states *or* worlds*;*
- *each* R^+_π *and* R^-_π *is a binary relation, called respectively the* positive *and the* negative π-accessibility relation, *and they are such that* $R^+_\pi, R^-_\pi \subseteq W \times W$*;*
- $N : \mathrm{Nom} \to W$ *is a function called* hybrid nomination *that assigns nominals to elements in* W *such that for any nominal* i, $N(i)$ *is the element of* W *named by* i*;*
- V^+ *and* V^- *are* hybrid valuations, *both with domain* Prop *and range* $\mathcal{P}(W)$, *such that* $V^+(p)$ *is the set of worlds where the propositional variable* p *holds, and* $V^-(p)$ *is the set of worlds where* $\neg p$ *holds.*

We will view each R^+_π as the set of pairs of worlds for which there is evidence of the presence of a transition via a modality π and each R^-_π as the set of pairs of worlds for which there is evidence of the lack of a transition via a modality π.

Semantics is formalized as follows:

Definition 3. *The double-belnapian satisfaction (for short* d-satisfaction*) relation* $\Vdash_{\mathrm{d}}$, *between a multistructure* $\mathcal{G} = (W, (R^+_\pi)_{\pi\in\mathrm{Mod}}, (R^-_\pi)_{\pi\in\mathrm{Mod}}, N, V^+, V^-)$, *a world* $w \in W$, *and a formula in* $\mathrm{Form}_{@,\supset}(\mathcal{L}_\pi)$ *is set as follows:*

- $\mathcal{G}, w \Vdash_{\mathrm{d}} p$ *iff* $w \in V^+(p)$*;*
- $\mathcal{G}, w \Vdash_{\mathrm{d}} i$ *iff* $w = N(i)$*;*
- $\mathcal{G}, w \Vdash_{\mathrm{d}} \neg p$ *iff* $w \in V^-(p)$*;*
- $\mathcal{G}, w \Vdash_{\mathrm{d}} \neg i$ *iff* $w \neq N(i)$*;*

- $\mathcal{G}, w \Vdash_{\mathrm{d}} \top$ *always;*
- $\mathcal{G}, w \Vdash_{\mathrm{d}} \bot$ *never;*
- $\mathcal{G}, w \Vdash_{\mathrm{d}} \neg\neg\varphi$ *iff* $\mathcal{G}, w \Vdash_{\mathrm{d}} \varphi$*;*
- $\mathcal{G}, w \Vdash_{\mathrm{d}} \varphi \wedge \psi$ *iff* $\mathcal{G}, w \Vdash_{\mathrm{d}} \varphi$ *and* $\mathcal{G}, w \Vdash_{\mathrm{d}} \psi$*;*
- $\mathcal{G}, w \Vdash_{\mathrm{d}} \neg(\varphi \wedge \psi)$ *iff* $\mathcal{G}, w \Vdash_{\mathrm{d}} \neg\varphi$ *or* $\mathcal{G}, w \Vdash_{\mathrm{d}} \neg\psi$*;*
- $\mathcal{G}, w \Vdash_{\mathrm{d}} \varphi \supset \psi$ *iff* $\mathcal{G}, w \Vdash_{\mathrm{d}} \varphi$ *implies* $\mathcal{G}, w \Vdash_{\mathrm{d}} \psi$*;*
- $\mathcal{G}, w \Vdash_{\mathrm{d}} \neg(\varphi \supset \psi)$ *iff* $\mathcal{G}, w \Vdash_{\mathrm{d}} \varphi$ *and* $\mathcal{G}, w \Vdash_{\mathrm{d}} \neg\psi$*;*
- $\mathcal{G}, w \Vdash_{\mathrm{d}} \varphi \vee \psi$ *iff* $[\mathcal{G}, w \Vdash_{\mathrm{d}} \varphi$ *or* $\mathcal{G}, w \Vdash_{\mathrm{d}} \psi]$
  and $[\mathcal{G}, w \Vdash_{\mathrm{d}} \neg\varphi$ *implies* $\mathcal{G}, w \Vdash_{\mathrm{d}} \psi]$
  and $[\mathcal{G}, w \Vdash_{\mathrm{d}} \neg\psi$ *implies* $\mathcal{G}, w \Vdash_{\mathrm{d}} \varphi]$*;*
- $\mathcal{G}, w \Vdash_{\mathrm{d}} \neg(\varphi \vee \psi)$ *iff* $[\mathcal{G}, w \Vdash_{\mathrm{d}} \neg\varphi$ *and* $\mathcal{G}, w \Vdash_{\mathrm{d}} \neg\psi]$
  or $[\mathcal{G}, w \nVdash_{\mathrm{d}} \varphi$ *and* $\mathcal{G}, w \Vdash_{\mathrm{d}} \neg\psi]$
  or $[\mathcal{G}, w \nVdash_{\mathrm{d}} \psi$ *and* $\mathcal{G}, w \Vdash_{\mathrm{d}} \neg\varphi]$*;*
- $\mathcal{G}, w \Vdash_{\mathrm{d}} \langle\pi\rangle\varphi$ *iff* $\exists w'(wR^{+}_{\pi}w'$ *and* $\mathcal{G}, w' \Vdash_{\mathrm{d}} \varphi)$*;*
- $\mathcal{G}, w \Vdash_{\mathrm{d}} [\pi]\varphi$ *iff* $\forall w'(wR^{+}_{\pi}w'$ *implies* $\mathcal{G}, w' \Vdash_{\mathrm{d}} \varphi)$*;*
- $\mathcal{G}, w \Vdash_{\mathrm{d}} \neg\langle\pi\rangle\varphi$ *iff* $\forall w'(\mathcal{G}, w' \Vdash_{\mathrm{d}} \varphi$ *implies* $wR^{-}_{\pi}w')$*;*
- $\mathcal{G}, w \Vdash_{\mathrm{d}} \neg[\pi]\varphi$ *iff* $\exists w'(w\not{R}^{-}_{\pi}w'$ *and* $\mathcal{G}, w' \Vdash_{\mathrm{d}} \neg\varphi)$*;*
- $\mathcal{G}, w \Vdash_{\mathrm{d}} @_i\varphi$ *iff* $\mathcal{G}, w' \Vdash_{\mathrm{d}} \varphi$*, where* $w' = N(i)$*;*
- $\mathcal{G}, w \Vdash_{\mathrm{d}} \neg@_i\varphi$ *iff* $\mathcal{G}, w' \Vdash_{\mathrm{d}} \neg\varphi$*, where* $w' = N(i)$*.*

$\mathcal{G}, w \Vdash_{\mathrm{d}} \varphi$ should be read as "φ is d-*satisfied* in the multistructure $\mathcal{G}$ at the world w".

We say that φ is *globally* d-*satisfied* if $\mathcal{G} \Vdash_{\mathrm{d}} \varphi$, where $\mathcal{G} \Vdash_{\mathrm{d}} \varphi$ if and only if $\mathcal{G}, w \Vdash_{\mathrm{d}} \varphi$ for all w in W.

Let Δ be a set of formulas in $\mathrm{Form}_{@,\supset}(\mathcal{L}_\pi)$. We say that a multistructure $\mathcal{G}$ is a *double-belnapian model* (for short d-*model*) of Δ if and only if $\mathcal{G} \Vdash_{\mathrm{d}} \delta$ for all $\delta \in \Delta$.

Observe that the definition of satisfiability for the disjunction of formulas incorporates the notion of disjunctive syllogism such that for the formula to hold, not only at least one of the disjuncts must hold, but also if the negation of one of the disjuncts holds, then the remainder of the formula when we remove that disjunct must hold as well.

The use of disjunctive syllogism is rather uncommon. A discussion about its use can be found in [1], and the reason we advocate in favor of its use in this logic is the same as Hunter and Besnard give for Quasi-classical logic [3]: the idea is that this definition links a disjunct and its complement, and preserves the meaning of the resolution principle.

However, the major novelty about this new logic is the interpretation of modal formulas $\langle\pi\rangle\varphi$, $[\pi]\varphi$ and their negations. Namely:

- $\langle\pi\rangle\varphi$ holds in a multistructure $\mathcal{G}$ at a world w if and only if there is evidence of a transition via a modality π from the world w to a world w' where φ holds.
  - ⋊ Thus if the formula $@_i\langle\pi\rangle j$ holds, then it means that there exists evidence of a transition via a modality π from the world named by the nominal i to the world named by the nominal j, $N(i)R^{+}_{\pi}N(j)$.

- $[\pi]\varphi$ holds in a multistructure $\mathcal{G}$ at a world w if and only if whenever there is evidence of a transition via a modality π from the world w to a world w', φ holds at w'.
  - $\rtimes$ Thus if the formula $@_i[\pi]\neg j$ holds, then it means that there is not evidence of a transition via a modality π from the world named by the nominal i to the world named by the nominal j, $N(i)\not R^+_\pi N(j)$.
- $\neg\langle\pi\rangle\varphi$ holds in a multistructure $\mathcal{G}$ at a world w if and only if whenever φ holds at a world w', there is evidence of the lack of a transition via a modality π from the world w to the world w'.
  - $\rtimes$ Thus if the formula $@_i\neg\langle\pi\rangle j$ holds, then it means that there is evidence of the lack of a transition via a modality π from the world named by the nominal i to the world named by the nominal j, $N(i)R^-_\pi N(j)$.
- $\neg[\pi]\varphi$ holds in a multistructure $\mathcal{G}$ at a world w if and only if there is a world w' such that there is not a negative transition from w to w' and where φ holds.
  - $\rtimes$ Thus if the formula $@_i\neg[\pi]\neg j$ holds, then it means that there is not evidence of the lack of a transition via a modality π from the world named by the nominal i to the world named by the nominal j, $N(i)\not R^-_\pi N(j)$.

Therefore not only do we allow local inconsistencies at the level of propositional variables – when both $@_ip$ and $@_i\neg p$ hold – but also consider it possible to have inconsistencies at the level of the accessibility relations – when both $@_i\langle\pi\rangle j$ and $@_i\neg\langle\pi\rangle j$ hold. Moreover, it is possible to have incomplete information at the level of propositional variables – when for example neither $@_ip$ nor $@_i\neg p$ hold – and at the level of the accessibility relations – when for example neither $@_i\langle\pi\rangle j$ nor $@_i\neg\langle\pi\rangle j$ hold.

Double-belnapian hybrid logic owes its name to the fact that we can extract a four-valued behaviour for propositional variables as well as for the underlying π-accessibility relations.

2.3 A Tableau System for Double-Belnapian Hybrid Logic

In order to provide an automated proof procedure, we need the following definitions:

Definition 4. *Given a hybrid (multimodal) similarity type* $\mathcal{L}_\pi = \langle \mathrm{Prop}, \mathrm{Nom}, \mathrm{Mod}\rangle$, *consider the set of signed formulas* $\mathrm{Form}^*_{@,\supset}(\mathcal{L}_\pi)$ *defined as*

$$\mathrm{Form}^*_{@,\supset}(\mathcal{L}_\pi) = \mathrm{Form}_{@,\supset}(\mathcal{L}_\pi) \cup \{\varphi^* \mid \varphi \in \mathrm{Form}_{@,\supset}(\mathcal{L}_\pi)\}.$$

The notion of d-satisfiability for a starred formula φ^* is the dual of the notion of d-satisfiability for the formula φ:

Definition 5. *We extend the satisfaction relation* $\Vdash_{\mathrm{d}}$ *to starred formulas as follows:*

$$\mathcal{G}, w \Vdash_{\mathrm{d}} \varphi^* \textit{ iff } \mathcal{G}, w \nVdash_{\mathrm{d}} \varphi$$

Global d-*satisfiability for the new formulas is defined following the same approach*, i.e.*:*

$$\mathcal{G} \Vdash_{\mathrm{d}} \varphi^* \text{ iff } \mathcal{G} \nVdash_{\mathrm{d}} \varphi$$

It easy to see that $\mathcal{G} \Vdash_{\mathrm{d}} \varphi^*$ if and only if it is false that $\forall w \in W,\ \mathcal{G}, w \Vdash_{\mathrm{d}} \varphi$ if and only if $\exists w \in W : \mathcal{G}, w \nVdash_{\mathrm{d}} \varphi$ if and only if $\exists w \in W : \mathcal{G}, w \Vdash_{\mathrm{d}} \varphi^*$.

The tableau system $\mathrm{T_D}$ is composed by the following rules:

For Non-starred Formulas:

$$\frac{\varphi}{@_i\varphi}\ (@_{\mathrm{I}}{}^{\mathrm{d}})(\mathrm{i}) \qquad \frac{@_i@_j\varphi}{@_j\varphi}\ (@_{\mathrm{E}}{}^{\mathrm{d}}) \qquad \frac{@_i(\varphi \wedge \psi)}{\begin{array}{c}@_i\varphi\\ @_i\psi\end{array}}\ (\wedge^{\mathrm{d}})$$

$$\frac{@_i(\varphi \vee \psi)}{\begin{array}{c|c|c|c|c|c|c} @_i\varphi & @_i\varphi & @_i\varphi & @_i\varphi & @_i\psi & @_i\psi & @_i\psi \\ (@_i\neg\varphi)^* & (@_i\neg\varphi)^* & (@_i\neg\psi)^* & @_i\psi & (@_i\neg\varphi)^* & (@_i\neg\psi)^* & (@_i\neg\varphi)^* \\ (@_i\neg\psi)^* & & @_i\psi & & (@_i\neg\psi)^* & & @_i\varphi \end{array}}\ (\vee^{\mathrm{d}})$$

$$\frac{@_i[\pi]\varphi,\ @_i\langle\pi\rangle j}{@_j\varphi}\ ([\pi]^{\mathrm{d}}) \quad \frac{@_i\langle\pi\rangle\varphi}{\begin{array}{c}@_i\langle\pi\rangle t\\ @_t\varphi\end{array}}\ (\langle\pi\rangle^{\mathrm{d}})(\mathrm{ii}) \qquad \frac{@_i(\varphi \supset \psi)}{(@_i\varphi)^* \mid @_i\psi}\ (\supset^{\mathrm{d}})$$

$$\frac{@_i\neg@_j\varphi}{@_j\neg\varphi}\ (\neg@^{\mathrm{d}}) \qquad \frac{@_i\neg(\varphi \wedge \psi)}{@_i\neg\varphi \mid @_i\neg\psi}\ (\neg\wedge^{\mathrm{d}}) \qquad \frac{@_i\neg(\varphi \vee \psi)}{\begin{array}{c|c|c} @_i\neg\varphi & @_i\varphi^* & @_i\psi^* \\ @_i\neg\psi & @_i\neg\psi & @_i\neg\varphi \end{array}}\ (\neg\vee^{\mathrm{d}})$$

$$\frac{@_i\neg[\pi]\varphi}{\begin{array}{c}@_i\neg[\pi]\neg t\\ @_t\neg\varphi\end{array}}\ (\neg[\pi]^{\mathrm{d}})(\mathrm{iii}) \quad \frac{@_i\neg\langle\pi\rangle\varphi,\ @_i\neg[\pi]\neg j}{(@_j\varphi)^*}\ (\neg\langle\pi\rangle^{\mathrm{d}}) \quad \frac{@_i\neg(\varphi \supset \psi)}{\begin{array}{c}@_i\varphi\\ @_i\neg\psi\end{array}}\ (\neg\supset^{\mathrm{d}})$$

$$\frac{@_i\neg\neg\varphi}{@_i\varphi}\ (\neg\neg^{\mathrm{d}}) \qquad \frac{@_i j,\ @_i\varphi}{@_j\varphi}\ (\mathrm{Nom}^{\mathrm{d}})(\mathrm{iv}) \qquad \frac{}{@_i i}\ (\mathrm{Id}^{\mathrm{d}})(\mathrm{v}) \quad \frac{@_i\neg\top}{@_i\bot}\ (\neg\top^{\mathrm{d}})$$

For Starred Formulas:

$$\frac{\varphi^*}{(@_t\varphi)^*}\ (@_{\mathrm{I}}^{*\mathrm{d}})(\mathrm{vi}) \qquad \frac{(@_i@_j\varphi)^*}{(@_j\varphi)^*}\ (@_{\mathrm{E}}^{*\mathrm{d}}) \qquad \frac{(@_i(\varphi \wedge \psi))^*}{(@_i\varphi)^* \mid (@_i\psi)^*}\ (\wedge^{*\mathrm{d}})$$

$$\frac{(@_i(\varphi \vee \psi))^*}{\begin{array}{c|c|c} (@_i\varphi)^* & @_i\neg\varphi & @_i\neg\psi \\ (@_i\psi)^* & (@_i\psi)^* & (@_i\varphi)^* \end{array}}\ (\vee^{*\mathrm{d}}) \quad \frac{(@_i(\varphi \supset \psi))^*}{\begin{array}{c}@_i\varphi\\ (@_i\psi)^*\end{array}}\ (\supset^{*\mathrm{d}}) \qquad \frac{(@_i[\pi]\varphi)^*}{\begin{array}{c}@_i\langle\pi\rangle t\\ (@_t\varphi)^*\end{array}}\ ([\pi]^{*\mathrm{d}})(\mathrm{vii})$$

$$\frac{(@_i\langle\pi\rangle\varphi)^*,\ @_i\langle\pi\rangle j}{(@_j\varphi)^*}\ (\langle\pi\rangle^{*\mathrm{d}}) \quad \frac{(@_i\neg(@_j\varphi))^*}{(@_j\neg\varphi)^*}\ (\neg@^{*\mathrm{d}}) \qquad \frac{(@_i\neg(\varphi \wedge \psi))^*}{\begin{array}{c}(@_i\neg\varphi)^*\\ (@_i\neg\psi)^*\end{array}}\ (\neg\wedge^{*\mathrm{d}})$$

$$\frac{(@_i\neg(\varphi \supset \psi))^*}{(@_i\varphi)^* \mid (@_i\neg\psi)^*}\ (\neg\supset^{*\mathrm{d}}) \qquad \frac{(@_i\neg[\pi]\varphi)^*, @_i\neg[\pi]\neg j}{(@_j\neg\varphi)^*}\ (\neg[\pi]^{*\mathrm{d}}) \quad \frac{(@_i\neg\langle\pi\rangle\varphi)^*}{\begin{array}{c}@_i\neg[\pi]\neg t\\ @_t\varphi\end{array}}\ (\neg\langle\pi\rangle^{*\mathrm{d}})\text{(vii)}$$

$$\frac{(@_i\neg(\varphi \vee \psi))^*}{\begin{array}{c|c|c|c|c|c|c} (@_i\neg\varphi)^* & (@_i\neg\varphi)^* & (@_i\neg\varphi)^* & (@_i\neg\varphi)^* & (@_i\neg\psi)^* & (@_i\neg\psi)^* & (@_i\neg\psi)^* \\ @_i\varphi & @_i\varphi & @_i\psi & (@_i\neg\psi)^* & @_i\varphi & @_i\psi & @_i\varphi \\ @_i\psi & & (@_i\neg\psi)^* & & @_i\psi & & (@_i\neg\varphi)^* \end{array}}\ (\neg\vee^{*\mathrm{d}})$$

$$\frac{(@_i\neg\neg\varphi)^*}{(@_i\varphi)^*}\ (\neg\neg^{*\mathrm{d}}) \qquad \frac{(@_i\varphi)^*}{@_i\neg\varphi}\ (\mathrm{Id}^{*\mathrm{d}})\text{(viii)}$$

(i) φ is not a satisfaction statement, i is in the branch;

(ii) $\varphi \notin \mathrm{Nom}$, t is a new nominal;

(iii) $\varphi \neq \neg i$ for all $i \in \mathrm{Nom}$, t is a new nominal;

(iv) for $@_i\varphi$ a literal;

(v) for i in the branch;

(vi) φ is not a satisfaction statement, t is a new nominal;

(vii) t is a new nominal;

(viii) $\varphi = j$ or $\varphi = \neg j$, where $j \in \mathrm{Nom}$; or $\varphi = \top$.

The rules ($@^{\mathrm{d}}_{\mathrm{I}}$), ($\mathrm{Id}^{\mathrm{d}}$), ($\mathrm{Nom}^{\mathrm{d}}$), ($[\pi]^{\mathrm{d}}$), ($\neg\langle\pi\rangle^{\mathrm{d}}$), ($\langle\pi\rangle^{*\mathrm{d}}$) and ($\neg[\pi]^{*\mathrm{d}}$) are called *non-destructive rules*. The remaining rules are called *destructive*. We distinguish between destructive and non-destructive rules for the same reason as in [6], so that in the systematic tableau construction algorithm, the application of destructive rules is restricted in such a way that a destructive rule is applied at most once to a formula (a destructive rule has exactly one formula in the premise – the converse is not true). As in [6], the classification of rules as destructive and non-destructive corresponds to a classification of formulas according to their form.

A tableau in this system will be denoted $\mathcal{T}_{\mathrm{D}}$.

Definition 6. *A* subformula *is defined by the following conditions:*

- *φ is a subformula of φ;*
- *if ψ^* is a subformula of φ, then so is ψ;*
- *if $\psi \wedge \delta$, $\psi \vee \delta$, or $\psi \supset \delta$ is a subformula of φ, then so are ψ and δ;*
- *if $@_i\psi$, $\neg\psi$, $[\pi]\psi$, or $\langle\pi\rangle\psi$ is a subformula of φ, then so is ψ.*

The tableau system $\mathrm{T_D}$ satisfies the following subformula property:

Theorem 1 (Subformula property). *If $@_i\varphi \in \mathcal{T}_D$, where φ is not a nominal, $\varphi \neq \langle\pi\rangle j$ and $\varphi \neq \neg[\pi]\neg j$ for $\pi \in \mathrm{Mod}$, $j \in \mathrm{Nom}$ or if $(@_i\varphi)^* \in \mathcal{T}_\mathrm{D}$, then in case $\varphi = \neg\psi$, either φ or ψ is a subformula of a root formula, otherwise φ is a subformula of a root formula.*

Proof. The proof can be obtained by checking each rule.

A binary relation between nominals naming the same worlds is set as previously and the definition for the inclusion of nominals is adapted as follows:

Definition 7. *Let Θ be a branch of a tableau and let Nom^Θ be the set of nominals occurring in the formulas of Θ. Define a binary relation $\sim^{\mathrm{d}}_\Theta$ on Nom^Θ by $i \sim^{\mathrm{d}}_\Theta j$ if and only if the formula $@_i j \in \Theta$.*

Definition 8. *Let i and j be nominals occurring on a branch Θ of a tableau in T_B. The nominal i is said to be* d-included in the nominal j with respect to Θ *if, for any subformula φ of a root formula, the following holds:*

- *if $@_i\varphi \in \Theta$, then $@_j\varphi \in \Theta$; and*
- *if $(@_i\varphi)^* \in \Theta$, then $(@_j\varphi)^* \in \Theta$; and*
- *if $@_i\neg\varphi \in \Theta$, then $@_j\neg\varphi \in \Theta$; and*
- *if $(@_i\neg\varphi)^* \in \Theta$, then $(@_j\neg\varphi)^* \in \Theta$.*

If i is d*-included in j with respect to Θ, and the first occurrence of j on Θ is before the first occurrence of i, then we write $i \subseteq^{\mathrm{d}}_\Theta j$.*

Definition 9 (Tableau construction). *Given a finite database $\Delta \subseteq \mathrm{Form}_{@,\supset}(\mathcal{L}_\pi)$ and a query $\varphi \in \mathrm{Form}_{@,\supset}(\mathcal{L}_\pi)$, one wants to verify if φ is a* d*-consequence of Δ. In order to do so, we define by induction a sequence $\mathcal{T}^0_\mathrm{D}, \mathcal{T}^1_\mathrm{D}, \mathcal{T}^2_\mathrm{D}, \cdots$ of finite tableaux in $\mathrm{T_D}$, each of which is embedded in its successor.*

Let $\mathcal{T}^0_\mathrm{D}$ be the finite tableau constituted by the formulas in Δ and φ^*. $\mathcal{T}^{n+1}_\mathrm{D}$ is obtained from $\mathcal{T}^n_\mathrm{D}$ if it is possible to apply an arbitrary rule to $\mathcal{T}^n_\mathrm{D}$ obeying the following three restrictions:

1. *If a formula to be added to a branch by applying a rule already occurs on the branch, then the addition of the formula is simply omitted.*
2. *After the application of a destructive rule to a formula occurrence φ on a branch, it is recorded that the rule was applied to φ with respect to the branch and the rule will not again be applied to φ with respect to the branch or any extension of it.*
3. *The existential rules $(\langle\pi\rangle^\mathrm{d})$, $(\neg[\pi]^\mathrm{d})$, $([\pi]^{*\mathrm{d}})$ and $(\neg\langle\pi\rangle^{*\mathrm{d}})$ are not applied to $@_i\langle\pi\rangle\varphi$, $@_i\neg[\pi]\varphi$, $(@_i[\pi]\varphi)^*$ nor to $(@_i\neg\langle\pi\rangle\varphi)^*$ on a branch Θ if there exists a nominal j such that $i \subseteq^{\mathrm{d}}_\Theta j$.*

Thus a formula cannot occur more than once on a branch, a destructive rule cannot be applied more once to the same formula and the third restriction are loop-check conditions.

The tableau construction algorithm is terminating, and the system is proved to be sound and complete.

Theorem 2 (Soundness). *The tableau rules are sound in the following sense: for any rule* $\dfrac{\Lambda}{\Sigma_1|\cdots|\Sigma_n}$, $n \geq 1$, *and any multistructure* $\mathcal{G}$,

$$\mathcal{G} \Vdash_{\mathrm{d}} \Lambda \textit{ implies } \mathcal{G} \Vdash_{\mathrm{d}} \Sigma_1 \textit{ or } \ldots \textit{ or } \mathcal{G} \Vdash_{\mathrm{d}} \Sigma_n$$

for Λ, $\Sigma_1, \ldots, \Sigma_n$ *sets of formulas in* $\mathrm{Form}^*_{@,\supset}(\mathcal{L}_\pi)$.

A branch is *closed* if and only if there is a formula ψ for which ψ and ψ^* are in that branch or if $@_i\bot$ or $@_i\neg i$ is in the branch for some nominal i. Otherwise the branch is open. A tableau is closed if and only if all of its branches are closed; otherwise the tableau is open.

In order to prove completeness, we prove that if a tableau has an open branch Θ, then there exists a model $\mathcal{G}^{\mathrm{d}}_{\Theta}$ and a world w where all root formulas are d-satisfied.

Theorem 3 (Model Existence). *Assume that the branch* Θ *is open. For any satisfaction statement* $@_i\varphi$ *which contains only nominals from* U^{d}, *there is a model* $\mathcal{G}^{\mathrm{d}}_{\Theta}$ *such that the following conditions hold:*

(i) if $@_i\varphi \in \Theta$, *then* $\mathcal{G}^{\mathrm{d}}_{\Theta}, [i]_{\approx^{\mathrm{d}}} \Vdash_{\mathrm{d}} \varphi$;
(ii) if $(@_i\varphi)^* \in \Theta$, *then* $\mathcal{G}^{\mathrm{d}}_{\Theta}, [i]_{\approx^{\mathrm{d}}} \nVdash_{\mathrm{d}} \varphi$.

Observe that root formulas that are satisfaction statements contain only nominals from U^{d}, therefore they are captured in this theorem. On the other hand, if a root formula φ (resp. φ^*) is not a satisfaction statement, the application of the rule ($@_{\mathrm{I}}{}^{\mathrm{d}}$) (resp. ($@^{*\mathrm{d}}_{\mathrm{I}}$)) turns it into one. Thus, by proving d-satisfiability of $@_i\varphi$ (resp. $(@_i\varphi)^*$) in a model $\mathcal{G}$, at a world w, where $i \in U^{\mathrm{d}}$, we are proving that there exists a model and a world where φ (resp. φ^*) is d-satisfied. Note also that ($@_{\mathrm{I}}{}^{\mathrm{d}}$) is applied to φ for every i in the branch, then there is at least one world where all root formulas are indeed d-satisfied.

There is a straightforward consequence relation in double-belnapian logic, defined as:

Definition 10 (Double-belnapian consequence relation). *Let* Δ *be a finite set of hybrid formulas called* database, *and* φ *be a hybrid formula called* query. *We say that* φ *is a* double-belnapian consequence of Δ, *for short* d-consequence *if and only if, for all multistructures* $\mathcal{G}$ *where all formulas in* Δ *are globally* d-*satisfied,* φ *is globally* d-*satisfied.*

Formally,

$$\Delta \Vdash_{\mathrm{D}} \varphi \textit{ iff } \forall \mathcal{G}\, (\mathcal{G} \Vdash_{\mathrm{d}} \Delta \Rightarrow \mathcal{G} \Vdash_{\mathrm{d}} \varphi)$$

In other words, φ is a consequence of Δ if and only if φ is globally d-satisfied in all multistructures that are d-models of Δ. It is clear that the consequence relation $\Vdash_{\mathrm{D}}$ is non-trivializable.

The following result holds:

Proposition 1. *For any set of formulas* $\Delta \in \mathrm{Form}_{@,\supset}(\mathcal{L}_\pi)$ *and any formula* $\varphi \in \mathrm{Form}_{@,\supset}(\mathcal{L}_\pi)$*, there is a tableau* τ_{D} *for a database* Δ *and query* φ *that is closed if and only if there is no model* $\mathcal{G}$ *such that* $\mathcal{G} \Vdash_{\mathrm{d}} \Delta$ *and* $\mathcal{G} \Vdash_{\mathrm{d}} \varphi^*$.

Example 1. *Let* $\Delta = \{@_i\langle\pi\rangle p, @_i[\pi]j, @_i\neg\langle\pi\rangle p\}$ *be a database and consider a query* $\varphi = @_i\neg\langle\pi\rangle j$.

Let us check if φ *is a dyadic consequence of* Δ *using the tableau-based decision procedure described in Proposition 1:*

$@_i\langle\pi\rangle p,\ @_i[\pi]j,\ @_i\neg\langle\pi\rangle p,\ (@_i\neg\langle\pi\rangle j)^*$	*1.*
$@_i\langle\pi\rangle t,\ @_t p$	*2. by* $(\langle\pi\rangle^{\mathrm{d}})$ *rule on 1*
$@_t j$	*3. by* $([\pi]^{\mathrm{d}})$ *rule on 1 and 2*
$@_j p$	*4. by* $(\mathrm{Nom}^{\mathrm{d}})$ *rule on 3 and 2*
$@_i\neg[\pi]\neg u, @_u j$	*5. by* $(\neg\langle\pi\rangle^{*\mathrm{d}})$ *rule on 1*
$@_i i, @_j j, @_t t, @_u u$	*6. by* $(\mathrm{Id}^{\mathrm{d}})$ *rule*
$@_j u$	*7. by* $(\mathrm{Nom}^{\mathrm{d}})$ *rule on 5 and 6*
$@_u p$	*8. by* $(\mathrm{Nom}^{\mathrm{d}})$ *rule on 7 and 4*
$(@_u p)^*$	*9. by* $(\neg\langle\pi\rangle^{\mathrm{d}})$ *rule on 1 and 5*
$\times$	

Since the tableau is closed, φ *is a dyadic consequence of* Δ.

Let us give some intuituion behind this result: (i) in a multistructure where $@_i\langle\pi\rangle p$ *holds, there is a world* w'*, which will be named by a nominal* t *such that* $N(i)R_\pi^+N(t)$ *and* $@_t p$ *holds; (ii) from* $@_i[\pi]j$*, we get that all positive* π*-transitions from* $N(i)$ *must lead to* $N(j)$*, thus* t *and* j *must name the same world; (iii) then since* $@_j p$ *holds, from the fact that* $@_i\neg\langle\pi\rangle p$ *must hold as well, it follows that* $N(i)R_\pi^-N(j)$.

We can also show that for all d-models transitivity of equality between nominals is globally d-satisfied:

Example 2. *Let* $\Delta = \{\}$ *and* $\varphi = (@_i j \wedge @_j k) \supset @_i k$.

The tableau-based decision procedure described in Proposition 1 yields the following:

$((@_i j \wedge @_j k) \supset @_i k)^*$	*1.*
$(@_t((@_i j \wedge @_j k) \supset @_i k))^*$	*2. by* $(@_{\mathrm{I}}^{*\mathrm{d}})$ *rule on 1*
$@_t(@_i j \wedge @_j k), (@_t(@_i k))^*$	*3. by* $(\supset^{*\mathrm{d}})$ *rule on 2*
$@_t(@_i j), @_t(@_j k)$	*4. by* $(\wedge^{\mathrm{d}})$ *rule on 3*
$@_i j, @_j k, (@_i k)^*$	*5. by* $(@_{\mathrm{E}}^{\mathrm{d}})$ *rule on 4,* $(@_{\mathrm{E}}^{*\mathrm{d}})$ *rule on 3*
$@_i i$	*6. by* $(\mathrm{Id}^{\mathrm{d}})$ *rule*
$@_j i$	*7. by* $(\mathrm{Nom}^{\mathrm{d}})$ *rule on 5 and 6 –* $@_i j, @_i i$
$@_i k$	*8. by* $(\mathrm{Nom}^{\mathrm{d}})$ *rule on 7 and 5 –* $@_j i, @_j k$
$\times$	

Since the tableau is closed, φ is a dyadic consequence of $\Delta = \{\}$ which means that φ is globally d-*satisfied in all* d-*models,* i.e., *φ is valid.*

2.4 Representation of Models via Diagrams

Let $\mathcal{L}_\pi(W)$ denote the expansion of $\mathcal{L}_\pi$ that ensures that all worlds are named by a nominal and let $\mathcal{G}(W)$ denote the natural expansion of the multistructure $\mathcal{G}$ to the hybrid multimodal similarity type $\mathcal{L}_\pi(W)$.

The diagram of a multistructure will be constituted by all *evidence* of what happens at specific states, all *evidence* about transitions and the lack of transitions, and finally all *evidence* about equalities between states; we introduce the notion of literal that will be used later:

Definition 11. *For a hybrid (multimodal) similarity type $\mathcal{L}_\pi = \langle \text{Prop}, \text{Nom}, \text{Mod}\rangle$, we define the set of d-literals over $\mathcal{L}_\pi$ as:*

$$\begin{aligned}\text{DLit}(\mathcal{L}_\pi) = \ & \{@_i p, @_i \neg p, @_i j, @_i \langle \pi \rangle j, @_i \neg \langle \pi \rangle j \mid i, j \in \text{Nom}, \\ & p \in \text{Prop}, \pi \in \text{Mod}\}.\end{aligned}$$

Definition 12. *Let $\mathcal{L}_\pi = \langle \text{Prop}, \text{Nom}, \text{Mod}\rangle$ be a hybrid (multimodal) similarity type, and $\mathcal{G} = (W, (R_\pi^+)_{\pi \in \text{Mod}}, (R_\pi^-)_{\pi \in \text{Mod}}, N, V^+, V^-)$ be a multistructure over $\mathcal{L}_\pi$. The* diagram *of $\mathcal{G}$, denoted by $\text{DDiag}(\mathcal{G})$, is the set of d-literals over $\mathcal{L}_\pi(W)$ that hold in $\mathcal{G}(W)$,* i.e.,

$$\text{DDiag}(\mathcal{G}) = \{\alpha \in \text{DLit}(\mathcal{L}_\pi(W)) \mid \mathcal{G}(W) \Vdash_{\text{d}} \alpha\}.$$

Two distinct multistructures over $\mathcal{L}_\pi$ with the same domain W induce two distinct diagrams (over $\mathcal{L}_\pi(W)$). Thus the diagram $\text{DDiag}(\mathcal{G})$ uniquely defines the multistructure $\mathcal{G}$.

We will use $\mathbb{D}(\Delta, W)$ to denote the set of dyadic diagrams of multistructures that are d-models of Δ with domain W over the hybrid multimodal similarity type $\mathcal{L}_\pi(W)$, where $\mathcal{L}_\pi$ contains the symbols occurring in Δ.

Example 3. *Suppose that we are given a map of a town, which for some reason contains imprecise information, namely it mentions that for some pairs of locations transitions are both possible and impossible, and for some other pairs it has no information. (For simplicity we consider a single modality which is then omitted.)*

Locations are named: a, b, c, d, e *(if they were not it would still be possible to assign them a new name). There are also variables* p *and* q *representing properties such as "there is a subway station" and "there is a pharmacy", that hold at some places and that are depicted in the map. The latter are also prone to inconsistency and incompleteness.*

The map is represented in the following figure:

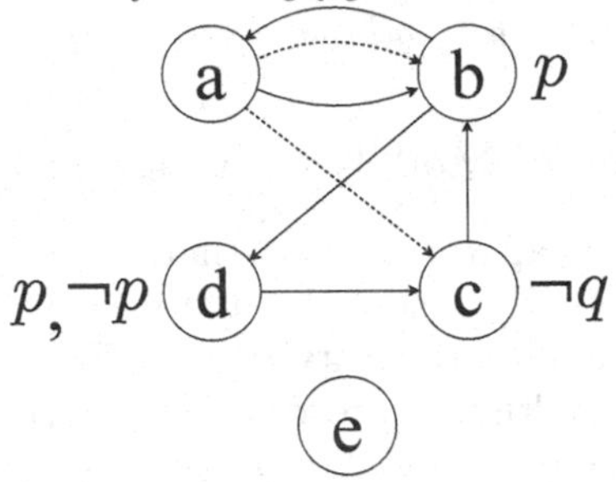

A full line indicates a transition and a dashed line indicates the lack of a transition.

This multistructure is represented by the following diagram:

$$\{@_{\mathrm{a}}\mathrm{a}, @_{\mathrm{b}}\mathrm{b}, @_{\mathrm{c}}\mathrm{c}, @_{\mathrm{d}}\mathrm{d}, @_{\mathrm{e}}\mathrm{e}, @_{\mathrm{b}}p, @_{\mathrm{c}}\neg q, @_{\mathrm{d}}p, @_{\mathrm{d}}\neg p, @_{\mathrm{a}}\Diamond \mathrm{b}, @_{\mathrm{a}}\neg\Diamond \mathrm{b}, @_{\mathrm{a}}\neg\Diamond \mathrm{c}, @_{\mathrm{b}}\Diamond \mathrm{a}, @_{\mathrm{b}}\Diamond \mathrm{d}, @_{\mathrm{c}}\Diamond \mathrm{b}, @_{\mathrm{d}}\Diamond \mathrm{c}\}$$

Recall that the definition of consequence relation says that a formula φ is a d*-consequence of a set of formulas Δ if and only if for all multistructures that are* d*-models of Δ, φ is* d*-satisfied. In this particular case, if we take the diagram of the map introduced to be our database Δ, the formula $@_{\mathrm{a}}\Diamond p$ is easily proved to be a* d*-consequence of it.*

If, however, one wants to check if a formula holds in *a particular multistructure, one should use as Δ not only its diagram – which talks about the* presence *of information – but also add all formulas that talk about the* absence *of information*[1]*, namely, if a formula $@_i p$, respectively $@_i\neg p$ and $@_i j$, is not part of the diagram, then the formula $(@_i p)^*$, respectively $(@_i\neg p)^*$ and $(@_i j)^*$, should be added to Δ; moreover, if a formula $@_i\langle\pi\rangle j$ or $@_i\neg\langle\pi\rangle j$ is not part of the diagram, then the formula $@_i[\pi]\neg j$, respectively $@_i\neg[\pi]\neg j$ should be added to Δ; lastly, for every nominal in the diagram $i_1,\ldots,i_n$, add the formula $i_1 \vee \ldots \vee i_n$. This construction is always feasible since the multistructures we are considering are finite.*

Following this algorithm, it is again easy (although it involves the addition of numerous formulas) to check that, even though $@_{\mathrm{a}}\neg\Diamond\neg q$ is not a consequence of the diagram of the map introduced, the formula holds true in *the map.*

In order to avoid unnecessary information when talking about a database, we introduce the notion of minimal model. Minimal models are those where each formula is absolutely necessary to keep it a *model*, according to the following definition:

Definition 13. *The set of minimal* d*-models with domain W for a set of hybrid formulas Δ is the set* $\mathrm{Min}\mathbb{D}(\Delta, W)$ *defined as:*

[1] Only for nominals, propositional variables and modalities already occurring in the diagram.

$$\text{Min}\mathbb{D}(\Delta, W) = \{\mathbb{M} \in \mathbb{D}(\Delta, W) \mid \textit{if } \overline{\mathbb{M}} \subset \mathbb{M} \textit{ then } \overline{\mathbb{M}} \notin \mathbb{D}(\Delta, W)\}.$$

Clearly, every d-model contains a minimal d-model, *i.e.*, for every d-model $\mathbb{M}_1$, there is a minimal d-model $\mathbb{M}_2$ such that $\mathbb{M}_2 \subseteq \mathbb{M}_1$; and if a variable $p \in \text{Prop}$ does not occur in Δ, then p does not occur in any minimal d-model.
No useful information is lost we use $\text{Min}\mathbb{D}(\Delta, W)$ instead of $\mathbb{D}(\Delta, W)$.

Given a set Δ of hybrid formulas, there is an algorithm that allows us to extract minimal d-models for Δ, each of them already represented by its dyadic diagram. The algorithm will resort to the tableau system introduced and comes as follows:

Algorithm 1. *In order to extract minimal* d*-models for* Δ *proceed as follows:*

1. *Build a terminal tableau whose root consists uniquely of all elements of* Δ *by applying the tableau rules of system* T_D*, where condition (iv) is restated as follows:*
(iv) for $@_i\varphi$ *a d-literal;*
together with the following extra rule:

$$\frac{@_i j,\ @_k\psi}{@_k(\psi[i/j])}(\text{Bridge}^\text{d})(i)$$

(i) $@_k\psi$ *is a dyadic literal;* $\psi[i/j]$ *means replace in* ψ *all occurrences of* i *with* j*.*

This extra rule is sound and ensures that we have indeed all d-literals that are d*-satisfied in our model.*
Consider only the open branches from now on.
2. *In order to determine minimal models with a certain number of worlds, combine nominals and/or add them in order to suit the number of worlds desired.*
3. *Apply the rules mentioned in step 1., treating the formulas introduced in step 2. as if they were root formulas, until a terminal tableau is reached.*
Repeat the instructions on step 2. about combining nominals in order to suit the number of worlds previously set.
Consider only the open branches.
4. *Finally, with the purpose of defining the positive and negative transitions between worlds, split each branch into subbranches such that each subbranch contains one way of combining the formulas* $@_i\langle\pi\rangle j$, $@_i[\pi]\neg j$ *and* $@_i\neg\langle\pi\rangle j$, $@_i\neg[\pi]\neg j$ *for all nominals* i *and* j *and modalities* π *occurring on the branch. Apply the rules indicated in step 1. until a terminal tableau is reached. Each new open branch defines the families of positive and negative accessibility relations* $(R^+_\pi)_{\pi\in\text{Mod}}$ *and* $(R^-_\pi)_{\pi\in\text{Mod}}$.
For each open branch copy the dyadic literals into a set which will be the dyadic diagram of a model for Δ*. Take the minimal models from among those.*

Proposition 2. *There are no minimal* d*-models for* Δ *other than those that are obtained from this algorithm.*

Proof. Suppose that $\mathbb{M}$ is the paraconsistent diagram of a multistructure $\mathcal{G}$ which is a minimal d-model for Δ and is such that $\mathbb{M} \not\subseteq \Theta$ for all open branches Θ, in the sense that for each branch Θ there exists a d-literal φ such that $\varphi \in \Theta$ and $\varphi \notin \mathbb{M}$.

Thus, for $\mathbb{M}$ under the conditions described, $\mathcal{G} \nVdash_{\mathrm{d}} \Theta$ for all Θ.

Recall that by the soundness theorem, for each rule $\dfrac{\Delta}{\Sigma_1|\ldots|\Sigma_n}$ and for any multistructure $\mathcal{G}$, $\mathcal{G} \Vdash_{\mathrm{d}} \Delta$ implies $\mathcal{G} \Vdash_{\mathrm{d}} \Sigma_1$ or $\ldots$ $\mathcal{G} \Vdash_{\mathrm{d}} \Sigma_n$. Therefore it follows that $\mathcal{G} \nVdash_{\mathrm{d}} \Delta$. So $\mathcal{G}$ is not a d-model for Δ, and therefore $\mathcal{G}$ cannot be a minimal d-model. Hence there is no such $\mathbb{M}$.

3 Conclusion

In this paper we introduced a new version of a paraconsistent and paracomplete hybrid logic which uses Belnap's logic as base: both propositional variables and accessibility relations are four-valued.

As opposed to other works combining paraconsistency with modal and hybrid logics at the level of accessibility relations, the version introduced does not take the usual modal operators $\langle\pi\rangle$ and $[\pi]$ as duals. The semantics presented is such that the hybrid multistructures can be described by a set of basic satisfaction statements.

This formal system seems to be useful to deal with graph-related problems, such as problems similar to that of the traveling salesman. We take the positive and negative accessibility relations and draw a map, where information about the presence and absence of a transition between places are explicitly depicted. By being given that map, the salesman should be able to choose a path that fulfills the requirements (in the form of a database) that he is given. A deeper study of applications of this logic is being made. Versions where the transitions are assigned weights is also a topic for further research.

Diana Costa acknowledges the support from the UK's Engineering and Physical Sciences Research Council - EPSRC (Grant number EP/R006865/1). Manuel A. Martins acknowledges the support from Fundação para a Ciência e a Tecnologia (FCT), within project UID/MAT/04106/2019 (CIDMA).

References

1. Arieli, O.: On the application of the disjunctive syllogism in paraconsistent logics based on four states of information. In: Proceedings of the Twelfth International Conference on Principles of Knowledge Representation and Reasoning, KR 2010, pp. 302–309. AAAI Press (2010)
2. Belnap, N.D.: A useful four-valued logic. In: Dunn, J.M., Epstein, G. (eds.) Modern Uses of Multiple-Valued Logic. D. Reidel (1977)
3. Besnard, P., Hunter, A.: Quasi-classical logic: non-trivializable classical reasoning from inconsistent information. In: Froidevaux, C., Kohlas, J. (eds.) ECSQARU 1995. LNCS, vol. 946, pp. 44–51. Springer, Heidelberg (1995). https://doi.org/10.1007/3-540-60112-0_6

4. Blackburn, P.: Representation, reasoning, and relational structures: a hybrid logic manifesto. Log. J. IGPL **8**(3), 339–365 (2000)
5. Braüner, T.: Axioms for classical, intuitionistic, and paraconsistent hybrid logic. J. Logic Lang. Inform. **15**(3), 179–194 (2006)
6. Braüner, T.: Hybrid Logic and its Proof-Theory. Springer, Dordrecht (2010). https://doi.org/10.1007/978-94-007-0002-4
7. Chechik, M., Devereux, B., Easterbrook, S., Gurfinkel, A.: Multi-valued symbolic model-checking. ACM Trans. Softw. Eng. Methodol. **12**(4), 371–408 (2003)
8. Costa, D., Martins, M.A.: Para consistency in hybrid logic. J. Log. Comput. **27**(6), 1825–1852 (2016)
9. Fitting, M.: Fixpoint semantics for logic programming a survey. Theor. Comput. Sci. **278**(1), 25–51 (2002). Mathematical Foundations of Programming Semantics 1996
10. Fitting, M.C.: Many-valued modal logics. Fundam. Inf. **15**(3–4), 235–254 (1991)
11. Hansen, J.U., Bolander, T., Braüner, T.: Many-valued hybrid logic. J. Log. Comput. **28**(5), 883–908 (2015)
12. Odintsov, S.P., Wansing, H.: Disentangling FDE-based paraconsistent modal logics. Stud. Logica **105**(6), 1221–1254 (2017)
13. Rivieccio, U., Jung, A., Jansana, R.: Four-valued modal logic: Kripke semantics and duality. J. Log. Comput. (2015)

Persuasive Argumentation and Epistemic Attitudes

Carlo Proietti[1,2] and Antonio Yuste-Ginel[3(✉)]

[1] Lund University, Lund, Sweden
[2] ILLC, University of Amsterdam, Amsterdam, The Netherlands
c.proietti@uva.nl
[3] University of Málaga, Málaga, Spain
antonioyusteginel@gmail.com

Abstract. This paper studies the relation between persuasive argumentation and the speaker's epistemic attitude. Dung-style abstract argumentation and dynamic epistemic logic provide the necessary tools to characterize the notion of persuasion. Within abstract argumentation, persuasive argumentation has been previously studied from a game-theoretic perspective. These approaches are blind to the fact that, in real-life situations, the epistemic attitude of the speaker determines which set of arguments will be disclosed by her in the context of a persuasive dialogue. This work is a first step to fill this gap. For this purpose we extend one of the logics of Schwarzentruber et al. with dynamic operators, designed to capture communicative phenomena. A complete axiomatization for the new logic via reduction axioms is provided. Within the new framework, a distinction between actual persuasion and persuasion from the speaker's perspective is made. Finally, we explore the relationship between the two notions.

Keywords: Argumentation frameworks · Dynamic Epistemic Logic · Persuasion and argument labellings

1 Introduction

Persuasion is probably the most relevant motivation of arguing and debating. Roughly defined, we could say that a piece of argumentation is persuasive whenever the speaker succeeds to align the hearer with her goal. Within the traditional divide of liberal arts of the trivium between *logic*, *grammar* and *rhetoric*, persuasive communication has been mostly the object of rhetoric (see [12]), with minor interest for its formal aspects. The main objective of this paper consists in studying persuasive argumentation using a well-known formal tool: abstract

The research activity of Antonio Yuste-Ginel is supported by MECD-FPU 2016/04113. Carlo Proietti gratefully acknowledges funding received from the European Commission (Marie Skłodowska-Curie Individual Fellowship 2016, 748421) and Sveriges Riksbanken (P16-0596:1) for his research.

L. Soares Barbosa and A. Baltag (Eds.): DaLí 2019, LNCS 12005, pp. 104–123, 2020.
https://doi.org/10.1007/978-3-030-38808-9_7

argumentation frameworks [10]. Abstract argumentation frameworks place ourselves in a dialectical perspective, where the strength of an argument is measured in terms of its relation to other arguments.[1] Besides, the notion of persuasion we are going to argue for can be read in dialectical terms too. Concretely, persuasion will be defined in terms of how the hearer assesses her arguments after the communication has taken place – and not in terms of her disposition to act in a certain way. For this purpose, we make use of the notion of *justification status* of an argument proposed by [24]. Hence, persuasion is going to be understood as a change in the hearer's justification status of a specific argument, the *issue* of the exchange, that fits the speaker communicative goal.

In addition to this dialectical flavour, our main conceptual contribution consists in taking into account the epistemic attitudes of the involved agents in order to provide a realistic notion of persuasive communication. An important antecedent in the study of persuasive communication from a formal perspective is [23], where dialogical logic is used to define different kinds of persuasive dialogues. Closer to our approach, previous works in abstract argumentation have investigated the question of persuasive argumentation from a game-theoretic point of view. Such approaches are mostly based on debate-game scenarios where the participants disclose arguments in turns, under the presupposition that they either know everything about the arguments available to their opponent [17] or that they don't consider them as relevant for their strategy [18]. These assumptions seem to be too strong when applied to real-life argumentative scenarios. First, communication does not necessarily unfolds as an exchange of single arguments in rigid turns. More importantly, it looks that it is precisely what the speaker thinks of the hearer's argumentative situation that makes her decide which arguments to disclose to persuade her. Indeed, there are cases in which, at an initial situation, the speaker can find a persuasive piece of argumentation but, due to her misinformation about the hearer, she ends up in a new situation in which the original goal of communication is not reachable any more.

Dynamic Epistemic Logic (DEL) is the mathematical study of informational changes [7], where information is understood in terms of the epistemic attitudes (knowledge and belief) of a set of agents. Previous works have studied relations between argumentation frameworks and epistemic logic [13,19–21]. For instance, [20,21] have focused on explaining the way that beliefs emerge from the set of arguments owned by an agent. Here, we introduce another problem: how the beliefs of the speaker determine the set of arguments that will be disclosed in the context of a discussion. For this aim, we propose a dynamic extension of one of the logics presented in [19], strongly related to the work of [2], that allows to reason about epistemic attitudes concerning the argumentative knowledge-base of other agents and about the effects of argumentative communication. In line with DEL, disclosure is encoded as a specific update of the model after an argument is announced. For our purposes we assume that the hearer is somehow "credulous": she will accept all the information that the speaker sends. As far

[1] See [14] for this notion of dialectics and [1] for its relation to argumentation frameworks.

as we know this is the first approach that combines tools imported both from AFs and DEL.[2] Its main contribution consists of a complete axiomatization of a dynamic logic of argumentative disclosure $\mathcal{L}^{!+}(A)$ and its doxastic/epistemic extensions.

The rest of this paper is organized as follows. Section 2.1 presents the preliminary concepts. In Sect. 2.2 we define communication within multi-agent frameworks and then introduce a notion of persuasion, understood as a change of the hearer's justification status of a given argument according to the speaker's goal. We also show how, in real-life situations, the information of the speaker about the hearer's information is crucial in order to perform persuasive argumentation. In Sect. 3 we extend one of the epistemic-argumentation logics of [19] with two dynamic modalities, meant to capture communicative phenomena. We provide a complete axiomatization for such extension via reduction axioms. In Sect. 4, we combine the AF tools with DEL to define the concept of epistemic-based persuasive arguments. We argue that this notion is more realistic than plain persuasion when applied to real-life argumentative scenarios. Finally, we discuss some relations between epistemic-based persuasion and plain persuasion. We close the paper by pointing out some future possible directions (Sect. 5).

2 Persuasive Communication

In this section we first recall the concepts that are needed for our notion of persuasion, namely, that of *argumentation framework*, its *multi-agent* version, *argument (complete) labelling* and *justification status*. Later on, we discuss how argumentative communication and persuasive argumentation can be modelled with the mentioned list of notions.

2.1 Preliminaries

Definition 1 (Argumentation Framework [10]**).** *An* argumentation framework *(AF, for short) is a pair* $(A, \rightsquigarrow)$ *where* $A \neq \emptyset$ *is a set of* arguments *and* $\rightsquigarrow \subseteq A \times A$ *is called the* attack *relation.*

For the purposes of this work we restrict our attention to *finite* AFs. Among others, AFs have been applied in several contexts to model multi-agent argumentative scenarios [4,16–19] where the agents' (partial) information is represented as a subgraph of a larger argumentative pool. Such scenarios are captured by the following definition.

Definition 2 (Multi-agent Argumentation Framework). *A* multi-agent argumentation framework *(MAF) for a non-empty and finite set of agents* Ag *is a triple* $(A, \rightsquigarrow, \{A_i\}_{i \in \mathsf{Ag}})$ *such that* $(A, \rightsquigarrow)$ *is an AF (called the* Universal Argumentation Framework *(UAF)) and* $A_i \subseteq A$*. Given a MAF and an agent* $i \in \mathsf{Ag}$*, agent* i*'s subgraph* *is defined as* $(A_i, \rightsquigarrow_i)$ *where* $\rightsquigarrow_i = \rightsquigarrow \cap (A_i \times A_i)$*.*

[2] Nevertheless, some papers [8,9] have combined tools from propositional dynamic logic and abstract argumentation. We will come back to them in the conclusions (Sect. 5).

Remark 1. Note that, given a MAF and an agent $i \in \mathsf{Ag}$, we have that $(A_i, \rightsquigarrow_i)$ is an AF. Note, also, that the way in which agents' subgraphs are defined amounts to assume, following [19], that agents share the same logical framework. That is to say, given two arguments $a, b \in A$, if the agent is aware of them, then she thinks that a attacks b if and only if it is actually the case that a attacks b. We add that this way of defining an agent's subgraph amounts also to assume that agents are somehow *ideal reasoners*: they cannot fail to see a conflict between arguments, e.g. an undercut or a rebuttal, where there is one.

In what follows, we restrict our attention to 2-agents AFs (2-AFs for short), i.e. we assume that $\mathsf{Ag} = \{1, 2\}$ and denote 2-AFs as $(A, \rightsquigarrow, A_1, A_2)$. Given a 2-AF, *a pointed 2-AF* is a tuple $(A, \rightsquigarrow, A_1, A_2, a)$ where $a \in A_1 \cap A_2$. In a pointed 2-AF $(A, \rightsquigarrow, A_1, A_2, a)$, the UAF $(A, \rightsquigarrow)$ is intended to represent all the relevant arguments about the issue a while each A_i is intended to represent the arguments that agent i is aware of.

The semantics of an AF $(A, \rightsquigarrow)$ is presented in terms of its *extensions* [10]. An extension of $(A, \rightsquigarrow)$ is a set of arguments $B \subseteq A$ that meets certain conditions to be an "acceptable" opinion. Typically, the minimal conditions for B are *conflict-freeness* (no $a, b \in B$ attack each other) and *defense* of its own arguments (for any c that attacks $b \in B$ there is some $b' \in B$ that attacks c). Any set that has these two properties is said to be *admissible*. Any admissible set that is equal to the set of arguments it defends is said to be *complete*. In [4,6] an alternative but equivalent approach to Dung's semantics is offered in terms of *labellings*. For our present purposes we only introduce the notion of a complete labelling,

Definition 3 ((Complete) Argument Labelling). *Let $(A, \rightsquigarrow)$ be an AF. An argument labelling is a total function $\mathcal{L} : A \to \{\mathsf{in}, \mathsf{out}, \mathsf{undec}\}$. Furthermore, a labelling $\mathcal{L}$ for $(A, \rightsquigarrow)$ is said to be* complete *iff for all $a \in A$ it holds that:*

- $\mathcal{L}(a) = \mathsf{in}$ *iff for all $c \in A$ s.t. $c \rightsquigarrow a$: $\mathcal{L}(c) = \mathsf{out}$*
- $\mathcal{L}(a) = \mathsf{out}$ *iff there is a $c \in A$ s.t $c \rightsquigarrow a$ and $\mathcal{L}(c) = \mathsf{in}$*

It is not difficult to show that, for any complete labelling, the set of arguments that are labelled in forms a complete extension and, viceversa, from any complete extension B we easily obtain a complete labelling where all and only the arguments in B are labelled in.

An AF $(A, \rightsquigarrow)$ may contain more than one complete extension. Based on this, [24] defines the justification status of an argument relative to an AF in terms of its membership to complete labellings.

Definition 4 (Justification Status). *Let $(A, \rightsquigarrow)$ be an AF and let $a \in A$. The* justification status *of a is the outcome yielded by the function $\mathcal{JS} : A \to \wp(\{\mathsf{in}, \mathsf{out}, \mathsf{undec}\})$ defined as:*

$$\mathcal{JS}(a) := \{\mathcal{L}(a) \mid \mathcal{L} \quad \textit{is a complete labelling of} \quad (A, \rightsquigarrow)\}$$

As noted in [24], two of the eight possible outcomes of $\mathcal{JS}$ are excluded. First, $\emptyset$ is never a possible outcome of $\mathcal{JS}$, since, as proved in [10], there is always at least a complete extension. Second, the value $\{\mathsf{in}, \mathsf{out}\}$ is also excluded from the range of $\mathcal{JS}$, since it can be proven that if $\mathsf{in}, \mathsf{out} \in \mathcal{JS}(a)$, then $\mathsf{undec} \in \mathcal{JS}(a)$. Let us denote by JS^* the set of the six possible justification status of an argument.

Notation. Let $(A, \rightsquigarrow, A_1, A_2, a)$ be a 2-AF, let $B \subseteq A$, we use $\mathcal{JS}^B(a)$ to refer to the justification status of a w.r.t. $(B, \rightsquigarrow \cap (B \times B))$. Note that $\mathcal{JS}^{A_i}(a)$ denotes the justification status of a for agent i. For the sake of readability, we always write $\mathcal{JS}_i(a)$ instead of $\mathcal{JS}^{A_i}(a)$.

The authors of [24] give the following names to the possible outcomes of $\mathcal{JS}$: $\{\mathsf{in}\}$ is called *strong accept*; $\{\mathsf{in}, \mathsf{undec}\}$ is called *weak accept*; $\{\mathsf{undec}\}$ is called *determined borderline*; $\{\mathsf{in}, \mathsf{out}, \mathsf{undec}\}$ is called *undetermined borderline*, $\{\mathsf{out}, \mathsf{undec}\}$ is called *weak reject* and $\{\mathsf{out}\}$ is called *strong reject*. The following total pre-order defines an acceptance hierarchy of an argument with respect to an AF:

$$\text{strong accept} > \text{weak accept} > \text{determined borderline} = \text{undetermined borderline} > \text{weak reject} > \text{strong reject}$$

2.2 Communication and Persuasion

For the sake of simplicity, we assume that 1 is the speaker (or sender), i.e., the one that is trying to persuade while 2 is the hearer (or receiver).

Definition 5 (Communication Step). *Given a pointed 2-AF $\mathcal{G} = (A, \rightsquigarrow, A_1, A_2, a)$ and set of arguments $B \subseteq A_1$, a* communication step *is a triple $(\mathcal{G}, B, \mathcal{G}^B)$ where $\mathcal{G}^B$ is called the* resulting pointed 2-AF *and it is defined as $\mathcal{G}^B := (A, \rightsquigarrow, A_1, A_2^B, a)$ where $A_2^B = A_2 \cup B$.*

Remark 2. First, agent 2 (the hearer) is assumed to always perform an *open update* [16], i.e., 2 always trusts 1 and incorporates all the received information into her subgraph. Second, the *disclosure policy* of 1 is left undecided, since our objective is to investigate how should 1 discloses her available information in order to persuade 2.

Note that $\mathcal{JS}^{A_i \cup B}(a)$ (see notation above) denotes the justification status of a for agent i after B has been communicated. For the sake of readability, we sometimes write $\mathcal{JS}_i^B(a)$ instead of $\mathcal{JS}^{A_i \cup B}(a)$. With these ingredients in mind, we are able to define persuasive sets of arguments as those that, after communicated, align the hearer's justification status with her intended goal.

Definition 6 (Persuasive Communication). *Let $(\mathcal{G}, B, \mathcal{G}^B)$ be a communication step and a let $\mathsf{goal} \in \mathsf{JS}^*$ be a goal of communication for the speaker. The set of arguments $B \subseteq A_1$ is said to be* persuasive *iff $\mathcal{JS}_2^B(a) = \mathsf{goal}$. Furthermore, a goal is said to be* achievable *through $B \subseteq A_1$ iff B is persuasive. In general, a goal is said to be achievable iff there is some B through which goal is achievable.*

Remark 3. Given a pointed 2-AF $(A, \rightsquigarrow, A_1, A_2, a)$ and a $\mathsf{goal} \in \mathsf{JS}^*$, we have that goal is achievable w.r.t. $(A, \rightsquigarrow, A_1, A_2, a)$ iff there is an $A'_2 \subseteq A$ such that: $A_2 \subseteq A'_2$, $A'_2 \setminus A_2 \subseteq A_1$ and $\mathcal{JS}^{A'_2}(a) = \mathsf{goal}$.

Note that persuasion is not always possible. In particular if $A_2 = A$ (2 has access to all relevant information) and $\mathsf{goal} \neq \mathcal{JS}_2(a)$ (the goal is not *trivial*), then we have that goal is not achievable: there is no $B \subseteq A_1$ s.t. $\mathcal{JS}_2^B(a) = \mathsf{goal}$. Besides, goal is not achievable when $\rightsquigarrow$ is well-founded in $(A, \rightsquigarrow, A_1, A_2, a)$ and goal is not $\{\mathsf{in}\}$ nor $\{\mathsf{out}\}$. As shown by [10], in such case there is only one complete extension (which is grounded, preferred and stable) in $(A, \rightsquigarrow)$ and in any of its possible subgraphs (since the relation $\rightsquigarrow$ is *a fortiori* well-founded there).

Our main objective can be reformulated now in more precise terms: given a pointed 2-AF $(A, \rightsquigarrow, A_1, A_2, a)$ and a $\mathsf{goal} \in \mathsf{JS}^*$, how can 1 select a persuasive set of arguments $B \subseteq A_1$? In order to define a persuasive disclosure policy for agent 1 (the speaker), we could adopt an external view and take into account all the relevant information (A, A_1 and A_2 together with $\rightsquigarrow$). If we adopt such a perspective, then a persuasive policy consists in selecting any set that produces persuasion. Nevertheless, this does not capture what agents do when they are actually trying to persuade another. In these cases, the speaker's information about the hearer's information is crucial to adopt a successful strategy. Let us make this point clear through the following example.

Example 1 (A bloody crime). A murder was committed in Amsterdam last night. The main suspect, called Mr. 1, is being interrogated by the famous detective Ms. 2. The suspect wants to persuade 2 that he is innocent (a), i.e., $\mathsf{goal} = \{\mathsf{in}\}$. Unfortunately for him, he was seen by several witnesses holding a bloody knife in his hands close to the crime scene (b). He does possess two potential alibis. First, 1 has a (well-known criminal) identical twin brother (c). Nevertheless, and unknown to Ms. 2, his twin brother was in Venice the night of the crime (f). Besides, 1 used to work in a butcher's nearby (d) but he was fired a week ago (e). Imagine that 2 owns e because she has done the proper interrogations before. Figure 1 represents a pointed 2-AF depicting the story. Note that $\mathcal{JS}_1(a) = \mathcal{JS}_2(a) = \{\mathsf{out}\}$ (both agents think that 1 is not innocent). Note also that 1 will succeed if he discloses c but he will fail if he discloses either d or $\{c, d\}$. Even more, if he discloses either d or $\{c, d\}$, then goal is not achievable in the resulting graph. This shows that 1's election is crucial in order to reach his goal (proving himself innocent). It also suggests that, within the art of persuasion, some mistakes turn out to be irreparable. In a real-life situation, 1 will chose between c and d according to his information about 2's information.

3 A Dynamic Epistemic Logic for Argumentation

A question arises naturally from Example 1: how could we represent 1's epistemic states (belief and knowledge) about 2's argumentative state? One simple way to do so, using tools imported from standard epistemic logic and awareness logic

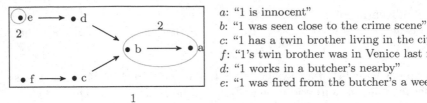

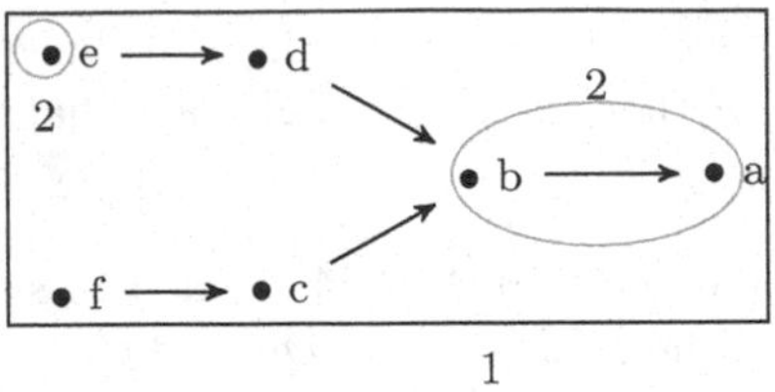

a: "1 is innocent"
b: "1 was seen close to the crime scene"
c: "1 has a twin brother living in the city"
f: "1's twin brother was in Venice last night"
d: "1 works in a butcher's nearby"
e: "1 was fired from the butcher's a week ago"

Fig. 1. A pointed 2-AF for Example 1.

[11], is offered in [19] under the name of $\mathcal{L}_1$. In order to avoid confusion, let us just simply call it $\mathcal{L}$. In this section, we first recall the syntax and semantics of $\mathcal{L}$. After that, we propose a dynamic extension of $\mathcal{L}$, named $\mathcal{L}^+$. $\mathcal{L}^+$ is designed to capture the notion of communication step (see Definition 5) within a DEL framework. We close the section by offering a complete axiomatization for the dynamic extension via reduction axioms.

3.1 Syntax and Semantics of $\mathcal{L}$

Given an AF $(A, \rightsquigarrow)$ and a finite set of agents Ag, the language $\mathcal{L}(A, \mathsf{Ag})$ is generated by the following Backus-Naur form (BNF, in what follows):

$$\varphi ::= \mathsf{owns}_i(a) \mid \neg\varphi \mid \varphi \wedge \varphi \mid \Box_i\varphi \qquad a \in A \quad i \in \mathsf{Ag}$$

$\mathsf{owns}_i(a)$ is intended to mean "i is aware of argument a" and $\Box_i\varphi$ is intended to mean "i believes (knows) that φ". In what follows, we assume that $\mathsf{Ag} = \{1, 2\}$ and restrict our attention to $\mathcal{L}(A)$.

Definition 7 (Model, Truth and Validity). *An* $\mathcal{L}(A)$-model *(or simply, a* model*) is a triple* $M = (W, \mathcal{R}, \mathcal{D})$ *where* $W \neq \emptyset$ *is a set of* possible worlds, $\mathcal{R} : \mathsf{Ag} \to \wp(W \times W)$ *assigns an* accessibility relation *to each agent, and* $\mathcal{D} : (\mathsf{Ag} \times W) \to \wp(A)$ *is an* awareness function, *intended to represent the set of arguments each agent is aware of at each world. For notational convenience, we abbreviate* $(w, v) \in \mathcal{R}(i)$ *as* $w\mathcal{R}_i v$ *and* $a \in \mathcal{D}(i, w)$ *as* $a \in \mathcal{D}_i(w)$. *Furthermore, we assume that for every* $i, j \in \mathsf{Ag}$ *and every* $w, u \in W$, *it holds that:*

1. *If* $w\mathcal{R}_i u$, *then* $\mathcal{D}_i(w) = \mathcal{D}_i(u)$
2. *If* $w\mathcal{R}_i u$, *then* $\mathcal{D}_j(u) \subseteq \mathcal{D}_i(w)$

Let us denote by $\mathcal{M}$ *the class of all models. Given a model* $M = (W, \mathcal{R}, \mathcal{D})$, *a pointed model is a pair* (M, w) *s.t.* $w \in W$. *Truth in pointed models is defined as usual for propositional connectives. We just make explicit the clauses for* owns_i *and* $\Box_i$*:*

$$M, w \models \mathsf{owns}_i(a) \textit{ iff } a \in \mathcal{D}_i(w)$$

$$M, w \models \Box_i\varphi \quad \textit{iff } M, w' \models \varphi \textit{ for all } w' \textit{ such that } w\mathcal{R}_i w'$$

A formula $\varphi \in \mathcal{L}(A)$ *is said to be* valid, *denoted by* $\models \varphi$, *iff it is true in all pointed models for* $\mathcal{L}(A)$.

Condition 1. means that awareness of arguments is fully introspective with respect to belief (knowledge). In other words, if an agent is aware of an argument, then she believes (knows) so and if she is not aware of an argument, then she believes (knows) so. Note that, if we assume that $\mathcal{R}_i$ is serial (which holds both for the standard notion of belief and knowledge), then Condition 1 also implies that $\models \Box_i \mathsf{owns}_i(a) \rightarrow \mathsf{owns}_i(a)$, i.e., if an agent believes (knows) that she is aware of an argument, then she is right. Condition 2, defined by the axiom $\neg\mathsf{owns}_i(a) \rightarrow \Box_i \neg\mathsf{owns}_j(a)$, captures the intuition according to which if an agent is not aware of an argument, then she thinks that no one else is aware of it.

Since we want to discuss both knowledge and belief, no restriction on $\mathcal{R}_i$ is imposed in Definition 7. Given an accessibility relation $\mathcal{R}_i$, we say that $\mathcal{R}_i$ is an *epistemic relation* iff it is a pre-order (reflexive and transitive) and we say that it is a *doxastic relation* iff it is serial, transitive and euclidean.

Let $((W, \mathcal{R}, \mathcal{D}), w)$ be a pointed model for $\mathcal{L}(A)$, we have that $(A, \rightsquigarrow, \mathcal{D}_1(w), \mathcal{D}_2(w))$ is a 2-AF (see Definition 2); let us call $(A, \rightsquigarrow, \mathcal{D}_1(w), \mathcal{D}_2(w))$ *the 2-AF induced by* (M, w). Furthermore, let $(A, \rightsquigarrow, \mathcal{D}_1(w), \mathcal{D}_2(w))$ be the 2-AF induced by (M, w), a *pointed 2-AF induced by* (M, w) is just a tuple $(A, \rightsquigarrow, \mathcal{D}_1(w), \mathcal{D}_2(w), a)$ s.t. $a \in \mathcal{D}_1(w) \cap \mathcal{D}_2(w)$. Note that a pointed model and one of its induced pointed 2-AFs represent both the argumentative situation of each agent with respect to a debate about a and their epistemic attitudes with respect to the other agent's argumentative situation. Analogously, let $\mathcal{G} = (A, \rightsquigarrow, A_1, A_2)$ be a 2-AF, *a pointed model for* $\mathcal{G}$ is a pointed model $((W, \mathcal{R}, \mathcal{D}), w)$ such that $A_1 = \mathcal{D}_1(w)$ and $A_2 = \mathcal{D}_2(w)$.

Proposition 1. *Let* $(A, \rightsquigarrow, A_1, A_2)$ *be a 2-AF. If* $A_i \nsubseteq A_j$, *then there does not exist any pointed model for* $(A, \rightsquigarrow, A_1, A_2)$ *s.t.* $\mathcal{R}_j$ *is reflexive.*

In other words, if j is not at least as well informed as i (in a strong sense of informedness [5]), then j cannot have any knowledge about $(A, \rightsquigarrow, A_1, A_2)$.

Example 2 (A bloody crime, revisited). Recall the story of Example 1 and the 2-AF shown in Fig. 1. A pointed model for it is shown in Fig. 2. Note that, since the relation $\rightsquigarrow$ is the same in every possible world, we can dispense with its representation. Nevertheless, awareness sets do change from world to world, so they must be included in the figure. Note that both $\mathcal{R}_1$ and $\mathcal{R}_2$ are doxastic relations. It is also simple to see that $M, w_0 \models \Box_1(\neg\mathsf{owns}_2(e)) \wedge \mathsf{owns}_2(e)$ (1 believes (wrongly) that 2 is not aware of e (the counter-argument to one of 1's alibis).

3.2 A Dynamic Extension of $\mathcal{L}$

Communication steps (see Definition 5) can be now represented in DEL style, as model transformers.

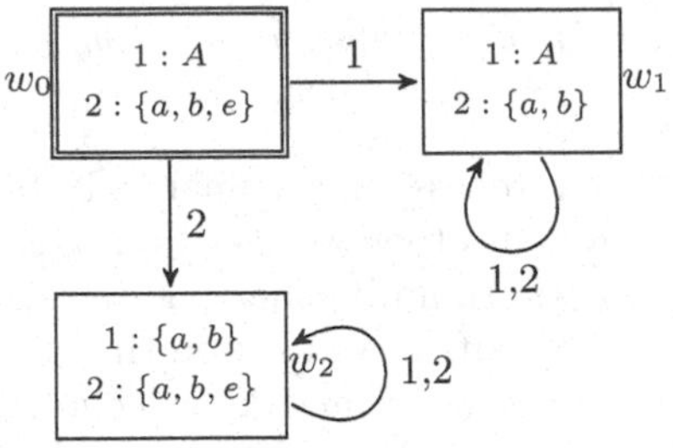

Fig. 2. Pointed model for the 2-AF of Fig. 1.

Definition 8 (Communication Model). *Given a pointed model* $(M, w) = ((W, \mathcal{R}, \mathcal{D}), w)$ *for* $\mathcal{L}(A)$*, the* communication pointed model $(M, w)^{+b} := ((W, \mathcal{R}, \mathcal{D}^{+b}), w)$ *shares domain, accessibility relations and distinguished world with* (M, w)*. The only difference is in the awareness function* $\mathcal{D}^{+b} : (\mathsf{Ag} \times W) \to \wp(A)$*, defined by cases for each* $i \in \mathsf{Ag}$ *and each* $v \in W$ *as follows:*

$$\begin{array}{ll} \mathcal{D}_i(v) \cup \{b\} & \text{if } b \in \mathcal{D}_1(w) \\ \mathcal{D}_i(v) & \text{otherwise} \end{array}$$

For notational convenience, we sometimes abbreviate $(M, w)^{+b}$ as M^{+b}, w.

Remark 4 ($(\cdot)^{+b}$ is a local update). This way of defining the updated model is somehow non-standard. Note that the function $(\cdot)^{+b}$ goes from *pointed models* to *pointed models*; and not from *models* to *models*, as it is the case in public announcement logics and logics with substitution operators [15,22]. Informally, the effect of an action changes if we move from one world to another, i.e., the precondition of the action is *local.*

Example 3 (Communication Models). Figure 3 extends the model of Fig. 2 and it shows the effects of the action $(\cdot)^{+d}$ when it is applied to different pointed models. Note that $(M, w_0)^{+d} \neq (M, w_0)$ but $(M, w_2)^{+d} = (M, w_2)$. Since the precondition of the action holds in w_0 ($d \in \mathcal{D}_1(w_0)$), we have that in the communication model $(M, w_0)^{+d}$ argument d has been added to the awareness sets of both agents in every world. However, if the action takes places in (M, w_2), where the precondition does not hold ($a \notin \mathcal{D}_1(w_2)$) the action $(\cdot)^{+d}$ has no effects.

We can easily go from the disclosure of single arguments to the disclosure of sets of arguments: given $B = \{b_1, ..., b_n\} \subseteq A$, define $(M, w)^{+B}$ as $(M, w)^{+b_1^{\cdot^{\cdot^{\cdot^{+b_n}}}}}$. In order to talk about the action $(\cdot)^{+a}$, we need to enrich the language with a dynamic modality. Define $\mathcal{L}^{+}(A)$ as the language generated by the following BNF:

$$\varphi ::= \mathsf{owns}_i(a) \mid \neg\varphi \mid \varphi \wedge \varphi \mid \Box_i \varphi \mid [+a]\varphi \qquad a \in A \quad i \in \mathsf{Ag}$$

For any $B = \{b_1, ..., b_n\} \subseteq A$, we define the shorthand $[+B]\varphi := [+b_1]...[+b_n]\varphi$. The notion of truth is extended to the new class of formulas as expected:

$$M, w \models [+b]\varphi \quad \text{ iff } \quad M^{+b}, w \models \varphi$$

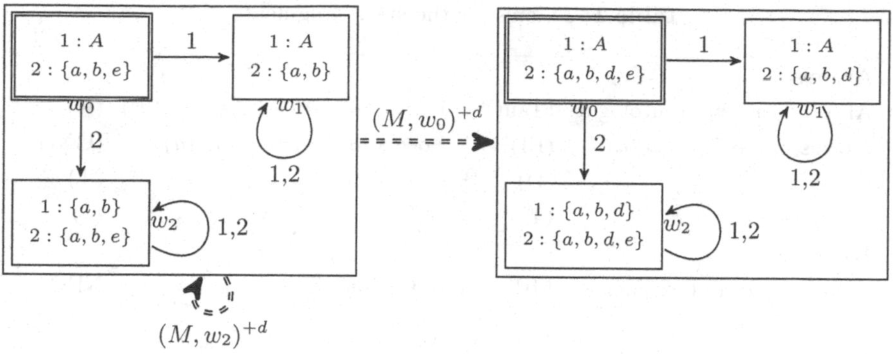

Fig. 3. Communication model

Remark 5. Definition 8 is enough to capture at least three of our intuitions. First, $M, w \vDash \mathsf{owns}_1(b)$ works as a precondition for the action to have any effect; intuitively, the speaker needs to be aware of what she communicates. Second, if $M, w \vDash \mathsf{owns}_1(b)$, then $M^{+b}, w \vDash \mathsf{owns}_2(b)$; i.e., if the precondition holds, then the hearer gets the communicated argument. Third, if $M, w \vDash \mathsf{owns}_1(b)$, then $M^{+b}, w \vDash \Box^k_{\mathsf{Ag}}(\mathsf{owns}_1(b) \wedge \mathsf{owns}_2(b))$ and any $k \in \mathbb{N}$; i.e. if the precondition holds, then the awareness of the communicated argument by both agents becomes common belief (knowledge). Note, however, that the communication model must be refined if we count with more than two agents and we want to model cases of private communication (for instance, by removing $\mathcal{R}$-arrows just for the speaker and the hearer).

3.3 Completeness

We provide an axiomatization for $\mathcal{L}^+(A)$. All systems are extensions of K, consisting of axioms $(Taut)$ and (K), and are closed under both inference rules (Table 1).

- A extends K with axioms (PI) and (GNI).[3]
- BA extends A with axioms (D), (4) and (5).
- KA extends A with axioms (T) and (4).

Besides, we denote by $\mathcal{M}^{\mathcal{K}}$ (resp. $\mathcal{M}^{\mathcal{B}}$) the class of all models where every $\mathcal{R}_i$ is an epistemic (resp. a doxastic) relation.

Theorem 1 (Soundness and Completeness for the Static Fragments). *The proof system* A *(respectively* AK*,* AB*) is sound and complete w.r.t the class of all models (resp. w.r.t.* $\mathcal{M}^{\mathcal{K}}$*,* $\mathcal{M}^{\mathcal{B}}$*).*

Proving soundness of all the mentioned systems is straightforward. Completeness proofs can be found in the Appendix.

[3] PI stands for *positive introspection* and GNI for *generalized negative introspection.* The latter captures standard negative introspection as a special case where the indexes i and j are the same.

Table 1. Axioms for the static fragments

Axioms			
All propositional tautologies	(Taut)	$\vdash \Box_i(\varphi \to \psi) \to (\Box_i\varphi \to \Box_i\psi)$	(K)
$\vdash \mathsf{owns}_i(a) \to \Box_i \mathsf{owns}_i(a)$	(PI)	$\vdash \neg\mathsf{owns}_i(a) \to \Box_i \neg\mathsf{owns}_j(a)$	(GNI)
$\vdash \neg\Box_i \bot$	(D)	$\vdash \Box_i\varphi \to \varphi$	(T)
$\vdash \Box_i\varphi \to \Box_i\Box_i\varphi$	(4)	$\vdash \neg\Box_i\varphi \to \Box_i\neg\Box_i\varphi$	(5)
Rules			
From $\varphi \to \psi$ and φ, infer ψ	MP	From φ infer $\Box_i\varphi$	NEC

Reduction Axioms for $[+a]$. Using Theorem 1, we obtain completeness results for the dynamic extensions (with $[+a]$ and its semantics) for all the three static logics (A, AK and AB). This is done by providing a set of reduction axioms for $[+a]$. Reduction axioms are valid formulas of the form $[a+]\varphi \leftrightarrow \psi$ s.t. the dynamic operator is "pushed inside" in the formula on the left side of the equivalence. A full set of reduction axioms plus the rule of substitution of equivalents enable us to find a provably equivalent formula in the static logic for every formula in the dynamic logic. The reader is referred to the Appendix and to [7,15] for further details.

In order to find the full set of reduction axioms for our new modality $[+a]$, we take a small detour. First, we show that $[+a]$ is definable in terms of another dynamic modality $[a!]$ (the *public announcement of argument* modality). Then, we offer the full set of reduction axioms for $[a!]$. We start by defining the new language. Given an AF $(A, \rightsquigarrow)$ and $\mathsf{Ag} = \{1, 2\}$, the language $\mathcal{L}^{!+}(A)$ is generated by the following BNF:

$$\varphi ::= \mathsf{owns}_i(a) \mid \neg\varphi \mid \varphi \wedge \varphi \mid [a!]\varphi \mid [+a]\varphi \qquad a \in A \quad i \in \mathsf{Ag}$$

The language $\mathcal{L}^{!}(A)$ is the result of removing the $[+a]\varphi$-clause.

Definition 9 (Announcement Model). *Given a model for* $\mathcal{L}(A)$, $M = (W, \mathcal{R}, \mathcal{D})$ *and an argument* $a \in A$, *let us define the* announcement model *as* $M^{a!} = (W, \mathcal{R}, \mathcal{D}^{a!})$ *that shares domain and accessibility relations with* M *and only varies in the awareness function, defined for every* $i \in \mathsf{Ag}$ *and every* $w \in W$ *as* $\mathcal{D}_i^{a!}(w) = \mathcal{D}_i(w) \cup \{a\}$.[4]

Remark 6. Note that both operations, $(\cdot)^{a+}$ and $(\cdot)^{a!}$, always return a model inside the same class (no matter if we pick up an arbitrary one from $\mathcal{M}$, $\mathcal{M}^{\mathcal{K}}$ or $\mathcal{M}^{\mathcal{B}}$). Since none of the operations alters the accessibility relation, we just have to check that Conditions 1 and 2 from Definition 7 are satisfied by any output of $(\cdot)^{a!}$ and $(\cdot)^{a+}$. Details are left to the reader.

[4] The operation $(\cdot)^{a!}$ can be understood as a special case of public substitution [15,22]. From the perspective of dynamic awareness logic [2], the same action can be understood in terms of the *consider* action, with the only difference that here arguments (and not formulas) are the content of announcements. A detailed comparison between the three operations is out of the scope of this paper.

Remark 6 assures that both $\mathcal{L}^{!+}$ and $\mathcal{L}^{!}$ are interpreted on the same class of models as $\mathcal{L}$. Now, the truth clauses for the remaining formulas are as before. As for $[a!]\varphi$, we add the following clause to the definition of truth:

$$M, w \models [a!]\varphi \quad \text{iff} \quad M^{a!}, w \models \varphi$$

Table 2 shows the full list of reduction axioms for $[+a]$ and $[a!]$.[5] The following proposition is crucial to obtain soundness and completeness for the dynamic extensions of the logics mentioned so far.

Proposition 2. *Schemata shown in Table 2 are valid and the rule SE preserves validity.*

We consider the axiom system $\mathsf{A}^{!+}$ (resp. $\mathsf{AK}^{!+}$ and $\mathsf{AB}^{!+}$) that extends A (resp. AK, AB) with the axioms and rule of Table 2.

Theorem 2 (Soundness and Completeness of $\mathcal{L}^{+!}$). *The axiom system $\mathsf{A}^{!+}$ (resp. $\mathsf{AK}^{!+}$ and $\mathsf{AB}^{!+}$) is sound and complete w.r.t. the class of models $\mathcal{M}$ (resp. $\mathcal{M}^{\mathcal{K}}$ and $\mathcal{M}^{\mathcal{B}}$).*

Table 2. Reduction axioms for $\mathcal{L}^{+!}(A)$

$\vdash [+a]\varphi \leftrightarrow (\mathsf{owns}_1(a) \rightarrow [a!]\varphi) \wedge (\neg\mathsf{owns}_1(a) \rightarrow \varphi)$	(Def+)
$\vdash [a!]\mathsf{owns}_i(a) \leftrightarrow \top$	(Atoms$^{=}$)
$\vdash [a!]\mathsf{owns}_i(b) \leftrightarrow \mathsf{owns}_i(b)$ where $a \neq b$	(Atoms$^{\neq}$)
$\vdash [a!]\neg\varphi \leftrightarrow \neg[a!]\varphi$	(Negation)
$\vdash [a!](\varphi \wedge \psi) \leftrightarrow ([a!]\varphi \wedge [a!]\psi)$	(Conjunction)
$\vdash [a!]\Box_i\varphi \leftrightarrow \Box_i[a!]\varphi$	(Box)
From $\varphi \leftrightarrow \psi$, infer $\delta \leftrightarrow \delta[\varphi/\psi]$	SE

4 Epistemic-Based Persuasive Arguments

In this section we combine the tools of Sect. 2 (AFs) and Sect. 3 (DEL) in order to define a notion of *persuasive argument based on the perspective of the speaker.* For this we need to take into account the speaker's epistemic situation. As our previous analysis suggests, "being persuasive from the speaker's perspective" does not guarantees actual persuasiveness (Definition 6), which heavily relies on external conditions. However, it is possible to provide sufficient conditions for the former to imply the latter. In other words, it is possible to isolate some epistemic conditions that are "safe" for the speaker, they guarantee that the communication is going to be persuasive. Let us first define persuasiveness from the speaker's perspective.

[5] In Table 2 $\delta[\varphi/\psi]$ is the result of substituting one or more occurrences of ψ in δ by φ.

Definition 10 (Epistemic-Based Persuasive Arguments). *Let (M, w) be a pointed model, let $(A, \rightsquigarrow, \mathcal{D}_1(w), \mathcal{D}_2(w), a)$ be a pointed 2-AF induced by (M, w) and let* $\mathsf{goal} \in \mathsf{JS}^*$ *be a goal of communication, we say that a set $B \subseteq \mathcal{D}_1(w)$ is* persuasive from 1's perspective *iff $\mathcal{JS}^{\mathcal{D}_2^{+B}(w')}(a) = \mathsf{goal}$ for all $w' \in W$ s.t. $w\mathcal{R}_1 w'$.*

Informally, a set of arguments is persuasive from the speaker's perspective iff it is persuasive in all her accessible AFs. An epistemic-based disclosure policy is just one that selects any set of arguments known (believed) to be persuasive by the speaker.

Definition 10 makes strong use of the notion of justification status. Consequently, epistemic-based persuasive sets cannot be described using $\mathcal{L}^+$. However, and due to the fact that we are working with finite AFs, we can get closer to this objective and express the "all accessible AFs" part of the definition. First, let us define the following shorthand in $\mathcal{L}(A)$:

$$\mathsf{2graph}(C) := \bigwedge_{a \in C} \mathsf{owns}_2(a) \wedge \bigwedge_{b \notin C} \neg \mathsf{owns}_2(b) \quad \text{for any} \quad C \subseteq A$$

The intuitive reading of 2graph is "C is 2's subgraph" and, indeed, it holds that $M, w \models \mathsf{2graph}(C)$ iff $C = \mathcal{D}_2(w)$. Again, since A is finite, we can fix an enumeration of its subsets $\wp(A) = \{A_1, ..., A_n\}$. With these two tools in mind, we can obtain:

Proposition 3. *Given a pointed model (M, w) for $\mathcal{L}(A)$, and a* $\mathsf{goal} \in \mathsf{JS}^*$ *we have that $B \subseteq A$ is persuasive from the speaker perspective iff there is an enumeration of the subsets of A, $\{A_1, ..., A_n\} = \wp(A)$ and an index m (with $1 \leq m \leq n$) s.t.:*

$$M, w \models \Box_1 [+B] \Big(\bigvee_{1 \leq i \leq m} \mathsf{2graph}(C_i) \bigwedge_{m < i \leq n} \neg \mathsf{2graph}(C_i) \Big)$$

and $\mathcal{JS}^{C_i}(a) = \mathsf{goal}$ for every $1 \leq i \leq m$.

It is immediate to show that if $\Box_1$ is not a factive attitude ($\mathcal{R}_1$ is not reflexive) then not any set that is persuasive from 1's perspective is ensured to be actually persuasive. More importantly, when the speaker lacks of knowledge about the hearer argumentative situation, she runs the risk of committing irreparable mistakes, as shown in the following example:

Example 4 (Wrong belief and persuasion). Recall the communication model depicted in Fig. 3. Let us assume that w_0 is the real world and recall that $\mathsf{goal} = \{\mathsf{in}\}$. Note that the set $\{d\}$ (the butcher's alibi) is persuasive from 1's perspective. Note, however, how she is wrong since we have that $\mathcal{JS}^{\mathcal{D}_2^{+d}(w_0)}(a) = \{\mathsf{out}\}$ (because 2 owns the counter-argument e). Even more, it can be easily shown that $\mathsf{goal} = \{\mathsf{in}\}$ is not achievable w.r.t. $(A, \mathcal{D}_1^{+d}(w_0), \mathcal{D}_2^{+d}(w_0), \rightsquigarrow)$, i.e. if 1 discloses d, he will not longer be able to persuade 2 of his innocence.

Remark 7 (Fully specific knowledge (belief) and epistemic-based persuasive sets). Note that $M, w \vDash \Box_1[+B]\mathsf{2graph}(C)$ can be read has "1 has fully specific knowledge (belief) about the effects of communicating B", i.e., the speaker is sure about what the hearer's subgraph will be after the communication. Note, also, that $M, w \vDash \Box_1[+B]\mathsf{2graph}(C)$ and $\mathcal{JS}^C(a) = \mathsf{goal}$ is a sufficient but not necessary condition for B to be persuasive from the speaker perspective in (M, w).

On the other side, it is immediate to show that if $\mathcal{R}_1$ is reflexive ($\Box_1$ is a factive attitude) then any set that is persuasive from 1's perspective is actually persuasive. However, factivity of $\Box_1$ is not a necessary condition for this. The next proposition shows that it is sufficient for the speaker to have a "good enough" belief in order to guarantee persuasion:

Proposition 4. *Given a pointed model (M, w) for $\mathcal{L}(A)$, let $B \subseteq A$ be persuasive from the speaker's perspective. Let A_i be the set of all a_i such that $M, w \vDash \mathsf{owns}_2(a_i) \land \neg\Box_1\mathsf{owns}_2(a_i)$. If $A_i \not\rightsquigarrow \mathcal{D}_2^{+B}(w) \setminus A_i$ then B is persuasive.*[6]

In other words, if the arguments 2 is aware of unbeknownst to 1 (e.g. e in our example) are such that they don't conflict with the set of arguments 2 is expected by 1 to have after communicating B, then the communication turns out to be persuasive. This is a consequence of the fact that the justification status of an argument a only depends on the *upstream* of a [24].

5 Closing Words and Future Work

Summing up, we defined persuasion based on the notion of *justification status* of an argument [24]. We then provided a dynamic extension for the logic $\mathcal{L}_1$ of [19] in order to capture the communicative aspects of persuasive argumentation. Furthermore, we have shown that the new logic is axiomatizable via reduction axioms. Using this logic, we distinguished persuasive arguments from epistemic-based persuasive arguments. We argued that the second notion is more realistic to model real-life argumentative scenarios. Finally, we discussed some of the epistemic conditions for a set of arguments to be actually persuasive.

There are several open branches for future work; let us just mention two of them. First, one of the main assumptions of our framework is that hearers always perform an *open update* [16], i.e., they incorporate whatever the speaker says into their AFs. Nevertheless, this is not the case in many situations, where the hearer might suspect that the speaker is acting dishonestly and, consequently, she might revise her AFs more prudently. Second, we recall that neither the notion of persuasion nor its epistemic-based counterpart are definable in the proposed logic. Augmenting the expressive power of the logic –using, for instance, similar techniques to those employed in [8,9]– in order to fully reason about persuasive argumentation inside the language looks a promising step for future work. Among

[6] Given an AF $(A, \rightsquigarrow)$ and two sets of arguments $B, C \subseteq A$, the attack relation is lifted from single arguments to sets of arguments as follows: $B \rightsquigarrow C$ iff $\exists b \in B, \exists c \in C(b \rightsquigarrow c)$.

other things, it might allow us to isolate not only sufficient epistemic conditions for a set of argument to be persuasive but also necessary ones.

Appendix: Notes and Proofs

Notes

Note 1. As mentioned, we have assumed that 1 is always the speaker while 2 is the hearer. Nevertheless, this logical setting can be easily generalized in order to model argumentative dialogues (where the role speaker/hearer changes in turns). Definition 8 should be extended to obtain a different operation $(\cdot)^a_i$ for each $i \in \mathsf{Ag}$ where the precondition is, consequently, $a \in \mathsf{owns}_i(w)$. Furthermore, the language must also be extended with the clause $[+_i a]\varphi$ for each $a \in A$, $i \in \mathsf{Ag}$. The completeness result presented below can be easily extended for such generalization.

Note 2 ($(\cdot)^{+b}$ as a global update). An alternative way of understanding the action $(\cdot)^{+b}$ (see Definition 7) such that the update becomes world-independent, i.e. $(\cdot)^{+b}$ goes from models to models, works as follows. First note that we still need a suitable notion of *actual world* so that we can express the precondition according to which the speaker has to be aware of b *in the actual world* for $(\cdot)^{+b}$ to have any effect. Hence, our former notion of *pointed model* is now simply called a *model*, i.e., a model is a tuple $M = (W, w, \mathcal{R}, \mathcal{D})$. A *pointed model* is now a pair $((W, w, \mathcal{R}, \mathcal{D}), v)$ where $v \in W$. Here w represents the actual world. The definition of $(\cdot)^{+b}$ stays the same (see Definition 8), but note that now the function $(\cdot)^{+b}$ goes from models to models. Finally, the notion of truth is redefined in *pointed models* as usual for the rest of the operators and it is the following one for $[+b]$:

$$(W, w, \mathcal{R}, \mathcal{D}), v \models [+b]\varphi \quad \text{iff} \quad (W, w, \mathcal{R}, \mathcal{D})^{+b}, v \models \varphi$$

Proofs

All the proofs follow standard methods. We just include some of them here for illustration.

Proposition 1

Proof. Let $\mathcal{G} = (A, \rightsquigarrow, A_i, A_j)$ be a 2-AF model, let (M, w) be a pointed model for $\mathcal{G}$, i.e., $A_i = \mathcal{D}_i(w)$ and $A_j = \mathcal{D}_j(w)$. Suppose, for the sake of contradiction, that $A_i \nsubseteq A_j$ but $\mathcal{R}_j$ is reflexive. We have that there is an argument $a \in A$ s.t. $a \in A_i$ but $a \notin A_j$ or equivalently $a \in \mathcal{D}_i(w)$ but $a \notin \mathcal{D}_j(w)$. But since $\mathcal{R}_j$ is reflexive, we know that $w\mathcal{R}_j w$. The last two assertions contradict Condition 2 of Definition 7.

Completeness of the Static Logics. Definition of deduction from assumptions ($\Gamma \vdash_* \varphi$), consistent set ($\Gamma \nvdash_* \bot$) (where $* \in \{\mathsf{A}, \mathsf{AK}, \mathsf{AB}\}$) and maximal consistency are standard [3]. Let us denote by $\mathfrak{MC}^*$ the class of all maximal consistent sets in $* \in \{\mathsf{A}, \mathsf{AK}, \mathsf{AB}\}$. When the context is clear or irrelevant, we just write $\mathfrak{MC}$.
For the proof of the next two claims, the reader is referred to [3] (p. 199).

Proposition 5 (Properties of MC-sets). *Let $\Gamma \in \mathfrak{MC}$:*

- *For every $\varphi \in \mathcal{L}(A)$: $\varphi \in \Gamma$ or $\neg\varphi \in \Gamma$*
- *If $\Gamma \vdash \varphi$, then $\varphi \in \Gamma$*

Lemma 1 (Lindenbaum). *Let $\Gamma \subseteq \mathcal{L}(A)$, if $\Gamma \nvdash \bot$, then there is a $\Gamma' \in \mathfrak{MC}$ s.t. $\Gamma \subseteq \Gamma'$.*

Definition 11 (Canonical Model). *Given a language $\mathcal{L}(A)$, define the canonical model $M^c = (W^c, \mathcal{R}^c, \mathcal{D}^c)$ as:*

$$W^c := \{\Gamma \subseteq \mathcal{L}(A) \mid \Gamma \in \mathfrak{MC}\}$$
$$\Gamma \mathcal{R}^c_i \Delta \quad \textit{iff} \quad \{\varphi \in \mathcal{L}(A) \mid \Box_i \varphi \in \Gamma\} \subseteq \Delta$$
$$a \in \mathcal{D}^c_i(\Gamma) \quad \textit{iff} \quad \mathsf{owns}_i(a) \in \Gamma$$

Lemma 2 (Canonicity). *Given $\mathcal{L}(A)$, its canonical model M^c is a model.*

Proof. All we need to show is that conditions 1 and 2 of Definition 7 are satisfied by M^c. For Condition 1, let us suppose that $\Gamma \mathcal{R}^c_i \Delta$ (*). Suppose that $a \in \mathcal{D}^c_i(\Gamma)$, by definition this is equivalent to $\mathsf{owns}_i(a) \in \Gamma$. From this we obtain $\Gamma \vdash \mathsf{owns}_i(a)$ and note that, by monotonicity of $\vdash$ and Ax (PI) we have that $\Gamma \vdash \mathsf{owns}_i(a) \rightarrow \Box_i \mathsf{owns}_i(a)$. Applying modus ponens we get $\Gamma \vdash \Box_i \mathsf{owns}_i(a)$. By Lemma 5 we have that $\Box_i \mathsf{owns}_i(a) \in \Gamma$. This, together with (*) and the definition of $\mathcal{R}^c_i$ implies $\mathsf{owns}_i(a) \in \Delta$ which is equivalent by definition of $\mathcal{D}^c$ to $a \in \mathcal{D}^c_i(\Delta)$. We have proven the left to right inclusion, for the right to left, the proof is analogous to Condition 2, where (GNI) is applied with $i = j$.
As for Condition 2, suppose $\Gamma \mathcal{R}^c_i \Delta$ (*). Suppose $a \in \mathcal{D}^c_j(\Delta)$. The latter is equivalent by definition to $\mathsf{owns}_j(a) \in \Delta$, which implies $\Delta \vdash \mathsf{owns}_j(a)$. Now, suppose, reasoning by contradiction, that $a \notin \mathcal{D}^c_i(\Gamma)$. This is equivalent by definition to $\mathsf{owns}_i(a) \notin \Gamma$. By Proposition 5 we have that $\neg\mathsf{owns}_i(a) \in \Gamma$ which implies $\Gamma \vdash \neg\mathsf{owns}_i(a)$. Using axiom (GNI) and MP we have that $\Gamma \vdash \Box_i \neg\mathsf{owns}_j(a)$. This, together with (*) and the definition of $\mathcal{R}^c$, implies $\neg\mathsf{owns}_j(a) \in \Delta$ and hence $\Delta \vdash \neg\mathsf{owns}_j(a)$ that contradicts the consistency of Δ. Therefore, $a \in \mathcal{D}^c_i(\Gamma)$.

Lemma 3 (Existence Lemma). *If $\Diamond_i \varphi \in \Gamma$, then there is a $\Delta \in W^c$ s.t. $\Gamma \mathcal{R}^c_i \Delta$ and $\varphi \in \Delta$.*

Since $\Box_i$ is a normal modal operator, the proof is completely standard. The reader is referred to [3] (pp. 200–201).

Lemma 4 (Truth Lemma). *For each $\Gamma \in W^c$ and and each $\varphi \in \mathcal{L}(A)$:*

$$\varphi \in \Gamma \quad \textit{iff} \quad M^c, \Gamma \models \varphi$$

Proof. The proof is by induction on the construction of φ (see [3] Chap. 4).

Finally Theorem 1 follows from the Truth Lemma by the typical argument.

Completeness for the Dynamic Extensions. For the completeness of $\mathsf{A}^{!+}$, $\mathsf{AK}^{!+}$ and $\mathsf{AB}^{!+}$, we apply the general method described in [15]. Let us show some of the details.

Proposition 2

Proof. Proving that SE preserves validity can be done by induction of the construction on φ. The proof is simple but long, so we leave it for the reader. Note that in standard awareness logic [11], this is not generally the case, since awareness sets do not need to be closed under logical equivalence. In $\mathcal{L}$, however, the range of awareness operators is restricted to arguments, and therefore soundness of SE is guaranteed.
As for the validity of the reduction axioms, let us just show two cases. Let (M, w) be a pointed model:

- $\models [+a]\varphi \leftrightarrow (\mathsf{owns}_1(a) \rightarrow [a!]\varphi) \wedge (\neg\mathsf{owns}_1(a) \rightarrow \varphi)$
  "$\rightarrow$". Suppose $M, w \models [+a]\varphi$. This is true iff $M^{+a}, w \models \varphi$. Let us reason by cases. If $a \notin \mathcal{D}_1(w)$, then the first conjunct is trivially true. For the second conjunct, note that if $a \notin \mathcal{D}_1(w)$, then $M^{+a}, w = M, w$. We can then substitute M^{+a}, w by M, w and obtain $M, w \models \varphi$ which implies $M, w \models \neg\mathsf{owns}_1(a) \rightarrow \varphi$. Now, if $a \in \mathcal{D}_1(a)$ then the second conjunct is trivially true. For the first conjunct we have that if $a \in \mathcal{D}_1(a)$, then $M^{+a}, w = M^{a!}, w$. By substituting equals in the hypothesis we obtain $M^{a!}, w \models \varphi$ which is equivalent by the semantic definition of $[a!]$ to $M, w \models [a!]\varphi$.
  "$\leftarrow$". This direction is analogous, each of the cases ($a \in \mathcal{D}_1(w)$ and $a \notin \mathcal{D}_1(w)$) makes one of the conjuncts trivially true and allows us to obtain the true consequent of the other. With that information is easy to deduce $M, w \models [+a]\varphi$.
- $\models [a!]\Box_i\varphi \leftrightarrow \Box_i[a!]\varphi$
  Suppose $M, w \models [a!]\Box_i\varphi$. This is true iff $M^{a!}, w \models \Box_i\varphi$ (Definition 9) iff $M^{a!}, w' \models \varphi$ for every w' s.t. $w\mathcal{R}_i w'$ (Definition 7) iff $M, w' \models [a!]\varphi$ for every w' s.t. $w\mathcal{R}_i w'$ (substituting equivalents of Definition 9 in the last assertion) iff $M, w \models \Box_i[a!]\varphi$ (Definition 7).

Definition 12 (Complexity measures).

+-depth *Define* $\overset{+}{n}$: $\mathcal{L}^{!+}(A) \rightarrow \mathbb{N}$ *that returns the number of nested* $[+a]$ *in* φ *for any* $a \in A$. *More detailed:* $\overset{+}{n}(\mathsf{owns}_i(a)) := 0$, $\overset{+}{n}(\star\varphi) := \overset{+}{n}(\varphi)$ *where* $\star \in \{\neg, \Box_i, [a!]\}$, $\overset{+}{n}(\varphi \wedge \psi) := max(\overset{+}{n}(\varphi), \overset{+}{n}(\psi))$ *and* $\overset{+}{n}([+a]\varphi) := 1 + \overset{+}{n}(\varphi)$.

Depth *Define* $d : \mathcal{L}^{!}(A) \rightarrow \mathbb{N}$ *as* $d(\mathsf{owns}_i(a)) = 0$, $d(\star\varphi) = 1 + d(\varphi)$ *where* $\star \in \{\neg, \Box_i, [a!]\}$ *and* $d(\varphi \wedge \psi) = max(d(\varphi), d(\psi))$.

O-depth *Define* $Od : \mathcal{L}^{!}(A) \rightarrow \mathbb{N}$ *that returns the number of nested* $[a!]$ *in* φ *for any* $a \in A$. *More detailed:* $Od(\mathsf{owns}_i(a)) = 0$, $Od(\neg\varphi) = Od(\Box_i\varphi) := Od(\varphi)$, $Od(\varphi \wedge \psi) := max(Od(\varphi), Od(\psi))$, *and* $Od([a!]\varphi) = 1 + Od(\varphi)$.

Ord *Define* $Ord : \mathcal{L}^{!}(A) \rightarrow \mathbb{N}$ *that returns the depth of the outermost occurrence of* $[a!]$. *More detailed:* $Ord(\mathsf{owns}_i(a)) := 0$, $Ord(\neg\varphi) =$

$Ord(\Box_i\varphi) := Ord(\varphi)$, $Ord(\varphi \wedge \psi) := max(Ord(\varphi), Ord(\psi))$, $Ord([a!]\varphi) = 1 + d(\varphi)$.

Lemma 5 (From $\mathcal{L}^{!+}(A)$ to $\mathcal{L}^{!}(A)$). *For every $\varphi \in \mathcal{L}^{!+}(A)$, there is a $\psi \in \mathcal{L}^{!}(A)$ s.t. $\vdash_{\mathsf{A}!+} \varphi \leftrightarrow \psi$.*

Proof. By induction on $\overset{+}{n}(\varphi)$. If $\overset{+}{n}(\varphi) = 0$, we have that $\varphi \in \mathcal{L}^{!}(A)$, and by (Taut) we have that $\vdash \varphi \leftrightarrow \varphi$, so we are done.

Assume as induction hypothesis that for every $\varphi \in \mathcal{L}^{!+}(A)$ s.t. $\overset{+}{n}(\varphi) \leq k$, there is a $\psi \in \mathcal{L}^{!}(A)$ s.t.: $\vdash_{\mathsf{A}+!} \varphi \leftrightarrow \psi$. Suppose $\overset{+}{n}(\varphi) = k+1$. Take every $\delta_i \in sub(\varphi)$ s.t. $\overset{+}{n}(\delta_i) \leq k$. Note that by induction hypothesis we have that there is a $\delta'_i \in \mathcal{L}^{!}(A)$ s.t.: $\vdash_{\mathsf{A}+!} \delta_i \leftrightarrow \delta'_i$. By SE we have that $\vdash \varphi \leftrightarrow \varphi[\delta_i/\delta'_i]$. Note that $\overset{+}{n}(\varphi[\delta_i/\delta'_i]) = 1$. It is easy to see that (Def+) and SE assures the existence of a formula $\psi \in \mathcal{L}^{!}(A)$ for every φ s.t $\overset{+}{n}(\varphi) = 1$ satisfying $\vdash_{\mathsf{A}+!} \varphi \leftrightarrow \psi$. In particular, we have that there is a $\psi \in \mathcal{L}^{!}(A)$ s.t.: $\vdash_{\mathsf{A}+!} \varphi[\delta_i/\delta'_i] \leftrightarrow \psi$. By transitivity of $\leftrightarrow$ we have that $\vdash_{\mathsf{A}+!} \varphi \leftrightarrow \psi$.

Remark 8. For every $\varphi \leftrightarrow \psi \in \{(Atoms^{=}) - (Box)\}$ it holds that $Ord(\varphi) > Ord(\psi)$.

Lemma 6. *For every $\varphi \in \mathcal{L}^{!}(A)$ s.t. $Od(\varphi) = 1$ there is a $\psi \in \mathcal{L}(A)$ s.t. $\vdash_{\mathsf{A}+!} \varphi \leftrightarrow \psi$.*

Proof. Suppose $Od(\varphi) = 1$, the rest of the proof is by induction on $Ord(\varphi)$.

For the basic case, suppose $Ord(\varphi) = 0$, then $\varphi \in \mathcal{L}(A)$ and $\vdash \varphi \leftrightarrow \varphi$, so we are done.

Suppose, as induction hypothesis, that for every $\varphi \in \mathcal{L}^{!}(A)$ s.t. $Ord(\varphi) \leq k$ there is a $\psi \in \mathcal{L}(A)$ s.t. $\vdash_{\mathsf{A}+!} \varphi \leftrightarrow \psi$. Now, suppose $Ord(\varphi) = k+1$. We have, by definition of Ord, that there is $[a!]\delta \in sub(\varphi)$ s.t. $Ord([a!]\delta) = k+1$. Note that, since $Od(\varphi) = 1$, then $Od([a!]\delta) = 1$ (there are no nested announcements in $[a!]\delta$) and therefore there is an axiom in Table 2 of the form $\vdash_{\mathsf{A}+!} [a!]\delta \leftrightarrow \delta'$. By Remark 8, $Ord([a!]\delta) > Ord(\delta')$. By the induction hypothesis we have that there is a $\sigma \in \mathcal{L}(A)$ s.t. $\vdash_{\mathsf{A}+!} \delta' \leftrightarrow \sigma$. By transitivity of $\leftrightarrow$ we have that $\vdash_{\mathsf{A}+!} [a!]\delta \leftrightarrow \sigma$ and, by SE, $\vdash_{\mathsf{A}+!} \varphi \leftrightarrow \varphi[[a!]\delta/\sigma]$. We can repeat the same argument for every $\delta_i \in sub(\varphi)$ s.t. $Ord(\delta_i) = k+1$. It is clear than the resulting formula ψ is in $\mathcal{L}(A)$ and that $\vdash_{\mathsf{A}+!} \varphi \leftrightarrow \psi$.

Lemma 7 (From $\mathcal{L}^{!}(A)$ to $\mathcal{L}(A)$). *For every $\varphi \in \mathcal{L}^{!}(A)$ there is a $\psi \in \mathcal{L}(A)$ s.t. $\vdash_{\mathsf{A}+!} \varphi \leftrightarrow \psi$.*

Proof. By induction on $Od(\varphi)$. The atomic case is straightforward since, if $Od(\varphi) = 0$, then $\varphi \in \mathcal{L}(A)$ and we are done. As for the inductive step, suppose as induction hypothesis that for every $\varphi \in \mathcal{L}^{!}(A)$ s.t $Od(\varphi) \leq k$ there is a $\psi \in \mathcal{L}(A)$ s.t. $\vdash_{\mathsf{A}+!} \varphi \leftrightarrow \psi$. Suppose $Od(\varphi) = k+1$. Then, there is a $\delta \in sub(\varphi)$ s.t. $Od(\delta) \leq k$. By the induction hypothesis we have that there is a $\delta' \in \mathcal{L}(A)$ s.t. $\vdash_{\mathsf{A}+!} \delta \leftrightarrow \delta'$ and by SE it holds that $\vdash_{\mathsf{A}+!} \varphi \leftrightarrow \varphi[\delta/\delta']$. We can repeat the same argument for every $\delta_i \in sub(\varphi)$ s.t. $Od(\delta_i) \leq k$. Note that, since $Od(\delta_i') = 0$, we have that $Od(\varphi[\delta_i/\delta_i']) = 1$ and by SE $\vdash_{\mathsf{A}+!} \varphi \leftrightarrow \varphi[\delta_i/\delta_i']$. By Lemma 6 we have that there is a $\psi \in \mathcal{L}(A)$ s.t. $\vdash_{\mathsf{A}+!} \varphi[\delta_i/\delta_i'] \leftrightarrow \psi$ and by transitivity of $\leftrightarrow$ it holds that $\vdash_{\mathsf{A}+!} \varphi \leftrightarrow \psi$.

Theorem 2

Proof. We prove completeness for $\mathsf{A}^{!+}$ w.r.t. $\mathcal{M}$, the other two cases are completely analogous. Let $\varphi \in \mathcal{L}^{!+}(A)$, suppose $\models \varphi$. By Lemmas 5 and 7 and transitivity of $\leftrightarrow$ we have that there is a $\psi \in \mathcal{L}(A)$ s.t. $\vdash_{\mathsf{A}+!} \varphi \leftrightarrow \psi$. From soundness of $\mathsf{A}^{+!}$ and the initial hypothesis it follows that $\models \psi$ and, by completeness of A we have that $\vdash_{\mathsf{A}} \psi$. Since $\mathsf{A}^{+!}$ is an extension of A, we have that $\vdash_{\mathsf{A}+!} \psi$. By SE we obtain $\vdash_{\mathsf{A}+!} \varphi$.

References

1. Beirlaen, M., Heyninck, J., Pardo, P., Straßer, C.: Argument strength in formal argumentation. IfCoLog J. Log. Their Appl. **5**(3), 629–675 (2018)
2. van Benthem, J., Velázquez-Quesada, F.R.: The dynamics of awareness. Synthese **177**(1), 5–27 (2010)
3. Blackburn, P., De Rijke, M., Venema, Y.: Modal Logic. Cambridge University Press, Cambridge (2002)
4. Caminada, M.: On the issue of reinstatement in argumentation. In: Fisher, M., van der Hoek, W., Konev, B., Lisitsa, A. (eds.) JELIA 2006. LNCS (LNAI), vol. 4160, pp. 111–123. Springer, Heidelberg (2006). https://doi.org/10.1007/11853886_11
5. Caminada, M., Sakama, C.: On the issue of argumentation and informedness. In: Otake, M., Kurahashi, S., Ota, Y., Satoh, K., Bekki, D. (eds.) JSAI-isAI 2015. LNCS, vol. 10091, pp. 317–330. Springer, Cham (2017). https://doi.org/10.1007/978-3-319-50953-2_22
6. Caminada, M.W., Gabbay, D.M.: A logical account of formal argumentation. Stud. Logica **93**(2–3), 109–145 (2009)
7. van Ditmarsch, H., van Der Hoek, W., Kooi, B.: Dynamic Epistemic Logic. Springer, Dordrecht (2007). https://doi.org/10.1007/978-1-4020-5839-4
8. Doutre, S., Herzig, A., Perrussel, L.: A dynamic logic framework for abstract argumentation. In: Baral, C., De Giacomo, G., Eiter, T. (eds.) Fourteenth International Conference on the Principles of Knowledge Representation and Reasoning. AAAI Press (2014)
9. Doutre, S., Maffre, F., McBurney, P.: A dynamic logic framework for abstract argumentation: adding and removing arguments. In: Benferhat, S., Tabia, K., Ali, M. (eds.) IEA/AIE 2017. LNCS (LNAI), vol. 10351, pp. 295–305. Springer, Cham (2017). https://doi.org/10.1007/978-3-319-60045-1_32
10. Dung, P.M.: On the acceptability of arguments and its fundamental role in nonmonotonic reasoning, logic programming and n-person games. Artif. Intell. **77**(2), 321–357 (1995)
11. Fagin, R., Halpern, J.Y.: Belief, awareness, and limited reasoning. Artif. Intell. **34**(1), 39–76 (1987)
12. Groarke, L.: Informal logic. In: Zalta, E.N. (ed.) The Stanford Encyclopedia of Philosophy. Metaphysics Research Lab, Stanford University, Spring 2017 edn. (2017)

13. Grossi, D., van der Hoek, W.: Justified beliefs by justified arguments. In: Baral, C., De Giacomo, G., Eiter, T. (eds.) Fourteenth International Conference on the Principles of Knowledge Representation and Reasoning. AAAI Press (2014)
14. Johnson, R.H.: Manifest Rationality: A Pragmatic Theory of Argument. Routledge, New York (2012)
15. Kooi, B.: Expressivity and completeness for public update logics via reduction axioms. J. Appl. Non-Classical Log. **17**(2), 231–253 (2007)
16. Proietti, C.: The dynamics of group polarization. In: Baltag, A., Seligman, J., Yamada, T. (eds.) LORI 2017. LNCS, vol. 10455, pp. 195–208. Springer, Heidelberg (2017). https://doi.org/10.1007/978-3-662-55665-8_14
17. Rahwan, I., Larson, K.: Argumentation and game theory. In: Simari, G., Rahwan, I. (eds.) Argumentation in Artificial Intelligence, pp. 321–339. Springer, Boston (2009). https://doi.org/10.1007/978-0-387-98197-0_16
18. Sakama, C.: Dishonest arguments in debate games. In: Verheij, B., Szeider, S., Woltran, S. (eds.) Frontiers in Artificial Intelligence and Applications. Computational Models of Argument, pp. 177–184. IOS Press (2012)
19. Schwarzentruber, F., Vesic, S., Rienstra, T.: Building an epistemic logic for argumentation. In: del Cerro, L.F., Herzig, A., Mengin, J. (eds.) JELIA 2012. LNCS (LNAI), vol. 7519, pp. 359–371. Springer, Heidelberg (2012). https://doi.org/10.1007/978-3-642-33353-8_28
20. Shi, C., Smets, S., Velázquez-Quesada, F.: Argument-based belief in topological structures. In: Lang, J. (ed.) Proceedings TARK 2017, vol. 251. Open Publishing Association (2017)
21. Shi, C., Smets, S., Velázquez-Quesada, F.R.: Beliefs supported by binary arguments. J. Appl. Non-Classical Log. **28**(2–3), 165–188 (2018)
22. Van Benthem, J., Van Eijck, J., Kooi, B.: Logics of communication and change. Inf. Comput. **204**(11), 1620–1662 (2006)
23. Walton, D., Krabbe, E.C.: Commitment in Dialogue: Basic Concepts of Interpersonal Reasoning. State University of New York Press, Albany (1995)
24. Wu, Y., Caminada, M.: A labelling-based justification status of arguments. Stud. Logic **3**(4), 12–29 (2010)

The Trace Modality

Dominic Steinhöfel(✉) and Reiner Hähnle

Department of Computer Science, TU Darmstadt, Darmstadt, Germany
{steinhoefel,haehnle}@cs.tu-darmstadt.de

Abstract. We propose the *trace modality*, a concept to uniformly express a wide range of program verification problems. To demonstrate its usefulness, we formalize several program verification problems in it: Functional Verification, Information Flow Analysis, Temporal Model Checking, Program Synthesis, Correct Compilation, and Program Evolution. To reason about the trace modality, we translate programs *and* specifications to *regular symbolic traces* and construct simulation relations on first-order symbolic automata. The idea with this uniform representation is that it helps to identify synergy potential—theoretically and practically—between so far separate verification approaches.

1 Introduction

Since the foundational work on program verification during the 1960s [17], the program verification tasks that were studied have much broadened beyond mere functional (partial or total) correctness. Basic variations include termination [14], reachability [25], and program synthesis [16]. Starting in the early 2000s, verification of *relational* properties of programs, such as information flow [8], correct compilation [21], or correctness of program transformations (refactoring) [12] has been in the focus of interest. Relational properties compare two programs having similar behavior. It is even more challenging to reason about programs having related, but intentionally *differing* behavior, such as in program evolution [13].

For all these tasks *dedicated* verification approaches were developed: dynamic logic [15], Hoare quadruples [30], self composition [4,8], product programs [3], etc. Usually, the verification problem to be solved is stated informally, and then the problem is *directly* formalized in the approach to be used for its solution. Hence, the formalism that a problem is stated in and the formalism where it is solved, are *conflated*. We consider this problematic for two reasons:

(1) **Premature commitment to a specific solution approach.** If one has invested to master a specific methodology, the temptation to solve *any* problem by modifying or extending the familiar is considerable, even if a different approach would have been more efficient, flexible, or easily extensible: The well-known "for a hammer the world consists of nails" effect.

This work was funded by the Hessian LOEWE initiative within the Software-Factory 4.0 project.

L. Soares Barbosa and A. Baltag (Eds.): DaLí 2019, LNCS 12005, pp. 124–140, 2020.
https://doi.org/10.1007/978-3-030-38808-9_8

(2) **Hard to detect commonalities and to transfer results.** One of the most powerful scientific stratagems is to detect structural similarity among different problem areas. This makes it possible to transfer insights and solutions from one problem space to another. In formal verification, this additionally opens the road to re-use of software tools for new tasks. To be able to spot commonalities, it is essential to know which aspects of a problem are genuinely new and hence require a novel approach. However, if a problem is *already formalized* in terms of a specific solution method, it is hard to identify commonality and analogy.

Experience with various software verification problems [1,8,14,28] let us realize that a small number of principles occur time and again in dedicated verification approaches: (1) *abstraction* of program runs in the sense of abstract interpretation [7]; (2) *approximation* of a set of program runs by a superset; (3) the capability to handle *schematic* programs, i.e. programs with unspecified parts. Abstraction makes it possible to compare programs written in different languages via a suitable abstraction of their traces. Approximation is needed to focus on a specific property and "forget" irrelevant information. Finally, to reason about program transformation (synthesis, compilation, refactoring, etc.) it is essential to be able to specify a program fragment in an unknown context. We propose a framework based on these principles that lets one express a wide variety of verification problems in a uniform, comparable manner.

We make only one assumption about the programs under verification: They must have a *trace semantics*, i.e. for an initial execution state s and a program p we can obtain the set of all traces ("program runs") that are possible when p is started in s. Our framework builds on the semantic notion of a *trace modality* $[\mathcal{C}_l \Vdash_\alpha \mathcal{C}_r]$, and a reasoning system based on *regular symbolic traces* and simulations on symbolic automata. The expression $[\mathcal{C}_l \Vdash_\alpha \mathcal{C}_r]$ is *valid* if the traces arising from the *implementation* $\mathcal{C}_l$ are *approximated* by the traces of the *specification* $\mathcal{C}_r$ after the *abstraction* step defined by α, where implementation and specification may be either programs (potentially containing *abstract contexts*) or formulas (e.g., in first-order or temporal logic). Symbolic traces approximate concrete traces. Our reasoning system translates implementation and specification to symbolic traces, transforms these to symbolic automata, and finally shows language inclusion by constructing a simulation relation "up to subsumption".

The paper is structured as follows. Section 2 defines elementary notions used in the paper. The semantics of the trace modality is described in Sect. 3, where we also formalize various verification tasks using the trace modality to demonstrate its expressiveness. In Sect. 4, we describe our reasoning system based on symbolic traces. Finally, Sect. 5 discusses related work, and Sect. 6 concludes the paper and describes future work opportunities. For space reasons, we moved some details of the paper (detailed examples, longer remarks) to an appendix, available at www.key-project.org/papers/trace-modality/.

2 Programs, Logic, Traces and Abstractions

We assume an imperative programming language $\mathcal{L}$ with the usual sequencing and assignment operators ";", "=". Programs may contain *schematic* statements, denoted with capital letters P, Q, etc. A program without schematic statements is called *concrete*. The set of concrete programs is $\mathcal{L}_0$. A program p with schematic statements represents the set Concr(p) of all well-formed $\mathcal{L}_0$-programs obtained by replacing each schematic statement in p with an arbitrary concrete statement.

At each point during the execution of a program $\mathtt{p} \in \mathcal{L}_0$ it is in a *state* $s \in \mathcal{S}$, mapping program variables to domain values. To model failed assertions, we distinguish a state $\perp$. We write $\mathcal{S}^\perp$ for $\mathcal{S} \cup \{\perp\}$. A *trace* τ is a possibly infinite sequence of states, denoted $s_0 s_1 \cdots s_n$ or $s_0 s_1 \cdots$ (the latter being infinite). For the empty trace we write ε and $\mathit{Traces} = (\mathcal{S}^\perp)^* \cup (\mathcal{S}^\perp)^\omega$ for the set of all traces. Predicate $\mathit{finite}(\tau)$ holds for finite traces and $\mathit{first}(\tau)$, $\mathit{last}(\tau)$ select a trace's first and final state (the latter is only defined for finite traces).

We assume a *trace semantics* $\mathrm{Tr}_s(\mathtt{p})$ that maps a *concrete* program $\mathtt{p} \in \mathcal{L}_0$ and initial state $s \in \mathcal{S}$ into the set of possible traces when p is started in s. When $\mathcal{L}_0$ is deterministic, this is a singleton. We define the set of all traces of $\mathtt{p} \in \mathcal{L}_0$ as $\mathrm{Tr}(\mathtt{p}) = \{\mathrm{Tr}_s(\mathtt{p}) \mid s \in \mathcal{S}\}$. If $\mathcal{P}$ is a set of concrete programs, then $\mathrm{Tr}(\mathcal{P}) = \{\mathrm{Tr}(\mathtt{p}) \mid \mathtt{p} \in \mathcal{P}\}$, similar for $\mathrm{Tr}_s(\mathcal{P})$. Now we define the semantics of a *schematic* program $\mathtt{p} \in \mathcal{L}$ as $\mathrm{Tr}(\mathrm{Concr}(\mathtt{p}))$ and $\mathrm{Tr}_s(\mathrm{Concr}(\mathtt{p}))$, respectively.

Let PVar denote the set of program variables and "$\circ$" the usual function composition operator. We define *abstraction operators* $\alpha : 2^{\mathit{Traces}} \to 2^{\mathit{Traces}}$ (in the sense of abstract interpretation [7]) on sets of traces $\mathcal{T}$:

Big-step abstraction: $\alpha_{big}(\mathcal{T}) = \{(s_0, s_n) \mid s_0 \cdots s_n \in \mathcal{T}\}$, i.e. the set of all pairs of the first and last state of any finite trace in $\mathcal{T}$. Observe that for infinite traces in $\mathcal{T}$, there is no corresponding pair in the abstracted set.

Observation abstraction: Let obs $\subseteq$ PVar, $s \in \mathcal{S}$, then $s \downarrow \mathrm{obs}$ is the state s restricted to values from obs. We define the *observation abstraction* relative to obs as $\alpha_{\mathrm{obs}}(\mathcal{T}) = \{(s_0 \downarrow \mathrm{obs})(s_1 \downarrow \mathrm{obs}) \cdots \mid s_0 s_1 \cdots \in \mathcal{T}\}$. For a concrete set of variables, for instance $\{\mathtt{x}\}$, we write $\alpha_{\{\mathtt{x}\}}$.

Data abstraction: Let α_d be an abstract operator on data types in p [7]. We define the *data abstraction* of a set of traces as $\alpha_d(\mathcal{T}) = \{\alpha_d(s_0)\alpha_d(s_1) \cdots \mid s_0 s_1 \cdots \in \mathcal{T}\}$, where the state $\alpha_d(s)(\mathtt{x}) = \alpha_d(s(\mathtt{x}))$ is defined pointwise.

Combination: Combine two abstractions α_1, α_2 by composition $\alpha_1 \circ \alpha_2$.

We use a standard first-order language with equality. It contains the usual propositional connectives and first-order quantifiers. Terms and formulas are standard, but we permit trace modality formulas $[\mathcal{T}_l \Vdash_\alpha \mathcal{T}_r]$ as atomic formulas. With Trm and Fml we denote the sets of all terms and formulas. The semantics of a formula is provided by a first-order structure K and a state $s \in \mathcal{S}$ that define the *validity* relation $K, s \models \varphi$ for each $\varphi \in$ Fml. For example, $K, s \models \varphi \to \psi$ iff *either* $K, s \not\models \varphi$, *or* $K, s \models \varphi$ and $K, s \models \psi$. Given $s \in \mathcal{S}$, write $s \models \varphi$ and say φ is *valid* for s if $K, s \models \varphi$ for all K. Write $\models \varphi$ and say that φ is *valid* if $s \models \varphi$ for all $s \in \mathcal{S}$. While K interprets *rigid* first-order functions and predicates, a state s assigns values to program variables that may *change* during execution. For the failure state $\bot$ we set $K, \bot \not\models \varphi$ for *any* K, φ.

We need `assert(`φ`)` and `assume(`φ`)` statements for asserting and assuming a first-order formula φ *in a program*. Our use cases are *program synthesis* for `assert` and *invariant reasoning* (appendix) for `assume` statements. For `assert`, we define $\mathrm{Tr}_s(\texttt{assert}(\varphi)) = \{s\}$ if $s \models \varphi$ and $\{\bot\}$ otherwise. The semantics of `assume` is defined as $\mathrm{Tr}_s(\texttt{assume}(\varphi)) = \{s\}$ if $s \models \varphi$ and $\emptyset$ otherwise. We define a full trace semantics for a simple $\mathcal{L}_0$-language in the appendix.

3 The Trace Modality

We define the *trace modality* $[\mathcal{T}_l \Vdash_\alpha \mathcal{T}_r]$, where the *implementation* $\mathcal{T}_l$ and *specification* $\mathcal{T}_r$ both are (possibly infinite) trace sets and α is a trace abstraction. It expresses that the specification is an approximation of the implementation relative to α. Its semantics is that the modality is *valid*, written $\models [\mathcal{T}_l \Vdash_\alpha \mathcal{T}_r]$, if $\alpha(\mathcal{T}_l) \subseteq \alpha(\mathcal{T}_r)$. We use *lifting functions* lift_l, lift_r that convert elements from the verification domain, such as programs or formulas, to trace sets. Formally:

Definition 1. *Let $\alpha : 2^{\mathit{Traces}} \to 2^{\mathit{Traces}}$ be a trace abstraction and $\mathcal{C}_l$, $\mathcal{C}_r$ elements of domains D_l, D_r with associated lifting functions $\mathit{lift}_{l/r} : \mathcal{S} \to D_{l/r} \to 2^{\mathit{Traces}}$. Then the trace modality $[\mathcal{C}_l \Vdash_\alpha \mathcal{C}_r]$ is valid in $s \in \mathcal{S}$, written $s \models [\mathcal{C}_l \Vdash_\alpha \mathcal{C}_r]$, iff $\alpha(\mathit{lift}_l(s)(\mathcal{C}_l)) \subseteq \alpha(\mathit{lift}_r(s)(\mathcal{C}_r))$.*

For readability, we omit lifting functions in the presentation and assume that verification domains have fixed lifting functions. We omit α if it is the identity.

Relation to Modal and Dynamic Logic. Like in modal and dynamic logic (DL) we can define a dual modality as follows: $\langle \mathcal{C}_l \Vdash_\alpha \mathcal{C}_r \rangle := \neg[\mathcal{C}_l \Vdash_\alpha \overline{\mathcal{C}_r}]$, where $\overline{\mathcal{C}_r}$ is the complement of $\mathcal{C}_r$. The semantics of this *diamond* trace modality can be phrased as: $s \models \langle \mathcal{C}_l \Vdash_\alpha \mathcal{C}_r \rangle$ iff there is a trace in $\alpha(\mathit{lift}_l(s)(\mathcal{C}_l))$ that is not in $\alpha(\overline{\mathit{lift}_r(s)(\mathcal{C}_r)})$. The axioms **N** (necessitation rule) and **K** (distribution axiom) of modal logic follow from Definition 1; axioms of Propositional Dynamic Logic (PDL) [15] also hold when defining suitable operators on trace sets (like sequencing and star). We refer to our discussion in the appendix (Remark 1) for these observations. Despite those similarities, the trace modality is strictly more general than DL. Specifications can originate from different verification domains; also a *program* can be a specification (we show several examples for this case later on) or a formula an implementation. Furthermore, we are not restricted to big-step reasoning. Because the notation $[p]p'$ would look strange for lengthy programs p' and to emphasize the mentioned differences between the trace modality and standard DL, we chose the notation also encapsulating the specification inside the box.

In the following, several verification tasks are described and formalized with the trace modality. We define suitable verification domains D, lifting functions lift_D, as well as abstractions. A summary table is in the appendix.

3.1 Functional Verification

In functional verification, one shows a given program $\mathtt{p} \in \mathcal{L}_0$ to satisfy a postcondition *Post* provided that a precondition *Pre* holds initially. The problem is frequently formalized with *Hoare triples* $\{Pre\}\mathtt{p}\{Post\}$ [17]. In DL [1,15], one writes $Pre \rightarrow [\mathtt{p}]Post$. We distinguish *partial correctness*, where *Post* is asserted to hold *if* p terminates, from *total correctness*, where it is also shown *that* p terminates. For the latter one can use the dual modality $\langle\mathtt{p}\rangle Post$.

Functional correctness is over the domain $D_{\mathcal{L}_0}$ for programs and D_{Fml} for first-order postconditions. We define lifting functions $\mathit{lift}_{\mathcal{L}_0}(s)(\mathtt{p}) := \mathrm{Tr}_s(\mathtt{p})$ and $\mathit{lift}_{\mathrm{Fml}}(s)(\varphi) := \{\tau \in \mathit{Traces} : \mathit{finite}(\tau) \wedge \mathit{first}(\tau) = s \wedge \mathit{last}(\tau) \models \varphi\}$ (all finite traces starting in s whose final state satisfies φ). Using the big-step abstraction, we can formalize (partial) functional correctness as $Pre \rightarrow [\mathtt{p} \Vdash_{\alpha_{big}} Post]$. Total correctness for *deterministic* programs is expressed as $Pre \rightarrow \langle\mathtt{p} \Vdash_{\alpha_{big}} Post\rangle$.

Example 1. Let p :=`j=i*i; while (i<j) { i=i*2; }`. It diverges iff the initial value of `i` is negative. One can prove postcondition $\mathit{even}(\mathtt{i})$ (with the obvious meaning) for p *if it terminates* (partial correctness). Thus, $s \models [\mathtt{p} \Vdash_{\alpha_{big}} \mathit{even}(\mathtt{i})]$ must hold in all $s \in \mathcal{S}$, i.e. $\alpha_{big}(\mathit{lift}_{\mathcal{L}_0}(s)(\mathtt{p})) \subseteq \alpha_{big}(\mathit{lift}_{\mathrm{Fml}}(s)(\mathit{even}(\mathtt{i})))$. If $s(\mathtt{i}) < 0$ then the set $\mathit{lift}_{\mathcal{L}_0}(s)(\mathtt{p})$ contains a single infinite trace. Therefore, $\alpha_{big}(\mathit{lift}_{\mathcal{L}_0}(s)(\mathtt{p})) = \emptyset$ and the subset relation holds. If $s(\mathtt{i}) \geq 0$, p has a single finite trace whose final state assigns an even value to `i` (either because $s(\mathtt{i})$ is 0, or because it is greater than 0, and the initial value was multiplied by 2 a number of times in the loop's body). Hence, $\alpha_{big}(\mathit{lift}_{\mathcal{L}_0}(s)(\mathtt{p}))$ contains a single pair (s, s_f) where s_f satisfies $\mathit{even}(\mathtt{i})$. It is in $\alpha_{big}(\mathit{lift}_{\mathrm{Fml}}(s)(\mathit{even}(\mathtt{i})))$ by defn. of $\mathit{lift}_{\mathrm{Fml}}$. We cannot show $s \models \langle\mathtt{p} \Vdash_{\alpha_{big}} \mathit{even}(\mathtt{i})\rangle$ for any s with $s(\mathtt{i}) < 0$, because then $\alpha_{big}(\mathit{lift}_{\mathcal{L}_0}(s)(\mathtt{p}))$ is empty and so cannot contain a trace not in $\alpha_{big}(\mathit{lift}_{\mathrm{Fml}}(s)(\mathit{even}(\mathtt{i})))$. However, $\models \mathtt{i} \geq 0 \rightarrow \langle\mathtt{p} \Vdash_{\alpha_{big}} \mathit{even}(\mathtt{i})\rangle$ is true. ◊

3.2 Information Flow Analysis

To prove that a given program treats secret inputs (for example, a password) confidentially, i.e. it does not inadvertently leak secret information, one can formally prove that it satisfies an *information flow policy*. In the simplest case such policies partition program variables into *low*-security variables that hold observable values and *high*-security ones whose values are secret. A policy imposes restrictions on the flow of values from *high* to *low* variables. A standard and very strong policy is *non-interference*: "Whenever two instances of the same program are run with equal *low* values and arbitrary *high* values, then the resulting *low* values are equal in the final state". This ensures that an attacker cannot learn anything about secret values by running the program with observable values. For simplicity, assume a program p contains exactly one low variable `l` and one high variable `h`, written $\mathtt{p}(\mathtt{l},\mathtt{h})$. Using *self composition* [4,8], this is formalized as a Hoare triple: If we can prove $\{\mathtt{l} \doteq \mathtt{l}'\}\mathtt{p}(\mathtt{l},\mathtt{h});\mathtt{p}(\mathtt{l}',\mathtt{h}')\{\mathtt{l} \doteq \mathtt{l}'\}$, p satisfies non-interference. It can also be directly expressed with the trace modality: $\models [\mathtt{p}(\mathtt{l},\mathtt{h}) \Vdash_{\alpha_{\{\mathtt{l}\}} \circ \alpha_{big}} \mathtt{p}(\mathtt{l},\mathtt{h}')]$. Note that the renaming of `l` to `l'` is then not necessary since programs are not composed, but evaluated separately. In the appendix, we discuss how *declassification* can be encoded with the trace modality.

Example 2. Let $\mathtt{p} := \mathtt{l=42;\ if\ (h>20)\ \{l=17;\}}$. This program does not satisfy non-interference, because the final value of the observable variable $\mathtt{l}$ depends on the initial value of $\mathtt{h}$. We prove that indeed, $\models [\mathtt{p}(\mathtt{l},\mathtt{h}) \Vdash_{\alpha_{\{\mathtt{l}\}} \circ \alpha_{big}} \mathtt{p}(\mathtt{l},\mathtt{h}')]$ does *not* hold, by showing that there is a state $s \in \mathcal{S}$ for which

$$(\alpha_{\{\mathtt{l}\}} \circ \alpha_{big})(\mathit{lift}_{\mathcal{L}_0}(s)(\mathtt{p}(\mathtt{l},\mathtt{h}))) \subseteq (\alpha_{\{\mathtt{l}\}} \circ \alpha_{big})(\mathit{lift}_{\mathcal{L}_0}(s)(\mathtt{p}(\mathtt{l},\mathtt{h}')))$$

is not true. Let s be such that $s(\mathtt{l}) = 0$, $s(\mathtt{h}) = 0$ and $s(\mathtt{h}') = 30$. Then the trace set of the implementation is $\{(\{\mathtt{l} \mapsto 0\}, \{\mathtt{l} \mapsto 42\})\}$ which is not contained in the set for the specification $\{(\{\mathtt{l} \mapsto 0\}, \{\mathtt{l} \mapsto 17\})\}$. ◊

3.3 Software Model Checking

Software Model Checking (SMC) [19] describes a wide range of techniques for analyzing *safety* or *liveness* properties of programs. Those techniques have in common that they focus on *automation* at cost of expressivity. Frequently, the goal is not to prove correctness relative to a specification, but rather to quickly uncover bugs or to generate high-coverage test cases. Recently, there has been a *convergence* between *model checking* and *deductive verification* techniques [26], as more mechanisms traditionally known from the latter field, such as abstraction [29], symbolic execution [23], etc., are integrated to achieve greater expressivity. On the other side, Bounded Model Checking (BMC) approaches, which limit state space exploration by a user-defined upper bound on loop unwindings, are well-known and successful, and finite space checkers such as SPIN [18] continue being used, e.g. in protocol verification. Properties of interest to SMC (e.g., the absence of memory faults) can usually be formalized in Temporal Logic (TL).

We introduce the domain D_{TL} for Linear Temporal Logic (LTL) formulas, lift_{TL} is the standard trace semantics for temporal logic (e.g., $\mathit{lift}_{TL}(s)(\Box p)$ is the set of all traces starting in s where p always holds). We exemplarily instantiate the trace modality to *Finite Space* MC. Finite space model checkers like SPIN exhaustively explore the state space of an abstract program model. This implies that the analysis starts from *a concrete input state* s and that no unbounded data structures are involved. We can formalize this problem as $s \models [\mathtt{p} \Vdash \varphi]$, where φ is an LTL formula. In the appendix, we show how to instantiate the trace modality to Bounded MC, Abstraction-Based MC and Symbolic Execution-Based MC. Model Checking tools for bug finding can be formalized with the diamond trace modality: They eagerly try to show $\models \langle \mathtt{p} \Vdash \neg\varphi \rangle$, i.e. there is a trace of $\mathtt{p}$ violating φ. Such a trace constitutes a counterexample which can be used to fix the program, and/or to create a useful test case.

So far, we considered *concrete* programs $\mathtt{p} \in \mathcal{L}_0$. The two subsequently discussed verification tasks are over *schematic* programs in $\mathcal{L}$.

3.4 Program Synthesis

Automated program synthesis starts with a specification of programs at a higher level than executable code. The latter is created (semi-)automatically from the specification. In [27], for instance, the user supplies a *scaffold* consisting of a functional specification $(Pre, Post)$, domain constraints defining the domains of expressions and guards, and a *schematic program* (called "flowgraph template") of the form $\bullet|*(T)|T;T$. Here, $\bullet$ is an acyclic fragment, T again a schematic program and $*(T)$ a loop with body T. The synthesizer infers *synthesis conditions*. These are satisfiable whenever there exists a valid program for the scaffold.

We encode $\bullet$ of the flowgraph template by programs $\mathtt{p} \in \mathcal{L}$ with schematic statements $\mathtt{P}, \mathtt{Q}, \ldots$, and define a new verification domain $D_\mathcal{L}$ with $\mathit{lift}_\mathcal{L}(s)(\mathtt{p}) := \mathrm{Tr}_s(\mathrm{Concr}(\mathtt{p}))$. Synthesis conditions are included in the intermediate program as suitable `assert(`φ`)` statements. When refining an intermediate program $\mathtt{p}$ to a more concrete program $\mathtt{p}'$, the property to show is $\models \mathit{Pre} \rightarrow [\mathtt{p}' \Vdash_{\alpha_{big}} \mathtt{p}]$: that $\mathtt{p}'$ is indeed a refinement of $\mathtt{p}$. In the appendix, we provide an example for the synthesis of a program computing integer square roots.

3.5 Correct Compilation

A compiler translates a program $\mathtt{p}$ in a source language into a program $\mathtt{c}$ of a target language, preserving the behavior of $\mathtt{p}$. The translation can introduce new program variables. Then, preservation of behavior is typically restricted to a set of *observable* variables *obs*. In *modular* compilation, a program $\mathtt{p}$ is given within an unspecified context. In this case both $\mathtt{p}$ and $\mathtt{c}$ are abstract. Correctness of compilation can be expressed as $\models [\mathtt{c} \Vdash_{\alpha_{obs} \circ \alpha_{big}} \mathtt{p}]$. If we want to enforce inclusion of the traces of $\mathtt{c}$ in the traces of $\mathtt{p}$, we can—for deterministic languages—use the diamond modality instead. In particular for non-deterministic languages, we can *additionally* prove the reverse direction $\models [\mathtt{p} \Vdash_{\alpha_{obs} \circ \alpha_{big}} \mathtt{c}]$.

The formalization makes the similarity to program synthesis explicit. Indeed, one could create a scaffold by extracting synthesis conditions from $\mathtt{p}$, and then try to infer $\mathtt{c}$ automatically. For example, in [28], a symbolic execution tree of the source program is "mined" to extract the target program. It is related to proof mining techniques used in program synthesis.

3.6 Program Evolution and Bug Fixing

Sometimes, the behavior of the "specification" should intentionally be *not* preserved. This situation occurs in program evolution, e.g., after manual or automatic bug fixing [22]: the patched program is supposed to exhibit the bug no longer, but no new bug is to be introduced. Similarly, in fault propagation analysis, an injected fault typically *will* change the behaviour of a program, but not arbitrarily. This problem is most naturally expressed as $\models [\mathtt{p}_{\mathit{fixed}} \Vdash_{\alpha_{bug} \circ \alpha_{big}} \mathtt{p}_{\mathit{bug}}]$, where behavioral differences are conveyed for a suitable abstraction α_{bug} suppressing buggy traces or relating them to corrected ones. We can go a step further and not just exclude buggy traces, but encode the *fix* by an abstraction α_{patch}. This is likely to produce a more reliable result asserting that apart from the fix, the programs behave equivalently, even for the formerly buggy paths. In the appendix, we discuss two alternative formalizations with an example.

4 Reasoning About the Trace Modality

We propose a reasoning algorithm based on *symbolic traces* for the trace modality. The idea is to lift all verification domains to a common language over symbolic traces that over-approximates the set of concrete traces produced by each lifting function. Abstractions are generalized to symbolic traces. Validity of the trace modality can then be established by *symbolic trace subsumption.* The symbolic traces we propose are a *regular* language. Hence, programs generally have to be over-approximated, for example, by loop invariant reasoning or bounded loop unwinding. Not all properties can be encoded in a regular symbolic trace language, such as complex Computation Tree Logic properties. Even so, the language is expressive enough to represent the problems formalized in Sect. 3, and problems encoded in it can be solved effectively (if the underlying first-order problems can be solved). We define symbolic stores, states and traces as follows:

Definition 2. *Let* $\mathtt{x} \in \mathrm{PVar}$, $t \in \mathrm{Trm}$, $\varphi \in \mathrm{Fml}$, *and* $\mathtt{P}$ *a schematic statement. The sets* SymSto *of* Symbolic Stores, SymState *of* Symbolic States, *and* SymTr *of* Symbolic Traces *are defined as follows in extended BNF:*

$$\begin{aligned} \mathrm{SymSto} &::= \mathtt{x} \text{ ``:=''} \, t \mid \mathit{sto}_{\mathtt{P}} \mid \mathrm{SymSto} \text{ ``||''} \, \mathrm{SymSto} \mid \text{``\{''} \, \mathrm{SymSto} \text{ ``\}''} \, \mathrm{SymSto} \\ \mathrm{SymState} &::= \varphi \mid \text{``(''} \, \mathrm{SymSto} \text{ ``,''} \, \varphi \text{ ``)''} \\ \mathrm{SymTr} &::= \mathrm{SymState} \mid \mathrm{SymTr} \, (\text{``;''} \mid \text{``+''}) \, \mathrm{SymTr} \mid \varphi \text{ ``!''} \mid \mathrm{SymTr} \text{ ``*''} \end{aligned}$$

Here an abstract *store* $\mathit{sto}_{\mathtt{P}}$ *represents an unknown state transition induced by a schematic* $\mathcal{L}$*-statement* $\mathtt{P}$. *The sets* SymSto_0, $\mathrm{SymState}_0$ *and* SymTr_0 *are defined as above, but do not contain abstract stores.*

Symbolic stores record changes to program variables. Elementary stores $\mathtt{x} := t$ represent states where the variable $\mathtt{x}$ attains the valuation of the (symbolic) term t. Symbolic stores sto_1, sto_2 are combined to a parallel store $\mathit{sto}_1 \,||\, \mathit{sto}_2$. If both assign a value to the same variable, the later assignment (in sto_2) "wins". A symbolic store sto_1 can be *applied* to a symbolic store sto_2, written $\{\mathit{sto}_1\}\mathit{sto}_2$. Left-hand sides in sto_2 are then evaluated in the states represented by sto_1. Combining two stores into one works by the *store concatenation operator* "$\circ$", defined as $\mathit{sto}_1 \circ \mathit{sto}_2 = \mathit{sto}_1 \,||\, \{\mathit{sto}_1\}\mathit{sto}_2$. We permit the application of symbolic stores to terms and formulas, with similar semantics. We write $\overrightarrow{\mathtt{x}} := \overrightarrow{t}$ for the store $\mathtt{x}_1 := t_1 \,||\, \ldots \,||\, \mathtt{x}_n := t_n$, where $\mathtt{x}_i$, t_i are the i-th components of $\overrightarrow{\mathtt{x}}$, $\overrightarrow{t}$.

Symbolic states consist of an (optional) symbolic store *sto* and path condition φ representing concrete states satisfying both φ and, if present, the assignments in *sto*. A symbolic trace is in the simplest case a sequence of symbolic states. The choice operator $+$ models nondeterministic choice as well as case distinctions for deterministic programs, depending on the path conditions of the argument

$$
\begin{aligned}
\mathsf{tval}_K:&\quad \mathrm{SymSto}_0 \to (\mathcal{S} \to \mathcal{S})\\
\mathsf{tval}_K(\mathtt{x} := t)(s)(\mathtt{y}) :=&\ \mathsf{val}(K, s; t) \text{ if } \mathtt{y} = \mathtt{x},\ s(\mathtt{y}) \text{ otherwise}\\
\mathsf{tval}_K(sto_1 \,||\, sto_2)(s) :=&\ \mathsf{tval}_K(sto_2)(\mathsf{tval}_K(sto_1)(s))\\
\mathsf{tval}_K:&\quad \mathrm{SymState}_0 \to 2^{\mathcal{S}}\\
\mathsf{tval}_K(\varphi) :=&\ \{s \in \mathcal{S} \mid K, s \models \varphi\}\\
\mathsf{tval}_K(sto, \varphi) :=&\ \{\mathsf{tval}_K(sto)(s) \mid K, s \models \varphi,\ s \in \mathcal{S}\}\\
\mathsf{tval}_K:&\quad \mathrm{SymTr}_0 \to 2^{\mathit{Traces}}\\
\mathsf{tval}_K(\tau_1; \tau_2) :=&\ \{\tau_1^0 \tau_2^0 \mid \tau_1^0 \in \mathsf{tval}_K(\tau_1) \setminus \{\cdots \bot\},\ \tau_2^0 \in \mathsf{tval}_K(\tau_2)\}\\
&\ \cup \{\bot \mid \tau_1^0 \bot \in \mathsf{tval}_K(\tau_1)\}\\
\mathsf{tval}_K(\tau_1 + \tau_2) :=&\ \mathsf{tval}_K(\tau_1) \cup \mathsf{tval}_K(\tau_2)\\
\mathsf{tval}_K(\varphi^!) :=&\ \begin{cases} \varepsilon & \text{if } \forall s \in \mathcal{S}:\ K, s \models \varphi \\ \bot & \text{otherwise} \end{cases}\\
\mathsf{tval}_K(\tau^*) :=&\ \{\tau_1^0 \tau_2^0 \cdots \tau_n^0 : \tau_i \in \mathsf{tval}_K(\tau),\ n \in \mathbb{N}\} \cup \{\varepsilon\}
\end{aligned}
$$

Fig. 1. The Valuation Function tval_K

traces. The trace $\varphi^!$, primarily used to model assertions, represents the empty trace if φ holds in the current state and the failure state otherwise. The traces τ^* represent all finite concrete traces in which all states satisfy τ. For instance, true* represents the set of all finite concrete traces. We do not include an operator τ^ω for infinite traces which would significantly complicate validity checking: One would have to separate terminating from non-terminating traces—which is undecidable—or consider only non-terminating runs.

A formal semantics for symbolic traces is based on a first-order structure K with domain D and interpretation I, as well as $s \in \mathcal{S}$. The *valuation function* $\mathsf{val}(K, s; \cdot)$ assigns to terms a value in D, to formulas "true" or "false." We write equivalently $K, s \models \varphi$ or $\mathsf{val}(K, s; \varphi) = \text{true}$, as well as $K, s \not\models \varphi$ or $\mathsf{val}(K, s; \varphi) = \text{false}$. The function $\mathsf{val}(K, s; \cdot)$ is defined as usual, except for the application of symbolic stores and the valuation of program variables. For $\mathtt{x} \in \mathrm{PVar}$, we define $\mathsf{val}(K, s; \mathtt{x}) = s(\mathtt{x})$. If $t \in \mathrm{Trm}$ and $sto \in \mathrm{SymSto}$, we define $\mathsf{val}(K, s; \{sto\}t) := \mathsf{val}(K, s'; t)$, where $s' = \mathsf{val}(K, s; sto)(s)$ (similarly for formulas). We define the trace valuation function tval_K first on *concrete* symbolic traces SymTr_0. It is parametric in a structure K that fixes the values of uninterpreted constant, function, and predicate symbols. The cumulative valuation function tval is canonically defined as $\mathsf{tval}(\tau) := \bigcup_K \mathsf{tval}_K(\tau)$.

Definition 3. *We inductively define the valuation function* tval_K*, overloaded for symbolic stores, states and traces, as in Fig. 1.*

Symbolic traces SymTr_0 are created for concrete programs $\mathcal{L}_0$. The symbolic evaluation of schematic programs in $\mathcal{L}$ creates abstract stores sto_{P} and path conditions C_{P} (details below). Intuitively, they represent *all possible symbolic stores and path conditions* that may arise from concrete program execution. We define their semantics by the union of the semantics of possible instantiations.

Definition 4. *Let* $\tau \in \mathrm{SymTr}$ *be a symbolic trace with occurrences of abstract stores* $sto_{\mathtt{P}_1}, \ldots, sto_{\mathtt{P}_n}$ *and path conditions* $C_{\mathtt{P}_1}, \ldots, C_{\mathtt{P}_n}$ *(with possibly multiple occurrences of each* $sto_{\mathtt{P}_i}$, $C_{\mathtt{P}_i}$*). We define* $\mathsf{tval}(\tau)$ *as the union* $\bigcup \mathsf{tval}(\tau_0)$ *of all* $\tau_0 \in \mathrm{SymTr}_0$ *that are obtained by instantiating all occurrences of* $sto_{\mathtt{P}_i}$, $C_{\mathtt{P}_i}$ *with concrete stores* $sto^0_{\mathtt{P}_i} \in \mathrm{SymSto}_0$ *and path conditions* $C^0_{\mathtt{P}_i} \in \mathrm{Fml}$.

Abstractions α are generalized to symbolic traces in the obvious manner, e.g., the big-step abstraction α_{big} takes the first and all final states of a trace. Symbolic representations of the lifting functions require more work. For a lifting function *lift*, we denote by *slift* its symbolic version. Like *lift*, *slift* takes a *symbolic* state and a verification domain construct and produces a *symbolic* trace.

Definition 5. *A symbolic lifting function slift is* correct *relative to lift if, for all* $s \in \mathrm{SymState}$ *and* $\sigma \in \mathsf{tval}(s)$, $\mathit{lift}(\sigma)(C) \subseteq \mathsf{tval}(\mathit{slift}(s)(C))$.

Symbolic lifting functions for first-order formulas are straightforward to define: $\mathit{slift}_{\mathrm{Fml}}(s)(\varphi) := \mathrm{true}^*;\varphi$. For LTL formulas, $\mathit{slift}_{TL}(s)$ maps (1) φ to "φ", (2) $\Box\varphi$ to "φ^*", (3) $\Diamond\varphi$ to "$\mathrm{true}^*;\varphi;\mathrm{true}^*$", and (4) $\varphi\,\mathcal{U}\,\psi$ to "$\varphi^*;\psi;\mathrm{true}^*$".

Defining symbolic lifting for programs means encoding symbolic execution. E.g., one can extract symbolic traces from a symbolic execution tree. Symbolic *traces* are more flexible, though, since they can encode non tree-like structures. The lifting function $\mathit{slift}_{\mathcal{L}_0}$ is defined as follows for assignments, if-else, assume and assert, and sequential composition (for those, it coincides with $\mathit{slift}^k_{\mathcal{L}_0}$ for BMC). W.l.o.g., we assume symbolic states to be of the form (sto, φ).

$$\begin{aligned}
\mathit{slift}_{\mathcal{L}_0}(sto,\varphi)(\mathtt{x=e}) &:= (sto \circ (\mathtt{x} := e), \varphi)\\
\mathit{slift}_{\mathcal{L}_0}(sto,\varphi)(\mathtt{if\,(g)}\ p_1\ \mathtt{else}\ p_2) &:= (\mathit{slift}_{\mathcal{L}_0}(sto, \varphi \wedge \{sto\}g))(p_1)\ +\\
&\ (\mathit{slift}_{\mathcal{L}_0}(sto, \varphi \wedge \neg\{sto\}g))(p_2)\\
\mathit{slift}_{\mathcal{L}_0}(sto,\varphi)(\mathtt{assume(}\psi\mathtt{)}) &:= (sto, \varphi \wedge \psi)\\
\mathit{slift}_{\mathcal{L}_0}(sto,\varphi)(\mathtt{assert(}\psi\mathtt{)}) &:= (\varphi \to \{sto\}\psi)^!\\
\mathit{slift}_{\mathcal{L}_0}(sto,\varphi)(p_1\,;\,p_2) &:= \{\tau_1;\tau_2 : \tau_1 \in \mathit{slift}_{\mathcal{L}_0}(sto,\varphi)(p_1),\\
&\ \tau_2 \in \mathit{slift}_{\mathcal{L}_0}(\mathit{last}(\tau_1))(p_2)\}
\end{aligned}$$

Symbolic lifting is more complex for loops, as usual in symbolic execution. Possible approaches are *loop unwinding* which generally does not terminate for loops with symbolic guards, *bounded unwinding* with a fixed upper bound on the number of unwinding steps, and *loop invariants*. In the appendix, we provide a more detailed discussion and define symbolic lifting for those cases.

To define $\mathit{slift}_{\mathcal{L}}$, we have to encode schematic statements P. We choose to do this with *abstract stores* $sto_{\mathtt{P}}$ that model state changes caused by schematic statements. We also admit *abstract formulas* $C_{\mathtt{P}}$ to model (unknown) path condition constraints arising from an abstract program P. We define:

$$\mathit{slift}_{\mathcal{L}}(sto,\varphi)(\mathtt{P}) := \mathrm{true}^*; (sto \circ sto_{\mathtt{P}}, \varphi \wedge \{sto \circ sto_{\mathtt{P}}\}C_{\mathtt{P}}) \quad \text{for all } \mathtt{P}.$$

The Algorithm for Checking Validity of Trace Modalities. When presented with a problem $[\mathcal{C}_l \Vdash_\alpha \mathcal{C}_r]$ and a symbolic state s_0, the algorithm evaluates in three phases whether $\alpha(\mathit{lift}_l(\sigma_0)(\mathcal{C}_l)) \subseteq \alpha(\mathit{lift}_r(\sigma_0)(\mathcal{C}_r))$ holds for all $\sigma_0 \in \mathsf{tval}(s_0)$:

(1) Convert $\mathcal{C}_{l/r}$ to symbolic traces $\tau^s_{l/r}$ using symbolic lifting functions $\mathit{slift}_{l/r}$ (as described above for first-order and LTL formulas, as well as $\mathcal{L}$-programs).
(2) Construct Symbolic Finite Automata (SFAs) $\mathsf{SFA}_{l/r}$ accepting the languages $\mathsf{tval}(\tau^s_{l/r})$, i.e. concrete traces represented by symbolic ones.
(3) Check whether the language accepted by SFA_l is *included* in the language accepted by SFA_r through construction of a *simulation relation.*

Transitions in an SFA are labeled with symbolic states that may represent infinitely many concrete states. For example, a transition labeled with "true" models a transition for *any* concrete state. Formally, we define SFA as:

Definition 6. *A* Symbolic Finite Automaton *is a tuple* $A = (Q, \Sigma, \delta, q_0, F)$ *of a finite set of states* Q*, an alphabet* $\Sigma \subseteq \mathcal{S}$*, a finite transition relation* $\delta \subseteq Q \times \text{SymState} \times Q$*, an initial state* $q_0 \in Q$ *and a set of accepting states* $F \subseteq Q$*. Automaton* A accepts *a concrete trace* $\sigma_1\sigma_2\cdots\sigma_n$ *if there is a path* $q_1 \xrightarrow{s_1} q_2 \xrightarrow{s_2} \cdots q_n \xrightarrow{s_n} q_{n+1}$ *in* A *such that* $q_{n+1} \in F$ *and for each* $i = 1, \ldots, n$ *it holds that* $\sigma_i \in \mathsf{tval}(s_i)$*. The* language $L(A)$ *of an SFA* A *is the set of all accepted traces.*

The construction of an SFA from symbolic traces (step (2)) is shown in Algorithm 2 in the appendix. Lemma 1 states the soundness of the algorithm.

Lemma 1. *Function* CREATESFA *in Algorithm 2 is correct:* $L(\text{CREATESFA}(\tau)) = \mathsf{tval}(\tau)$ *holds for all* $\tau \in \text{SymTr}$.

Simulation relations on automata for checking language inclusion [24] and the complexity of crating them [10] have been studied before. Our notion is non-standard, though, since we use symbolic automata with *first-order* transitions. It is not sufficient to relate edges with identical labels or to use existing *propositional* symbolic approaches. Instead, we try to *prove* that an edge in the specification automaton *subsumes* an edge in the implementation automaton. We define symbolic state subsumption as follows.

Definition 7. *Let* $s_i = (\mathit{sto}_i, \varphi_i)$*,* $i = 1, 2$ *be symbolic states. Let* $\overrightarrow{\mathtt{x}_i}$ *be the left-hand sides of* sto_i*,* subst *be a substitution of abstract symbols in* s_2 *not occurring in* s_1 *with concrete symbols; i.e. uninterpreted constants, function symbols, abstract stores, abstract path conditions are replaced with terms, stores, and formulas. Let* P *be a fresh predicate with arity* $|\overrightarrow{\mathtt{x}_2}|$*. Then* s_2 subsumes s_1 *iff*

(SUB1) *all variables in* $\overrightarrow{\mathtt{x}_2}$ *are also contained in* $\overrightarrow{\mathtt{x}_1}$ *and*
(SUB2) *there is a substitution* subst *such that:*
$$\models \varphi_1 \wedge \{\mathit{sto}_1\}P(\overrightarrow{\mathtt{x}_2}) \rightarrow \mathit{subst}(\{\mathit{sto}_1\}\varphi_2 \wedge \{\mathit{sto}_2\}P(\overrightarrow{\mathtt{x}_2})) \ .$$

For states without stores omit the $\{sto_i\}$. *In the following, we write* $s_1 \sqsubseteq s_2$ *if* s_2 *subsumes* s_1, *and* $s_1 \sqsubseteq_{subst} s_2$ *to make the substitution subst for (SUB2) explicit.*

Example 3. Let $s_1 = (\mathtt{x} := 17 \,||\, \mathtt{y} := 42 \,||\, \mathtt{z} := 2, \mathrm{true})$. It is subsumed by $s_2 = (\mathtt{x} := c, c \geq 0)$, since (SUB2) holds for $subst := (c \mapsto 17)$:

$$\begin{aligned} & \models \{\mathtt{x} := 17\}P(\mathtt{x}) \rightarrow (c \mapsto 17)(\{\mathtt{x} := 17\}c \geq 0 \wedge \{\mathtt{x} := c\}P(\mathtt{x})) \\ \text{follows from } & \models \{\mathtt{x} := 17\}P(\mathtt{x}) \rightarrow (\{\mathtt{x} := 17\}17 \geq 0 \wedge \{\mathtt{x} := 17\}P(\mathtt{x})) \\ \text{follows from } & \models P(17) \rightarrow (17 \geq 0 \wedge P(17)) \end{aligned}$$

which is true (w.l.o.g. we omit parts of the store of s_1 that do not occur in the target formula). Two more small examples are in Example 8 (appendix). ◊

Lemma 2. *For* s_1, $s_2 \in \mathrm{SymState}$, $s_1 \sqsubseteq s_2$ *implies* $\mathsf{tval}(s_1) \subseteq \mathsf{tval}(s_2)$.

Subsumption can also be used to establish whether, for a concrete state σ and symbolic state s, it holds that $\sigma \in \mathsf{tval}(s)$ which is needed for the acceptance criterion of SFAs (Definition 6): for the symbolic state $s' = (\overrightarrow{\mathbf{x_s}} := \sigma(\overrightarrow{\mathbf{x_s}}), \mathrm{true})$, where $\overrightarrow{\mathbf{x_s}}$ are the left-hand sides of the store of s, it is sufficient to prove $s' \sqsubseteq s$.

Now we can define the notion of *a Subsumption Simulation Relation (SSR)*, a simulation relation on SFAs based on subsumption.

Definition 8. *A* Subsumption Simulation Relation *between SFAs* $A_i = (Q_i, \Sigma, \delta_i, q_0^i, F_i)$, $i = 1, 2$, *is any relation* $R \subseteq Q_1 \times Q_2$ *satisfying*

$$\begin{aligned} \text{(SR1)} \quad & \forall q_1 \in Q_1, q_2 \in Q_2, s, q_1' \in Q_1, \\ & \quad ((R(q_1, q_2) \wedge (q_1, s, q_1') \in \delta_1) \implies \\ & \quad\quad \exists q_2' \in Q_2, s', (R(q_1', q_2') \wedge (q_2, s', q_2') \in \delta_2 \wedge s \sqsubseteq s')) \\ \text{(SR2)} \quad & (q_0^1, q_0^2) \in R \end{aligned}$$

Definition 8 equals the "safety simulation relation" of [10], except for the highlighted conjunct $s \sqsubseteq s'$ in (SR1). Constructing an SSR additionally requires to find a suitable substitution and to call a prover showing subsumption. Since SSRs are closed under union and (SR2) is monotone, one can compute R by repeatedly deleting pairs from $Q_1 \times Q_2$ that locally do not satisfy (SR1), and then check whether the result satisfies (SR2) [10]. For each local check, we might have to substitute abstract symbols in the specification automaton. The subsequent lemma, also stated in [10] for their similar notion, establishes a sufficient condition between simulation relations and language inclusion.

Lemma 3. *If there is an SSR between SFAs* A_1 *and* A_2, *then* $L(A_1) \subseteq L(A_2)$.

Our top-level algorithm EVALUATE is shown in Algorithm 1. In the final step it tries to find an SSR. Only if this was successful, it returns YES. Function FINDSSR (Algorithm 1) starts with an "initial simulation" produced by function INITSIM (Algorithm 3, appendix) instead of the cross product to save expensive subsumption checks. During the filtering to derive an SSR, it maintains a *set* of substitutions *substs*, since there might be multiple options. Function SUBSUMPTION(s, s', *substs*) (Algorithm 4, appendix) tries to find compatible

Algorithm 1. Evaluation of a Trace Modality Formula using SSRs

function EVALUATE(s_0, $[\mathcal{C}_l \Vdash_\alpha \mathcal{C}_r]$)
  $\tau_l \leftarrow \alpha(\mathit{slift}_l(s_0)(\mathcal{C}_l))$, $\tau_r \leftarrow \alpha(\mathit{slift}_r(s_0)(\mathcal{C}_r))$ ▷ Step (1)
  $A_l \leftarrow$ CREATESFA(τ_l), $A_r \leftarrow$ CREATESFA(τ_r) ▷ Step (2)
  if $(q_0^l, q_0^r) \in$ FINDSSR(A_l, A_r) **then return** YES ▷ Step (3)
  else return UNKNOWN **end if**
end function

function FINDSSR($(Q_l, \Sigma, \delta_l, q_0^l, F_l)$, $(Q_r, \Sigma, \delta_r, q_0^r, F_r)$)
  $R \leftarrow$INITSIM(Q_l, Q_r, δ_l, δ_r), *substs* $\leftarrow \{\lambda x.x\}$, *changed* $\leftarrow$ *true*
  while *changed* = *true* **do**
    changed $\leftarrow$ *false*
    for all $(q_l, q_r) \in R$, $(q_l, s, q_l') \in \delta_l$ **do**
      if $\exists (q_r, s', q_r') \in \delta_r$ s.t. SUBSUMPTION(s, s', *substs*) $\neq \emptyset$) **then**
      substs $\leftarrow$ SUBSUMPTION(s, s', *substs*) ▷ (for all such s')
      else $R \leftarrow R \setminus (q_l, q_r)$, *changed* $\leftarrow$ *true* **end if**
    end for
  end while
  return R
end function

extensions subst' of the substitutions in *substs* by first applying an existing substitution and then finding another one for yet uninstantiated abstract symbols. If there is no such substitution, e.g., since one would have to instantiate the same abstract symbol with different values, the original substitution is dropped. We do not further specify the process of finding substitutions; a naive approach could try to instantiate abstract symbols with all combinations of terms occurring as right-hand sides in the store of s. An example application of Algorithm 1 is shown in the appendix. Lemma 4 below states correctness of the FINDSSR. The subsequent main theorem follows from Lemmas 1 to 4 and the usage of correct symbolic lifting functions (Definition 5).

Lemma 4. *Function* FINDSSR *(Algorithm 1) is correct: For SFAs A_1, A_2, it holds that any SSR R found by* FINDSSR(A_1, A_2) *satisfies (SR1).*

Theorem 1. *Function* EVALUATE *(Algorithm 1) is correct: For all $s_0 \in$ SymState,* EVALUATE(s_0, $[\mathcal{C}_1 \Vdash_\alpha \mathcal{C}_2]$) = YES *only if, for all $\sigma \in \mathsf{tval}(s_0)$, $\sigma \models [\mathcal{C}_1 \Vdash_\alpha \mathcal{C}_2]$.*

5 Related Work

We compare our work to (1) logics based on traces and (2) approaches unifying program verification techniques. De Giacomo & Vardi [9] propose a Regular Temporal Specification language RE_f that is syntactically similar to our symbolic traces, but ranges over *propositional* formulas while our atoms are first-order symbolic states. They show that RE_f has the same expressiveness as Monadic Second-order Logic (MSO) and is strictly more expressive than LTL on finite traces. They define Linear-time Dynamic Logic LDL_f, having the same expressivity as RE_f, but allowing logical connectives like negation. Reasoning in LDL_f is also translated to automata. They mention, but do not detail, the possibility to "capture finite executions of programs [...] (in a propositional variant [...])", which is exactly what we do—but not restricted to a propositional variant. In addition, we incorporate *abstract programs* to reason about *classes* of programs. It would be interesting to investigate whether we could use a variant of LDL_f to embed symbolic traces conveniently into logic formulas.

Beckert & Bruns [5] combine dynamic logic and first-order temporal logic to a *Dynamic Trace Logic*. They have a trace-based semantics for a while language and provide a sequent calculus to reason about temporal properties (not preceded by symbolic lifting). The calculus rules depend on the top-level operator of the first-order LTL post condition. This leads quite complex loop invariant rules. Also, the approach is not directly applicable to other verification domains, e.g., relational verification. Our approach is more flexible, because there is no syntactic constraint between the left and right-hand side of the trace modality.

Din et al. [11] propose a trace semantics for the actor-based concurrent language ABS. Traces are "locally abstract, globally concrete": at the local (e.g., method) level, symbolic traces are used. These are primarily a *semantic* notion, facilitating a modular semantics for a concurrent language, while our symbolic traces are *syntactic* entities. The authors briefly sketch a program logic with trace formulas, but leave the notion of trace formulas abstract.

Regarding area (2), Kamburjan [20] proposes the *behavioral modality* aiming to integrate existing analyses and sharing some aspects with the trace modality. It asserts that a statement in a concurrent language meets a behavioral specification consisting of a *type* and a *translation* of the type into an MSO formula. This is the case if that formula holds for all traces generated by the statement. Important differences to our approach include: (a) The behavioral modality *syntactically* integrates analyses on the *same program class*, while the trace modality is mainly a *general semantic framework*, (b) the "translation" of [20] projects to MSO and is thus less expressive than lifting to arbitrary trace sets. The trace modality can also be used to combine verification techniques. Two specifications can semantically be combined by forming the intersection of the trace sets. For reasoning about combinations, we could use product constructions on SFAs.

Some systems do not provide a common semantics for verification domains, but a framework to *implement* different analyses. They usually represent verification problems in an Intermediate Language (IL) and interface to different provers. Boogie [2] and Why3 [6] both are an IL and tool for deductive program verification. They are used as backends by verifiers for languages like C and Java. Our "IL" is the regular symbolic trace language, which, compared to Boogie and WhyML, is less usable for direct programming, more abstract and less expressive (e.g., we cannot directly write loops, but have to use invariants). Yet, the syntactic notion of symbolic traces is closely related to the semantic notion of the trace modality, allowing *formalizing* and *proving* a problem in a closely related framework. Moreover, the trace modality can easily express other problems than "standard" post condition verification. Our algorithm also interfaces to different provers: Which one to use in the subsumption step is left open.

6 Conclusion and Outlook

We presented the trace modality, a novel formalism for expressing many practical problems of sequential program verification. It relates two elements of the same or different domains, e.g., programs, first-order assertions, or temporal logic formulas. Programs can be abstract and represent classes of concrete programs. We demonstrate the usefulness of the trace modality by providing formalizations of various verification problems: Functional Verification, Information Flow Analysis, Model Checking, Program Synthesis, Compilation, and Program Evolution. Our uniform reasoning system translates programs and formulas to regular symbolic traces and then reduces the problem to the construction of simulation relations between finite automata with symbolic transitions. Similar to the semantics of the trace modality, this approach is parametric in the translation to symbolic traces and the abstraction operator. Although regular symbolic traces have already been proposed before as both a specification mechanism and semantic representation, our work is the first we know of connecting both aspects. This facilitates flexible reasoning about programs and specifications in different combinations: A program can even serve as the specification of a formula.

We hope that our uniform formalization helps to uncover synergy potential between so far separate areas in the field of program verification. Moreover, the practical potential of a system based on symbolic traces supporting different verification techniques, for example, program synthesis and deductive verification, is huge. For instance, after a failed proof attempt of a postcondition, one could try synthesis techniques for stepwise refinement of the postcondition to an abstract program. MC and deductive verification techniques could work hand in hand to treat loops, by unwinding, k-induction, abstract interpretation-based techniques, etc. Finally, the idea of "patch abstraction" for program evolution could help in proof reuse, by applying the patches also to existing proofs.

Apart from investigating these ideas, we plan to implement our reasoning algorithm for symbolic traces and to examine different existing trace languages, like linear-time dynamic logic, which might lead to more intuitive or more expressive representations. Also, we project to extend our framework to non-deterministic, in particular, to concurrent programming languages.

References

1. Ahrendt, W., Beckert, B., et al. (eds.): Deductive Software Verification - The KeY Book. LNCS, vol. 10001. Springer, Cham (2016). https://doi.org/10.1007/978-3-319-49812-6

2. Barnett, M., Chang, B.-Y.E., DeLine, R., Jacobs, B., Leino, K.R.M.: Boogie: a modular reusable verifier for object-oriented programs. In: de Boer, F.S., Bonsangue, M.M., Graf, S., de Roever, W.-P. (eds.) FMCO 2005. LNCS, vol. 4111, pp. 364–387. Springer, Heidelberg (2006). https://doi.org/10.1007/11804192_17
3. Barthe, G., Crespo, J.M., Kunz, C.: Relational verification using product programs. In: Butler, M., Schulte, W. (eds.) FM 2011. LNCS, vol. 6664, pp. 200–214. Springer, Heidelberg (2011). https://doi.org/10.1007/978-3-642-21437-0_17
4. Barthe, G., D'Argenio, P.R., et al.: Secure information flow by self-composition. In: Proceedings of CSFW-17, pp. 100–114. IEEE Computer Society (2004)
5. Beckert, B., Bruns, D.: Dynamic logic with trace semantics. In: Bonacina, M.P. (ed.) CADE 2013. LNCS (LNAI), vol. 7898, pp. 315–329. Springer, Heidelberg (2013). https://doi.org/10.1007/978-3-642-38574-2_22
6. Bobot, F., Filliâtre, J.C., et al.: Why3: shepherd your herd of provers. In: Boogie 2011: First International Workshop on IVL, pp. 53–64 (2011)
7. Cousot, P., Cousot, R.: Abstract interpretation: a unified lattice model for static analysis of programs by construction or approximation of fixpoints. In: 4th Symposium of POPL, pp. 238–252. ACM Press, January 1977
8. Darvas, Á., Hähnle, R., Sands, D.: A theorem proving approach to analysis of secure information flow. In: Hutter, D., Ullmann, M. (eds.) SPC 2005. LNCS, vol. 3450, pp. 193–209. Springer, Heidelberg (2005). https://doi.org/10.1007/978-3-540-32004-3_20
9. De Giacomo, G., Vardi, M.Y.: Linear temporal logic and linear dynamic logic on finite traces. In: Proceedings of 23rd IJCAI, pp. 854–860 (2013)
10. Dill, D.L., Hu, A.J., Wong-Toi, H.: Checking for language inclusion using simulation preorders. In: Larsen, K.G., Skou, A. (eds.) CAV 1991. LNCS, vol. 575, pp. 255–265. Springer, Heidelberg (1992). https://doi.org/10.1007/3-540-55179-4_25
11. Din, C.C., Hähnle, R., Johnsen, E.B., Pun, K.I., Tapia Tarifa, S.L.: Locally abstract, globally concrete semantics of concurrent programming languages. In: Schmidt, R.A., Nalon, C. (eds.) TABLEAUX 2017. LNCS (LNAI), vol. 10501, pp. 22–43. Springer, Cham (2017). https://doi.org/10.1007/978-3-319-66902-1_2
12. Garrido, A., Meseguer, J.: Formal specification and verification of Java refactorings. In: Proceedings of 6th SCAM, pp. 165–174. IEEE Computer Society (2006)
13. Godlin, B., Strichman, O.: Regression verification: proving the equivalence of similar programs. Softw. Test. Verif. Reliab. **23**(3), 241–258 (2013)
14. Hähnle, R., Heisel, M., Reif, W., Stephan, W.: An interactive verification system based on dynamic logic. In: Siekmann, J.H. (ed.) CADE 1986. LNCS, vol. 230, pp. 306–315. Springer, Heidelberg (1986). https://doi.org/10.1007/3-540-16780-3_99
15. Harel, D., Tiuryn, J., et al.: Dynamic Logic. MIT Press, Cambridge (2000)
16. Heisel, M.: Formalizing and implementing Gries' program development method in dynamic logic. Sci. Comput. Program. **18**(1), 107–137 (1992)
17. Hoare, C.A.R.: An axiomatic basis for computer programming. Commun. ACM **12**(10), 576–580 (1969)
18. Holzmann, G.J.: The model checker SPIN. IEEE Trans. SE **23**(5), 279–295 (1997)
19. Jhala, R., Majumdar, R.: Software model checking. ACM Comput. Surv. **41**(4), 21:1–21:54 (2009)
20. Kamburjan, E.: Behavioral program logic. In: Cerrito, S., Popescu, A. (eds.) TABLEAUX 2019. LNCS (LNAI), vol. 11714, pp. 391–408. Springer, Cham (2019). https://doi.org/10.1007/978-3-030-29026-9_22
21. Leroy, X.: Formal verification of a realistic compiler. Comm. ACM **52**(7), 107–115 (2009)

22. Monperrus, M.: Automatic software repair: a bibliography. ACM Comput. Surv. **51**(1), 17:1–17:24 (2018)
23. Păsăreanu, C.S., Visser, W.: Verification of Java programs using symbolic execution and invariant generation. In: Graf, S., Mounier, L. (eds.) SPIN 2004. LNCS, vol. 2989, pp. 164–181. Springer, Heidelberg (2004). https://doi.org/10.1007/978-3-540-24732-6_13
24. Rauch Henzinger, M., Henzinger, T.A., et al.: Computing simulations on finite and infinite graphs. In: Proceedings of 36th Symposium on FoCS, pp. 453–462. IEEE (1995)
25. Reps, T.W., Horwitz, S., et al.: Precise interprocedural dataflow analysis via graph reachability. In: Proceedings of 22nd POPL, pp. 49–61 (1995)
26. Shankar, N.: Combining model checking and deduction. Handbook of Model Checking, pp. 651–684. Springer, Cham (2018). https://doi.org/10.1007/978-3-319-10575-8_20
27. Srivastava, S., Gulwani, S., et al.: From program verification to program synthesis. In: Proceedings of 37th POPL, pp. 313–326 (2010)
28. Steinhöfel, D., Hähnle, R.: Modular, correct compilation with automatic soundness proofs. In: Margaria, T., Steffen, B. (eds.) ISoLA 2018. LNCS, vol. 11244, pp. 424–447. Springer, Cham (2018). https://doi.org/10.1007/978-3-030-03418-4_25
29. Visser, W., Havelund, K., et al.: Model checking programs. Autom. Softw. Eng. **10**(2), 203–232 (2003)
30. Yang, H.: Relational separation logic. Theoret. CS **375**(1–3), 308–334 (2007)

Iterative Division in the Distributive Full Non-associative Lambek Calculus

Igor Sedlár(✉)

The Czech Academy of Sciences, Institute of Computer Science,
Pod Vodárenskou věží 271/2, Prague, Czech Republic
sedlar@cs.cas.cz

Abstract. We study an extension of the Distributive Full Non-associative Lambek Calculus with iterative division operators. The iterative operators can be seen as representing iterative composition of linguistic resources or of actions. A complete axiomatization of the logic is provided and decidability is established via a proof of the finite model property.

Keywords: Distributive Full Non-associative Lambek Calculus · Dynamic logic · Iterated composition · Lambek Calculus · Transitive closure

1 Introduction

Operators of the Lambek Calculus [16] were designed to represent types of linguistic expressions. The "product" operator • articulates the internal structure of expressions—an expression is of type $A \bullet B$ if it is a result of *concatenating* an expression of type A with an expression of type B, in that order. The left and right "division" operators, \ and /, describe the behaviour of expressions under concatenations—an expression x is of type $A \backslash B$ if, for all expressions y of type A, the concatenation yx is of type B; similarly for B/A and xy. The interpretation of product in terms of concatenation of strings requires the product operation to be associative, which also entails some particular properties of the division operators.

The Lambek operators admit more general interpretations as well. For instance, we may read them in terms of *merging pieces of information* or *composing linguistic resources*; see [18, p. 350] or [13, p. 10]. On this interpretation, $A \backslash B$ denotes resources x such that if x is composed with an "input" resource of type A, then the result is a resource of type B; similarly B/A denotes resources x such that any composition of a resource of type A with "input" x will result in a resource of type B. Adopting the perspective of arrow logic [2,26], the division

This work is supported by the Czech Science Foundation grant number GJ18-19162Y. The author is grateful to Andrew Tedder and three anonymous reviewers for useful comments.

L. Soares Barbosa and A. Baltag (Eds.): DaLí 2019, LNCS 12005, pp. 141–154, 2020.
https://doi.org/10.1007/978-3-030-38808-9_9

operators can also be seen as describing *composition of actions*. On this interpretation, $A\backslash B$ denotes actions x such that any action consisting of performing an action of type A and then performing x is an action of type B; B/A denotes actions x such that performing x and then performing an action of type A is always of type B.

Assuming either of these interpretations, it is natural to consider *iterated composition* in addition to "one-off" composition represented by the Lambek division operators. As an example of iterated composition, take a linguistic resource y and an arbitrary non-empty finite sequence $x_1, \ldots, x_n$ of resources of type A, and compose y with input x_1, then compose the result with input x_2 and so on. With an *iterative* left division operator at hand, say $\backslash\!\!\backslash$, we could denote by $A \backslash\!\!\backslash B$ resources y such that iterated composition of y with any non-empty sequence of resources $x_1, \ldots, x_n$ of type A, as indicated above, is guaranteed to result in a resource of type B. As another example, take an action y and a finite non-empty sequence $x_1, \ldots, x_n$ of actions of type A. Perform x_1 after y, then perform x_2 and so on. With an iterative right division operator at hand, say $/\!\!/$, we could denote by $B /\!\!/ A$ actions y such that performing any sequence of actions of type A after y, as indicated above, is guaranteed to result in an action of type B. Iterative composition can be seen as a generalization of action iteration in dynamic logic; the former corresponds to a binary modality while the latter to a unary one. Accordingly, the question concerning the result of iterated composition can be seen as a question concerning "correctness" of iterative composition with respect to specific postconditions.

Example 1. Suppose we want to know if the core beliefs of some agent, say Ann, concerning some topic of interest, are "immune" to fake news concerning the topic. We can rephrase this by asking if exposing Ann consecutively to any number of fake news related to the topic changes her core beliefs concerning the topic. This is a question concerning iterated composition—let y represent Ann's initial belief state, let A denote fake news concerning the given topic and let B denote belief states that support Ann's initial core beliefs concerning the topic; the question is whether combining y consecutively with any $x_1, \ldots, x_n$ of type A results in a belief state of type B.

Example 2. Suppose we have programmed a robot to perform certain tasks under specific observed conditions, for example re-arranging objects in a warehouse. For security reasons, we want to know if any "legal" sequence of the robot's actions can lead to a situation endangering the human workers in the warehouse. Again, we have here an issue pertaining to iterated composition—the question is whether, given some initial action y, all sequences of actions of the type "legal" performed consecutively after y constitute an action of type "not endangering the human workers".

Note that $A \backslash\!\!\backslash B$, interpreted as above, intuitively corresponds to an infinite conjunction of formulas $A\backslash B$, $A\backslash(A\backslash B)$, $A\backslash(A\backslash(A\backslash B))$ and so on; similarly $B /\!\!/ A$ corresponds to an infinite conjunction of B/A, $(B/A)/A$ and so on. On the assumption that composition (product) is associative, the former series of formulas is equivalent to $A\backslash B$, $(A \bullet A)\backslash B$, $\big(A \bullet (A \bullet A)\big)\backslash B$ and so on; and similarly for the latter series of formulas. Hence, on the assumption of associativity, iterative division of both kinds can be formalised using a transitive-only version of the "continuous" Kleene star opertor familiar from regular languages; see especially Pratt's Action Logic [21], Kozen's $*$-cointinuous action lattices [12] or van Benthem's Dynamic Arrow Logic [1]. As "the Kleene plus" of A, A^+, intuitively represents $A \vee (A \bullet A) \vee \big(A \bullet (A \bullet A)\big) \vee \ldots$, "repeated considerations of information of type A resulting in B" (the first example), i.e. $A \backslash\!\backslash B$, can be formalized as $A^+\backslash B$ and "repeating A-type actions with result B" (the second example), i.e. $B /\!/ A$, as B/A^+.

However, the assumption of associativity, necessary for the reduction of iterative division to the Kleene operator, is problematic for at least two reasons. Firstly, it has been shown that associativity often leads to undecidability. Buszkowski [5] and Palka [20] have shown that the logic of all $*$-continuous action lattices (the ones where, roughly, Kleene star is equivalent to an infinite disjunction) is undecidable; Kuznetsov [15] established recently that the logic of all action lattices is undecidable as well. His proof applies also to Pratt's Action Logic. It follows from the results of [14] that Associative Dynamic Arrow Logic is undecidable.

Secondly, associativity of composition is problematic on some information-related and channel-theoretic interpretations of the Lambek Calculus; see e.g. [24,25] for more details. Lambek [17] provides motivation for getting rid of associativity even on the original linguistic interpretation of his calculus. (On this interpretation, the object of study are "bracketed strings" over an alphabet—in presence of associativity, brackets can be omitted).

Thus a natural question arises concerning a formalization of iterative composition in the more general non-associative setting. In this paper we extend the Distributive Non-associative Lambek Calculus with primitive iterative division operators $\backslash\!\backslash$ and $/\!/$, representing the two kinds of iterative composition outlined in the above examples. Whe show that the resulting logic is decidable and we provide a sound and complete axiomatization for it. Our starting point is the relational semantics for the Distributive Non-associative Lambek Calculus in the style of Došen [8] using a ternary accessibility relation. In Sect. 2 we use this semantics to give satisfaction clauses for formulas with $\backslash\!\backslash$ and $/\!/$. In Sect. 3 we provide a weakly complete axiomatization of the theory of all such models and prove that the theory is decidable. In the concluding Sect. 4 we discuss variants and extensions of our basic logic and point out some possible directions of future work.

Related Work. Bimbó and Dunn [4] provide a relational semantics for Pratt's Action Logic (a logic containing versions of the Lambek division operators along with the Kleene star) and for the related logic of Kleene Algebras [11]. Non-associative versions of Kleene algebra were studied in [7] with a motivation coming from temporal logic. The iterative division operators studied in the present paper seem to be new, although definable in existing frameworks on the assumption of associativity.

2 Relational Models and Iteration

A *Došen frame* is $F = \langle S, R \rangle$, where S is a non-empty set ("states") and R is a ternary relation on S. States can be seen, for instance, as linguistic resources. On that interpretation, $Rstu$ means that composing resource t with input s might result in resource u (composition is in general non-deterministic). States can also be seen as actions, in which case $Rstu$ is taken to mean that action u may be decomposed into s followed by t (as in arrow logic) or, more generally, as saying that performing t after s may give u.

Fix a denumerable set Pr of propositional variables, intuitively representing some basic features of states. A *Došen model* is $M = \langle S, R, V \rangle$ where V is a function from Pr to subsets of S; $V(p)$ is the set of states having feature p. We say that $\langle S, R, V \rangle$ is a model based on frame $\langle S, R \rangle$.

Various formal languages can be used to express complex features of states. Our basic language is the Lambek language with bounded-lattice connectives $\mathcal{L}_{[\backslash, \bullet, /, \wedge, \vee, \top, \bot]}$, concisely denoted as $\mathcal{L}_0$, containing zero-ary operators $\top$ ("top", "truth") and $\bot$ ("bottom", "falsity") and binary operators $\backslash$ ("left division"), $\bullet$ ("product", "fusion"), $/$ ("right division"), $\wedge$ ("meet", "conjunction") and $\vee$ ("join", "disjunction"). The set of $\mathcal{L}_0$-*formulas* (over Pr) is defined as usual. *Sequents* are ordered pairs of formulas. For each M, we define the *satisfaction relation* $\models_M$ between states of the model and formulas as follows:

$s \models_M p$ iff $s \in V(p)$;
$s \models_M \top$ for all s; $s \not\models_M \bot$ for all s;
$s \models_M A \wedge B$ iff $s \models_M A$ and $s \models_M B$;
$s \models_M A \vee B$ iff $s \models_M A$ or $s \models_M B$;
$s \models_M A \bullet B$ iff there are t, u such that $Rtus$ and $t \models_M A$ and $u \models_M B$;
$s \models_M A \backslash B$ iff, for all t and u, if $Rtsu$ and $t \models_M A$, then $u \models_M B$;
$s \models_M B/A$ iff, for all t and u, if $Rstu$ and $t \models_M A$, then $u \models_M B$.

A sequent $A \vdash B$ is *valid in* M iff $s \models_M A$ implies $s \models_M B$ for all states s of M; $A \vdash B$ is *valid in a frame* F iff it is valid in all models based on the frame. For each language $\mathcal{L}$ considered in this paper, the $\mathcal{L}$-*theory* of a class of frames is the set of sequents of $\mathcal{L}$-formulas valid in each frame belonging to the class.

Informally, formulas express types of states; $s \models_M A$ is read as "s is of type A (in M)". Sequents express type dependency; $A \vdash B$ is valid in M iff all states of type A are of type B (in M).

We use the standard [22] notation

$$Rstuv := \exists x(Rstx \;\&\; Rxuv) \qquad Rs(tu)v := \exists x(Rsxv \;\&\; Rtux)$$

Let $\bar{x}$ be a finite non-empty list of states $\langle x_1, \dots, x_n \rangle$, which we call a "path of length n". We define

$$R\overleftarrow{x}\,st := \exists y_1, \dots, y_{n-1}\big(Rx_1sy_1 \wedge \big(\bigwedge_{1 \le i \le n-2} Rx_{i+1}y_iy_{i+1}\big) \wedge Rx_ny_{n-1}t\big)$$

$$Rs\overrightarrow{x}\,t := \exists y_1, \dots, y_{n-1}\big(Rsx_1y_1 \wedge \big(\bigwedge_{1 \le i \le n-2} Ry_ix_{i+1}y_{i+1}\big) \wedge Ry_{n-1}x_nt\big)$$

(Hence, if $\bar{x} = \langle x_1, x_2 \rangle$, then $R\overleftarrow{x}st$ is $\exists y(Rx_1sy \wedge Rx_2yt)$, i.e. $Rx_2(x_1s)t$, whereas $Rs\overrightarrow{x}t$ is $\exists y(Rsx_1y \wedge Ryx_2t)$, i.e. Rsx_1x_2t .)

We say that $\bar{x} = \langle x_1, \ldots, x_n \rangle$ satisfies A in M, notation $\bar{x} \models_M A$, iff $x_i \models_M A$ for all $i \in \{1, \ldots, n\}$. We define

$$A\backslash^1 B := A\backslash B \quad A\backslash^{n+1} B := A\backslash(A\backslash^n B) \quad B/^1 A := B/A \quad B/^{n+1} A := (B/^n A)/A$$

Note that $A\backslash^n B$ denotes a type of object such that, if n inputs of type A are consecutively combined with the given object, then the result will be of type B; $B/^n A$ has a similar meaning. The iterative division operators we are after can be seen, informally, as corresponding to infinite conjunctions:

$$\bigwedge_{1 \leq n} A\backslash^n B \qquad \bigwedge_{1 \leq n} B/^n A$$

Of course, these are not really formulas of our language as conjunctions are finite. Hence, we need to express iterative division in some other way.

Lemma 1. *Let $\bar{x} = \langle x_1, \bar{z} \rangle$. Then*

(a) $\bar{x} \models_M A$ only if $\bar{z} \models A$;
(b) $R\overleftarrow{x}st$ only if Rx_1sy_1 and $R\overleftarrow{z}x_1t$ for some y_1;
(c) $Rs\overrightarrow{x}t$ only if Rsx_1y_1 and $Rx_1\overleftarrow{z}t$ for some y_1.

Proof. Item (a) is obvious. (b) follows from the assumption that $z_i = x_{i+1}$ and the definition of $Rs\overrightarrow{x}t$. (c) is established similarly.

Proposition 1.

(a) $s \models_M A\backslash^n B$ iff, for all paths $\bar{x}$ of length n and all t, if $R\overleftarrow{x}st$ and $\bar{x} \models_M A$, then $t \models_M B$.
(b) $s \models_M B/^n A$ iff, for all paths $\bar{x}$ of length n and all t, if $Rs\overrightarrow{x}t$ and $\bar{x} \models_M A$, then $t \models_M B$.

Proof. Induction on n. Both base cases $n = 1$ are straightforward consequences of the satisfaction clauses for the division operators. Next, we show that if (a) holds for $k \in \{1, \ldots, n-1\}$, then it holds for $k+1$; a similar claim about (b) is established analogously. Firstly, assume that $s \models A\backslash^{k+1} B$ and we have $\bar{x} = \langle x_1, \ldots, x_{k+1} \rangle = \langle x_1, \bar{z} \rangle$ such that $R\overleftarrow{x}st$ and $\bar{x} \models A$. We have to show that $t \models B$. By the definition of $A\backslash^{k+1} B$, we have $s \models A\backslash(A\backslash^k B)$ and by the definition of $R\overleftarrow{x}st$ we have Rx_1sy_1 and $R\overleftarrow{z}y_1t$ for some y_1. Hence, $y_1 \models A\backslash^k B$ by the satisfaction clause for left division and so $t \models B$ by the induction hypothesis ($\bar{z}$ is obviously a path of length k). Secondly, we show that if $s \not\models A\backslash^{k+1} B$, then there is a path $\bar{x}$ of length $k+1$ such that $R\overleftarrow{x}st$, $\bar{x} \models A$ and $t \not\models B$. If $s \not\models A\backslash^{k+1} B$, then $s \not\models A\backslash(A\backslash^n B)$ by the definition of $A\backslash^{k+1} B$. Hence, there are x, y such that $Rxsy$, $x \models A$ and $y \not\models A\backslash^k B$. The latter means, by the induction hypothesis, that there is a sequence $\bar{z}$ of length k and a state t such that $R\overleftarrow{z}yt$ and $\bar{z} \models A$ while $t \not\models B$. But $\bar{x} = \langle x, \bar{z} \rangle$ is a sequence of length $k+1$ satisfying A such that $R\overleftarrow{z}st$.

The proposition provides a lead as to the appropriate satisfaction conditions for iterated versions of the division operators to which we now turn.

The Lambek language with distributive bounded-lattice connectives and iterative division operators $\mathcal{L}_{[\backslash,\bullet,/,\backslash\!\backslash,/\!\!/,\wedge,\vee,\top,\bot]}$, denoted also as $\mathcal{L}_1$, adds to $\mathcal{L}_0$ two binary operators $\backslash\!\backslash$ ("iterative left division") and $/\!\!/$ ("iterative right division"). A *finite path* of elements of a model is a path $\bar{x}$ of length n for some natural number $n \geq 1$. The satisfaction relation, when extended to $\mathcal{L}_1$, is assumed to satisfy the following new clauses:

$s \models_M A\backslash\!\backslash B$ iff, for all t and finite paths $\bar{x}$, if $R\overleftarrow{\bar{x}}st$ and $\bar{x} \models_M A$, then $t \models_M B$;
$s \models_M B/\!\!/A$ iff, for all t and finite paths $\bar{x}$, if $Rs\overrightarrow{\bar{x}}t$ and $\bar{x} \models_M A$, then $t \models_M B$.

Validity is defined as before.

Proposition 2. *The following sequents are valid in all Došen frames:*

(a) $A\backslash\!\backslash B \wedge A\backslash\!\backslash C \vdash A\backslash\!\backslash(B \wedge C)$ *and* $B/\!\!/A \wedge C/\!\!/A \vdash (B \wedge C)/\!\!/A$;
(b) $A\backslash\!\backslash B \vdash A\backslash B \wedge A\backslash(A\backslash\!\backslash B)$ *and* $B/\!\!/A \vdash B/A \wedge (B/\!\!/A)/A$;
(c) $A\backslash B \wedge A\backslash(A\backslash\!\backslash B) \vdash A\backslash\!\backslash B$ *and* $(B/\!\!/A)/A \wedge B/A \vdash B/\!\!/A$.

The following rules preserve validity in Došen models:

(d) $\dfrac{A \vdash B \quad C \vdash D}{B\backslash\!\backslash C \vdash A\backslash\!\backslash D}$ *and* $\dfrac{A \vdash B \quad C \vdash D}{C/\!\!/B \vdash D/\!\!/A}$;
(e) $\dfrac{A \vdash B\backslash A}{A \vdash B\backslash\!\backslash A}$ *and* $\dfrac{A \vdash A/B}{A \vdash A/\!\!/B}$.

Proof. We show just the $\backslash\!\backslash$-parts of (b), (c) and (e). (b) Firstly, it is clear that $A\backslash\!\backslash B \vdash A\backslash B$ is valid (consider paths of length 1). Secondly, fix s, take some t, u and assume that there are x and $\bar{z}$ satisfying A such that $Rxst$ and $R\overleftarrow{\bar{z}}tu$. We have to prove that $u \models B$. It is clear that $R\overleftarrow{\langle x, \bar{z}\rangle}su$ and $\langle x, \bar{z}\rangle \models A$; hence if $s \models A\backslash\!\backslash B$, then $u \models B$ and so, in general, $s \models A\backslash(A\backslash\!\backslash B)$.

(c) Assume that $s \models A\backslash(A\backslash\!\backslash B) \wedge A\backslash B$ and take some finite path $\bar{x}$ satisfying A such that $R\overleftarrow{\bar{x}}st$. We have to show that $t \models B$. If $\bar{x} = \langle x \rangle$, then this follows from the assumption that $s \models A\backslash B$. If $\bar{x} = \langle x, \bar{z}\rangle$, then $R\overleftarrow{\bar{z}}yt$ and $y \models A\backslash\!\backslash B$ by Lemma 1 and the assumption $s \models A\backslash(A\backslash\!\backslash B)$; it then follows readily that $t \models B$.

To prove (e), assume that $s \models_M A$ and $R\overleftarrow{\bar{x}}st$ for some $\bar{x} \models_M B$ and t. We have to show that $t \models_M A$. By the definition of $R\overleftarrow{\bar{x}}st$, there are $y_1, \ldots, y_{n-1}$ such that

$$Rx_1sy_1 \wedge \bigwedge_{1 \leq i \leq n-2} Rx_{i+1}y_iy_{i+1} \wedge Rx_ny_{n-1}t$$

If A entails $B\backslash A$ in M, then $y_i \models_M A$ for all $i \in \{1, \ldots, n-1\}$. Hence, $y_{n-1} \models_M B\backslash A$ and so $t \models_M A$.

Remark 1. We may define the *left transitive closure* R^{+l} of R stepwise as follows:

$$R^1 := R$$
$$R^{n+1} := \{\langle s, t, u\rangle \mid \exists xy(Rsyu \wedge R^nxty)\}$$
$$R^{+l} := \bigcup_{1 \leq n} R^n$$

The right transitive closure R^{+r} of R may be defined similarly. It is interesting to note that the implication

$$s \vDash_M A \backslash\!\backslash B \implies \Big(\forall t, u(R^{+l}tsu \wedge t \vDash_M A \Rightarrow u \vDash_M B\Big) \tag{1}$$

is not valid in general, although the converse implication is valid. (A similar claim holds for R^{+r} and $B /\!/ A$.) To see the former, take a model where $R = \{\langle x, s, y\rangle, \langle t, y, u\rangle\}$ and $V(p) = \{t\}, V(q) = \emptyset$. Then $R^{+l} = \{\langle t, s, u\rangle\}$, so the consequent of (1) fails for $A = p$ and $B = q$. However, there are no finite paths $\bar{x}$ such that $R\overleftarrow{\bar{x}}\, su$ and $\bar{x} \vDash A$ (only $\langle x, t\rangle$ satisfies the former condition, but p fails in x), so vacuously $s \vDash p \backslash\!\backslash q$. To see the latter, observe that if $R\overleftarrow{\bar{x}}\, su$ and x is the last element of $\bar{x}$, then $R^{+l}xsu$.

We note that

$$A \backslash\!\backslash C \wedge B \backslash\!\backslash C \vdash (A \vee B) \backslash\!\backslash C \quad \text{and} \quad C /\!/ A \wedge C /\!/ B \vdash C /\!/ (A \vee B)$$

are not valid; the reader is invited to find a counterexample as an exercise.

3 Completeness and Decidability

In this section we provide a sound and (weakly) complete axiomatization of the $\mathcal{L}_1$-theory of all Došen frames and we show the theory to be decidable via a finite canonical model construction. Our technique derives from [19]; it is a variant of the finite canonical model construction often used in completeness proofs for logics with fixpoint operators such as epistemic logics with common knowledge or Propositional Dynamic Logic.

Let us consider the following axiom system, denoted as *IDFNL*:

Distributive lattice axioms

$$A \vdash A \qquad A \vdash \top \qquad \bot \vdash A$$
$$A \wedge B \vdash A \qquad A \wedge B \vdash B \qquad A \vdash A \vee B \qquad B \vdash A \vee B$$
$$A \wedge (B \vee C) \vdash (A \wedge B) \vee (A \wedge C)$$

Residuation rules

$$\frac{A \bullet B \vdash C}{B \vdash A \backslash C} \qquad \frac{B \vdash A \backslash C}{A \bullet B \vdash C} \qquad \frac{A \bullet B \vdash C}{A \vdash C / B} \qquad \frac{A \vdash C / B}{A \bullet B \vdash C}$$

Iteration axioms

$$A \backslash\!\backslash B \wedge A \backslash\!\backslash C \vdash A \backslash\!\backslash (B \wedge C) \qquad B /\!/ A \wedge C /\!/ A \vdash (B \wedge C) /\!/ A$$
$$A \backslash\!\backslash B \vdash A \backslash B \wedge A \backslash (A \backslash\!\backslash B) \qquad B /\!/ A \vdash B / A \wedge (B /\!/ A) / A$$
$$A \backslash B \wedge A \backslash (A \backslash\!\backslash B) \vdash A \backslash\!\backslash B \qquad (B /\!/ A) / A \wedge B / A \vdash B /\!/ A$$

Distributive lattice rules

$$\frac{A \vdash B \quad A \vdash C}{A \vdash B \wedge C} \qquad \frac{A \vdash C \quad B \vdash C}{A \vee B \vdash C} \qquad \frac{A \vdash B \quad B \vdash C}{A \vdash C}$$

Iteration rules

$$\frac{A \vdash B \quad C \vdash D}{B \backslash\!\backslash C \vdash A \backslash\!\backslash D} \qquad \frac{A \vdash B \quad C \vdash D}{C /\!/ B \vdash D /\!/ A} \qquad \frac{A \vdash B \backslash A}{A \vdash B \backslash\!\backslash A} \qquad \frac{A \vdash A / B}{A \vdash A /\!/ B}$$

Theorems are defined as usual. We write $A \longrightarrow B$ instead of "$A \vdash B$ is provable in *IDFNL*" for the rest of the paper.

Remark 2. If the sequence of symbols "$A\backslash$" is seen as a formula-indexed unary modality $[A]$, the special case "$(A \vee B)\backslash$" is seen as a choice modality $[A \cup B]$ and the special case "$A\backslash\!\backslash$" is seen as a transitive-closure modality $[A^+]$, then some of the iteration axioms and rules correspond to variants of Segerberg's axioms for Propositional Dynamic Logic; see [9, ch. 7], for example. (A similar claim applies to "$/A$", which we leave out of the present discussion). It follows from the residuation rules that (i) $[A]$ is a regular modality in the sense of [6,23]—$[A]B \wedge [A]C$ entails $[A](B \wedge C)$; (ii) $[A]$ is a monotonic modality—if B entails C, then $[A]B$ entails $[A]C$; (iii) $[A]$ is a normal modality—$[A]\top$ is entailed by $\top$. For similar reasons, $[A^+]$ can also be seen as a normal, regular and monotonic modality.

The residuation rules also imply that "choice" $[A \cup B]$ satisfies the usual PDL reduction axiom, according to which $[A \cup B]C$ is equivalent to $[A]C \wedge [B]C$. The second iteration rule corresponds to the *Loop Invariance Rule* of PDL according to which A entails $[B^+]A$ in case A entails $[B]A$. The second and third iteration axiom together say that $[A^+]B$ is a fixed point of the function $f : C \mapsto [A]B \wedge [A]C$.[1] Note that $[A^+]B$ is not a fixed point of $f' : C \mapsto [A]C$ (we are dealing with a version of transitive closure—but recall Remark 1—not reflexive transitive closure).

As noted earlier, the dual of the first iteration axiom does not hold; this is reminiscent of the situation in PDL where, transposed to our setting, $[A^+ \cup B^+]C$ is not equivalent to $[(A \cup B)^+]C$.

Given Remark 2, it is not surprising that completeness and decidability results concerning our logic with iterative division operators can be established using arguments similar to the proofs for Propositional Dynamic Logic. Given that we are working in a setting without Boolean negation, we find the approach of Nishimura [19] particularly suitable. We augment our variation of Nishimura's argument with usual techniques pertaining to relational semantics of substructural logics [22].

Let L be any extension of Distributive Lattice Logic. The notion of a prime L-theory is defined as expected (a set of formulas closed under conjunction and provable sequents that has the disjunction property). An independent L-pair is an ordered pair of sets of formulas Γ, Δ such that there are no finite $\Gamma' \subseteq \Gamma$, $\Delta' \subseteq \Delta$ such that $\bigwedge \Gamma' \longrightarrow \bigvee \Delta'$ (in L). Recall that $\bigwedge \emptyset := \top$ and $\bigvee \emptyset := \bot$. We will rely on the following well-known result:

[1] Strictly speaking, this function should be defined on the equivalence classes of formulas.

Lemma 2 (Pair Extension). *Let L be an extension of the Distributive Lattice Logic and let $\langle \Gamma, \Delta \rangle$ be an independent L-pair. Assume that Φ is a set of formulas such that $\Gamma \cup \Delta \subseteq \Phi$. There is an independent L-pair $\langle \Gamma', \Delta' \rangle$ such that $\Gamma \subseteq \Gamma'$, $\Delta \subseteq \Delta'$ and $\Gamma' \cup \Delta' = \Phi$.*

Proof. Essentially [22, pp. 92–95].

Corollary 1. *If L is an extension of Distributive Lattice Logic and $\langle \Gamma, \Delta \rangle$ is an independent L-pair, then there is a prime L-theory Σ such that $\Gamma \subseteq \Sigma$ and $\Delta \cap \Sigma = \emptyset$.*

Proof. Lemma 2 in the case Φ is the whole language; in that case Γ' is a prime theory (see [22, Lemma 5.16]).

The *restriction* of $\langle \Gamma, \Delta \rangle$ to Σ is $\langle \Gamma \cap \Sigma, \Delta \cap \Sigma \rangle$. We say that $\langle \Gamma, \Delta \rangle$ is a *full* pair iff $\Gamma \cup \Delta$ is the set of all formulas.

Definition 1 (Closure). *A set of formulas Φ is the closure of a set of formulas Φ' iff it is the smallest set of formulas such that*

1. *$\Phi' \subseteq \Phi$;*
2. *$\top, \bot \in \Phi$;*
3. *Φ is closed under subformulas;*
4. *If $A \backslash\!\!\backslash B \in \Phi$, then $A \backslash B \in \Phi$;*
5. *If $B /\!\!/ A \in \Phi$, then $B / A \in \Phi$.*

If Φ is the closure of Φ, then we say that Φ is closed.

Lemma 3. *The closure of any finite set is finite.*

Definition 2 (Finite canonical model). *Let Φ be a finite closed set. The model M_Φ is defined as follows.*

- *S_Φ is the set of independent IDFNL-pairs $a = \langle a_{in}, a_{out} \rangle$ such that $a_{in} \cup a_{out} = \Phi$ (note that $a_{in} \cap a_{out} = \emptyset$ by definition of independent pair); we often write "$A \in a$" instead of "$A \in a_{in}$" and "$a \vdash A$" instead of "$\bigwedge a_{in} \longrightarrow A$";*
- *$R_\Phi abc$ iff, for all $A, B \in \Phi$, if $a \vdash A$ and $b \vdash A \backslash B$, then $c \vdash B$ (note that, if $C \in \Phi$, then $a \vdash C$ iff $C \in a$);*
- *if $p \in \Phi$, then $a \in V_\Phi(p)$ iff $p \in a$; otherwise $V_\Phi(p) = \emptyset$.*

The satisfaction relation $\models_\Phi$ is defined in the usual manner.

We note that the restriction to *finite* closed sets is required by our strategy in proving the next lemma for $\backslash\!\!\backslash$ and $/\!\!/$.

Lemma 4 (Truth Lemma). *For all M_Φ, $E \in \Phi$ and $z \in M_\Phi$, $E \in z$ iff $z \models_\Phi E$.*

Proof. Induction on the complexity of E. The base case holds by definition and the cases for constants and lattice connectives are easily established using the Distributive lattice axioms and rules. The cases for the Lambek connectives are established using standard arguments [22]; we give the ones for $\backslash$ and $\bullet$ in full, just in case. We mostly omit the subscript Φ in the rest of the proof.

$E = A\backslash B$. $A\backslash B \in b$ implies $b \vDash A\backslash B$ by the definition of R_Φ. Conversely, if $A\backslash B \notin b$, then we reason as follows. Firstly, $\langle\{C \mid b \vdash A\backslash C\}, \{B\}\rangle$ is an independent pair and so there is, by the Pair Extension Lemma 2, a full independent pair $\langle \Gamma, \Delta\rangle$, such that Γ extends $\{C \mid b \vdash A\backslash C\}$ and $B \in \Delta$. The restriction $c = \langle c_{in}, c_{out}\rangle$ of $\langle \Gamma, \Delta\rangle$ to Φ is clearly in S_Φ. Next, take the pair $\langle\{A\}, \{D \mid \exists C \notin \Gamma : b \vdash D\backslash C\}\rangle$; this pair is independent, for otherwise $b \vdash A\backslash \bigvee C_i$ for some disjunction of $C_i \notin \Gamma$ and thus some $C_i \in \Gamma$ by the construction of Γ, leading to a contradiction. Hence, there is a full independent pair $\langle \Sigma, \Theta\rangle$ such that $A \in \Sigma$ and Θ extends $\{D \mid \exists C \notin \Gamma : b \vdash D\backslash C\}$. The restriction $a = \langle a_{in}, a_{out}\rangle$ of $\langle \Sigma, \Theta\rangle$ to Φ is in S_Φ. Moreover, $R_\Phi abc$; for take $D, C \in \Phi$ such that $b \vdash D\backslash C$ and $c \nvdash C$. The latter means that $C \notin \Gamma$, but then $a \nvdash D$ by the construction of a. The case $E = B/A$ is established similarly.

$E = A \bullet B$. If $b \vdash B$, then $b \vdash A\backslash(A \bullet B)$ since $B \longrightarrow A\backslash(A \bullet B)$ by residuation. If also $a \vdash A$, then $Rabc$ implies $c \vdash A \bullet B$ by the definition of R_Φ. Hence, $c \vDash A \bullet B$ implies $c \vdash A \bullet B$. The converse implication is established as follows. Assume that $c \vdash A \bullet B$. Then c is extended by a full independent pair $\langle \Gamma, \Delta\rangle$. The pair $\langle\{B\}, \{C \mid \Gamma \nvdash A \bullet C\}\rangle$ is easily shown to be independent; thus it is extended by some full independent pair $\langle \Sigma, \Theta\rangle$ with a restriction b to Φ. The pair $\langle\{A\}, \{C \mid \exists D \in \Sigma : \Gamma \nvdash C \bullet D\}\rangle$ is also easily shown to be independent and thus extended by a full independent pair with a restriction a to Φ. It is clear that $a \vdash A$ and $b \vdash B$. It remains to show that $R_\Phi abc$. If $a \vdash C$ and $b \vdash C\backslash D$, for some $C, D \in \Phi$, then $\Gamma \vdash C \bullet (C\backslash D)$ by the construction of a and b. Hence, $\Gamma \vdash D$ and so $c \vdash D$. Consequently, $c \vdash A \bullet B$ implies $c \vDash A \bullet B$.

$E = A\backslash\!\!\backslash B$. First we prove that if $A\backslash\!\!\backslash B \in a$, $R\overleftarrow{x}ab$ for some $\bar{x}$ of length n and $A \in x_i$ for all $i \in \{1, \ldots, n\}$, then $B \in b$. If $\bar{x} = \langle x\rangle$, then we have $Rxab$ and, by the second $\backslash\!\!\backslash$-axiom and the definition of closure, $A\backslash B \in a$. Hence, $B \in b$ by the definition of the canonical R. Now assume that $\bar{x}$ of length $n \geq 2$. The assumption $R\overleftarrow{x}ab$ means that there are $y_1, \ldots, y_{n-1}$ such that

$$Rx_1ay_1 \wedge \bigwedge_{1 \leq i \leq n-2} Rx_{i+1}y_iy_{i+1} \wedge Rx_ny_{n-1}b$$

Since $A\backslash\!\!\backslash B \longrightarrow A\backslash(A\backslash\!\!\backslash B)$ by the second $\backslash\!\!\backslash$-axiom and both A and $A\backslash\!\!\backslash B$ are in Φ, we have $A\backslash\!\!\backslash B \in y_i$ for all $i \in \{1, \ldots, n-1\}$. Since $A\backslash\!\!\backslash B \longrightarrow A\backslash B$ by the second $\backslash\!\!\backslash$-axiom, $A\backslash B \in y_{n-1}$ and so $B \in b$ by the definition of R.

The converse claim is established as follows. Assume that $a \vDash_\Phi A\backslash\!\!\backslash B$. We define ($\bar{x}_n$ means that path $\bar{x}$ is of length n)

$$Y := \Big\{y \mid (\exists n \exists \bar{x}_n)\big(R\overleftarrow{x}ay \wedge (\forall i \in \{1, \ldots, n\})(A \in x_i)\big)\Big\}$$

$$\varphi_Y := \bigvee_{b \in Y} \big(\bigwedge b_{in}\big)$$

(Note that if $Y = \emptyset$, then φ_Y is $\bot$.) We sometimes write "Y" instead of "φ_Y"and let the context disambiguate.

We first show that $\varphi_Y \longrightarrow A\backslash\varphi_Y$ (here we need the assumption that Y is finite). If not, then $\exists b \in Y$ such that $b \nvdash A\backslash Y$. It follows that $\bigwedge\{C \mid b \vdash A\backslash C\} \not\longrightarrow Y$. (Since $b \vdash A\backslash \bigwedge\{C \mid b \vdash A\backslash C\}$.) So, by the Pair Extension Lemma, there is a prime theory Γ containing all C such that $b \vdash A\backslash C$ and disjoint from the set of disjuncts of φ_Y. Now take the independent pair $\langle\{A\}, \{D \mid \exists C \notin \Gamma : b \vdash D\backslash C\}\rangle$ (for the proof of independence, see the argument in case $E = A\backslash B$); there is $d \in S$ such that $A \in d_{in}$ and $\{D \mid \exists C \notin \Gamma : b \vdash D\backslash C\} \cap \Phi \subseteq d_{out}$ by the Pair Extension Lemma. Define $c_{in} := \Gamma \cap \Phi$ and c_{out} as the complement of c_{in} relative to Φ. It is easily seen that $Rdbc$, for if $C \in \Phi$ and $C \notin c$, then $C \notin \Gamma$ and so, if $d \vdash D$ for some $D \in \Phi$, then $b \nvdash D\backslash C$ by the construction of d. Since $A \in d$ and $b \in Y$, we have $c \in Y$ and so $c \vdash Y$. But then $Y \in \Gamma$, which is impossible by the construction of Γ.

Hence, $Y \longrightarrow A\backslash Y$ and so, by the second $\backslash\!\!\backslash$-rule, $Y \longrightarrow A\backslash\!\!\backslash Y$. Since all elements of Y contain B, we have $Y \longrightarrow B$ and so $Y \longrightarrow A\backslash\!\!\backslash B$. It can be shown similarly as above that $a \vdash A\backslash Y$; but since $A\backslash Y \longrightarrow A\backslash B \wedge A\backslash(A\backslash\!\!\backslash B) \longrightarrow A\backslash\!\!\backslash B$, we obtain $a \vdash A\backslash\!\!\backslash B$. This means that $A\backslash\!\!\backslash B \in a$.

The claim for $E = B/\!\!/A$ is established similarly.

Theorem 1. *IDFNL is a sound and weakly complete axiomatization of the* $\mathcal{L}_1$*-theory of all Došen frames.*

Proof. Soundness is an easy exercise; completeness follows from the construction of the finite canonical model (for each $A \not\longrightarrow B$, take as Φ the closure of $\{A, B\}$ and construct M_Φ) and the Truth Lemma 4 in conjunction with the Pair Extension Lemma 2 (if $A \not\longrightarrow B$, then there is a in M_Φ such that $A \in a_{in}$ and $B \in a_{out}$; by the Truth Lemma, there is a state in M_Φ satisfying A that does not satisfy B).

Theorem 2. *The* $\mathcal{L}_1$*-theory of all Došen frames is decidable.*

Proof. The proof of Theorem 1 entails axiomatizability and completeness with respect to a recursively enumerable class of models (finite Došen models).

4 Conclusion

In this article we have put forward a decidable extension of the Distributive Full Non-associative Lambek Calculus that allows to reason about the effects of iterative composition (of bracketed expressions in Lambek's sense, or more generally of linguistic resources or actions). We have achieved this by extending DFNL with two primitive iterative division operators $\backslash\!\!\backslash$ and $/\!\!/$ and by providing a complete axiomatization and establishing the finite model property. (In fact, we have established *bounded* finite model property, from which decidability follows independently of the axiomatization.)

In the rest of this section, we discuss some of our design choices and plans for future work. Firstly, the reader may wonder why we have left out the discussion of an "iterative product" operator with respect to which $\backslash\!\backslash$ and $/\!/$ would be residuated. In fact, we suspect that there is not a single such operator; technically speaking, the iterative division operators "look at" two different accessibility relations. This will be investigated in more detail in the future.

Concerning our choice of the language, we note that the presence of $\top, \bot$ is motivated by technical considerations. In our proof of the Truth Lemma for the iterative division operators, the set Y may be empty in which case φ_Y is not well defined without $\bot$ in the language. In order to obtain the Truth Lemma for $\bot$, we need $\top$. (When it comes to the informal interpretation of these constants, $\top$ can be read as the trivial type of linguistic resource or action—all objects are of this type; and $\bot$ can be read as the inconsistent type—no object is of this type.)

Our work is motivated by the interest of studying iterated composition in non-associative settings. We have presented the basic logic of such settings, but it is interesting also to look at its extensions, especially those where composition has some "natural" properties. Some of these are familiar from the literature on the Lambek Calculus. For instance, it is not hard to show that the extension of *IDFNL* with the Weak contraction axiom

$$A \wedge A\backslash B \vdash B$$

is a sound and weakly complete axiomatization of the theory of Došen frames satisfying reflexivity $Rsss$ and that this theory is decidable. This frame condition reflects the idea that composing an object with itself may always result in the object itself. This is again plausible in some cases, but not in general (action composition is a counterexample).

Similarly, the extension of *IDFNL* with the Weak commutativity axiom

$$A \bullet B \vdash B \bullet A$$

is a sound and weakly complete axiomatization of the theory of all frames such that $Rstu$ implies $Rtsu$; this theory is decidable as well. The frame condition is reflecting the idea that the order of composition is immaterial when it comes to the output. (This may be the case for some special cases of composition, but not in general—think of action composition as an example.)

Some natural assumptions, however, go beyond the limits of the present framework. For instance, if composition is thought of as *information update* and formulas are seen as expressing information *entailed by* states, then it is plausible to assume the Success axiom

$$A\backslash B \vdash A\backslash(A \wedge B)$$

expressing the notion that "update with A" results in a state entailing A. Many notions of update studied in the epistemic logic literature share this feature (e.g. public announcements or belief revision), but it can be shown that the Success axiom is *not canonical* when the present notion of a canonical model is assumed. To repair this, we would have to add a partial information order

$\leq$ (as in the Routley–Meyer semantics for relevant logics [22]) and assume that $Rstu \implies s \leq u$. This can be done, but it would make the semantics more complicated.

There are also other properties of composition not usually studied in the context of the Lambek Calculus (or substructural logics in general), but natural when the present setting is seen as a generalization of various logics of epistemic dynamics. For instance, in Public Announcement Logic it is assumed that if it is possible to compose information s as input with information t (to publicly announce s in the context of t), then s has to be "true" with respect to t. This may be seen as corresponding to $Rstu \implies s \leq t$. For more on frame properties corresponding to various notions of information update (in the setting of normal modal logic), see [3,10].

In the future, we would like to take a closer look at the variants of our basic logic discussed above.

References

1. van Benthem, J.: A note on dynamic arrow logic. In: van Eijck, J., Visser, A. (eds.) Logic and Information Flow, pp. 15–29. MIT Press (1994)
2. van Benthem, J.: Logic and the flow of information. In: Prawitz, D., Skyrms, B., Westerståhl, D. (eds.) Logic, Methodology and Philosophy of Science IX, Studies in Logic and the Foundations of Mathematics, vol. 134, pp. 693–724. Elsevier (1995). https://doi.org/10.1016/S0049-237X(06)80070-4
3. Benthem, J.: Two logical faces of belief revision. In: Trypuz, R. (ed.) Krister Segerberg on Logic of Actions. OCL, vol. 1, pp. 281–300. Springer, Dordrecht (2014). https://doi.org/10.1007/978-94-007-7046-1_13
4. Bimbó, K., Dunn, J.M.: Relational semantics for Kleene logic and action logic. Notre Dame J. Formal Logic **46**(4), 461–490 (2005). https://doi.org/10.1305/ndjfl/1134397663
5. Buszkowski, W.: On action logic: equational theories of action algebras. J. Logic Comput. **17**(1), 199–217 (2006). https://doi.org/10.1093/logcom/exl036
6. Chellas, B.: Modal Logic. An Introduction. Cambridge University Press, Cambridge (1980)
7. Desharnais, J., Möller, B.: Non-associative Kleene algebra and temporal logics. In: Höfner, P., Pous, D., Struth, G. (eds.) RAMICS 2017. LNCS, vol. 10226, pp. 93–108. Springer, Cham (2017). https://doi.org/10.1007/978-3-319-57418-9_6
8. Došen, K.: A brief survey of frames for the Lambek Calculus. Math. Logic Q. **38**(1), 179–187 (1992). https://doi.org/10.1002/malq.19920380113
9. Harel, D., Kozen, D., Tiuryn, J.: Dynamic Logic. MIT Press, Cambridge (2000)
10. Holliday, W.H., Hoshi, T., Icard III, T.F.: A uniform logic of information dynamics. In: Bolander, T., Braüner, T., Ghilardi, S., Moss, L. (eds.) Advances in Modal Logic 2012, pp. 348–367. College Publications (2012)
11. Kozen, D.: A completeness theorem for Kleene algebras and the algebra of regular events. Inf. Comput. **110**(2), 366–390 (1994). https://doi.org/10.1006/inco.1994.1037
12. Kozen, D.: On action algebras. In: Logic and Information Flow, pp. 78–88. MIT Press (1994)

13. Kurtonina, N.: Frames and labels. A modal analysis of categorial inference. Ph.D. thesis, Utrecht University (1994)
14. Kurucz, Á., Németi, I., Sain, I., Simon, A.: Decidable and undecidable logics with a binary modality. J. Logic Lang. Inf. **4**(3), 191–206 (1995). https://doi.org/10.1007/BF01049412
15. Kuznetsov, S.: The logic of action lattices is undecidable. In: 34th Annual ACM/IEEE Symposium on Logic in Computer Science, LICS 2019, Vancouver, BC, Canada, 24–27 June 2019, pp. 1–9 (2019). https://doi.org/10.1109/LICS.2019.8785659
16. Lambek, J.: The mathematics of sentence structure. Am. Math. Mon. **65**(3), 154–170 (1958)
17. Lambek, J.: On the calculus of syntactic types. In: Jakobson, R. (ed.) Structure of Language and Its Mathematical Aspects, pp. 166–178. AMS, Providence (1961)
18. Moortgat, M.J.: Multimodal linguistic inference. J. Logic Lang. Inf. **5**(3), 349–385 (1996). https://doi.org/10.1007/BF00159344
19. Nishimura, H.: Semantical analysis of constructive PDL. Publ. Res. Inst. Math. Sci. **18**(2), 847–858 (1982). https://doi.org/10.2977/prims/1195183579
20. Palka, E.: An infinitary sequent system for the equational theory of *-continuous action lattices. Fundamenta Informaticae **78**(2), 295–309 (2007)
21. Pratt, V.: Action logic and pure induction. In: van Eijck, J. (ed.) JELIA 1990. LNCS, vol. 478, pp. 97–120. Springer, Heidelberg (1991). https://doi.org/10.1007/BFb0018436
22. Restall, G.: An Introduction to Substrucutral Logics. Routledge, London (2000)
23. Segerberg, K.: An Essay in Classical Modal Logic. Filosofiska Föreningen Och Filosofiska Institutionen Vid Uppsala Universitet, Uppsala (1971)
24. Sequoiah-Grayson, S.: Epistemic closure and commutative, nonassociative residuated structures. Synthese **190**(1), 113–128 (2013). https://doi.org/10.1007/s11229-010-9834-z
25. Tedder, A.: Channel composition and ternary relation semantics. IFCoLog J. Logics Appl. **4**(3), 731–735 (2017)
26. Venema, Y.: A crash course in arrow logic. In: Marx, M., Pólos, L., Masuch, M. (eds.) Arrow Logic and Multi-Modal Logic, pp. 3–34. Center for the Study of Language and Information, Stanford (1997)

Resource Separation in Dynamic Logic of Propositional Assignments

Joseph Boudou[1], Andreas Herzig[1](✉), and Nicolas Troquard[2]

[1] IRIT, CNRS, Toulouse, France
herzig@irit.fr
[2] Free University of Bozen-Bolzano, Bolzano, Italy

Abstract. We extend dynamic logic of propositional assignments by adding an operator of parallel composition that is inspired by separation logics. We provide an axiomatisation via reduction axioms, thereby establishing decidability. We also prove that the complexity of both the model checking and the satisfiability problem stay in PSPACE.

Keywords: Dynamic logic · Separation logic · Propositional assignments · Parallel composition

1 Introduction

It is notoriously delicate to extend Propositional Dynamic Logic PDL with an operator of parallel composition of programs. Several attempts were made in the literature: Abrahamson as well as Mayer and Stockmeyer studied a semantics in terms of interleaving [MS96]; Peleg and Goldblatt modified the interpretation of programs from a relation between possible worlds to a relation between possible worlds and sets thereof [Pel87, Gol92]; Balbiani and Vakarelov studied the interpretation of parallel composition of programs π_1 and π_2 as the intersection of the accessibility relations interpreting π_1 and π_2 [BV03]. However, it seems fair to say that there is still no consensus which of these extensions is the 'right' one.

Dynamic Logic of Propositional Assignments DL-PA [BHT13, BHST14] is a version of Propositional Dynamic Logic PDL whose atomic programs are assignments of propositional variables p to true or false, respectively written $+p$ and $-p$. We and coauthors have shown that many knowledge representation concepts and formalisms can be captured in DL-PA, such as update and revision operations [Her14], database base fusion and repair operations [FHR19], planning [HMNDBW14, HMV19], lightweight dynamic epistemic logics [CS15, CHM+16, CS17], and judgment aggregation [NGH18]. The mathematical properties of DL-PA are simpler than those of PDL, in particular, the Kleene star can be eliminated [BHT13] and satisfiability and model checking are both PSPACE complete [BHST14].

In this paper we investigate how dynamic logic can be extended with a program operator of parallel composition $\pi_1||\pi_2$ of two programs π_1 and π_2 that is inspired by separation logic. The latter was proposed in the literature

L. Soares Barbosa and A. Baltag (Eds.): DaLí 2019, LNCS 12005, pp. 155–170, 2020.
https://doi.org/10.1007/978-3-030-38808-9_10

as an account of concurrency, e.g. by Brookes and by O'Hearn [O'H04, Bro04, Bro07, BO16]. Their Concurrent Separation Logic is characterised by two main principles:

1. When two programs are executed in parallel then the state of the system is partitioned ('separated') between the two programs: the perception of the state and its modification is viewed as being local to each of the two parallel programs. Each of them therefore has a partial view of the global state. This in particular entails that parallelism in itself does not modify the state of the system: the parallel execution of two programs that do nothing does not change the state. This means that the formula $\varphi \to [\top?||\top?]\varphi$ should be valid, where "?" is the test operator. These tests $\varphi?$ differ from standard PDL tests; this will be explained when we discuss what system states should look like.
2. The execution of a parallel program $\pi_1||\pi_2$ should be insensitive to the way the components of π_1 and π_2 are interleaved. So "race conditions" [BO16] must be avoided: the execution should not depend on the order of execution of atomic actions in π_1 and π_2, where we consider tests to be atomic, too. Here we interpret this in a rather radical way: when there is a race condition between two programs then they cannot be executed in parallel. For example, the parallel program $+p||-p$ where $+p$ makes p true and $-p$ makes p false is inexecutable because there is a conflict: the two possible interleavings $+p; -p$ and $-p; +p$ are not equivalent. We even consider that $+p||+p$ and $p?||+p$ are inexecutable, which some may consider a bit over-constrained.

Together, the above two principles entail that the dynamic logic formula

$$[(\pi_1; \varphi_1?)||(\pi_2; \varphi_2?)](\varphi_1 \wedge \varphi_2)$$

should be valid. If we replace φ_1 by p and φ_2 by $\neg p$ then the above tells us that $(\pi_1; p?)||(\pi_2; \neg p?)$ is inexecutable. So the program $\pi_1; (p?||\pi_2); \neg p?$ that is obtained from it by interleaving should be inexecutable, too.

We have not yet said what one should understand by a DL-PA system state. A previous approach of ours only considered the separation of valuations, i.e., of truth values of propositional variables [Her13]. Two separating conjunctions in the style of separation logic were defined on such models. This however did not allow us to define an adjoint implication as usually done in the separation logic literature, which was somewhat unsatisfactory. The paper [HMV19] has richer models where valuations are supplemented by information about writability of variables, supposing that a variable can only be assigned by a program when it is writable. Splitting and merging of such models can be defined in a natural way, thus providing a meaningful interpretation of parallel composition. We here push this program further and consider models having moreover information about readability of variables. We suppose that writability implies readability[1] and

[1] As suggested by one of the reviewers, it may be relaxed and one may suppose that a program can only modify a variable without being able to read its value. This would simplify the presentation of the logic; however, we believe that our inclusion constraint is natural in most applications.

that a variable can only be tested if it is readable. So our tests $\varphi?$ differ from standard PDL tests and also from DL-PA tests in that their executability depends on whether the relevant variables are readable. In particular, while $\langle p?\rangle\top \to p$, remains valid, its converse $p \to \langle p?\rangle\top$ becomes invalid in our logic.

The paper is organised as follows. In Sect. 2 we define models and the two ternary relations 'split' and 'merge' on models. In Sect. 3 we define the language of our logic and in Sect. 4 we give the interpretation of formulas and programs. In Sect. 5 we axiomatise the valid formulas by means of reduction axioms and in Sect. 6 we establish that the satisfiability problem is PSPACE complete. Section 7 concludes.

2 Models and Their Splitting and Merging

Let $\mathbb{P}$ be a countable set of propositional variables. A model is a triple $\mathsf{m} = \langle \mathsf{Rd}, \mathsf{Wr}, \mathsf{V}\rangle$ where Rd, Wr, and V are subsets of $\mathbb{P}$ such that $\mathsf{Wr} \subseteq \mathsf{Rd}$. The idea is that Rd is the set of readable variables, Wr is the set of writable variables, and V is a valuation: its elements are true, while those of its complement $\mathbb{P} \setminus \mathsf{V}$ are false. The constraint that $\mathsf{Wr} \subseteq \mathsf{Rd}$ means that writability implies readability.

Two models $\mathsf{m}_1 = \langle \mathsf{Rd}_1, \mathsf{Wr}_1, \mathsf{V}_1\rangle$ and $\mathsf{m}_2 = \langle \mathsf{Rd}_2, \mathsf{Wr}_2, \mathsf{V}_2\rangle$ are *RW-compatible* if and only if writable variables of one model and the readable variables of the other do not interfere, i.e., if and only if $\mathsf{Wr}_1 \cap \mathsf{Rd}_2 = \mathsf{Wr}_2 \cap \mathsf{Rd}_1 = \emptyset$. For example, $\mathsf{m}_1 = \langle\{p\}, \{p\}, \emptyset\rangle$ and $\mathsf{m}_2 = \langle\{p\}, \emptyset, \emptyset\rangle$ are not RW-compatible: in m_1, some program π_1 modifying the value of p may be executable, while for programs executed in m_2, the value of p may differ depending on whether it is read before or after the modification by π_1 took place.

As writability implies readability, RW-compatibility of m_1 and m_2 implies $\mathsf{Wr}_1 \cap \mathsf{Wr}_2 = \emptyset$.

We define ternary relations $\lhd$ ('split') and $\rhd$ ('merge') on models as follows:

$\mathsf{m} \lhd {}^{\mathsf{m}_1}_{\mathsf{m}_2}$ iff m_1 and m_2 are RW-compatible, $\mathsf{Rd} = \mathsf{Rd}_1 \cup \mathsf{Rd}_2$, $\mathsf{Wr} = \mathsf{Wr}_1 \cup \mathsf{Wr}_2$, and $\mathsf{V} = \mathsf{V}_1 = \mathsf{V}_2$

${}^{\mathsf{m}_1}_{\mathsf{m}_2} \rhd \mathsf{m}$ iff m_1 and m_2 are RW-compatible, $\mathsf{Rd} = \mathsf{Rd}_1 \cup \mathsf{Rd}_2$, $\mathsf{Wr} = \mathsf{Wr}_1 \cup \mathsf{Wr}_2$, $\mathsf{V}_1 \setminus \mathsf{Wr} = \mathsf{V}_2 \setminus \mathsf{Wr}$, and $\mathsf{V} = (\mathsf{V}_1 \cap \mathsf{Wr}_1) \cup (\mathsf{V}_2 \cap \mathsf{Wr}_2) \cup (\mathsf{V}_1 \cap \mathsf{V}_2)$

For example, for $\mathsf{m} = \langle \mathsf{Rd}, \mathsf{Wr}, \mathsf{V}\rangle$ we have $\mathsf{m} \lhd {}^{\mathsf{m}}_{\mathsf{m}_2}$ for every $\mathsf{m}_2 = \langle \mathsf{Rd}_2, \emptyset, \mathsf{V}\rangle$ such that $\mathsf{Rd}_2 \subseteq \mathbb{P} \setminus \mathsf{Wr}$. Observe that, contrarily to splitting, merging does not keep the valuation constant: it only keeps constant the non-modifiable part $\mathsf{V} \setminus \mathsf{Wr}$ of the valuation V and puts the results of the allowed modifications of Wr together. These modifications cannot conflict because m_1 and m_2 are RW-compatible. Figure 1 illustrates each of these two operations by an examples. The checks that are performed in the merge operation are reminiscent of the self composition technique in the analysis of secure information flows [DHS05, SG16].[2]

[2] We are grateful to Rainer Hähnle for pointing this out to us.

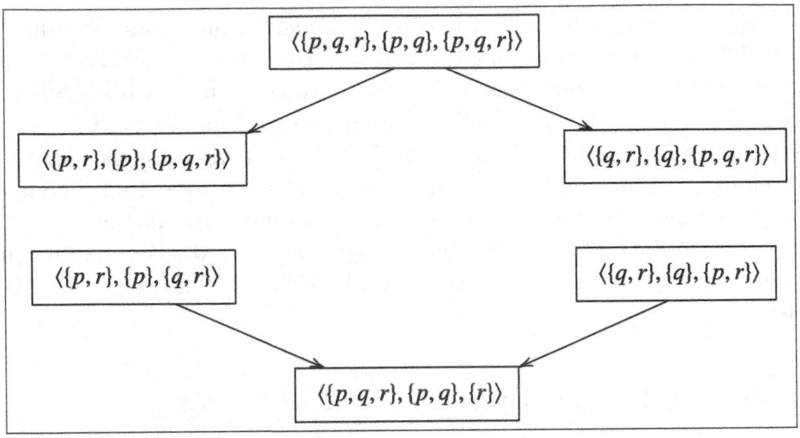

Fig. 1. Examples of split and merge operations: the top half illustrates the split of the model $\langle\{p,q,r\},\{p,q\},\{p,q,r\}\rangle$ into $\langle\{p,r\},\{p\},\{p,q,r\}\rangle$ and $\langle\{q,r\},\{q\},\{p,q,r\}\rangle$; the bottom half illustrates the merge of the models $\langle\{p,r\},\{p\},\{p,q,r\}\rangle$ and $\langle\{q,r\},\{q\},\{p,q,r\}\rangle$ into $\langle\{p,q,r\},\{p,q\},\{r\}\rangle$.

The set Rd of readable variables of a model m induces an indistinguishability relation between models:

$$\mathsf{m} \sim \mathsf{m}' \text{ iff } \mathsf{Rd} = \mathsf{Rd}', \mathsf{Wr} = \mathsf{Wr}', \mathsf{V} \cap \mathsf{Rd} = \mathsf{V}' \cap \mathsf{Rd}'$$

So m and m′ are indistinguishable if (1) they have the same readable and writable variables and (2) the valuations are identical as far as their readable parts are concerned. This relation will serve to interpret tests: the test $\varphi?\!\!?$ of a formula φ is conditioned by its truth in all read-indistinguishable models, i.e., in all models where the readable variables have the same truth value.

3 Language

We use $p, q, \ldots$ for variables in the set of propositional variables $\mathbb{P}$. Formulas and programs are defined by the following grammar, where p ranges over $\mathbb{P}$:

$$\varphi ::= p \mid \top \mid \neg\varphi \mid \varphi \vee \varphi \mid \langle\pi\rangle\varphi$$
$$\pi ::= +p \mid -p \mid \mathtt{r}{+}p \mid \mathtt{r}{-}p \mid \mathtt{w}{+}p \mid \mathtt{w}{-}p \mid \varphi? \mid \varphi?\!\!? \mid \pi;\pi \mid \pi \cup \pi \mid \pi^* \mid \pi || \pi$$

The program $+p$ makes p true and $-p$ makes p false. The executability of these two programs is conditioned by the writability of p. The program $\mathtt{r}{+}p$ makes p readable and $\mathtt{r}{-}p$ makes p unreadable; similarly, $\mathtt{w}{+}p$ makes p writable and $\mathtt{w}{-}p$ makes p non-writable. We suppose that these four programs are always executable. The program $\varphi?$ is the PDL test that φ, that we call *exogeneous*; $\varphi?\!\!?$ is the *endogeneous* test that φ: it is conditioned by the readability of the relevant variables of φ.

The formula $[\pi]\varphi$ abbreviates $\neg\langle\pi\rangle\neg\varphi$. Given an integer $n \geq 0$, the program π^n is defined inductively by $\pi^0 = \top?$ and $\pi^{n+1} = \pi; \pi^n$. Similarly, $\pi^{\leq n}$ is defined by $\pi^{\leq 0} = \top?$ and $\pi^{\leq n+1} = \top? \cup (\pi; \pi^{\leq n})$. The program **if** φ **then** π abbreviates $(\varphi?; \pi) \cup \neg\varphi?$. For a finite set of variables $P = \{p_1, \ldots, p_n\}$ and associated programs $\{\pi_1(p_1), \ldots, \pi_n(p_n)\}$, we are going to use the notation $;_{p \in P}\ \pi(p)$ to denote the sequence $\pi_1(p_1); \cdots; \pi_n(p_n)$, in some order. We will make use of this notation with care to guarantee that the ordering of the elements of P does not matter.

The set of propositional variables occurring in a formula φ is noted $\mathbb{P}(\varphi)$ and the set of those occurring in a program π is noted $\mathbb{P}(\pi)$. For example, $\mathbb{P}(p \vee \langle +q \rangle \neg r) = \{p, q, r\}$.

4 Semantics

Let $\mathsf{m} = \langle \mathsf{Rd}, \mathsf{Wr}, \mathsf{V} \rangle$ be a model. Formulas are interpreted as sets of models:

$$
\begin{array}{ll}
\mathsf{m} \models \top & \\
\mathsf{m} \models p & \text{iff } p \in \mathsf{V}, \text{ for } p \in \mathbb{P} \\
\mathsf{m} \models \neg\varphi & \text{iff } \mathsf{m} \not\models \varphi \\
\mathsf{m} \models \varphi \vee \psi & \text{iff } \mathsf{m} \models \varphi \text{ or } \mathsf{m} \models \psi \\
\mathsf{m} \models \langle\pi\rangle\varphi & \text{iff there is a model } \mathsf{m}' \text{ such that } \mathsf{m}[\![\pi]\!]\mathsf{m}' \text{ and } \mathsf{m}' \models \varphi
\end{array}
$$

Programs are interpreted as relations on the set of models:

$$
\begin{array}{ll}
\mathsf{m}[\![+p]\!]\mathsf{m}' & \text{iff } \mathsf{Rd}' = \mathsf{Rd},\ \mathsf{Wr}' = \mathsf{Wr},\ \mathsf{V}' = \mathsf{V} \cup \{p\}, \text{ and } p \in \mathsf{Wr} \\
\mathsf{m}[\![-p]\!]\mathsf{m}' & \text{iff } \mathsf{Rd}' = \mathsf{Rd},\ \mathsf{Wr}' = \mathsf{Wr},\ \mathsf{V}' = \mathsf{V} \setminus \{p\}, \text{ and } p \in \mathsf{Wr} \\
\mathsf{m}[\![\mathtt{r}{+}p]\!]\mathsf{m}' & \text{iff } \mathsf{Rd}' = \mathsf{Rd} \cup \{p\},\ \mathsf{Wr}' = \mathsf{Wr}, \text{ and } \mathsf{V}' = \mathsf{V} \\
\mathsf{m}[\![\mathtt{r}{-}p]\!]\mathsf{m}' & \text{iff } \mathsf{Rd}' = \mathsf{Rd} \setminus \{p\},\ \mathsf{Wr}' = \mathsf{Wr} \setminus \{p\}, \text{ and } \mathsf{V}' = \mathsf{V} \\
\mathsf{m}[\![\mathtt{w}{+}p]\!]\mathsf{m}' & \text{iff } \mathsf{Rd}' = \mathsf{Rd} \cup \{p\},\ \mathsf{Wr}' = \mathsf{Wr} \cup \{p\}, \text{ and } \mathsf{V}' = \mathsf{V} \\
\mathsf{m}[\![\mathtt{w}{-}p]\!]\mathsf{m}' & \text{iff } \mathsf{Rd}' = \mathsf{Rd},\ \mathsf{Wr}' = \mathsf{Wr} \setminus \{p\}, \text{ and } \mathsf{V}' = \mathsf{V} \\
\mathsf{m}[\![\varphi?]\!]\mathsf{m}' & \text{iff } \mathsf{m} = \mathsf{m}' \text{ and } \mathsf{m} \models \varphi \\
\mathsf{m}[\![\varphi\text{?`}]\!]\mathsf{m}' & \text{iff } \mathsf{m} = \mathsf{m}' \text{ and } \mathsf{m}'' \models \varphi \text{ for every } \mathsf{m}'' \text{ such that } \mathsf{m}'' \sim \mathsf{m} \\
\mathsf{m}[\![\pi_1; \pi_2]\!]\mathsf{m}' & \text{iff there is an } \mathsf{m}'' \text{ such that } \mathsf{m}[\![\pi_1]\!]\mathsf{m}'' \text{ and } \mathsf{m}''[\![\pi_2]\!]\mathsf{m}' \\
\mathsf{m}[\![\pi_1 \cup \pi_2]\!]\mathsf{m}' & \text{iff } \mathsf{m}[\![\pi_1]\!]\mathsf{m}' \text{ or } \mathsf{m}[\![\pi_2]\!]\mathsf{m}' \\
\mathsf{m}[\![\pi^*]\!]\mathsf{m}' & \text{iff there is an } n \geq 0 \text{ such that } \mathsf{m}[\![\pi]\!]^n\mathsf{m}' \\
\mathsf{m}[\![\pi_1 || \pi_2]\!]\mathsf{m}' & \text{iff there are } \mathsf{m}_1, \mathsf{m}_2, \mathsf{m}'_1, \mathsf{m}'_2 \text{ such that } \mathsf{m} \lhd {}^{\mathsf{m}_1}_{\mathsf{m}_2}, {}^{\mathsf{m}'_1}_{\mathsf{m}'_2} \rhd \mathsf{m}', \\
& \quad \mathsf{m}_1[\![\pi_1]\!]\mathsf{m}'_1,\ \mathsf{Rd}_1 = \mathsf{Rd}'_1,\ \mathsf{Wr}_1 = \mathsf{Wr}'_1,\ \mathsf{V}_1 \setminus \mathsf{Wr}_1 = \mathsf{V}'_1 \setminus \mathsf{Wr}'_1, \\
& \quad \mathsf{m}_2[\![\pi_2]\!]\mathsf{m}'_2,\ \mathsf{Rd}_2 = \mathsf{Rd}'_2,\ \mathsf{Wr}_2 = \mathsf{Wr}'_2,\ \mathsf{V}_2 \setminus \mathsf{Wr}_2 = \mathsf{V}'_2 \setminus \mathsf{Wr}'_2
\end{array}
$$

In the interpretation of assignments of atomic formulas we require propositional variables to be modifiable, while readability and writability can be modified unconditionally. When a variable is made writable then it is made readable, too, in order to guarantee the inclusion constraint on models; similarly when a variable is made unreadable.

The interpretation of parallel composition $\pi_1||\pi_2$ is such that both π_1 and π_2 only modify 'their' variables: parallel composition $\pi_1||\pi_2$ of two programs π_1 and

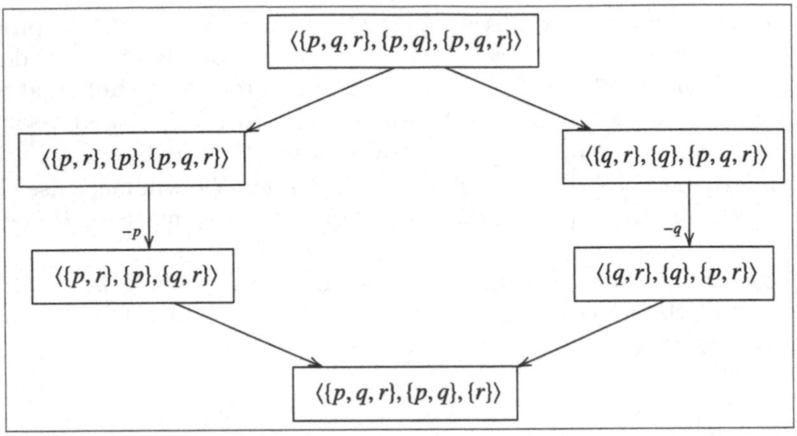

Fig. 2. Illustration of an execution of $-p||-q$ at the model $\langle\{p,q,r\},\{p,q\},\{p,q,r\}\rangle$.

π_2 relates two models m and m' when the following conditions are satisfied: (1) m can be split into m_1 and m_2; (2) the execution of π_1 on m_1 may lead to m_1' and the execution of π_2 on m_2 may lead to m_2'; (3) m_1' and m_2' can be merged into m'. Moreover, (4) the modifications are legal: π_1 and π_2 neither change readability nor writability, and each of them only modifies variables that were allocated to it by the split.

Figure 2 illustrates the interpretation of the parallel program $-p||-q$. Some more examples follow.

Example 1. Suppose $\mathsf{m} = \langle\mathsf{Rd},\mathsf{Wr},\mathsf{V}\rangle$ with $\mathsf{Wr} = \mathsf{Rd} = \mathsf{V} = \{p,q,r\}$. Then $\mathsf{m}' = \langle\mathsf{Rd},\mathsf{Wr},\mathsf{V}'\rangle$ with $\mathsf{V}' = \{p,r\}$ is the only model such that $\mathsf{m}[\![+p||-q]\!]\mathsf{m}'$.

The next example illustrates the last condition (4) in the interpretation of parallel composition.

Example 2. The program $+p||(\mathtt{w}{+}p;-p;\mathtt{r}{-}p)$ cannot be executed on the model $\mathsf{m} = \langle\{p\},\{p\},\{p\}\rangle$. Indeed, suppose there are m_1 and m_2 such that $\mathsf{m} \lhd {\mathsf{m}_1 \atop \mathsf{m}_2}$ and suppose $+p$ is executed on m_1 and $\mathtt{w}{+}p;-p;\mathtt{r}{-}p$ on m_2. For $+p$ to be executable we must have $p \in \mathsf{Wr}_1$, and therefore $p \notin \mathsf{Wr}_2$ (and a fortiori $p \notin \mathsf{Rd}_2$). So $\mathsf{m}_1 = \langle\{p\},\{p\},\{p\}\rangle$ and $\mathsf{m}_2 = \langle\emptyset,\emptyset,\{p\}\rangle$. Then $\mathsf{m}_1' = \mathsf{m}_1$ is the only model such that $\mathsf{m}_1[\![+p]\!]\mathsf{m}_1'$; and $\mathsf{m}_2' = \langle\emptyset,\emptyset,\emptyset\rangle$ is the only model such that $\mathsf{m}_2[\![\mathtt{w}{+}p;-p;\mathtt{r}{-}p]\!]\mathsf{m}_2'$. These two models cannot be merged: $\mathsf{V}_2' \setminus \mathsf{Wr}_2' = \emptyset$ fails to be equal to $\mathsf{V}_2 \setminus \mathsf{Wr}_2 = \{p\}$.

Let us finally explain the different semantics of the two test operators of our logic.

Example 3. Suppose m is such that $p \notin \mathsf{Rd}$ and $p \in \mathsf{V}$. Then the program $p?$ is executable at m because $p \in \mathsf{V}$. In contrast, there is no m' such that $\mathsf{m}[\![p?\!\!?]\!]\mathsf{m}'$, the reason being that there is always an m'' such that $\mathsf{m} \sim \mathsf{m}''$ and $p \notin \mathsf{V}''$. So $p?\!\!?$ fails at m.

In practice, parallel programs should only contain endogeneous tests in order to avoid that a subprogram accesses the truth value of a variable that is not among its readable variables. Actually we have kept PDL tests for technical reasons only: we could not formulate some of the reduction axioms without them.

Satisfiability and validity of formulas are defined in the expected way.

Example 4. The formulas $\varphi \to [\top ?\!?||\top ?\!?]\varphi$, $[+p||-p]\bot$, $[+p||+p]\bot$ and $[p?\!?||+p]\bot$ whose programs were mentioned in the introduction are all valid.

The formulas $\langle +p\rangle\top$ and $\langle -p\rangle\top$ both express that p is writable. Similarly, $\langle p?\!?\rangle\top$ expresses that p is true and readable, and $\langle \neg p?\!?\rangle\top$ expresses that p is false and readable; therefore $\langle p?\!?\rangle\top \vee \langle \neg p?\!?\rangle\top$ expresses that p is readable. This will be instrumental in our axiomatisation.

5 Axiomatisation via Reduction Axioms

We axiomatise the validities of our logic by means of reduction axioms, as customary in dynamic epistemic logics [vDvdHK07]. These axioms transform every formula into a boolean combination of propositional variables and formulas of the form $\langle +p\rangle\top$ and $\langle p?\!?\rangle\top \vee \langle \neg p?\!?\rangle\top$. The former expresses that p is writable: we abbreviate it by $\mathtt{w}_p$. The latter expresses that p is readable: we abbreviate it by $\mathtt{r}_p$.

We start by eliminating all the program operators from formulas, where the elimination of parallel composition is done by sequentialising it while keeping track of the values of the atoms. After that step, the only remaining program operators either occur in formulas of the form $\mathtt{r}_p$ or $\mathtt{w}_p$, or are assignments of the form $\langle +p\rangle$, $\langle -p\rangle$, $\langle \mathtt{r}{+}p\rangle$, $\langle \mathtt{r}{-}p\rangle$, $\langle \mathtt{w}{+}p\rangle$, or $\langle \mathtt{w}{-}p\rangle$. The assignments can be distributed over the boolean operators, taking advantage of the fact that all of them are deterministic modal operators (validating the Alt_1 axiom $\langle \pi\rangle\varphi \to [\pi]\varphi$). Finally, sequences of such modalities facing a propositional variable can be transformed into boolean combinations of readability and writability statements $\mathtt{r}_p$ and $\mathtt{w}_p$. The only logical link between these statements is that writability of p implies readability of p. This is captured by the axiom schema $\mathtt{w}_p \to \mathtt{r}_p$.

The sequentialisation of parallel composition uses copies of variables, so we start by introducing that notion. We then define some programs and formulas that will allow us to formulate the reduction axioms more concisely.

5.1 Copies of Atomic Propositions

We are going to need fresh copies of each propositional variable, one per occurrence of the parallel composition operator. In order to keep things readable we neglect that the index of the copies should be attached to programs and denote the copies of the variable p by $p^{\mathbf{k}}$, where $\mathbf{k}$ is some integer. In principle we should introduce a bijection between the indexes $\mathbf{k}$ and the subprogram they are attached to; we however do not do so to avoid overly complicated notations.

Given a set of propositional variables $P \subseteq \mathbb{P}$ and an integer $\mathbf{k} \in \{1,2\}$, we define the set of copies $P^{\mathbf{k}} = \{p^{\mathbf{k}} : p \in P\}$.

5.2 Useful Programs

Let $P \subseteq \mathbb{P}$ be some finite set of propositional variables. Figure 3 lists four programs that will be useful to concisely formulate the reduction axioms. We comment on them in the sequel.

$$
\begin{aligned}
\mathit{copyV}^{\mathbf{k}}(P) &= \mathop{;}_{p\in P} ((p?; +p^{\mathbf{k}}) \cup (\neg p?; -p^{\mathbf{k}}))\\
\mathit{splitRW}(P) &= \mathop{;}_{p\in P} (\mathtt{r}{-}p^1; \mathtt{r}{-}p^2;\\
&\qquad \textbf{if } \mathtt{w}_p \textbf{ then } (\mathtt{w}{+}p^1 \cup \mathtt{w}{+}p^2);\\
&\qquad \textbf{if } \mathtt{r}_p \wedge \neg \mathtt{w}_p \textbf{ then } (\mathtt{r}{+}p^1 \cup \mathtt{r}{+}p^2 \cup (\mathtt{r}{+}p^1; \mathtt{r}{+}p^2)))\\
\mathit{copybackRW}^{\mathbf{k}}(P) &= \mathop{;}_{p\in P} ((\neg \mathtt{r}_{p^{\mathbf{k}}}?; \mathtt{r}{-}p) \cup\\
&\qquad (\mathtt{r}_{p^{\mathbf{k}}} \wedge \neg \mathtt{w}_{p^{\mathbf{k}}}?; \mathtt{r}{+}p; \mathtt{w}{-}p) \cup\\
&\qquad (\mathtt{w}_{p^{\mathbf{k}}}?; \mathtt{w}{+}p))\\
\mathit{mergeRW}(P) &= \mathop{;}_{p\in P} (\textbf{if } \mathtt{r}_{p^1} \textbf{ then } \mathtt{r}{+}p \,;\, \textbf{if } \mathtt{w}_{p^1} \textbf{ then } \mathtt{w}{+}p)
\end{aligned}
$$

Fig. 3. Useful programs, for $P \subseteq \mathbb{P}$ and $\mathbf{k} \in \{1,2\}$

The $\mathit{copyV}^{\mathbf{k}}(P)$ program assigns the truth value of each variable $p \in P$ to its copy $p^{\mathbf{k}}$.

The $\mathit{splitRW}(P)$ program simulates the split operation by nondeterministically assigning two copies of each read and write variable in a way such that a counterpart of the RW-compatibility constraint $\mathsf{Wr}_1 \cap \mathsf{Rd}_2 = \mathsf{Wr}_2 \cap \mathsf{Rd}_1 = \emptyset$ is guaranteed. Note that the assignments $\mathtt{w}{+}p^{\mathbf{k}}$ also make $p^{\mathbf{k}}$ readable.

The $\mathit{copybackRW}^{\mathbf{k}}(P)$ program will be executed after the split and before the subprogram $\pi_{\mathbf{k}}$ in order to make the readable and writable variables be all those p that $\mathit{splitRW}(P)$ has assigned to $\pi_{\mathbf{k}}$.

The $\mathit{mergeRW}(P)$ program simulates the merge operation by reinstating all those read- and write-atoms that had been allocated to the first subprogram in the sequentialisation.

Observe that in the sequential compositions $\mathop{;}_{p\in P}(\ldots)$ occurring in the above programs, the order of the variables does not matter. Observe also that the only endogeneous tests on the right hand side occur in readability statements $\mathtt{r}_p$ (which abbreviate $\langle p?\!\!?\rangle\top \vee \langle \neg p?\!\!?\rangle\top$).

Lemma 1. $\mathsf{m}[\![\mathit{copyV}^{\mathbf{k}}(P)]\!]\mathsf{m}'$ *if and only if* $\mathsf{Rd}' = \mathsf{Rd}$, $\mathsf{Wr}' = \mathsf{Wr}$, *and* $\mathsf{V}' = (\mathsf{V} \setminus P^{\mathbf{k}}) \cup (\mathsf{V} \cap P)^{\mathbf{k}}$.

Lemma 2. *For all models* m *and* m' *and all sets of propositional variables* P, *the following three are equivalent:*

$$
\begin{aligned}
\langle\varphi?\rangle\psi &\leftrightarrow \psi\wedge\varphi\\
\langle\varphi\mathbf{?}\rangle\psi &\leftrightarrow \psi\wedge[\,;_{p\in\mathbb{P}(\varphi)}\,(\mathbf{if}\ \neg\mathtt{r}_p\ \mathbf{then}\ (+p\cup -p))]\varphi\\
\langle\pi_1;\pi_2\rangle\varphi &\leftrightarrow \langle\pi_1\rangle\langle\pi_2\rangle\varphi\\
\langle\pi_1\cup\pi_2\rangle\varphi &\leftrightarrow \langle\pi_1\rangle\varphi\vee\langle\pi_2\rangle\varphi\\
\langle\pi^*\rangle\varphi &\leftrightarrow \langle\pi^{\leq 2^{|\mathbb{P}(\varphi)|}}\rangle\varphi\\
\langle\pi_1\|\pi_2\rangle\varphi &\leftrightarrow \langle \mathit{splitRW}(\mathbb{P}(\pi_1)\cup\mathbb{P}(\pi_2));\\
&\qquad \mathit{copybackRW}^1(\mathbb{P}(\pi_1)); \mathit{copyV}^1(\mathbb{P}(\pi_1)); \pi_1;\\
&\qquad\qquad \mathit{NochangeRW}^1(\mathbb{P}(\pi_1))?; \mathit{OkChangeV}^1(\mathbb{P}(\pi_1))?;\\
&\qquad \mathit{copybackRW}^2(\mathbb{P}(\pi_2)); \mathit{copyV}^2(\mathbb{P}(\pi_2)); \pi_2;\\
&\qquad\qquad \mathit{NochangeRW}^2(\mathbb{P}(\pi_2))?; \mathit{OkChangeV}^2(\mathbb{P}(\pi_2))?;\\
&\qquad \mathit{mergeRW}(\mathbb{P}(\pi_1))\rangle\,\varphi
\end{aligned}
$$

Fig. 4. Reduction axioms for program operators

1. $\mathsf{m}[\![\mathit{splitRW}(P)]\!]\mathsf{m}'$;
2. *for* $\mathbf{k}\in\{1,2\}$, $\mathsf{Rd}\setminus P^{\mathbf{k}}=\mathsf{Rd}'\setminus P^{\mathbf{k}}$, $\mathsf{Wr}\setminus P^{\mathbf{k}}=\mathsf{Wr}'\setminus P^{\mathbf{k}}$, $\mathsf{V}=\mathsf{V}'$, *and for all* $p\in P$,
  - $p\in\mathsf{Rd}$ *iff* ($p^{\mathbf{1}}\in\mathsf{Rd}'$ *or* $p^{\mathbf{2}}\in\mathsf{Rd}'$),
  - $p\in\mathsf{Wr}$ *iff* ($p^{\mathbf{1}}\in\mathsf{Wr}'$ *or* $p^{\mathbf{2}}\in\mathsf{Wr}'$),
  - *if* $p^{\mathbf{1}}\in\mathsf{Wr}'$ *then* $p^{\mathbf{2}}\notin\mathsf{Rd}'$, *and if* $p^{\mathbf{2}}\in\mathsf{Wr}'$ *then* $p^{\mathbf{1}}\notin\mathsf{Rd}'$;
3. *there are* $\mathsf{m}_1,\mathsf{m}_2$ *such that* $\mathsf{m}\lhd{}^{\mathsf{m}_1}_{\mathsf{m}_2}$ *and for* $\mathbf{k}\in\{1,2\}$:
  - $\mathsf{Rd}_{\mathbf{k}}=(\mathsf{Rd}\setminus P)\cup\{p\in P: p^{\mathbf{k}}\in\mathsf{Rd}'\}$,
  - $\mathsf{Wr}_{\mathbf{k}}=(\mathsf{Wr}\setminus P)\cup\{p\in P: p^{\mathbf{k}}\in\mathsf{Wr}'\}$,
  - $\mathsf{V}_{\mathbf{k}}=\mathsf{V}=\mathsf{V}'$.

Lemma 3. $\mathsf{m}[\![\mathit{copybackRW}^{\mathbf{k}}(P)]\!]\mathsf{m}'$ *if and only if:*
- $\mathsf{Rd}'=(\mathsf{Rd}\setminus P)\cup\{p\in P: p^{\mathbf{k}}\in\mathsf{Rd}\}$,
- $\mathsf{Wr}'=(\mathsf{Wr}\setminus P)\cup\{p\in P: p^{\mathbf{k}}\in\mathsf{Wr}\}$, *and*
- $\mathsf{V}'=\mathsf{V}$.

Lemma 4. $\mathsf{m}[\![\mathit{mergeRW}(P)]\!]\mathsf{m}'$ *if and only if:*
- $\mathsf{Rd}'=\mathsf{Rd}\cup\{p\in P: p^{\mathbf{1}}\in\mathsf{Rd}\}$,
- $\mathsf{Wr}'=\mathsf{Wr}\cup\{p\in P: p^{\mathbf{1}}\in\mathsf{Wr}\}$, *and*
- $\mathsf{V}'=\mathsf{V}$.

5.3 Useful Formulas

The following formulas will be of use in reduction axioms:

$$
\mathit{NochangeRW}^{\mathbf{k}}(P)=\bigwedge_{p\in P}\big((\mathtt{r}_p\leftrightarrow\mathtt{r}_{p^{\mathbf{k}}})\wedge(\mathtt{w}_p\leftrightarrow\mathtt{w}_{p^{\mathbf{k}}})\big)
$$

$$
\mathit{OkChangeV}^{\mathbf{k}}(P)=\bigwedge_{p\in P}\big(\neg\mathtt{w}_p\to(p\leftrightarrow p^{\mathbf{k}})\big)
$$

$$\begin{array}{ll}
\langle +p\rangle\top \leftrightarrow \mathtt{w}_p & \langle -p\rangle\top \leftrightarrow \mathtt{w}_p \\
\langle \mathtt{r}{+}p\rangle\top \leftrightarrow \top & \langle \mathtt{r}{-}p\rangle\top \leftrightarrow \top \\
\langle \mathtt{w}{+}p\rangle\top \leftrightarrow \top & \langle \mathtt{w}{-}p\rangle\top \leftrightarrow \top \\
\langle +p\rangle\neg\varphi \leftrightarrow \mathtt{w}_p \wedge \neg\langle +p\rangle\varphi & \langle -p\rangle\neg\varphi \leftrightarrow \mathtt{w}_p \wedge \neg\langle -p\rangle\varphi \\
\langle \mathtt{r}{+}p\rangle\neg\varphi \leftrightarrow \neg\langle \mathtt{r}{+}p\rangle\varphi & \langle \mathtt{r}{-}p\rangle\neg\varphi \leftrightarrow \neg\langle \mathtt{r}{-}p\rangle\varphi \\
\langle \mathtt{w}{+}p\rangle\neg\varphi \leftrightarrow \neg\langle \mathtt{w}{+}p\rangle\varphi & \langle \mathtt{w}{-}p\rangle\neg\varphi \leftrightarrow \neg\langle \mathtt{w}{-}p\rangle\varphi \\
\langle +p\rangle(\varphi\vee\psi) \leftrightarrow \langle +p\rangle\varphi \vee \langle +p\rangle\psi & \langle -p\rangle(\varphi\vee\psi) \leftrightarrow \langle -p\rangle\varphi \vee \langle -p\rangle\psi \\
\langle \mathtt{r}{+}p\rangle(\varphi\vee\psi) \leftrightarrow \langle \mathtt{r}{+}p\rangle\varphi \vee \langle \mathtt{r}{+}p\rangle\psi & \langle \mathtt{r}{-}p\rangle(\varphi\vee\psi) \leftrightarrow \langle \mathtt{r}{-}p\rangle\varphi \vee \langle \mathtt{r}{-}p\rangle\psi \\
\langle \mathtt{w}{+}p\rangle(\varphi\vee\psi) \leftrightarrow \langle \mathtt{w}{+}p\rangle\varphi \vee \langle \mathtt{w}{+}p\rangle\psi & \langle \mathtt{w}{-}p\rangle(\varphi\vee\psi) \leftrightarrow \langle \mathtt{w}{-}p\rangle\varphi \vee \langle \mathtt{w}{-}p\rangle\psi
\end{array}$$

Fig. 5. Reduction axioms for boolean operators

The first is true if and only if readability and writability statements have the same value for every p in P and its copy $p^{\mathbf{k}}$.

5.4 Reduction Axioms for Program Operators

The reduction axioms for program operators are in Fig. 4. Those for sequential and nondeterministic composition and for exogeneous tests (PDL tests) are as in PDL. That for endogeneous tests $\varphi⁇$ varies the truth values of the non-readable variables of φ. That for the Kleene star is familiar from DL-PA. That for parallel composition $\pi_1||\pi_2$ executes π_1 and π_2 in sequence: it starts by splitting up readability and writability between the two programs, then executes π_1, checks whether π_1 didn't change the readability and writability variables and whether all truth value changes it brought about are legal, and finally executes π_2 followed by the same checks for π_2.

Observe that the validity of the reduction axiom for $||$ relies on the fact that the copies $p^{\mathbf{1}}$ and $p^{\mathbf{2}}$ that are introduced by the program $splitRW(\mathbb{P}(\pi_1) \cup \mathbb{P}(\pi_2))$ are fresh. One may also note that the length of the right hand side can be shortened by restricting $\mathbb{P}(\pi_{\mathbf{k}})$ to the propositional variables that are assigned by $\pi_{\mathbf{k}}$, i.e., to elements $p \in \mathbb{P}$ such that $+p$ or $-p$ occurs in $\pi_{\mathbf{k}}$.

The exhaustive application of the equivalences of Fig. 4 from the left to the right results in formulas whose program operators are either endogeneous tests occurring in a readability statement $\mathtt{r}_p = \langle p⁇\rangle\top \vee \langle\neg p⁇\rangle\top$, or assignments of the form $\mathtt{r}{+}p$, $\mathtt{r}{-}p$, $\mathtt{w}{+}p$, $\mathtt{w}{-}p$, $+p$, or $-p$. (We recall that the last but one, $+p$, may also be written as $\mathtt{w}_p$.)

5.5 Reduction Axioms for Boolean Operators

We now turn to modal operators $\langle\pi\rangle$ where π is of the form $\mathtt{r}{+}p$, $\mathtt{r}{-}p$, $\mathtt{w}{+}p$, $\mathtt{w}{-}p$, $+p$, or $-p$. They are deterministic and can therefore be distributed over the boolean operators. The corresponding reduction axioms are in Fig. 5.

We note that in the first equivalence $\langle +p\rangle\top \leftrightarrow \mathtt{w}_p$, the right hand side actually abbreviates the left hand side. We nevertheless state it in order to

$$\langle +p\rangle q \leftrightarrow \begin{cases} \mathtt{w}_p & \text{if } q = p \\ \mathtt{w}_p \wedge q & \text{otherwise} \end{cases} \qquad \langle -p\rangle q \leftrightarrow \begin{cases} \bot & \text{if } q = p \\ \mathtt{w}_p \wedge q & \text{otherwise} \end{cases}$$

$$\langle \mathtt{r}{+}p\rangle q \leftrightarrow q \qquad \langle \mathtt{r}{-}p\rangle q \leftrightarrow q$$

$$\langle \mathtt{w}{+}p\rangle q \leftrightarrow q \qquad \langle \mathtt{w}{-}p\rangle q \leftrightarrow q$$

$$\langle +p\rangle \mathtt{r}_q \leftrightarrow \mathtt{w}_p \wedge \mathtt{r}_q \qquad \langle -p\rangle \mathtt{r}_q \leftrightarrow \mathtt{w}_p \wedge \mathtt{r}_q$$

$$\langle \mathtt{r}{+}p\rangle \mathtt{r}_q \leftrightarrow \begin{cases} \top & \text{if } q = p \\ \mathtt{r}_q & \text{otherwise} \end{cases} \qquad \langle \mathtt{r}{-}p\rangle \top \leftrightarrow \begin{cases} \bot & \text{if } q = p \\ \mathtt{r}_q & \text{otherwise} \end{cases}$$

$$\langle \mathtt{w}{+}p\rangle \mathtt{r}_q \leftrightarrow \mathtt{r}_q \qquad \langle \mathtt{w}{-}p\rangle \mathtt{r}_q \leftrightarrow \mathtt{r}_q$$

$$\langle +p\rangle \mathtt{w}_q \leftrightarrow \mathtt{w}_p \wedge \mathtt{w}_q \qquad \langle -p\rangle \mathtt{w}_q \leftrightarrow \mathtt{w}_p \wedge \mathtt{w}_q$$

$$\langle \mathtt{r}{+}p\rangle \mathtt{w}_q \leftrightarrow \mathtt{w}_q \qquad \langle \mathtt{r}{-}p\rangle \mathtt{w}_q \leftrightarrow \mathtt{w}_q$$

$$\langle \mathtt{w}{+}p\rangle \mathtt{w}_q \leftrightarrow \begin{cases} \top & \text{if } q = p \\ \mathtt{w}_q & \text{otherwise} \end{cases} \qquad \langle \mathtt{w}{-}p\rangle \mathtt{w}_q \leftrightarrow \begin{cases} \bot & \text{if } q = p \\ \mathtt{w}_q & \text{otherwise} \end{cases}$$

Fig. 6. Reduction axioms for assignments

highlight that the exhaustive application of these reduction axioms results in sequences of atomic assignments facing either propositional variables or $\mathtt{w}_p$ or $\mathtt{r}_q$. These sequences are going to be reduced in the next step.

5.6 Reduction Axioms for Assignments

When atomic programs face propositional variables or readability and writability statements then the modal operator can be eliminated (sometimes introducing a writability statement $\mathtt{w}_p$). The reduction axioms doing that are in Fig. 6.

As announced, the exhaustive application of the above equivalences results in boolean combinations of propositional variables and readability and writability statements.

5.7 Soundness, Completeness, and Decidability

Let us call $\mathsf{DL\text{-}PA}^{||}$ our extension of DL-PA with parallel composition. Its axiomatisation is made up of

- an axiomatisation of propositional logic;
- the equivalences of Sects. 5.4, 5.5, and 5.6;
- the inclusion axiom schema $\mathtt{w}_p \to \mathtt{r}_p$, which is an abbreviation of the formula $\langle +p\rangle\top \to (\langle p?\rangle\top \vee \langle \neg p?\rangle\top)$;
- the rule of equivalence $RE(\langle\pi\rangle)$ "from $\varphi \leftrightarrow \psi$ infer $\langle\pi\rangle\varphi \leftrightarrow \langle\pi\rangle\psi$".

The inference rules preserve validity and the axioms are valid:

Theorem 1. *The axiomatisation of* $\mathsf{DL\text{-}PA}^{||}$ *is sound: if* φ *is provable with the axiomatics of* $\mathsf{DL\text{-}PA}^{||}$ *then it is* $\mathsf{DL\text{-}PA}^{||}$ *valid.*

As to completeness, the reduction axioms of Sects. 5.4, 5.5, and 5.6 allow us to transform any formula into an equivalent boolean combination of propositional variables and readability and writability statements. (Their application requires the rule of replacement of equivalents, which is derivable because we have rules of equivalence for all the connectives of the language, in particular the above $RE(\langle\pi\rangle)$.) Let φ be the resulting formula. Then φ has a $\mathsf{DL\text{-}PA}^{||}$ model if and only if

$$\varphi \wedge \bigwedge_{p \in \mathbb{P}} (\mathtt{w}_p \to \mathtt{r}_p)$$

has a model in propositional logic, where in propositional logic, $\mathtt{r}_p$ and $\mathtt{w}_p$ are considered to be arbitrary propositional variables; so there is a priori no connection between them nor with the propositional variable p.

Theorem 2. *The axiomatisation of* $\mathsf{DL\text{-}PA}^{||}$ *is complete: if* φ *is* $\mathsf{DL\text{-}PA}^{||}$ *valid then it is provable in the axiomatics of* $\mathsf{DL\text{-}PA}^{||}$.

Based on the reduction of $\mathsf{DL\text{-}PA}^{||}$ formulas to boolean formulas (and the transformation of $\mathtt{r}_p$ and $\mathtt{w}_p$ from abbreviations into propositional variables), we may check the satisfiability of $\mathsf{DL\text{-}PA}^{||}$ formulas by means of propositional logic SAT solvers. This is however suboptimal because reduction may result in a formula that is super-exponentially longer than the original formula. In the next section we explore another route.

6 Complexity via Translation into DL-PA

We establish PSPACE complexity of $\mathsf{DL\text{-}PA}^{||}$ satisfiability and model checking by translating formulas and programs to Dynamic Logic of Propositional Assignments DL-PA. The language of the latter is the fragment of that of $\mathsf{DL\text{-}PA}^{||}$: it has neither endogeneous tests, nor readability and writability assignments, nor parallel composition. So the language of DL-PA is built by the following grammar:

$$\varphi ::= p \mid \top \mid \neg\varphi \mid (\varphi \vee \varphi) \mid \langle\pi\rangle\varphi$$
$$\pi ::= +p \mid -p \mid \varphi? \mid (\pi;\pi) \mid (\pi \cup \pi) \mid \pi^*$$

None of the operators of the language refers to the Rd-component or the Wr-component of models. The interpretation of DL-PA formulas and programs therefore only requires a valuation V.

Our translation from $\mathsf{DL\text{-}PA}^{||}$ to DL-PA eliminates endogeneous tests and parallel composition. This is done in a way that is similar to their reduction axioms of Fig. 4. It moreover transforms readability and writability statements into special propositional variables $\mathtt{r}_p$ and $\mathtt{w}_p$, similar to the reduction axioms of Fig. 6.

To make this formal, let the set of *atomic formulas* be

$$\mathbb{X} = \mathbb{P} \cup \{\mathtt{w}_p \ : \ p \in \mathbb{P}\} \cup \{\mathtt{r}_p \ : \ p \in \mathbb{P}\}.$$

Given a set of propositional variables $P \subseteq \mathbb{P}$, $\mathbb{R}_P = \{\mathtt{r}_p : p \in P\}$ is the associated set of read-variables and $\mathbb{W}_P = \{\mathtt{w}_p : p \in P\}$ is the associated set of write-variables. So $\mathbb{X} = \mathbb{P} \cup \mathbb{R}_\mathbb{P} \cup \mathbb{W}_\mathbb{P}$. As before, the set of propositional variables occurring in a formula φ is noted $\mathbb{P}(\varphi)$ and the set of those occurring in a program π is noted $\mathbb{P}(\pi)$. This now includes the p's in $\mathtt{r}_p$ and $\mathtt{w}_p$. For example, $\mathbb{P}(p \wedge \langle +w_q \rangle \neg \mathtt{r}_p) = \{p, q\}$.

We translate the DL-PA$^{||}$ programs $\mathtt{r}{+}p$, $\mathtt{r}{-}p$, $\mathtt{w}{+}p$, and $\mathtt{w}{-}p$ into the DL-PA programs $+\mathtt{r}_p$, $-\mathtt{r}_p$, $+\mathtt{w}_p$ and $-\mathtt{w}_p$. Moreover, we have to 'spell out' that $-\mathtt{w}_p$ has side effect $-\mathtt{r}_p$ and that $+\mathtt{r}_p$ has side effect $+\mathtt{w}_p$. So the programs of Fig. 3 become the following DL-PA programs:

$$\begin{aligned}
copyV^{\mathbf{k}}(P) &= ;_{p \in P} \; \big((p?; +p^{\mathbf{k}}) \cup (\neg p?; -p^{\mathbf{k}})\big) \\
splitRW(P) &= ;_{p \in P} \; \big((-\mathtt{w}_{p^1}; -\mathtt{r}_{p^1}); (-\mathtt{w}_{p^2}; -\mathtt{r}_{p^2}); \\
&\qquad \textbf{if } \mathtt{w}_p \textbf{ then } \big((+\mathtt{w}_{p^1}; +\mathtt{r}_{p^1}) \cup (+\mathtt{w}_{p^2}; +\mathtt{r}_{p^2})\big); \\
&\qquad \textbf{if } \mathtt{r}_p \wedge \neg \mathtt{w}_p \textbf{ then } \big(+\mathtt{r}_{p^1} \cup +\mathtt{r}_{p^2} \cup (+\mathtt{r}_{p^1}; +\mathtt{r}_{p^2})\big)\big) \\
copybackRW^{\mathbf{k}}(P) &= ;_{p \in P} \; \big((\neg \mathtt{r}_{p^{\mathbf{k}}}?; -\mathtt{r}_p; -\mathtt{w}_p) \;\cup \\
&\qquad (\mathtt{r}_{p^{\mathbf{k}}} \wedge \neg \mathtt{w}_{p^{\mathbf{k}}}?; +\mathtt{r}_p; -\mathtt{w}_p) \;\cup \\
&\qquad (\mathtt{w}_{p^{\mathbf{k}}}?; +\mathtt{w}_p; +\mathtt{r}_p)\big) \\
mergeRW(P) &= ;_{p \in P} \; (\textbf{if } \mathtt{r}_{p^1} \textbf{ then } +\mathtt{r}_p \; ; \; \textbf{if } \mathtt{w}_{p^1} \textbf{ then } +\mathtt{w}_p)
\end{aligned}$$

The useful formulas of Sect. 5.3 remain unchanged, except that readability and writability statements are no longer DL-PA$^{||}$ abbreviations, but are now DL-PA propositional variables.

Given a DL-PA$^{||}$ program or formula, its translation into DL-PA basically follows the reduction axiom for endogeneous tests ⁇ and parallel composition $||$ of Fig. 4. We replace:

1. all occurrences of φ⁇ by $[;_{p \in \mathbb{P}(\varphi)} \; (\textbf{if } \neg \mathtt{r}_p \textbf{ then } (+p \cup -p))]\varphi?$
2. all occurrences of $\pi_1 || \pi_2$ by

$$\begin{aligned}
&splitRW(\mathbb{P}(\pi_1) \cup \mathbb{P}(\pi_2)); \\
&copybackRW^1(\mathbb{P}(\pi_1)); copyV^1(\mathbb{P}(\pi_1)); \pi_1; NochangeRW^1(\mathbb{P}(\pi_1))?; OkChangeV^1(\mathbb{P}(\pi_1))?; \\
&copybackRW^2(\mathbb{P}(\pi_2)); copyV^2(\mathbb{P}(\pi_2)); \pi_2; NochangeRW^2(\mathbb{P}(\pi_2))?; OkChangeV^2(\mathbb{P}(\pi_2))?; \\
&mergeRW(\mathbb{P}(\pi_1))
\end{aligned}$$

3. all occurrences of $\mathtt{r}{+}p$, $\mathtt{r}{-}p$, $\mathtt{w}{+}p$, and $\mathtt{w}{-}p$ by the DL-PA programs $+\mathtt{r}_p$, $-\mathtt{r}_p$, $+\mathtt{w}_p$ and $-\mathtt{w}_p$, for $p \in \mathbb{P}$
4. all occurrences of $-\mathtt{w}_p$ by $-\mathtt{w}_p; -\mathtt{r}_p$ and all occurrences of $+\mathtt{r}_p$ by $+\mathtt{r}_p; +\mathtt{w}_p$, for $p \in \mathbb{P}$

Let $t(\varphi)$ be the translation of the DL-PA$^{||}$ formula φ. Remember that in $t(\varphi)$, the variables $\mathtt{r}_p$ and $\mathtt{w}_p$ are considered to be arbitrary propositional variables.

Theorem 3. *A* $\mathsf{DL\text{-}PA}^{||}$ *formula* φ *is* $\mathsf{DL\text{-}PA}^{||}$*-satisfiable if and only if the* DL-PA *formula* $t(\varphi) \wedge \bigwedge_{p \in \mathbb{P}(\varphi)}(\mathtt{w}_p \rightarrow \mathtt{r}_p)$ *is* DL-PA *satisfiable.*

As the length of $t(\varphi)$ is polynomial in that of φ, it follows that $\mathsf{DL\text{-}PA}^{||}$ model and satisfiability checking are both PSPACE complete.

7 Conclusion

We have added to Dynamic Logic of Propositional Assignments DL-PA a parallel composition operator in the spirit of separation logics. To that end we have augmented DL-PA valuations by readability and writability information. We have adopted a stricter stance on race conditions than in the approach of [HMV19] where e.g. the program $+p||+p$ is executable. We have provided a complete axiomatisation in terms of reduction axioms, ensuring at the same time decidability. We have also proved PSPACE complexity via a translation to DL-PA.

The mathematical properties of $\mathsf{DL\text{-}PA}^{||}$ compare favourably with the high complexity or even undecidability of the separation logics in the literature. They also compare favourably with those of other extensions of dynamic logic by a separating parallel composition operator that were proposed in the literature [BdFV11, VVB14, BB18]. Just as ours, the latter line of work is in the spirit of separation logic, having splitting and merging operations that are defined on system states. The axiomatisation that was introduced and studied in [BB18] is restricted to the star-free fragment and the authors had to add propositional quantifiers in order to make parallel composition definable. This contrasts with the simplicity of our axiomatisation of $\mathsf{DL\text{-}PA}^{||}$ that we obtained by adding reduction axioms to the axiomatisation of DL-PA. Just as DL-PA can be viewed as an instance of PDL—the interpretation of atomic programs moves from PDL's abstract relation between states to concrete updates of valuations—, $\mathsf{DL\text{-}PA}^{||}$ can be viewed as an instance of the logic of [BdFV11] where the interpretation of parallel composition no longer resorts to an abstract relation $\star$ associating three states, but instead has concrete functions that split and merge valuations and that are constrained by readability and writability information.

Acknowledgements. The paper benefitted from comments and remarks from the reviewers as well as from the attendees of DaLí 2019, in particular Alexandru Baltag, Raul Fervari, Rainer Hähnle and Dexter Kozen. We did our best take their comments into account.

Andreas Herzig's work was done in the framework of the ANR project "Cognitive Planning in Persuasive Multimodal Communication" (CoPains).

References

[BB18] Balbiani, P., Boudou, J.: Iteration-free PDL with storing, recovering and parallel composition: a complete axiomatization. J. Log. Comput. **28**(4), 705–731 (2018)

[BdFV11] Benevides, M.R.F., de Freitas, R.P., Viana, J.P.: Propositional dynamic logic with storing, recovering and parallel composition. Electr. Notes Theor. Comput. Sci. **269**, 95–107 (2011)

[BHST14] Balbiani, P., Herzig, A., Schwarzentruber, F., Troquard, N.: DL-PA and DCL-PC: model checking and satisfiability problem are indeed in PSPACE. CoRR, abs/1411.7825 (2014)

[BHT13] Balbiani, P., Herzig, A., Troquard, N.: Dynamic logic of propositional assignments: a well-behaved variant of PDL. In: Kupferman, O. (ed.) Logic in Computer Science (LICS). IEEE (2013)

[BO16] Brookes, S., O'Hearn, P.W.: SIGLOG News. Concurrent separation logic **3**(3), 47–65 (2016)

[Bro04] Brookes, S.: A semantics for concurrent separation logic. In: Gardner, P., Yoshida, N. (eds.) CONCUR 2004. LNCS, vol. 3170, pp. 16–34. Springer, Heidelberg (2004). https://doi.org/10.1007/978-3-540-28644-8_2. [GY04]

[Bro07] Brookes, S.: A semantics for concurrent separation logic. Theor. Comput. Sci. **375**(1–3), 227–270 (2007)

[BV03] Balbiani, P., Vakarelov, D.: PDL with intersection of programs: a complete axiomatization. J. Appl. Non-Class. Log. **13**(3–4), 231–276 (2003)

[CHM+16] Cooper, M.C., Herzig, A., Maffre, F., Maris, F., Régnier, P.: A simple account of multi-agent epistemic planning. In: Kaminka, G.A., et al. (eds.) ECAI 2016–22nd European Conference on Artificial Intelligence, The Hague, The Netherlands, 29 August–2 September 2016, Volume 285 of Frontiers in Artificial Intelligence and Applications, pp. 193–201. IOS Press (2016)

[CS15] Charrier, T., Schwarzentruber, F.: Arbitrary public announcement logic with mental programs. In: Weiss, G., Yolum, P., Bordini, R.H., Elkind, E. (eds.) Proceedings of the 2015 International Conference on Autonomous Agents and Multiagent Systems, AAMAS 2015, Istanbul, Turkey, 4–8 May 2015, pp. 1471–1479. ACM (2015)

[CS17] Charrier, T., Schwarzentruber, F.: A succinct language for dynamic epistemic logic. In: Larson, K., Winikoff, M., Das, S., Durfee, E.H. (eds.) Proceedings of the 16th Conference on Autonomous Agents and MultiAgent Systems, AAMAS 2017, São Paulo, Brazil, 8–12 May 2017, pp. 123–131. ACM (2017)

[DHS05] Darvas, Á., Hähnle, R., Sands, D.: A theorem proving approach to analysis of secure information flow. In: Hutter, D., Ullmann, M. (eds.) SPC 2005. LNCS, vol. 3450, pp. 193–209. Springer, Heidelberg (2005). https://doi.org/10.1007/978-3-540-32004-3_20

[FHR19] Feuillade, G., Herzig, A., Rantsoudis, C.: A dynamic logic account of active integrity constraints. Fundamenta Informaticae **169**(3), 179–210 (2019)

[Gol92] Goldblatt, R.: Parallel action: concurrent dynamic logic with independent modalities. Studia Logica **51**(3/4), 551–578 (1992)

[GY04] Gardner, P., Yoshida, N. (eds.): CONCUR 2004 - Concurrency Theory, 15th International Conference, London, UK, August 31 – 3 September 2004, Proceedings, Volume 3170 of Lecture Notes in Computer Science. Springer, Heidelberg (2004)

[Her13] Herzig, A.: A simple separation logic. In: Libkin, L., Kohlenbach, U., de Queiroz, R. (eds.) WoLLIC 2013. LNCS, vol. 8071, pp. 168–178. Springer, Heidelberg (2013). https://doi.org/10.1007/978-3-642-39992-3_16

[Her14] Herzig, A.: Belief change operations: a short history of nearly everything, told in dynamic logic of propositional assignments. In: Baral, C., De Giacomo, G. (eds.) Proceedings of KR 2014. AAAI Press (2014)

[HMNDBW14] Herzig, A., Menezes, V., De Barros, L.N., Wassermann, R.: On the revision of planning tasks. In: Schaub, T. (ed.) European Conference on Artificial Intelligence (ECAI), August 2014

[HMV19] Herzig, A., Maris, F., Vianey, J.: Dynamic logic of parallel propositional assignments and its applications to planning. In: Kraus, S. (ed.) Proceedings of the Twenty-Eighth International Joint Conference on Artificial Intelligence, IJCAI 2019, Macao, China, 10–16 August 2019, pp. 5576–5582. ijcai.org (2019)

[MS96] Mayer, A.J., Stockmeyer, L.J.: The complexity of PDL with interleaving. Theor. Comput. Sci. **161**(1&2), 109–122 (1996)

[NGH18] Novaro, A., Grandi, U., Herzig, A.: Judgment aggregation in dynamic logic of propositional assignments. J. Log. Comput. **28**(7), 1471–1498 (2018)

[O'H04] O'Hearn, P.W.: Resources, concurrency and local reasoning. Gardner and Yoshida, pp. 49–67

[Pel87] Peleg, D.: Concurrent dynamic logic. J. ACM **34**(2), 450–479 (1987)

[SG16] Scheben, C., Greiner, S.: Information flow analysis. Deductive Software Verification – The KeY Book. LNCS, vol. 10001, pp. 453–471. Springer, Cham (2016). https://doi.org/10.1007/978-3-319-49812-6_13

[vDvdHK07] van Ditmarsch, H.P., van der Hoek, W., Kooi, B.: Dynamic Epistemic Logic. Kluwer Academic Publishers (2007)

[VVB14] Veloso, P.A.S., Veloso, S.R.M., Benevides, M.R.F.: PDL for structured data: a graph-calculus approach. Logic J. IGPL **22**(5), 737–757 (2014)

Stit Semantics for Epistemic Notions Based on Information Disclosure in Interactive Settings

Aldo Iván Ramírez Abarca(✉) and Jan Broersen

Utrecht University, 3512 JK Utrecht, The Netherlands
{a.i.ramirezabarca,J.M.broersen}@uu.nl

Abstract. We characterize four types of agentive knowledge using a stit semantics over branching discrete-time structures. These are *ex ante* knowledge, *ex interim* knowledge, *ex post* knowledge, and know-how. The first three are notions that arose from game-theoretical analyses on the stages of information disclosure across the decision making process, and the fourth has gained prominence both in logics of action and in deontic logic as a means to formalize ability. In recent years, logicians in AI have argued that any comprehensive study of responsibility attribution and blameworthiness should include proper treatment of these kinds of knowledge. This paper intends to clarify previous attempts to formalize them in stit logic and to propose alternative interpretations that in our opinion are more akin to the study of responsibility in the stit tradition. The logic we present uses an extension with knowledge operators of the Xstit language, and formulas are evaluated with respect to branching discrete-time models. We also present an axiomatic system for this logic, and address its soundness and completeness.

1 Introduction

For logicians of action and obligation, there is little debate as to the intuition that agentive responsibility has an important epistemic component. In interactive settings, what agents know before and after a choice of action needs to be taken into account when ascribing responsibility and/or culpability for an outcome. Aiming to model the different degrees of culpability according to judicial practice with a stit formalism, Broersen introduced in [5] a logic of 'knowingly doing'. Next, a comprehensive study of three kinds of game knowledge (*ex ante, ex interim,* and *ex post*) was provided by Lorini et al. in [15] with the goal of formalizing both responsibility attribution and some attribution-emotions related to it – like guilt or blame. They also used stit for it, just as Horty and Pacuit recently did in [13], where new epistemic operators are added to basic stit in order to model *ex interim* knowledge and epistemic ability (or know-how). Even more recently, Horty used in [12] the same novel epistemic operators to provide a logic of epistemic obligations, to which [7] constitutes a reply. Additionally, other attempts to model individual and collective know-how in a stit-like fashion can

L. Soares Barbosa and A. Baltag (Eds.): DaLí 2019, LNCS 12005, pp. 171–189, 2020.
https://doi.org/10.1007/978-3-030-38808-9_11

be found in [17], where the authors take inspiration from Coalition Logic and use transition systems to account for a given group of agents' ability to bring about an outcome by voting. We mention this in the introduction rather than including it in a section for related work because the present paper has two main objectives, and they both stem from the context of the existing literature in epistemic stit: (1) we want to point out the areas for which the mentioned works overlap, clarifying their differences and shortcomings, and (2) we want to offer new stit formalizations for *know-how*, *ex ante, ex interim*, and *ex post* knowledge, targeting components of them which we believe are essential in an analysis of responsibility.

Within game theory and epistemic logic, there is a degree of agreement regarding characteristics of the four kinds of knowledge we have mentioned. In broad terms, these characteristics are the following. ***Ex ante*** knowledge concerns the information that is available to the agents regardless of their choices of action at a given moment. It is commonly thought to be the knowledge that the agents have *before* they choose any of their available actions and execute them. ***Ex interim* knowledge** can be seen as the knowledge that is private to an agent after choosing an action but before knowing the concurrent choices of other agents. ***Ex post* knowledge** concerns the information that is disclosed to the agents after everybody reveals their choices of action and executes them. **Know-how** concerns the epistemic ability of bringing about a particular outcome.

The paper is structured as follows. Since the logic we favor is an extension of Xstit [6,23], in Sect. 2 we deal with the examples that motivated our choice of syntax and semantics and introduce these two aspects of the logic. In Sect. 3 we present the definitions for *ex ante, ex interim, ex post* knowledge, and know-how that we want to formalize and give their characterizations as formulas built with specific combinations of the operators in our language. We compare these new interpretations with the previous ones by dissecting the examples from the preceding section. In Sect. 4 we introduce an axiomatic system for the developed logic and mention its soundness and completeness results, after which we conclude.

2 An Example Involving Four Kinds of Game Knowledge

We intend to give a formal overview for settings of interactive decisions. Different agents will have different epistemic status and they can act *concurrently*. This means that our models include the layouts of formal games with *incomplete* and *imperfect* information,[1] as well as of concurrent game structures (CGS's)

[1] In [1] Ågotnes et al. write: "In game theory, two different terms are traditionally used to indicate lack of information: 'incomplete' and 'imperfect' information. Usually, the former refers to uncertainties about the game structure and rules, while the latter refers to uncertainties about the history, current state, etc. of the specific *play of the game*.".

(see [1,4]) and epistemic transition systems (see [16,17]). Consider the following example, built as a variation of Horty's puzzles for epistemic ability [13] and inspired by the film *Mission: Impossible 6.*

Example 1. A bomb squad consisting of three members (*ethan*, *luther*, and *benji*) faces a complex bomb situation. Terrorists threaten to blow up a facility with two bombs (L and B) remotely connected to each other. If the squad defuses one bomb before the other, then the latter is programmed to set off. The terrorists who planted the bombs start a countdown. If the countdown ends both bombs go off. Each bomb has a remote activation system with two main wires, a red one and a green one. Moreover, each bomb has its own detonator, and these detonators include a fail-safe mechanism that makes it possible for the bombs to be disarmed. The squad figures out that there are *three* ways to successfully defuse the two bombs: (1) If they activate the fail-safe mechanisms of *both* detonators, the squad needs to cut both red wires simultaneously. (2) If they manage to activate the fail-safe mechanism for the detonator of bomb L but not of bomb B, they need to cut the red wire of L and the green one of B simultaneously. (3) The reverse situation of the above item in case they only manage to activate the fail-safe mechanism for the detonator of bomb B. In other words, cutting the red wire of a bomb without the previous activation of the fail-safe mechanism in its detonator makes it go off. Cutting the green wire *with* previous activation of the fail-safe mechanism also makes it go off. If neither fail-safe mechanism is activated, both bombs go off. If any of these bombs goes off, the explosion is so powerful that it is impossible to ascertain which bomb went off or if both did.

After the countdown starts, agent *ethan* is commissioned with the task of retrieving the detonators. Agents *luther* and *benji* have to afterwards synchronize the cutting of wires in order to disarm bombs L and B, respectively. A malfunction in the squad's telecom gear causes for them to lose all communication with each other, so *luther* and *benji* do not know whether *ethan* has retrieved one detonator, both of them, or none. Regardless, they know that they need to synchronize the cutting of both bombs' main wires *just before* the countdown ends. We explore the following alternatives: *(a)* Unbeknownst to *luther* and *benji*, *ethan* succeeds in retrieving only the detonator for bomb B. They synchronize the cutting of the wires, and since it is statistically better for both *luther* and *benji* to cut the two red wires, they do so. Bomb L goes off. *(b)* Unbeknownst to *benji*, *luther* finds out what *ethan* did. However, *luther* is actually an undercover associate of the terrorists, so he decides to go on with the cutting of the red wire so that bomb L goes off.

It is convenient to have visual representations of our examples, and stit logic allows us to draw diagrams of them when seen as models. In order to be precise about such models, we introduce the syntax and semantics of the stit logic that we will use before addressing the diagrams. As mentioned before, it is an extension of Xstit logic.[2]

Definition 1 (Syntax KXstit). *Given a finite set Ags of agent names and a countable set of propositions P such that $p \in P$ and $\alpha \in Ags$, the grammar for the formal language $\mathcal{L}_{\mathsf{KX}}$ is given by:*

$$\varphi := p \mid \neg\varphi \mid \varphi \wedge \psi \mid \Box\varphi \mid X\varphi \mid Y\varphi \mid [\alpha]\varphi \mid [Ags]\varphi \mid K_\alpha\varphi$$

$\Box\varphi$ is meant to express the 'historical necessity' of φ ($\Diamond\varphi$ abbreviates $\neg\Box\neg\varphi$). X is the 'next moment' operator and Y is the 'last moment' operator. $[\alpha]\varphi$ stands for 'α sees to it that φ'. $[Ags]\varphi$ stands for 'the grand coalition Ags sees to it that φ'. K_α is the epistemic operator for α. Observe that $\mathcal{L}_{\mathsf{KX}}$ is built with the *instantaneous* action operators $[\alpha]$ and $[Ags]$. We have done so because this expressive language simplifies the axiomatization process for our logic. However, we restrict our treatment of the four kinds of agentive knowledge to 'actions that take effect in the next moment', which are characterized by formulas of the form $[\alpha]X\varphi$ and $[Ags]X\varphi$. Therefore, we work with a fragment of $\mathcal{L}_{\mathsf{KX}}$. In what follows, we abbreviate the combination $[\alpha]X$ by $[\alpha]^X$ and the combination $[Ags]X$ by $[Ags]^X$ (see [23] for a similar approach of the matter).

As for the semantics, the structures with respect to which we evaluate the formulas of $\mathcal{L}_{\mathsf{KX}}$ are based on *epistemic branching discrete-time frames.*

Definition 2 (Epistemic branching discrete-time (BDT) frames). *A tuple of the form $\langle T, \sqsubset, \mathbf{Choice}, \{\sim_\alpha\}_{\alpha \in Ags}\rangle$ is called an* epistemic branching discrete-time frame *iff*

- *T is a non-empty set of* moments *and $\sqsubset$ is a strict partial ordering on T satisfying 'no backward branching'. Each maximal $\sqsubset$-chain is called a* history, *which represents a way in which time evolves. H denotes the set of all histories, and for each $m \in T$, $H_m := \{h \in H; m \in h\}$. Tuples $\langle m, h\rangle$ are called* situations *iff $m \in T$, $h \in H$, and $m \in h$. We call the frames 'discrete-time' because $(T, \sqsubset)$ must meet these requirements:* (a) *For every $m \in T$ and $h \in H_m$, there exists a unique moment m^{+h} such that $m \sqsubset m^{+h}$ and $m^{+h} \sqsubseteq m'$ for every $m' \in h$ such that $m \sqsubset m'$.* (b) *For every $m \in T$ and $h \in H_m$, there exists a unique moment m^{-h} such that $m^{-h} \sqsubset m$ and $m' \sqsubseteq m^{-h}$ for every $m' \in h$ such that $m' \sqsubset m$.*[3]
- **Choice** *is a function that maps each α and m to a partition $\mathbf{Choice}^m_\alpha$ of H_m. The cells of these partitions represent the actions that are available to each agent at moment m. For $m \in T$ and $h \in H_m$ we denote by $\mathbf{Choice}^m_{Ags}(h)$ the set $\bigcap_{\alpha \in Ags} \mathbf{Choice}^m_\alpha(h)$, and we take $\mathbf{Choice}^m_{Ags} := \{\mathbf{Choice}^m_{Ags}(h); h \in H_m\}$, which is the partition of actions available to the grand coalition.* **Choice**

[2] Xstit was developed by Broersen in [5] on the conceptual assumption that the effects of performing an action are not instantaneous. Rather, an action that is chosen at a given moment will bring about effects only in the next.

[3] Observe that these definitions, coupled with the fact that histories are linearly ordered, imply that for every $m \in T$ and $h \in H_m$, $(m^{-h})^{+h} = m$ and $(m^{+h})^{-h} = m$.

must satisfy the following constraints. (NC) *or 'no choice between undivided histories': for all $h, h' \in H_m$, if $m' \in h \cap h'$ for some $m' \sqsupset m$, then $h \in L$ iff $h' \in L$ for every $L \in \mathbf{Choice}^m_\alpha$.* (IA) *or 'independence of agency': a function s on Ags is called a* selection function *at m if it assigns to each α a member of $\mathbf{Choice}^m_\alpha$. If we denote by $\mathbf{Select}^m$ the set of all selection functions at m, then we have that for every $m \in T$ and $s \in \mathbf{Select}^m$, $\bigcap_{\alpha \in Ags} s(\alpha) \neq \emptyset$ (see [3] for a discussion of the property).*

- *For each $\alpha \in Ags$, $\sim_\alpha$ is an equivalence relation on the set of* situations, *meant to express the epistemic indistinguishability relation for α. At this point, the only condition we impose on these relations is* (NoF) *or 'no forget condition': For every $m \in T$, $h \in H_m$, and $\alpha \in Ags$, if $\langle m^{+h}, h\rangle \sim_\alpha \langle m_*, h_*\rangle$, then $\langle m, h\rangle \sim_\alpha \langle m_*^-, h_*\rangle$.*

Definition 3. *An epistemic BDT model $\mathcal{M}$ consists of the tuple that results from adding a valuation function $\mathcal{V}$ to an epistemic BDT frame, where $\mathcal{V} : P \to 2^{T \times H}$ assigns to each atomic proposition a set of moment-history pairs. Relative to a model $\mathcal{M}$, the semantics for the formulas of $\mathcal{L}_{KX}$ is defined recursively by the following truth conditions, evaluated at a situation $\langle m, h\rangle$:*

$$
\begin{array}{ll}
\mathcal{M}, \langle m,h\rangle \models p & \textit{iff } \langle m,h\rangle \in \mathcal{V}(p)\\
\mathcal{M}, \langle m,h\rangle \models \neg\varphi & \textit{iff } \mathcal{M}, \langle m,h\rangle \not\models \varphi\\
\mathcal{M}, \langle m,h\rangle \models \varphi \wedge \psi & \textit{iff } \mathcal{M}, \langle m,h\rangle \models \varphi \textit{ and } \mathcal{M}, \langle m,h\rangle \models \psi\\
\mathcal{M}, \langle m,h\rangle \models \Box\varphi & \textit{iff } \forall h' \in H_m, \mathcal{M}, \langle m,h'\rangle \models \varphi\\
\mathcal{M}, \langle m,h\rangle \models X\varphi & \textit{iff } \mathcal{M}, \langle m^{+h},h\rangle \models \varphi\\
\mathcal{M}, \langle m,h\rangle \models Y\varphi & \textit{iff } \mathcal{M}, \langle m^{-h},h\rangle \models \varphi\\
\mathcal{M}, \langle m,h\rangle \models [\alpha]\varphi & \textit{iff } \forall h' \in \mathbf{Choice}^m_\alpha(h), \mathcal{M}, \langle m,h'\rangle \models \varphi\\
\mathcal{M}, \langle m,h\rangle \models [Ags]\varphi & \textit{iff } \forall h' \in \mathbf{Choice}^m_{Ags}(h), \mathcal{M}, \langle m,h'\rangle \models \varphi\\
\mathcal{M}, \langle m,h\rangle \models K_\alpha\varphi & \textit{iff } \forall \langle m',h'\rangle \textit{ s.t. } \langle m,h\rangle \sim_\alpha \langle m',h'\rangle,\\
 & \quad \mathcal{M}, \langle m',h'\rangle \models \varphi.
\end{array}
$$

Satisfiability, validity on a frame, and general validity are defined as usual. We write $|\varphi|^m$ to refer to the set $\{h \in H_m; \mathcal{M}, \langle m,h\rangle \models \varphi\}$.

With the definitions provided in Definition 3 we can analyze the cases in Example 1 as epistemic BDT models. A diagram for Example 1(a) is included in Fig. 1.

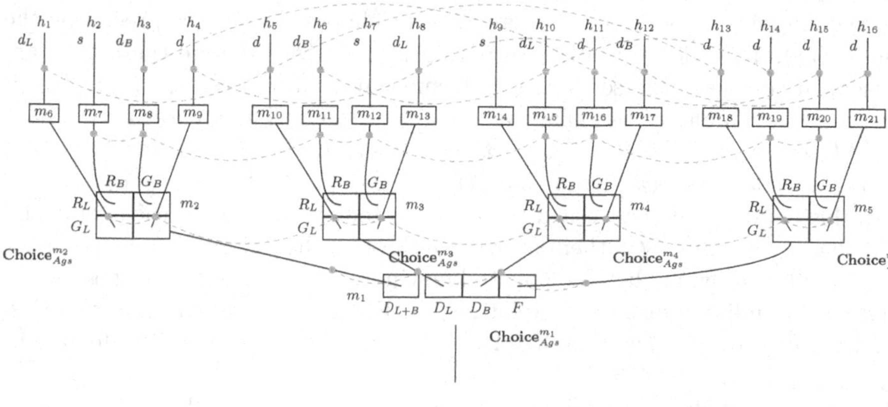

Fig. 1. Example 1(a) with epistemic status of *luther*

The diagram represents the different possibilities in which time may evolve from the point the bomb squad sets out to defuse the bombs onward. Each history stands for one of these relevant possibilities, according to the actions taken by the agents. We take d_L and d_B to denote the propositions 'bomb L detonates' and 'bomb B detonates', respectively, and we abbreviate $d_L \wedge d_B$ with d. We take s to denote the proposition 'the bombs are defused'. These are true or false depending on the moment/history pair of evaluation. For instance, at situation $\langle m_2, h_4\rangle$ the bombs have not detonated ($\mathcal{M}, \langle m_2, h_4\rangle \models \neg d_L \wedge \neg d_B$), but in the next moment they have ($\mathcal{M}, \langle m_9, h_4\rangle \models d$). For clarity, we have labeled the actions available to the agents within the choice partitions of each moment. Label D_{L+B} stands for 'activating the fail-safe mechanism of both detonators' (similarly for D_L and D_B), F stands for 'failing to secure a detonator', R_L (R_B) stands for 'cutting the red wire of bomb L (B)', and G_L (G_B) stands for 'cutting the green wire of bomb L (B)'. In epistemic BDT models all agents in Ags get to choose from their 'available' actions at *every* moment/history pair. In our example, Ags is made up of $ethan$, $luther$ and $benji$. However, $luther$ and $benji$ cannot choose anything at moment m_1, so we take it that their available actions both lie within the trivial partition, meaning that $\mathbf{Choice}^{m_1}_{luther} = \mathbf{Choice}^{m_1}_{benji} = \{H_{m_1}\}$. Similarly, we have that $\mathbf{Choice}^{m_i}_{ethan} = \{H_{m_i}\}$ for m_2, m_3, m_4, and m_5.

In both cases (a) and (b) of Example 1, at moment m_1 $ethan$ 'chooses' an action and executes it with effects in the next moment. The set of 'next moments' for m_1 comprises m_2, m_3, m_4, and m_5. The histories running through each of these are partitioned according to the choices of action available to $luther$ and $benji$. The frame condition *independence of agency* makes the partitions-layout look like a game in normal form, modelling concurrent choice of action. Observe that although this example presupposes that there is a single next state per action profile, this need not be the case for the general models.[4]

In both cases (a) and (b) of Example 1, at moments m_2, m_3, m_4, and m_5 the available actions for $luther$ are either R_L or G_L, and the available actions for $benji$ are either R_B or G_B. A given outcome will ensue according to which action profile is chosen by Ags –at these moments, only $luther$ and $benji$'s choices are relevant. For example, let us suppose that at moment m_4, $benji$ cuts the red wire (he chooses R_B), and $luther$ chooses to cut the green one (he chooses G_L). This means that we constrain H_{m_4} to $\{h_9\}$, where the bombs are defused. In this case, the semantics in Definition 3 implies that $\mathcal{M}, \langle m_4, h_9\rangle \models [Ags]^X s$. As examples of formulas involving traditional Xstit operators, we have that $\mathcal{M}, \langle m_1, h_2\rangle \models X(\neg d_L \wedge \neg d_B)$, that $\mathcal{M}, \langle m_1, h_{10}\rangle \models X[luther]^X d_L$, that $\mathcal{M}, \langle m_4, h_{11}\rangle \not\models Y[Ags]^X d$, and that $\mathcal{M}, \langle m_3, h_7\rangle \models Y\Diamond X[luther]^X d_L$.

In this paper we are concerned with the epistemic structure of the agents and with what it says about *(a)* their knowledge through the different stages of choice of action, and *(b)* what they are able to knowingly do. The epistemic structure is given by the indistinguishability relations. In Fig. 1 we represent $luther$'s indistinguishability relation in Example 1(a) with blue dashed lines. We focus our

[4] Models that satisfy the condition that for every $m \in T$ and $h \in H_m$, if $h' \in \mathbf{Choice}^m_{Ags}(h)$ then $m^{+h} = m^{+h'}$ are called *deterministic* (see [6,21]).

study on the epistemic structures of *luther* and *benji*, since it is only because of them that cases (a) and (b) of Example 1 are different. Although *ethan* is also endowed with an indistinguishability relation over the set of situations in our BDT structure, we omit its analysis. The explanation is the following. At moment m_1 *luther* (and *benji*, for that matter) does not know what *ethan* does. At moments m_2, m_3, m_4, and m_5, we observe that *luther* is able to distinguish between either cutting the red or the green wire of his bomb. If we take the proposition r_L to mean 'the red cable has been cut in bomb L', then we have that $\mathcal{M}, \langle m_i, h\rangle \models K_{luther}[luther]^X r_L \vee K_{luther}[luther]^X \neg r_L$ for $i \in \{2,3,4,5\}$ and $h \in H_{m_i}$.[5] So *in this example* we assume that *luther* (and *benji*) knowingly performs his available actions in the sense of knowingly performing the actions labeled by R_L and G_L. However – and this is essential in our treatment of knowledge – this is not mandatory for all our frames. Observe that our example still accounts for the possibility that agents bring about certain outcomes without knowingly doing so. In Example 1 (a), we have that even if $\mathcal{M}, \langle m_4, h_{10}\rangle \models [luther]^X d_L$, it is the case that $\mathcal{M}, \langle m_4, h_{10}\rangle \models \Box\neg K_{[luther]}[luther]^X d_L$ (there is no way in which *luther* knowingly sets a bomb off). At moments m_6–m_{21}, although the fate of the bombs has been decided, agents may still be uncertain about the exact cause of the explosion in the cases where *luther* and *benji* have not both cut the green wire of their respective bomb. We use the epistemic structures of the agents at these moments in order to illustrate instances of *ex post* knowledge. Observe, for example, that $\mathcal{M}, \langle m_{11}, h_6\rangle \models \neg K_{luther} Y[benji]^X d_B$.

3 *Ex Ante*, *Ex interim*, *Ex Post*, and Know-How

Recent trends in modelling responsibility by way of 'knowingly doing' and epistemic ability ('know-how') base these two notions on the differential knowledge across the stages of decision making. In this section we describe diverse interpretations that authors have given in the past to the four kinds of knowledge, and we compare them with our own versions. As mentioned in the introduction, we have two goals in mind. One is to clarify overlapping intuitions for the work done in epistemic stit and address the shortcomings of previous analyses. The other is to present new formal characterizations that we believe are more akin to modelling responsibility with stit.

As we see it, we are modelling agents' *uncertainty* in strategic interaction. The branching-time theory and language of action that lies at the heart of stit allows us to do this neatly, being flexible enough to address different angles of agentive uncertainty. For this work we discern the following levels of uncertainty, in clear correlation with the four kinds of knowledge: *(a) Uncertainty about previous actions. (b) Uncertainty about the nature and effects of one's own actions. (c) Uncertainty about other agents' actions. (d) Uncertainty about the effects of joint*

[5] This is related to a property that epistemic game theorists call "knowledge of one's own action", a feature which we will address in Sect. 3, when we compare the different interpretations of knowledge and their implications. Although it holds in this example, we do not enforce it in all BDT frames.

actions. The essence of our criticism to previous proposals also underlies what we strive for the most in *our* semantics: *flexibility*. We want for the epistemic stit models to be flexible enough to address both coarse- and fine-grained kinds of uncertainty in interactive settings.

***Ex ante* Knowledge.** It is commonly thought of as the kind of knowledge that an agent has *regardless* of its choice of action at a given moment (see [2,15]). Previous renditions of the concept in epistemic stit all try to model this quality, but from somewhat different viewpoints. To illustrate the knowledge that *we* intend to formalize, consider our Example 1. In case (a), at situation $\langle m_4, h_{10}\rangle$ – which we have taken as an actual situation – neither *luther* nor *benji* has *ex ante* knowledge that *ethan* activated the fail-safe mechanism in the detonator for bomb B. In case (b), on the contrary, *luther* does know it *ex ante*. Therefore, we favor the view that if an agent has certainty about previous actions, it is easier for that agent to discern things *ex ante*.

Lorini et al. present in [15] an epistemic stit logic with three operators for *ex ante, ex interim,* and *ex post* knowledge: $K_\alpha^{\bullet\circ\circ}$, $K_\alpha^{\circ\bullet\circ}$, and $K_\alpha^{\circ\circ\bullet}$, respectively. They base the semantics of all three of them on primitive epistemic indistinguishability relations for *ex ante* knowledge. The respective intersections of these relations with those of individual and collective action –themselves resulting from a structure of action labels– yield then Lorini et al.'s versions of *ex interim* and *ex post* knowledge. Their treatment follows game theory's natural assumption that *ex interim* knowledge refines *ex ante*, and that *ex post* knowledge in turn refines *ex interim*. We can safely suppose that this is the reason why they take the semantics for *ex ante* knowledge as the starting point of all three. Although the main problems with Lorini et al.'s system will be discussed when we deal with *ex interim* knowledge, we mention here that the fact that the authors do not enforce any connection between *ex ante* knowledge and historical necessity poses a problem for identifying what an agent knows *ex ante* with the knowledge that is present regardless of that agent's choice of action. In other words, Lorini et al.'s system admits situations in which at a given moment and along a given history an agent knows φ *ex ante*, but if the agent 'changes' its choice of action then it would stop knowing φ (in Lorini et al.'s logic, $K_\alpha^{\bullet\circ\circ}\varphi \to \Box K_\alpha^{\bullet\circ\circ}\varphi$ is not valid).[6]

In [13] and [10], Horty and Pacuit and Herzig and Troquard, respectively, tackle a notion of *ex ante* knowledge with epistemic stit in similar ways. It is only under the light of their full systems that we find fault in both approaches, which we address when dealing with *ex interim* knowledge and know-how.

Our Version: We take α's *ex ante* knowledge to be all the truths *about the next moment* that, regardless of its current choice of action, α knows to be independent of that choice of action. Let $\mathcal{M} = \langle T, \sqsubset, \mathbf{Choice}, \{\sim_\alpha\}_{\alpha\in Ags}\rangle$ be an *epistemic BDT frame* and φ of $\mathcal{L}_{\mathsf{KX}}$. We say that at situation $\langle m, h\rangle$, α has

[6] In [15] (p. 1320), Remark 2.6 actually states that the authors do not intend for agents to consider all their available choices epistemically *possible* in the *ex ante* sense, but this leads precisely into having choice-dependent *ex ante* knowledge.

ex ante knowledge of φ iff $\mathcal{M}, \langle m, h\rangle \models \Box K_\alpha \Box X\varphi$. For instance, we can see that in our Example 1, if we again take f_B to denote the proposition 'the fail-safe mechanism of bomb B has been activated', we get that $\mathcal{M}, \langle m_4, h_{10}\rangle \not\models \Box K_{luther}\Box XY f_B$ for case (a), and that $\mathcal{M}, \langle m_4, h_{10}\rangle \models \Box K_{luther}\Box XY f_B$ for case (b).

Two points must be made. First, we observe that we have modelled an *individual* version of *ex ante* knowledge, with no explicit mention of whether there is a collective counterpart or whether *ex ante* knowledge is already collective in nature from the start. There is a sense in which *ex ante* knowledge has been thought as strictly non-private information. Aumann and Dreze, for instance, state that at the *ex ante* stage of differential information environments, no agent should have any private knowledge ([2], p. 80). This entails that *ex ante* knowledge should then be seen as an instance of group knowledge. Above we studied an individual version, and we then model Aumann and Dreze's *ex ante* knowledge with $\Box C\Box X\varphi$, where C stands for the operator for common knowledge for the grand coalition Ags in the language L_{KX}. Second, Duijf points out in [8] (Chap. 3) that it is important to account for the temporal dimension of *ex ante* knowledge, where this is seen as the knowledge that agents have *before* they and the others engage in choices of action. Our account does acknowledge such temporal dimension insofar it is given within Xstit logic, and thus the information that agents have *ex ante* is available *before* the effects of choices of action take place.

***Ex interim* Knowledge.** It is assumed that at the *ex interim* stage of decision making, an agent's available information expands its *ex ante* knowledge by taking into account *its* choice of action, though not yet the other agents' ones. If an agent knows φ *ex interim*, then the agent is certain about the fact that φ will occur after the performance of its choice of action and regardless of what other agents choose. For instance, in Example 1(b) *luther* knows *ex interim* that bomb L will go off after he chooses R_L. We side by the intuition that if an agent has some certainty about the effects of its own actions, then it is easier for that agent to discern things *ex interim*.[7]

For Lorini et al., the information available to an agent *ex interim* is not only independent of the other agents' choices of action, but also *must* make agents discern which action they are taking. This means that in Lorini et al.'s formalization agents will always be able to know *ex interim* the action they perform and can never be uncertain at the *ex interim* stage about the difference between actions that have different labels. The condition can be expressed – in the terminology of [15] – by use of propositional constants representing the execution of action labels: if for every action label A and α we take p_A^α to denote the proposition 'The action A is performed by α', then the following formula is valid in Lorini et al.'s system: $p_A^\alpha \rightarrow K^{\circ\bullet\circ} p_A^\alpha$. Although the property is to a

[7] We still want to allow for situations in which agents do not always have certainty about the actions that they choose even after choosing them. As will be seen later, this distinguishes our interpretation of *ex interim* knowledge from epistemic game theory's traditional one.

certain extent in keeping with epistemic game theory, we find it constraining in the context of epistemic stit. For instance, in Example 1 we may want to model a situation in which *ethan* does not know the difference between detonator L and detonator B but still activates the fail-safe mechanism of one of them. We would like to say that in this case *ethan* is not able to discern *ex interim* whether he chose to activate the mechanism for bomb L or for bomb B, but according to Lorini et al.'s formalization this would be impossible. The constraint is all the more problematic because of its consequences for Lorini et al.'s treatment of responsibility/culpability attribution: in their formalism, agents will always be morally responsible for performing a given action, without being able to excuse themselves from moral responsibility by claiming that they were uncertain about which action they chose. Observe also that the constraint implies that *ex ante* certainty of the present moment forces agents to know all the consequences of their actions, so options for modelling excusability are restricted.

In [13] Horty and Pacuit work with similar ideas to Lorini et al.'s when it comes to the relationship between *ex interim* knowledge and action labels. With the goal of disambiguating the sense of epistemic ability from that of causal ability in stit, they base a version of know-how on novel semantics for *ex interim* knowledge. In order to deal with both *ex interim* knowledge and know-how, Horty & Pacuit extend basic stit with syntactic and semantic components. Syntactically, they introduce the operator $[\ldots kstit]$ to encode agentive *ex interim* knowledge and add it to a language that includes operators $\mathcal{K}_\alpha$ for epistemic indistinguishability, operators $[\alpha\ stit]$ for the traditional Chellas-stit notion of action, and $\Box$ for historical necessity. The semantics for formulas involving $[\ldots kstit]$ uses *action types* under the premise that actions of the same *type* might lead to different outcomes in different moments. At a given moment and along a given history, α knowingly sees to it that φ iff at all moments that are epistemically indistinguishable for α to the one of evaluation, α's execution of the same action type enforces φ.[8] As mentioned in [7], the use of types brings three unfavorable constraints: (1) In order for $[\ldots kstit]$ to be an **S5** operator, the primitive epistemic indistinguishability relations – those supporting the operators $\mathcal{K}_\alpha$ – must ensue not between moment-history pairs but between moments. This limits the class of models to those in which knowledge is moment-dependent and for which agents will not be able to know that they perform a given action.[9] This leads Horty & Pacuit into identifying $\mathcal{K}_\alpha\varphi$ with α's *ex ante* knowledge of φ, but then a shortcoming is that both instances of knowledge ($\mathcal{K}_\alpha$ and $[\alpha\ kstit]$) satisfy what we call the 'own action condition' (`OAC`). This condition is semantically stated by the following rule: for every situation $\langle m_*, h_*\rangle$, if $\langle m_*, h_*\rangle \sim_\alpha \langle m, h\rangle$ for

[8] Formally, $\mathcal{M}, \langle m, h\rangle \models [\alpha\ kstit]\varphi$ iff for every $\langle m', h'\rangle$ such that $\langle m, h\rangle \sim_\alpha \langle m', h'\rangle$, $Exn_{m'}(Lbl^\alpha(\langle m, h\rangle)) \subseteq |\varphi|^{m'}$, where Lbl_α is a function that maps a situation to the action type of the action token being performed at that situation, and $Exn_{m'}$ is a partial function that maps types to their corresponding tokens at moment m'.

[9] Horty & Pacuit's models satisfy the following constraint: if $\langle m, h\rangle \sim_\alpha \langle m', h'\rangle$, then $\langle m, h_*\rangle \sim_\alpha \langle m', h'_*\rangle$ for every $h_* \in H_m$, $h'_* \in H_{m'}$, which, under reflexivity of $\sim_\alpha$, corresponds syntactically to the axiom schema $\mathcal{K}_\alpha\varphi \to \Box\varphi$.

some $\langle m, h\rangle$, then $\langle m_*, h'_*\rangle \sim_\alpha \langle m, h\rangle$ for every $h'_* \in \mathbf{Choice}_\alpha^{m_*}(h_*)$. It implies the validity of the formulas $\mathcal{K}_\alpha\varphi \to [\alpha\ stit]\varphi$ and $[\alpha\ kstit]\varphi \to [\alpha\ stit]\varphi$. In Horty & Pacuit's formalism, then, there is no sense whatsoever in which agents can know more than what they bring about.[10] (2) Just as with Lorini et al., the semantics for $[\ldots kstit]$ entails that agents cannot have uncertainty about the actions they perform at the *ex interim* stage. (3) Indistinguishable moments must offer the same available types.[11] The problem with this constraint, which we call 'uniformity of available action types' (UAAT), is technical in nature: it cannot be characterized syntactically *in their logic* without producing an infinite axiomatization. This is due to the fact that performing a certain action type can only be expressed syntactically with propositional constants.

In [10] Herzig and Troquard present a version of *ex interim* knowledge under the term *dynamic knowledge* in order to give semantics for know-how, as Horty & Pacuit. They extend the language of basic Xstit with a modal operator $[\ldots Kstit]$ for this dynamic knowledge. Contrary to Lorini et al. and Horty & Pacuit, it is for the semantics of formulas involving *this* operator that they use primitive epistemic indistinguishability relations, and they define the truth conditions *both* for action ($[\alpha\ Stit]\varphi$) and for static knowledge ($\Box[\alpha\ Kstit]\varphi$) in terms of it. Still, their formalization ends up working in a similar way to Horty & Pacuit's. First, their versions of knowledge – both static and dynamic – satisfy (OAC), so again there is no sense in which agents can know more than what they bring about. Second, they restrict to situations for which agents cannot be uncertain about the actions they choose. Lastly, they favor a condition of uniformity that corresponds to Horty & Pacuit's (UAAT).

In [8], Duijf has an interesting proposal that somewhat resembles Herzig and Troquard's. Duijf thinks that a primitive indistinguishability relation that links moment-history pairs in instantaneous stit characterizes a kind of knowledge that we may already call *ex interim*. What distinguishes his interpretation from Herzig & Troquard's – as well as from Horty & Pacuit's, for that matter – is that Duijf's *ex interim* knowledge is flexible enough to deal both with cases of uncertainty about one's action (it is not the case that agents *must* know their

10 To see how this constraint thwarts an analysis of the interaction between knowledge and action, consider our Example 1, and assume that at moment m_4, for instance, we want to say that *luther* knows *in some sense* –not in an *ex ante* or *ex interim* sense, though– what *benji* will choose. Therefore, *luther* should in principle be able to somehow distinguish h_9 from h_{12}, and h_{10} from h_{11}. However, in presence of (OAC), this cannot be the case (see [8] (Chap. 3) for a more elaborate discussion about the undesirability of this property in epistemic stit).

11 In all the treatments of game knowledge that we presently review, virtually nobody disagrees with some version of this constraint. In the case of the approaches from game theory, ATL, and Coalition Logic, the premise is very much related to the concept of 'uniform strategies'. We will address it further when analyzing versions of know-how. It is worth mentioning that Lorini et al. remain vague about the subject. The examples they present all presuppose the condition, but they do not demand it explicitly or even refer to it. If they were to enforce it, it would bring the same technical problem as in Horty and Pacuit's [13].

actions *ex interim*) – which accounts for possibility of a more coarse-grained knowledge – and with cases for which agents know more than what they bring about – which accounts for instances of fine-grained knowledge.[12] However, it may be a bit too flexible, for it allows situations in which an agent knows *ex interim* that another agent is bringing about something that is not settled, which is clearly dependent on the other agent's choice. Denoting Duijf's operator for *ex interim* knowledge by $\mathbb{K}_\alpha$ and the traditional Chellas-stit operators by $[\alpha]$, the formula $\mathbb{K}_\alpha[\beta]\varphi \wedge \neg\Box\varphi$ is satisfiable in Duijf's logic. It might be surprising that Lorini et al.'s version of *ex interim* knowledge also does not satisfy (OAC), so a comparable criticism can be advanced. In fact, their formalism is such that agents could have *ex ante* knowledge of what other agents are bringing about, something atypical.

Our Version: We identify *ex interim* knowledge with Broersen's notion of 'knowingly doing' [6], so that an agent knows φ *ex interim* iff it knowingly sees to it that φ happens in the next moment. Thus, let $\mathcal{M}$ be an *epistemic BDT model* and φ of $\mathcal{L}_{\mathsf{KX}}$. We say that at situation $\langle m, h\rangle$, α has *ex interim* knowledge of φ iff $\mathcal{M}, \langle m, h\rangle \models K_\alpha[\alpha]^X\varphi$. In Example 1(b) we get that *luther* knowingly sees to it that bomb L goes off, so that he knows *ex interim* that bomb L will go off ($\mathcal{M}, \langle m_4, h_{10}\rangle \models K_{luther}[luther]^X d_L$.) In contrast, in case (a) we have that $\mathcal{M}, \langle m_4, h_{10}\rangle \models \neg K_{luther}[luther]^X d_L$, so that *luther* in fact sets bomb L off, but not knowingly and thus without *ex interim* knowledge about it. As for how our notion of *ex interim* knowledge deals with the constraints that we have criticized in the reviewed literature, we advance two important remarks:

1. We do not impose any condition on the primitive epistemic indistinguishability relations that would exclude uncertainty of one's own action in the *ex interim* stage, so we allow for cases of coarse-grained knowledge that have clear implications for responsibility/culpability attribution in stit logic. In particular, full certainty about the moment of evaluation does not imply that agents will know the effects of all their current actions.
2. Our system is flexible enough so that agents can *in some sense* know more than what they bring about. Since we do not impose (OAC) for our traditional knowledge semantics, we account for instances of finer-grained knowledge. However, agents *cannot* know *ex interim* more than what they bring about (reflexivity of the primitive indistinguishability relations entails that $K_\alpha[\alpha]^X\varphi \to [\alpha]^X\varphi$ is valid with respect to the class of our frames).[13]

***Ex post* Knowledge.** At the last stage of information disclosure, it is revealed to the agents which choices of action they engaged in. Game theorists call the

[12] Duijf does not demand for his models to validate (OAC). However, as we will point out when addressing his formalization of know-how, Duijf does enforce a constraint corresponding to Horty & Pacuit's (UAAT).

[13] Comparing our version with Duijf's, we observe that we exclude situations where agents can know *ex interim* that other agents will see to it that φ in the next moment without it being settled that φ will hold in the next moment, while we had seen he does not. $K_\alpha[\alpha]^X Y[\beta]^X\varphi \to \Box X\varphi$ is valid with respect to the class of our frames.

knowledge that arises at this point *ex post* knowledge. This is commonly seen as including facts that hold after constraining the possible histories to the epistemic equivalents of the choice profile of the grand coalition. Although Aumann and Dreze assume that at the *ex post* stage "all information is revealed to all" ([2], p. 80), we take it to mean *all information ensuing from disclosing the agents' choices.* Game theorists also describe *ex post* knowledge as the kind of knowledge that can be attained *after* all the agents have performed their 'strategies', which adds a temporal dimension to the concept and thus increases its ambiguity. In our view, if the agents have some certainty about the effects of joint action, then it is easier for them to know things *ex post.* In Example 1(a), we consider as instances of *ex post* knowledge at the actual situation the facts that *Ags* caused a bomb to go off and did so *unknowingly.* We do not consider that it should also be *ex post* knowledge the fact that actually it was *luther* who set off the bomb and that it was bomb L.

Out of all the papers that we have reviewed so far, only [15] includes some treatment for *ex post* knowledge in epistemic stit. There, the relation that provides semantics for formulas involving $K_\alpha^{\circ\circ\bullet}$ is built by intersecting the primitive relation for *ex ante* knowledge with the relation for collective action of the grand coalition – itself the intersection of the agents' relations for individual action (see Definitions 2 and 3 for the corresponding semantics of $[Ags]^X\varphi$). A point to be made is that the instantaneous nature of their action semantics fails to make allowance for an analysis of the temporal dimension of this kind of knowledge. For instance, their semantics does not admit situations for which an agent knows *ex post* that it brought about φ without the agent also knowing *ex interim* that it brought about φ ($K_\alpha^{\circ\circ\bullet}[\alpha\ \mathbf{stit}]\varphi \to K_\alpha^{\circ\bullet\circ}[\alpha\ \mathbf{stit}]\varphi$ turns out to be valid with respect to their frames, where $[\alpha\ \mathbf{stit}]$ are the traditional Chellas-stit operators given in their notation).

Our Version(s): In our semantics, we propose a version for individual *ex post* knowledge in the following way. Let $\mathcal{M}$ be an *epistemic BDT frame* and φ of $\mathcal{L}_{\mathsf{KX}}$. We say that at situation $\langle m, h\rangle$, φ is *ex post* knowledge of α iff $\mathcal{M}, \langle m, h\rangle \models X\ K_\alpha\ Y\ [Ags]^X\varphi$. In this way, in Example 1(a) we get that $\mathcal{M}, \langle m_4, h_{10}\rangle \models X\ K_{luther/benji}\ Y\ [Ags]^X d_L \vee d_B$. For case (b) we get that $\mathcal{M}, \langle m_4, h_{10}\rangle \models \neg X\ K_{benji}\ Y\ [Ags]^X(Y[luther]^X d_L)$ (*benji* does not know even *ex post* that *luther* set off bomb L).[14]

[14] Other interesting cases appear in the non-actual situations where the bombs were defused. In Example 1(a), for instance, if we take f_B to denote the proposition 'the fail-safe mechanism of bomb B has been activated', then $\mathcal{M}, \langle m_4, h_9\rangle \models \neg K_{luther/benji}(Y[ethan]^X f_B)$ and $\mathcal{M}, \langle m_4, h_9\rangle \models X\ K_{luther/benji}\ Y\ [Ags]^X (Y\ Y[ethan]^X f_B)$ (*luther* and *benji realize ex post* that *ethan* secured the detonator for bomb B). Observe that, contrary to Lorini et al.'s formalization, ours does account for cases where an agent knows *ex post* that it brought about φ without knowing *ex interim* that it would bring about φ: $X\ K_\alpha\ Y\ [Ags]^X Y[\alpha]^X\varphi \to K_\alpha[\alpha]^X\varphi$ is not valid with respect to our frames.

Endowed with our three versions of differential knowledge according to the stages of decision making, we can see how they interact with each other. Complying with the customary game theoretical view, we have that *ex post* refines *ex interim*, which in turn refines *ex ante*.

Proposition 1. *Let* $\mathcal{M}$ *be an* epistemic branching discrete-time frame, φ *of* $\mathcal{L}_{KX}$, *and* $\alpha \in Ags$. *We have that* $\mathcal{M} \models \Box K_\alpha \Box X \varphi \rightarrow K_\alpha [\alpha]^X \varphi$ *and* $\mathcal{M} \models K_\alpha [\alpha]^X \varphi \rightarrow X\ K_\alpha\ Y\ [Ags]^X \varphi$.

Know-How. When we talk about know-how we refer to the so-called *practical* or *procedural knowledge* of an agent that takes 'actions' rather than propositions as content (see [8], Chap. 3).[15] The intuition is that an agent knows how to do something iff it has the procedural knowledge of bringing about that something. We are not engaging in a circular argument here, for the second statement can be described with precise definitions for 'knowledge', 'action', and 'possibility'. Still, we acknowledge that there is a lively debate in the literature as to what being able to bring about a certain outcome exactly means, and the question of what it means to be *epistemically able* only builds on that first debate (see [1,6,8,13,16,17,22]). Presently, we base the conceptual reach of know-how on the approach of epistemic stit. Much like Horty and Pacuit in [13], we are concerned with situations in which agentive knowledge yields differences between what agents can bring about, on one hand, and what they can bring about *knowingly*, on the other. Consider Example 1 and the differences between case (a) and case (b). In case (a), we would like to say that *luther* and *benji* do not know how to save the facility. Whether being *causally* able to perform an action that they know will save the facility is equal to knowing how to save it or not is very much open to debate, but the reader will agree that at least it is necessary for knowing how. Broersen, Herzig and Troquard, Horty and Pacuit, Naumov and Tao, Ågotnes et al., and Duijf all agree with this, and [10] and [13] in fact characterize their versions of know-how exactly as the possibility of bringing about a certain outcome knowingly. In what follows, we focus our study of previous literature on *individual* know-how, leaving its collective counterpart for future endeavors.

---

[15] According to [8], in [9] Fantl draws the outlines of know-how by distinguishing it from two other kinds of knowledge: *knowledge by acquaintance* and *propositional knowledge* (know-that). Setting aside for the moment the concept of knowledge by acquaintance, [8] proposes that the essential difference between know-how and know-that lies in the content they take. We side by this interpretation, where procedural knowledge concerns actions, and propositional knowledge concerns propositions. Such a disambiguation identifies the concept of know-how that we study with Wang's *goal-directed* know-how. This is related to the debate introduced by Ryle [19] as to whether know-how can be reduced to know-that or not, where *intellectualists* think it can be reduced and *anti-intellectualists* think it cannot.

Horty and Pacuit [13] and [12] work on the assumption that an agent is epistemically able to do something iff it is able to have *ex interim* knowledge of that something. Their goal is to formally disambiguate simplified versions of the different cases of our Example 1. Using a logic endowed with the operator $[\dots kstit]$ that we reviewed before, they define know-how as the historical possibility of *ex interim* knowledge. We have already commented on the problems of their system.

Another related approach to know-how is given by Herzig and Troquard in the already mentioned [10]. Herzig and Troquard use their dynamic knowledge operator $[\dots Kstit]$ to state that an agent knows how to see to it that φ (in the next moment) iff it is historically necessary that the agent knowingly enforces the possibility to knowingly bring about φ: at situation $\langle m, h\rangle$, α knows how to see to it that φ iff $\langle m, h\rangle \models \Box[\alpha\ Kstit]\Diamond[\alpha\ Kstit]X\varphi$. In our view, Herzig & Troquard's treatment of know-how is successful to a certain extent, but their models are constrained by (OAC) and by the condition of uniformity corresponding to Horty & Pacuit's (UAAT), as we established before. Somewhat connected to Herzig and Troquard's version, Duijf presents in [8] a simple and elegant stit theory of know-how that ultimately characterizes individual know-how by stating that at situation $\langle m, h\rangle$, α knows how to see to it that φ iff $\langle m, h\rangle \models \mathbb{K}_\alpha\Diamond\mathbb{K}_\alpha[\alpha]\varphi$ – where $\mathbb{K}_\alpha$ are the operators for Duijf's version of *ex interim* knowledge and $[\alpha]$ are the traditional Chellas-stit operators. As we saw, Duijf rejects imposing condition (OAC) on his frames, so his logic admits finer-grained renditions of knowledge. However, just as in Herzig & Troquard's proposal, the condition of uniformity of available actions – which in Duijf's system is syntactically expressed by the axiom schema $\Diamond\mathbb{K}_\alpha[\alpha]\varphi \to \mathbb{K}_\alpha\Diamond[\alpha]\varphi$ – yields that his formula for know-how is equivalent to $\Diamond\mathbb{K}_\alpha[\alpha]\varphi$.[16]

Our Version: Let $\mathcal{M}$ be an *epistemic branching discrete-time frame* and φ of $\mathcal{L}_{\mathsf{KX}}$. We say that at situation $\langle m, h\rangle$, α knows how to see to it that φ iff $\langle m, h\rangle \models \Box K_\alpha\Diamond K_\alpha[\alpha]^X\varphi$. So we propose that an agent knows how to see to it

[16] Duijf does not comment on such equivalence, whose deduction – in Duijf's system – comes from the following argument. Turns out to be the case that the validity of $\Diamond\mathbb{K}_\alpha[\alpha]\varphi \to \mathbb{K}_\alpha\Diamond[\alpha]\varphi$ entails the validity of $\Diamond\mathbb{K}_\alpha\varphi \to \mathbb{K}_\alpha\Diamond\varphi$ in Duijf's logic. This last schema, denoted by $(Unif - H)$, is the syntactic counterpart of a condition that we call 'uniformity of historical possibility', and in light of it we have that

1. $\vdash \mathbb{K}_\alpha[\alpha]\varphi \to \mathbb{K}_\alpha\mathbb{K}_\alpha[\alpha]\varphi$	Substitution of axiom (4) for $\mathbb{K}_\alpha$
2. $\vdash \Diamond\mathbb{K}_\alpha[\alpha]\varphi \to \Diamond\mathbb{K}_\alpha\mathbb{K}_\alpha[\alpha]\varphi$	Modal logic on 1
3. $\vdash \Diamond\mathbb{K}_\alpha\mathbb{K}_\alpha[\alpha]\varphi \to \mathbb{K}_\alpha\Diamond\mathbb{K}_\alpha[\alpha]\varphi$	Substitution of $(Unif - H)$ for α
4. $\vdash \Diamond\mathbb{K}_\alpha[\alpha]\varphi \to \mathbb{K}_\alpha\Diamond\mathbb{K}_\alpha[\alpha]\varphi$	Propositional logic 2, 4.

The other direction is straightforward, by axiom (T) for $\mathbb{K}_\alpha$. A similar deduction can be provided to ensure that Herzig & Troquard's $\Box[\alpha\ Kstit]\Diamond[\alpha\ Kstit]\varphi$ is reducible to $\Diamond[\alpha\ Kstit]\varphi$.

that φ if it has *ex ante* knowledge of the possibility of knowing *ex interim* (or knowingly doing) φ.[17] In this way, in Example 1(a) we have that $\mathcal{M}, \langle m_4, h_{10} \rangle \not\models \Box K_{luther} \Diamond K_{luther} [luther]^X s$ (*luther* does not know how to defuse the bombs), whereas in case (b) we have that $\mathcal{M}, \langle m_4, h_{10} \rangle \models \Box K_{luther} \Diamond K_{luther} [luther]^X d_L$ (*luther* knows how to set off a bomb). Since in both cases, *luther* ultimately does set off a bomb, we consider case (a) as a situation where he should be excused from moral responsibility of the explosion, while case (b) is one where he should be held morally responsible for it.[18]

4 Axiomatization

Definition 4 (Proof system). *Let Λ be the proof system defined by the following axioms and rules of inference:*

- (Axioms) *All classical tautologies from propositional logic. The* **S5** *axiom schemata for* $\Box$, $[\alpha]$, $[Ags]$, *and* K_α. *The following axiom schemata for the interactions of formulas with the given operators:*

[17] We observe that if we were to incorporate a condition of uniformity of available actions into our logic (as we do in the axiomatization), it would be equivalent to the semantic condition known as 'uniformity of historical possibility' ($\texttt{Unif} - \texttt{H}$), which says that for every situation $\langle m_*, h_* \rangle$, if $\langle m_*, h_* \rangle \sim_\alpha \langle m, h \rangle$ for some $\langle m, h \rangle$, then for every $h'_* \in H_{m_*}$ there exists $h' \in H_m$ such that $\langle m_*, h'_* \rangle \sim_\alpha \langle m, h' \rangle$. Under this condition, which corresponds syntactically to the schema $\Diamond K_\alpha \varphi \to K_\alpha \Diamond \varphi$, we would have two important consequences: our formula for *ex ante* knowledge would be equivalent to $\Box K_\alpha X \varphi$, and our formula for know-how would be equivalent to $\Diamond K_\alpha [\alpha]^X \varphi$.

[18] Although we focus our comparisons on the previous work within epistemic stit, it is worth discussing some of the approaches to the concept in the epistemic extensions of ATL and Coalition Logic (see [1,11]), for the ideas behind the syntax and semantics for know-how in these logics are similar to those of stit. For instance, Naumov and Tao and Ågotnes et al. – in [17] and [1], respectively – share many intuitions with Horty and Pacuit. The notion of know-how they both formalize is characterized by the statement that an agent knows how to bring about φ at a given state s iff there exists a 'strategy' a such that in all states that are epistemically indistinguishable to s for the agent, 'strategy' a will lead to states at which φ holds. In other words, an agent knows how to do something if there exists a way for the agent to knowingly enforce φ. [17] and [1] use different interpretations for the word 'strategy'. While in the former the authors refer to an action label in single-step transitions, Ågotnes et al. use the term as is done in ATL, where strategies are functions that assign to each agent and state a pertinent transition. Regardless of the difference, their formalization of know-how depends on the same reasoning: an agent would know how to do φ iff there exists a uniform strategy such that at all epistemically indistinguishable states, the transition assigned by the strategy leads to a state at which φ holds. In both accounts, we face again the idea of uniformity.

$$Y X\varphi \leftrightarrow \varphi \qquad (In1)$$
$$X Y\varphi \leftrightarrow \varphi \qquad (In2)$$
$$X\varphi \leftrightarrow \neg X \neg\varphi \qquad (DET.S.X)$$
$$Y\varphi \leftrightarrow \neg Y \neg\varphi \qquad (DET.S.Y)$$
$$\Box\varphi \rightarrow [\alpha]\varphi \qquad (SET)$$
$$[\alpha]X\varphi \rightarrow [\alpha]X\Box\varphi \qquad (NA)$$
$$[Ags]X\varphi \rightarrow [Ags]X\Box\varphi \qquad (NAgs)$$
$$[\alpha]\varphi \rightarrow [Ags]\varphi \qquad (GA)$$

For $m \geq 1$ *and pairwise distinct* $\alpha_1, \ldots, \alpha_m$,

$$\bigwedge_{1\leq i\leq n} \Diamond[\alpha_i]p_i \rightarrow \Diamond\left(\bigwedge_{1\leq i\leq n}[\alpha_i]p_i\right) \qquad (IA)$$
$$K_\alpha X\varphi \rightarrow X K_\alpha\varphi \qquad (NoF)$$
$$\Diamond K_\alpha p \rightarrow K_\alpha \Diamond p \qquad (Unif-H)$$

- (Rules of inference) *Modus Ponens, Substitution, and Necessitation for the modal operators.*

We define Λ_n *as the axiom system constructed by adding axiom* $(AgsPC_n)$ *to* Λ, *where*

$$\bigwedge_{1\leq k\leq n} \Diamond\left(\left(\bigwedge_{1\leq i\leq k-1} \neg\varphi_i\right) \wedge [Ags]\varphi_k\right) \rightarrow \bigvee_{1\leq k\leq n} \varphi_k \qquad (AgsPC_n).$$

Following [5] and [18], we will show that the axiom system Λ_n is sound and complete with respect to the general multi-modal Kripke models, which Payette calls 'irregular' in [18]. However, we conjecture that there is no problem in using unraveling techniques as in [20] to transform these general Kripke models into those of Definition 2 in a truth-preserving way.

Proposition 2. *The system* Λ_n *is sound and complete with respect to the class of Kripke-exstit* n*-models.*

The proof of soundness is straightforward. For completeness, we proceed in three steps. In the first step, we prove completeness with respect to Kripke models that are *super-additive*, meaning those for which each action available to *Ags* is included in an intersection of individual actions but is not necessarily the same as such intersection (see [20] for their exact definition). In the second step, we prove completeness with respect to Kripke super-additive models where the temporal relations are irreflexive. In the last step, we use a technique similar to Schwarzentruber's construction in [20] and Lorini's in [14] to prove completeness with respect to the class of actual models, meaning those for which each action available to *Ags* is the same as an intersection of individual actions. The full proof is long and technical, and for reasons of space we cannot include it here. It can be found in the arXiv.org version of the present work and in a forthcoming issue of the full paper with proofs.

5 Conclusion

In this work, we carefully reviewed previous renditions of four kinds of agentive knowledge (*ex ante*, *ex interim*, *ex post,* and know-how) in epistemic stit theory. Motivated by examples that demand a notion of flexibility of the epistemic component in analyses of responsibility attribution, we presented a new logic for them. We find that our versions offer a fine background for building a nuanced theory of responsibility based on the influence of knowledge on action and decision.

References

1. Ågotnes, T., Goranko, V., Jamroga, W., Wooldridge, M.: Knowledge and ability. In: van Ditmarsch, H., Halpern, J., van der Hoek, W., Kooi, B. (eds.) Handbook of Epistemic Logic, pp. 543–589. College Publications (2015)
2. Aumann, R.J., Dreze, J.H.: Rational expectations in games. Am. Econ. Rev. **98**(1), 72–86 (2008)
3. Belnap, N., Perloff, M., Xu, M.: Facing the Future: Agents and Choices in Our Indeterminist World. Oxford University Press, Oxford (2001)
4. Boudou, J., Lorini, E.: Concurrent game structures for temporal STIT logic. In: Proceedings of the 17th International Conference on Autonomous Agents and MultiAgent Systems, pp. 381–389. International Foundation for Autonomous Agents and Multiagent Systems (2018)
5. Broersen, J.: A complete STIT logic for knowledge and action, and some of its applications. In: Baldoni, M., Son, T.C., van Riemsdijk, M.B., Winikoff, M. (eds.) DALT 2008. LNCS, vol. 5397, pp. 47–59. Springer, Heidelberg (2009). https://doi.org/10.1007/978-3-540-93920-7_4
6. Broersen, J.: Deontic epistemic STIT logic distinguishing modes of mens rea. J. Appl. Log. **9**(2), 137–152 (2011)
7. Broersen, J., Ramírez Abarca, A.I.: Formalising oughts and practical knowledge without resorting to action types. In: Proceedings of the 17th International Conference on Autonomous Agents and MultiAgent Systems, pp. 1877–1879. International Foundation for Autonomous Agents and Multiagent Systems (2018)
8. Duijf, H.: Let's do it!: collective responsibility, joint action, and participation. Ph.D. thesis, Utrecht University (2018)
9. Fantl, J.: Knowing-how and knowing-that. Philos. Compass **3**(3), 451–470 (2008)
10. Herzig, A., Troquard, N.: Knowing how to play: uniform choices in logics of agency. In: Proceedings of the Fifth International Joint Conference on Autonomous Agents and Multiagent Systems, pp. 209–216. ACM (2006)
11. van der Hoek, W., Wooldridge, M.: Cooperation, knowledge, and time: alternating-time temporal epistemic logic and its applications. Stud. Logica. **75**(1), 125–157 (2003)
12. Horty, J.: Epistemic oughts in STIT semantics. In: Deontic Logic and Normative Systems. Proceedings of DEON 2018, pp. 157–176 (2016)
13. Horty, J., Pacuit, E.: Action types in STIT semantics. Rev. Symb. Log. (2017, forthcoming)
14. Lorini, E.: Temporal logic and its application to normative reasoning. J. Appl. Non-Class. Log. **23**(4), 372–399 (2013)

15. Lorini, E., Longin, D., Mayor, E.: A logical analysis of responsibility attribution: emotions, individuals and collectives. J. Log. Comput. **24**(6), 1313–1339 (2014)
16. Naumov, P., Tao, J.: Coalition power in epistemic transition systems. In: Proceedings of the 16th Conference on Autonomous Agents and MultiAgent Systems, pp. 723–731. International Foundation for Autonomous Agents and Multiagent Systems (2017)
17. Naumov, P., Tao, J.: Together we know how to achieve: an epistemic logic of know-how. arXiv preprint arXiv:1705.09349 (2017)
18. Payette, G.: Decidability of an Xstit logic. Stud. Logica. **102**(3), 577–607 (2014)
19. Ryle, G.: The Concept of Mind. Routledge, Abingdon (2009)
20. Schwarzentruber, F.: Complexity results of STIT fragments. Stud. Logica. **100**(5), 1001–1045 (2012)
21. Van De Putte, F., Tamminga, A., Duijf, H.: Doing without nature. In: Baltag, A., Seligman, J., Yamada, T. (eds.) LORI 2017. LNCS, vol. 10455, pp. 209–223. Springer, Heidelberg (2017). https://doi.org/10.1007/978-3-662-55665-8_15
22. Wang, Y.: A logic of knowing how. In: van der Hoek, W., Holliday, W.H., Wang, W. (eds.) LORI 2015. LNCS, vol. 9394, pp. 392–405. Springer, Heidelberg (2015). https://doi.org/10.1007/978-3-662-48561-3_32
23. Xu, M.: Combinations of STIT with ought and know. J. Philos. Log. **44**(6), 851–877 (2015). https://doi.org/10.1007/s10992-015-9365-7. http://dx.doi.org/10.1007/s10992-015-9365-7

Bringing Belief Base Change into Dynamic Epistemic Logic

Marlo Souza[1(✉)] and Álvaro Moreira[2]

[1] Institute of Mathematics and Statistics, Federal University of Bahia - UFBA, Av. Adhemar de Barros, S/N, Ondina, Salvador, BA, Brazil
marlo@dcc.ufba.br

[2] Institute of Informatics, Federal University of Rio Grande do Sul - UFRGS, Av. Bento Gonçalves, Porto Alegre, RS 9500, Brazil
alvaro.moreira@inf.ufrgs.br

Abstract. AGM's belief revision is one of the main paradigms in the study of belief change operations. In this context, belief bases (prioritised bases) have been primarily used to specify the agent's belief state. While the connection of iterated AGM-like operations and their encoding in dynamic epistemic logics have been studied before, few works considered how well-known postulates from iterated belief revision theory can be characterised by means of belief bases and their counterpart in dynamic epistemic logic. Particularly, it has been shown that some postulates can be characterised through transformations in priority graphs, while others may not be represented that way. This work investigates changes in the semantics of Dynamic Preference Logic that give rise to an appropriate syntactic representation for its models that allow us to represent and reason about iterated belief base change in this logic.

1 Introduction

Belief Change is the study of how an epistemic agent comes to change her mind after acquiring new information. While changes in mental attitudes is a well-studied topic in the literature, the integration of such changes as operations within logics of beliefs, obligations, etc. is a somewhat recent development.

Inspired by the Dutch School, several dynamic logics for information change have been proposed [5,32] which can be connected to the study Belief Change. In particular, Girard [14] proposes Dynamic Preference Logic (DPL) which has been applied to study generalisations of belief revision *a la* AGM [14,15]. Interestingly, [29] have proposed using DPL as a tool to investigate different classes of belief change operators.

Belief Base Change is the area that studies Belief Change based on syntactic representations of the agent's epistemic commitments. The area arises from Hansson's [17] criticism of the use of deductively closed sets of formulas to represent an agent's epistemic state in the AGM paradigm. Recently, the notion of belief base has been extended into similar (and more expressive) structures such as e-bases [28], epistemic entrenchments [27], priority graphs [23] and others.

L. Soares Barbosa and A. Baltag (Eds.): DaLí 2019, LNCS 12005, pp. 190–205, 2020.
https://doi.org/10.1007/978-3-030-38808-9_12

While connections between Belief Base Change and Belief Change have been investigated in the literature [9,10,18], they rely mainly on one-shot changes, thus, are not able to clarify the behaviour of iterated changes. As such, it is necessary to establish which formal properties these belief base change operations satisfy in a dynamic sense, as studied in the literature of Iterated Belief Change [8,19,25].

The relationship between priority graphs (and similar structures) and preference relations has been widely investigated in the literature [3,23]. Logics relating notions of belief/preference based on syntactic representations, such as priority graphs, and semantic representations, have been studied before by authors such as Levesque [20], Van Benthem et al. [33] and Lorini [24]. More yet, it has been shown that several well-known dynamic operators for preference change can be characterised by means of transformations on such structures [3,31,33].

Souza et al. [30] have taken one step in the direction of connecting Belief Base Change and Iterated Belief Change by characterising well-known postulates as conditions that must be satisfied by transformations on priority graphs. These authors show, however, that an important class of postulates cannot be represented that way, demonstrating that there is an expressiveness gap between priority graphs and preference models concerning the dynamic aspects of the logic.

In this work, we aim to shorten the expressiveness gap between preference models and priority graphs. We show that for an appropriate restriction of the class of models, we can provide syntactic structures (called grounded priority graphs) able to encode all the information contained in a preference model, i.e. not only the information relative to the ordering among the possible worlds but also extensional information on which worlds are epistemically possible. As such, we can study operations of belief change based on preference models as transformations on grounded priority graphs. As a result, we obtain the representation of two postulates shown by Souza et al. [30] to not be representable in such a manner. We also obtain a characterisation of relevant priority graph transformations, i.e., transformations that may be used to represent belief change operators, a problem that was left open in previous works, such as [23,30,31].

This work is structured as follows: in Sect. 2, we present the background theory on Iterated Belief Change; in Sect. 3, we present Dynamic Preference Logic, as well as the relevant connections between preference models and priority graphs in the literature. We also prove some fundamental representation results, which strengthen the ones in the literature, based on the definition of preference model we propose. In Sect. 4, we employ DPL to study Iterated Belief Change operators through transformations on priority graphs. In this section, we provide a characterisation of relevant priority graph transformations, and we use them to characterise important belief change postulates which could not be represented by previous methods. Finally, in Sect. 5, we provide some final considerations, reflecting on the epistemological limitations of our logic, as well as possible future work and applications.

2 Dynamic and Iterated Belief Change

AGM's work [1] focused on postulating minimal requirements for belief change operations in order to describe rational ways of changing one's beliefs.

Among the three basic operations studied by AGM, only expansion can be univocally defined. The operations of revision and contraction, on the other hand, are constrained by a set of postulates, usually referred to as AGM postulates, that define a class of suitable change operators, representing different rational ways in which an agent can change her beliefs.

It has been argued that AGM's approach lacks a clear semantic interpretation. Based on Lewis' models for counterfactual reasoning [21], Grove [16] provided a possible-world semantics to AGM operations for a (supraclassical and monotonic) logic $\mathcal{L}$. He shows that for any belief revision operator $*$ satisfying the AGM postulates and any belief set B, there is a system of spheres $S_B = \langle W, \leq \rangle$, in which W is a set of models for the language $\mathcal{L}$, such that $w \in Min_{\leq} W$ iff $w \vDash B$ and $[\![B * \varphi]\!]_{S_B} = Min_{\leq}[\![\varphi]\!]_{S_B}$. As such, compliance to AGM's postulates can be semantically characterised by postulate FAITH below, which states the minimal worlds on the revised epistemic state of the agent are exactly the minimal worlds satisfying a certain property φ that the agent has come to believe to be true, on changes in Grove's models [25]:

(FAITH) $w \in Min_{\leq}[\![\varphi]\!]$ iff $w \in Min_{\leq_{*\varphi}} W$

It has been pointed out that AGM belief revision says very little about how to change one agent's beliefs repeatedly. In fact, it has been observed that the AGM approach allows some counter-intuitive behaviour in the iterated case [8]. To remedy this deficiency, Darwiche and Pearl [8] propose a set of additional postulates that further constrain the behaviour of revision operators. Furthermore, the authors analyse the proposal by Boutilier [6] of Natural Revision. To model this operation, they propose the postulate of *conditional belief minimisation* CB, which states that the conditional beliefs of the agent (which are not related to the property being revised) are maintained.

(CB) If $w, w' \notin Min_{\leq}[\![\varphi]\!]$, then $w \leq w'$ iff $w \leq_{*\varphi} w'$.

Darwiche and Pearl use this postulate to characterise the operation of Natural Revision showing thus that this is only an example of their broader notion of iterated belief change.

Definition 1 (Natural Revision). *Let $\leq \subseteq W \times W$ be a plausibility relation and φ a propositional formula. The Natural Revision of $\leq$ by φ is the plausibility relation $\leq_{*\varphi} \subseteq W \times W$ satisfying* FAITH *and* CB.

Based on criticism by Freund and Lehman [11], Nayak et al. [25], however, show that DP postulates are incompatible with the original AGM postulates. To solve this problem, they propose the notion of dynamic revision operator, in which a belief revision changes not only the belief set of the agent but the operation itself, i.e., the agent's epistemic state. This distinction between *static* and *dynamic* operators has been observed to be relevant in works such as that of Van Benthem [32] and Baltag and Smets [5], or that of Lindström and Rabinowicz [22], in which AGM-like static revision can be seen as a counterfactual reasoning while dynamic revision is modelled as an epistemic action changing the agent's epistemic state.

In this work, we explore the characterisation of Belief Change postulates within Dynamic Preference Logic using both the proof theory of the logic and its characterisation through transformations on belief bases, understood here as priority graphs. To do this, in the following section, we introduce Dynamic Preference Logic, the logic that we will use to reason about Belief Change.

3 Dynamic Preference Logic

Preference Logic is a modal logic of transitive and reflexive frames. It has been applied to model a plethora of phenomena in Deontic Logic [33], Epistemic Logic [5], etc. Dynamic Preference Logic (DPL) [14] is the result of "dynamifying" Preference Logic, i.e., extending it with dynamic modalities allowing the study of dynamic phenomena of attitudes such as Beliefs, Obligations, Preferences, etc.

We begin our presentation with the language and semantics of Preference Logic, which we will later "dynamify".

Definition 2. *Let P be a finite set of propositional letters. We define the language $\mathcal{L}_{\leq}(P)$ by the following grammar (where $p \in P$):*

$$\varphi ::= p \mid \neg\varphi \mid \varphi \wedge \varphi \mid A\varphi \mid [\leq]\varphi \mid [<]\varphi$$

We will often refer to the language $\mathcal{L}_{\leq}(P)$ simply as $\mathcal{L}_{\leq}$ by supposing the set P is fixed. Also, we will denote the language of propositional formulas by $\mathcal{L}_0(P)$ or simply $\mathcal{L}_0$. Girard [14] has proposed a semantics for DPL based on Kripke frames with a reflexive and transitive accessibility relation. However, as pointed out earlier, Souza et al. [30] show that for this class of models, some belief change operators cannot be represented by means of the manipulation of syntactic representations of these models, presented later in this section. For this reason, we propose a variation of the notion of preference models that, we show, possess good representational properties from a dynamic point of view.

Definition 3. *A conditionally-grounded preference model is a tuple $M = \langle W, \leq, v\rangle$ where $W \subseteq 2^P$ is a set of possible worlds, $\leq$ is a reflexive and transitive relation over W, and $v : P \to 2^W$, s.t. $w \in v(p)$ iff $p \in w$, is a valuation function.*

In such a model, the accessibility relation $\leq$ represents an ordering of the possible worlds according to the preferences of a certain agent. As such, given two possible worlds $w, w' \in W$, we say that w is at least as preferred as w' if, and only if, $w \leq w'$.

Notice that in Definition 3, we require that $W \subseteq 2^P$, i.e., possible worlds are possible propositional valuations. This requirement has important expressiveness consequences for the logic. Particularly, one expressiveness consequence can be seen in Theorem 7, a stronger version of a representation theorem due to Liu [23].

The choice of restriction in the class of models we present in this work stems from two reasons: these models are more connected with Grove's proposal of models for belief change, in which possible worlds were maximal consistent theories of the logic - in the propositional classical logic case, it is equivalent to valuations - and the fact that, as showed by Andersen et al. [2], for conditional logics defined over linear preference model, any (linear) preference model is modally equivalent to a conditionally-grounded (linear) preference model[1]. From their work, we also know that the logic of degrees of belief, which can be encoded within Preference Logic, is more expressive than the logic of conditional beliefs, which suggests that the restriction on the models has important expressibility consequences for our logic.

Since, in this work, our investigation only concerns those postulates which are defined by means of conditions on Grove models, usually based on the notion of conditional belief, we do not believe this expressive limitation of the logic will be of great concern. We nevertheless discuss these limitations in our Final Considerations. In the following, we will refer to conditionally-grounded preference models simply as preference models, for the sake of the presentation.

The interpretation of the formulas over these models is defined as usual. Here, we only present the interpretations for the modalities, since the semantics of the propositional connectives is clear. They are interpreted as

$$\begin{array}{lll} M, w \vDash A\varphi & \text{iff} & \forall w' \in W : M, w' \vDash \varphi \\ M, w \vDash [\leq]\varphi & \text{iff} & \forall w' \in W : w' \leq w \Rightarrow M, w' \vDash \varphi \\ M, w \vDash [<]\varphi & \text{iff} & \forall w' \in W : w' < w \Rightarrow M, w' \vDash \varphi \end{array}$$

As usual, we will refer as $\langle\leq\rangle\varphi$ and $\langle<\rangle\varphi$ to the formulas $\neg[\leq]\neg\varphi$ and $\neg[<]\neg\varphi$, respectively, as commonly done in modal logic. Also, given a model M and a formula φ, we use the notation $[\![\varphi]\!]_M$ to denote the set of all the worlds in M satisfying φ. When it is clear which model we are referring to, we will denote the same set by $[\![\varphi]\!]$. Also, as usual, we will refer as $M \vDash \varphi$ to the fact that for any world w in the model, it holds that $M, w \vDash \varphi$.

As the concept of most preferred worlds satisfying a given formula φ will be of great use in modelling some interesting phenomena in this logic, we define a formula encompassing this exact concept.

[1] The authors consider only linear models in their work and, a priori, it is not clear whether their modal equivalence result can be extended to pre-orders in general. Nevertheless, it indicates that conditionally-grounded models preserve a great deal of conditional information held in general preference models and, as such, constitute an interesting subclass of models to be studied for this logic. Our results in this work only support this conclusion by showing that, for considering this subclass of models, we can obtain interesting representation results that allow computational exploration of DPL in diverse areas.

Definition 4. *We define the formula $\mu\varphi \equiv \varphi \wedge \neg\langle<\rangle\varphi$ that is satisfied by exactly the most preferred worlds satisfying φ, i.e., $[\![\mu\varphi]\!]_M = Min_{\leq}[\![\varphi]\!]_M$.*

3.1 Preferences and Priorities

The relation between preference relations and their representations as orderings over formulas (priority orderings, or entrenchment relations) has been extensively studied in the literature [3,12,13]. Liu [23] explore this relationship to propose a syntactic representation of preference models, called priority graphs (or P-graphs for short) which can be used to reason about conditional preferences in DPL [33]. With this connection, we will be able to investigate well-known postulates of Iterated Belief Change, defined over preference relations as those in preference models, using operations on priority graphs, thus connecting belief base change operations and iterated belief revision.

Definition 5 [23]. *Let P be a countable set of propositional symbols and $\mathcal{L}_0(P)$ the language of classical propositional sentences over the set P. A priority graph is a tuple $G = \langle \Phi, \prec\rangle$ where $\Phi \subset \mathcal{L}_0(P)$, is a finite set of propositional sentences and $\prec$ is a strict partial order on Φ.*

It is easy to see that from a priority graph, we can construct a preference model by taking the preference relation induced by such a graph.

Definition 6. *Let $G = \langle \Phi, \prec\rangle$ be a P-graph and $M = \langle W, \leq, v\rangle$ be a preference model. We say that M is induced by G iff for any $w, w' \in W$ it holds that*

$$w \leq w' \quad \textit{iff} \quad \forall\varphi \in \Phi : ((w' \models \varphi \Rightarrow w \models \varphi) \textit{ or } \exists\psi \in \Phi : \psi \prec \varphi,\ w \models \psi, \textit{and } w' \not\models \psi)$$

Clearly, given a P-graph $G = \langle \Phi, \prec\rangle$, the relation $\leq$ satisfying the condition in Definition 6 is reflexive. Notice that it is also transitive since for any words w, w', w'', if $w \leq w'$ and $w' \leq w''$ then for any φ'' that w'' satisfies, then either w' satisfies it or there is some φ' that w' satisfies and w'' doesn't and $\varphi' \prec \varphi$. Similarly, since $w \leq w'$ there is some φ that w satisfies and w' doesn't and $\varphi \prec \varphi'$. Notice that, since Φ is finite, we can take the minimal φ' and φ for which these properties hold, from which we can conclude that w'' cannot satisfy φ, otherwise either $w \not\leq w'$ or $w' \not\leq w''$. Thus, by transitivity of $\prec$, $w \leq w''$.

The induction of preference models from P-graphs raises the question about the relations between these two structures. Liu [23] shows that any preference frame, i.e., any set of worlds with a reflexive and transitive accessibility relation, is induced by some P-graph. This result cannot be strengthened to preference models, however, since by fixing a certain valuation, it is easy to construct a model for which there is no P-graph that induces it - it suffices to have two worlds w and w' which satisfy the same propositional literals and $w < w'$. Since no propositional formula can distinguish the world w from w', no P-graph can express the order $w < w'$. Within the class of preference models defined in this work, we can strengthen further this result showing that any conditionally-grounded preference model is induced by a P-graph.

Theorem 7. *Any preference model $M = \langle W, \leq, v\rangle$ is induced by a priority graph $G = (\Phi, \prec)$.*

Proof. Take $C_M = \{[w] \mid [w] = \{w' \in W \text{ s.t. } w' \leq w \text{ and } w \leq w'\}\}$, we define the characteristic formula of a cluster $[w]$, the formula $\varphi_{[w]} = \bigvee_{w' \in [w]} \bigwedge_{p \in P} p(w')$ s.t. $p(w') = p$ if $M, w' \vDash p$ and $p(w') = \neg p$, otherwise. With that, construct $G_M = \langle \Phi, \prec\rangle$ on the following way.

- $\Phi = \{\varphi_{[w]} \mid [w] \in C_M\}$
- $\varphi \prec \psi$ iff there are $w, w' \in W$ s.t. $M, w \vDash \varphi$ and $M, w' \vDash \psi$ and $w < w'$.

Notice that each world w in the model satisfies exactly one formula of Φ and only worlds in the same cluster, i.e., equally preferable to each other, satisfy the same formula Φ, since the formula $\varphi_{[w]}$ is a disjunction of the characteristic formulas $\varphi_{w'}$ of the worlds in the cluster $[w]$. As such, it clearly holds that for any $w, w' \in W$, $w \leq w'$ iff either $\varphi_{[w]} = \varphi_{[w']}$ or $\varphi_{[w]} \prec \varphi_{[w']}$. We call G_M the canonical P-graph inducing M. □

Notice that not necessarily two P-graphs that induce the same preference model are equal (or isomorphic in some sense), since, as can be easily seen from Definition 6, any submodel of a preference model induced by some P-graph G is also induced by G. As such, preference models are underdetermined, in a sense, by P-graphs and two preference models with substantially distinct canonical models can be induced by the same P-graph.

Fact 8. *Let $G = \langle \Phi, \prec\rangle$ be a P-graph and let also $M = \langle W, \leq, v\rangle$ be a preference model induced by G. For any preference model $M' = \langle W', \leq', v'\rangle$ s.t. $W' \subseteq W$, $\leq' = \leq_{|W'}$ and $v' = v_{|W'}$, M' is induced by G.*

4 Iterated Belief Change and Dynamic Preference Logic

In this section, we investigate the relationship between the postulates satisfied by iterated belief change operators discussed in Sect. 2 and their characterisation inside Dynamic Preference Logic.

We define a dynamic operation on a preference model as any operation that takes a preference model and a formula and changes the preference relation of the model.

Definition 9 [29]. *We say $\star$ is a dynamic operator on preference models if for any preference model $M = \langle W, \leq, v\rangle$ and formula $\varphi \in \mathcal{L}_0$, we have that $\star(M, \varphi) = \langle W, \leq_\star, v\rangle$. In other words, an operation on preference models is called a dynamic operator iff it only changes the relation of the preference model. We will use $M_{\star\varphi}$ to denote the model $\star(M, \varphi)$.*

Given a dynamic operator $\star$, we extend the language $\mathcal{L}_\leq$ with formulas $[\star\varphi]\xi$. Here, we point out some abuse of notation, since we use $\star$ as both a dynamic operator defined as a function and as a symbol in the object language to define the modality $[\star\varphi]$ - which will correspond to the application of this operator $\star$ to the model.

Definition 10. *Let $\star$ be a dynamic operator. We define the language $\mathcal{L}_{\leq}(\star)$ as the smallest set containing $\mathcal{L}_{\leq}$ and all formulas $[\star\varphi]\xi$, with $\varphi \in \mathcal{L}_0$ and $\xi \in \mathcal{L}_{\leq}(\star)$.*

Given a preference model $M = \langle W, \leq, v \rangle$, the semantics of formulas $[\star\varphi]\xi$ of $\mathcal{L}_{\leq}(\star)$ is as follows

$$M, w \models [\star\varphi]\xi \quad \text{iff} \quad M_{\star\varphi}, w \models \xi$$

Notice that, in this work, we are only interested in belief changing operators, i.e., those changing the plausibility the agent attributes to each epistemically possible world, not creating any new knowledge about the world[2].

Liu et al. [23,33] show that some dynamic belief operators can also be described by means of changes in the priority graphs representing the agent's belief base. In the following, $\mathbb{G}(P)$ denotes the set of all priority graphs constructed over a set P of propositional symbols.

Definition 11. *We call a graph transformation any function $\dagger : \mathbb{G}(P) \times \mathcal{L}_0(P) \to \mathbb{G}(P)$.*

A P-graph transformation is, thus, a transformation in the agent's belief base, as represented by a priority graph. Since P-graphs and preference models are translatable into one another, it is easy to connect P-graph transformations and dynamic operators as well.

Definition 12 [30]. *Let $\star$ be a dynamic operator and $\dagger$ be a P-graph transformation. We say $\star$ is induced by $\dagger$ if for any preference model M and any P-graph G, if M is induced by G then the preference model $\star(M, \varphi)$ is induced by the P-graph $\dagger(G, \varphi)$, where φ is any propositional formula in $\mathcal{L}_0(P)$.*

Some difficulties may arise in this connection since the relationship between P-graphs and preference models is not univocal, as exemplified by Fact 8. We will deal with some of these difficulties in this section through the definition of a more suitable syntactic representation of conditionally-grounded preference models in Subsect. 4.2.

Particularly, it is clear that not all P-graph transformations induce dynamic operators. The reason for this is that, since P-graphs are syntactic representations of preferences, different P-graphs may induce the same preference models. As such, if the P-graph transformation changes these equivalent P-graphs in inconsistent ways, no dynamic operator can satisfy the condition of Definition 12.

For example, a graph transformation that changes the graph $p \prec q$ into the graph $p \prec q$ and the graph $p \wedge q \prec p \wedge \neg q \prec \neg p \wedge q \prec \neg p \wedge \neg q$ into

[2] As helpfully pointed out by one of the reviewers, since our agents are introspective in the sense that agents know about their beliefs, the belief change operations investigated in this work do change the agent's knowledge, but only in the sense that they change their knowledge about their epistemic state, not their knowledge about the world or current state of affairs. This is an important distinction in the class of operations studied.

$p \wedge q \prec \neg p \wedge q \prec p \wedge \neg q \prec \neg p \wedge \neg q$ cannot induce any dynamic operator since the original graphs are equivalent, i.e., induce the same models, but the resulting graphs are not. As such, Souza et al. [30] define the notion of relevant graph transformation.

Definition 13 [30]. *We say that a P-graph transformation † is relevant if there is some dynamic operator ⋆ that is induced by it.*

4.1 Characterising Relevant Graph Transformations

While some earlier representation results by Liu [23] guarantee the existence of relevant P-graphs, Souza et al. [30] did not provide means to identify which graph transformations are relevant or not. To provide such conditions, we need to formalise the notion of equivalence between P-graphs discussed above.

Definition 14. *Let G_1 and G_2 be two P-graphs, we say G_1 and G_2 are φ-equivalent, symbolically $G_1 \equiv_\varphi G_2$, iff they induce the same preference models of a formula φ, i.e., for any preference model M, if $M \models \varphi$, then G_1 induce M iff G_2 induce M.*

The idea of φ-equivalence is that two graphs induce the same models when restricted to a certain class of models - represented by a formula φ. Clearly, it holds that two P-graphs are equivalent (in the sense that they induce the same models) when they are $\top$-equivalent.

Now, by Proposition 15 below, we have that not only relevant graph transformations preserve φ-equivalence between P-graphs, but this is a sufficient condition for a transformation to be relevant. This is a direct consequence of the Fact 8 presented in Sect. 3.

Proposition 15. *Let $\dagger : \mathbb{G}(P) \times \mathcal{L}_0(P) \to \mathbb{G}(P)$ be a P-graph transformation, the following statements are equivalent:*

1. *† is relevant;*
2. *for any P-graphs G_1, G_2 and propositional formula φ, if $G_1 \equiv_\psi G_2$ for some propositional formula ψ, then $\dagger(G_1, \varphi) \equiv_\psi \dagger(G_2, \varphi)$.*

Proof. Notice that the proof that statement 1 implies statement 2 is trivial by Definition 12. The other implication follows easily by defining for any model $M = \langle W, \leq, v\rangle$ and propositional formula φ, the result $*(M, \varphi) = M' = \langle W, \leq', v\rangle$ s.t. $\leq'$ is induced by the graph $\dagger(G, \varphi)$, where G is the canonical P-graph inducing M. We must show that † induces ⋆, i.e., that for any P-graph inducing M, the result of its transformation by † must induce M'.

Take a P-graph G' that induces M. Take the formula

$$\psi_M = \left(\bigvee_{w \in W} \varphi_w\right) \wedge \left(\bigwedge_{w \in 2^P \setminus W} \neg\varphi_w\right),$$

where given a propositional valuation w,

$$\psi_w = \left(\bigwedge_{p \in w} p \wedge \bigwedge_{p \in P \setminus w} \neg p \right).$$

Clearly, for any model $M' = \langle W', \leq', v' \rangle$, $M' \vDash \varphi_M$ iff $W' \subseteq W$. As such, by Fact 8, it is easy to see that $G \equiv_{\psi_M} G'$. Since $\dagger$ preserves ψ_M-equivalence, then $\dagger(G, \varphi) \equiv_{\psi_M} \dagger(G', \varphi)$. Since dynamic operators don't change the set of possible worlds, clearly $M' \vDash \psi_M$ and, as such, it must be induced by G'. □

While the notion of φ-equivalence clarifies the necessary behaviour for a graph transformation to be relevant, it is yet not completely clear how to decide whether a transformation preserves φ-equivalence. Since, by Fact 8, we know that a P-graph induces all submodels of some model it induces, to verify if two graphs are φ-equivalent, it suffices to verify if they induce the same model in the limiting case, i.e., the model containing all and only the valuations that satisfy φ.

Proposition 16. *Let G_1 and G_2 be P-graphs and let $\varphi \in \mathcal{L}_0$ be a propositional formula. We have that $G_1 \equiv_\varphi G_2$ iff there is some preference model $M = \langle [\![\varphi]\!]_0, \leq, v \rangle$, where $[\![\varphi]\!]_0$ stands for the set of all propositional valuations satisfying φ, s.t. M is induced both by G_1 and G_2.*

Proof (Sketch of the proof). It suffices to see that, given the restriction in the class of models considered in Definition 3, any model is composed by a subset of propositional valuations in 2^P. As such, for any model $M = \langle W, \leq, v \rangle$ induced by a P-graph G, it must be the case that there is a canonical induced model $M_G = \langle 2^P, \leq_G, v_G \rangle$ induced by M_G s.t. $\leq \subseteq \leq_G$ - by Definition 6. From there, it is easy to see that $G_1 \equiv_\varphi G_2$ iff $M_{G_1} = M_{G_2}$, as defined above, considering only those valuations that satisfy φ in the canonical induced model.

With this result, we have a tool to verify whether a P-graph transformation is relevant, i.e., induces some dynamic operator. Notice that, since the number of preference models for a finite set P of propositional symbol is also finite, and since there is only a finite amount of semantically distinct propositional formulas over this symbol set, verifying if a graph transformation is relevant is decidable (and, in fact, exponential on the number of propositional symbols in P).

4.2 Overcoming P-Graphs Expressibility Gaps

Souza et al. [29] show that the proof theory of DPL can be used to characterise Belief Change postulates. More yet, they study which postulates can also be represented by conditions on graph transformations, such as DP-1. We say a graph transformation satisfies a postulate if all dynamic operators induced by it satisfy this postulate.

To characterise belief change postulates using graph transformations, Souza et al. [30] provide a set of constraints on transformations that guarantee satisfaction to some postulates.

Unfortunately, the authors also show that some important postulates from Iterated Belief Revision cannot be characterised by P-graph transformations, as is the case of CB[3]. However, Natural Revision, which satisfies postulates FAITH and CB, is definable in DPL.

Fact 17 [30]. *No relevant P-graph transformation* $\dagger : \mathbb{G}(P) \times \mathcal{L}_0(P) \to \mathbb{G}(P)$ *satisfies both* FAITH *and* CB.

The reason for such a result is that some dynamic operators are defined by means of the minimal worlds in the model satisfying some property. It has been shown, however, that such a property cannot be encoded employing P-graphs [31]. As such, to overcome the expressiveness gap between dynamic operators and graph transformation, we propose a restriction on the class of models in DPL semantics (corresponding to the requirement that $W \subseteq 2^P$ in Definition 3) and, below, a variation of the notion of priority graph which, together, guarantee that transformations on priority graphs can appropriately characterise these postulates.

Definition 18. *We call grounded P-graph a structure* $G = \langle \varphi, \Phi, \prec \rangle$*, s.t.* $\varphi \in \mathcal{L}_0$ *is a consistent propositional formula and* $\langle \Phi, \prec \rangle$ *is a P-graph. We also say that* G *is grounded by* φ*.*

The main reason for the lack of expressiveness of P-graphs to define dynamic operations is that a P-graph encodes only information on the structure of the accessibility relation of the models induced by it. The extension of such a model, i.e., which worlds are indeed possible, is not encoded within a P-graph. As such, from the structure of the P-graph, it is not possible to determine which worlds are minimal in the induced models. In Definition 18, we complement a P-graph with the information φ, which will be used to define exactly which worlds exist in the induced models.

Definition 19. *Let* $G = \langle \varphi, \Phi, \prec \rangle$ *be a grounded P-graph, we say that the preference model* $M = \langle W, \leq, v \rangle$ *is induced by* G *iff* $W = [\![\varphi]\!]_0$ *and* $\leq$ *is induced by the P-graph* $\langle \Phi, \prec \rangle$*.*

Notice that, by Definition 19, a grounded P-graph induces exactly one preference model in which the possible worlds are exactly the propositional valuations satisfying the formula φ which grounds it. With that addition, we can determine, based solely on the structure of a grounded P-graph, what are the minimal worlds in the induced model that satisfy some formula. To construct a graph-based codification for a formula representing such worlds, based on the work of [33], we will use the notion of maximal paths in a graph.

[3] Other interesting examples have been previously provided by Souza et al. [31], showing that some iterated contraction operators cannot be characterised by P-graphs transformations, unless when restricted to a special class of preference models, which they call broad models.

Definition 20. *Let $G = \langle \varphi, \Phi, \prec \rangle$ be a grounded P-graph, $\sigma = \langle \xi_1, \cdots, \xi_n \rangle$ be a maximal chain of nodes in G, and let ψ be a propositional formula, we define the formula $\mu_\sigma(\psi)$ representing the minimal worlds in the induced model satisfying ψ as $\mu_\sigma(\psi) = \mu_\sigma^n(\psi)$, where:*

$$\mu_\sigma^i(\psi) = \begin{cases} \varphi \wedge \psi & \textit{if } i = 0 \\ \xi_i \wedge \mu_\sigma^{i-1}(\psi) & \textit{if } i > 0 \textit{ and } \xi_i \wedge \mu_\sigma^{i-1}(\psi) \not\vdash \bot \\ \mu_\sigma^{i-1}(\psi) & \textit{otherwise} \end{cases}$$

Notice that in Definition 20, the formula $\mu_sigma^i(\psi)$ corresponds to the maximal (ordered) conjunction of formulas ξ_j in the path $\sigma = \langle \xi_1, \cdots, \xi_n \rangle$ that is consistent with φ and *psi*. Since all possible worlds satisfying φ exist in any model M induced by a grounded P-graph $G = \langle \varphi, \Phi, \prec \rangle$, if there is a minimal world in M satisfying ψ, it must satisfy the formula $\mu_sigma(\psi)$ for some maximal path σ in G. With that, it is easy to construct a propositional formula from a grounded P-graph that is satisfied exactly by the minimal ψ-worlds in the model induced by it.

Proposition 21. *Let $G = \langle \varphi, \Phi, \prec \rangle$ be a grounded P-graph, let Σ be the set of all maximal chains of nodes in G, and let $M = \langle W, \leq, v \rangle$ be the preference model induced by G. For any world $w \in W$, it holds that*

$$M, w \models \mu_G(\psi) \quad \textit{iff} \quad w \in Min_{\leq}[\![\psi]\!]$$

where $\mu_G(\psi) = \bigvee_{\sigma \in \Sigma} \mu_\sigma(\psi)$

Proposition 21 shows that, differently then what happens for P-graphs by Fact 30 of [31], grounded P-graphs completely define the minimal worlds of their induced conditionally-grounded models. Since the aforementioned fact is used to prove that well-known contraction operators, as well as postulates CB and FAITH, cannot be represented by P-graph transformations, if we consider grounded P-graphs and conditionally-grounded P-graphs, we can provide a representation result for these postulates - and other similar postulates characterised by minimal worlds in a model.

We do point out that, in this work, we do not allow grounded P-graph transformations to change the grounding of the graph, similar to the condition that dynamic operators cannot change the set of possible worlds of the model. Formally we would need to redefine notions such as P-graph transformation to reinforce this restriction. For space constraints, however, we will refrain from doing so.

Finally, we can characterise CB using both the proof theory of DPL and grounded P-graph transformations.

Proposition 22. *Let $\star$ be a dynamic operator on preference models satisfying* FAITH. *The operator $\star$ satisfies* CB *if, and only if, the axiom schemata below are valid in $\mathcal{L}_{\leq}(\star)$.*

$$
\begin{array}{ll}
[\star\varphi]p & \leftrightarrow p \\
[\star\varphi](\xi \wedge \xi) & \leftrightarrow [\star\varphi]\xi \wedge [\star\varphi]\xi \\
[\star\varphi]\neg\xi & \leftrightarrow \neg[\star\varphi]\xi \\
[\star\varphi]A\xi & \leftrightarrow A[\star\varphi]\xi \\
[\star\varphi][\leq]\xi & \leftrightarrow A(\mu\varphi \rightarrow [\star\varphi]\xi) \wedge (\neg\mu\varphi \rightarrow [\leq][\star\varphi]\xi) \\
[\star\varphi][<]\xi & \leftrightarrow \mu\varphi \vee \neg\mu\varphi \rightarrow (A(\mu\varphi \rightarrow [\star\varphi]\xi) \wedge [<][\star\varphi]\xi) \\
[\leq][\star\varphi]\xi & \rightarrow \neg\mu\varphi \rightarrow ([\star\varphi][\leq](\neg\mu\varphi \rightarrow \xi)) \\
[<][\star\varphi]\xi & \rightarrow \neg\mu\varphi \rightarrow ([\star\varphi][<](\neg\mu\varphi \rightarrow \xi))
\end{array}
$$

Proof (Sketch of the Proof). The first implication is straight-forward, by showing that each axiom holds for any preference model M and dynamic operation $\star$ satisfying CB and FAITH. It suffices to notice that for any world w, if it is a minimal φ-world, it will become a minimal world in the revised model $M_{\star\varphi}$, by FAITH. If it is not, for any world w' s.t. $w' \leq w$, it holds that $w' \leq_\star w$, by CB, and for any minimal φ-world w', $w' < w$ by FAITH.

The other implication can be easily shown by observing that for any world in a preference model (in fact, for any set of worlds) there is a propositional formula ξ that is satisfied only by this world (the worlds in this set). With that, and the fact that for any propositional formula ξ and dynamic operator $\star$ it holds in DPL that $\xi \equiv [\star\varphi]\xi$, it is easy to use the axioms above to show that if $\star$ satisfies the postulates above, then it satisfies CB and FAITH.

Postulate CB can be represented by means of grounded P-graph transformations in the following way.

Proposition 23. *Let $\dagger : \mathbb{G}(P) \times \mathcal{L}_0(P) \rightarrow \mathbb{G}(P)$ be a relevant grounded P-graph transformation. $\dagger$ satisfies* CB *iff for all grounded P-graph $G = \langle\varphi, \Phi, \prec\rangle$ and propositional formula $\psi \in \mathcal{L}_0$, it holds that $\dagger(G, \psi)$ is φ-equivalent to the grounded P-graph $G' = \langle\varphi, \Phi_\dagger, \prec_\dagger\rangle$ satisfying:*

1. *For all $\xi \in \Phi$, there is some $\xi' \in \Phi_\dagger$ s.t.*
   (a) $\varphi \wedge \xi \equiv \varphi \wedge \xi'$ and
   (b) $\forall \alpha' \in \Phi_\dagger$, if $\alpha' \prec_\dagger \xi'$ then
   $\alpha' \equiv \mu_G(\psi)$ or
   there is $\alpha \in \Phi$ s.t. $\varphi \wedge \alpha \equiv \varphi \wedge \alpha'$ and $\alpha \prec \xi$;
2. *For all $\xi' \in \Phi_\dagger$, $\xi' \equiv \mu_G(\psi)$ or there is some $\xi \in \Phi$ s.t.*
   (a) $\varphi \wedge \xi \equiv \varphi \wedge \xi'$ and
   (b) $\forall \alpha \in \Phi$, if $\alpha \prec \xi$ then there is $\alpha' \in \Phi_\dagger$ s.t.
   $\varphi \wedge \alpha \equiv \varphi \wedge \alpha'$ and
   $\alpha' \prec_\dagger \xi'$.

Similarly, we can characterise FAITH using grounded P-graph transformations:

Proposition 24. *Let $\dagger : \mathbb{G}(P) \times \mathcal{L}_0(P) \rightarrow \mathbb{G}(P)$ be a relevant grounded P-graph transformation. $\dagger$ satisfies* FAITH *if for all grounded P-graph $G = \langle\varphi, \Phi, \prec\rangle$ and propositional formula $\psi \in \mathcal{L}_0$, it holds that $\dagger(G, \psi)$ is φ-equivalent to the grounded P-graph $G' = \langle\varphi, \Phi_\dagger, \prec_\dagger\rangle$ satisfying:*

1. $\mu_G(\psi) \in \Phi_\dagger$;
2. For all $\xi \in \Phi$, $\mu_G(\psi) \prec_\dagger \xi$.

Notice that while in this work we were able to provide characterisations of both CB and FAITH using grounded P-graphs, giving similar representations to belief contractions postulates [26] would be considerably more difficult. The reason for this is that contraction postulates describe constraints that are more fine-grained than those described by revision postulates. As a result, commonly, the restrictions imposed by such postulates would be described by properties on the paths in the resulting grounded P-graph.

Given the space constraints, we will not explore the representation of these operations in this work, but we do point out that a characterisation of Lexicographic Contraction using P-graphs - which works for our models - has been provided by Souza et al. [31] in their investigation on contraction operations using DPL. As such, this codification can provide clues for a characterisation of the contraction postulates using graph transformations.

5 Final Considerations

This work has investigated changes in the semantics of Dynamic Preference Logic and Priority Graphs to tackle the expressiveness gap for dynamic properties between dynamic operators over preference models and P-graph transformations. As such, this work can be seen as a step further in the attempt to provide a semantic foundation for the study on Relational Belief Change using Dynamic Preference Logic, as done by Girard et al. [14,15] and Souza et al. [29–31].

Notice that the class of models used in this work is not the same classes used in previous works [14,29]. As highlighted before, one of the contributions of this work is precisely investigating an appropriate class of models for DPL that could give rise to good representation results employing (grounded) priority graphs. Notice that the class of models used by us is closely related to Grove's [16] models of AGM Belief Change.

From an epistemological point of view, since possible worlds are interpreted as epistemically possible, our models are capable of representing the notion of an agent having some knowledge *about* the world (what is epistemically necessary) and her beliefs regarding the state of the world. The restriction in Definition 3 that $W \subseteq 2^P$ states that each possible state of affairs is identified about what is true on the observable properties of the world (represented by propositional symbols). This means that the agent cannot conceive two different state of affairs that are phenomenically identical. This may have important implications in the representation power of our logic regarding auto-epistemic phenomena. This fact highlights the importance of investigating introspective phenomena within Belief Revision Theory to understand the expressive limitations of the theory and its postulates.

As future work, we intend to study how our framework connects to the study of Non-Monotonic Belief Change, as studied by [7]. Since preference models can be used to define conditional preferences and non-monotonic rules, we believe our semantic framework is ideal for providing a semantic perspective on the work of these authors. This connection is important to understand reasoning about change based on non-monotonic rules, such as in the case of goal-oriented reasoning in agent programs [34].

We point out that, while we focused on the study of belief changing operations, specifically those that do not the change the agent's knowledge about the world, the results obtained here point to the fact that this framework can be used to study more general belief change operations, such as Public Announcements and those studied by Girard and Rott by means of General Dynamic Dynamic Logic programs [15]. It is not clear, however, if this approach could be connected with the study of more general relation changing operations available in the literature, such as those studied by Areces et al. [4].

References

1. Alchourrón, C.E., Gärdenfors, P., Makinson, D.: On the logic of theory change: partial meet contraction and revision functions. J. Symb. Log. **50**(2), 510–530 (1985)
2. Andersen, M.B., Bolander, T., van Ditmarsch, H., Jensen, M.H.: Bisimulation and expressivity for conditional belief, degrees of belief, and safe belief. Synthese **194**(7), 2447–2487 (2017)
3. Andréka, H., Ryan, M., Schobbens, P.Y.: Operators and laws for combining preference relations. J. Log. Comput. **12**(1), 13–53 (2002)
4. Areces, C., Fervari, R., Hoffmann, G.: Relation-changing modal operators. Log. J. IGPL **23**(4), 601–627 (2015)
5. Baltag, A., Smets, S.: A qualitative theory of dynamic interactive belief revision. Texts Log. Games **3**, 9–58 (2008)
6. Boutilier, C.: Revision sequences and nested conditionals. In: Proceedings of the 13th International Joint Conference on Artificial Intelligence, vol. 93, pp. 519–531. Morgan Kaufmann, New York (1993)
7. Casini, G., Fermé, E., Meyer, T., Varzinczak, I.: A semantic perspective on belief change in a preferential non-monotonic framework. In: Sixteenth International Conference on Principles of Knowledge Representation and Reasoning (2018)
8. Darwiche, A., Pearl, J.: On the logic of iterated belief revision. Artif. Intell. **89**(1), 1–29 (1997)
9. Fermé, E., Garapa, M., Reis, M.D.L.: On ensconcement and contraction. J. Log. Comput. **27**(7), 2011–2042 (2017)
10. Fermé, E., Krevneris, M., Reis, M.: An axiomatic characterization of ensconcement-based contraction. J. Symb. Log. **18**(5), 739–753 (2008)
11. Freund, M., Lehmann, D.: Belief revision and rational inference. Technical report 94–16, Leibniz Center for Research in Computer Science, Institute of Computer Science, Hebrew University of Jerusalem (1994)
12. Gärdenfors, P., Makinson, D.: Revisions of knowledge systems using epistemic entrenchment. In: Proceedings of the 2nd Conference on Theoretical Aspects of Reasoning About Knowledge, pp. 83–95. Morgan Kaufmann Publishers Inc. (1988)
13. Georgatos, K.: To preference via entrenchment. Ann. Pure Appl. Log. **96**(1–3), 141–155 (1999)

14. Girard, P.: Modal logic for belief and preference change. Ph.D. thesis, Stanford University (2008)
15. Girard, P., Rott, H.: Belief revision and dynamic logic. In: Baltag, A., Smets, S. (eds.) Johan van Benthem on Logic and Information Dynamics. OCL, vol. 5, pp. 203–233. Springer, Cham (2014). https://doi.org/10.1007/978-3-319-06025-5_8
16. Grove, A.: Two modelings for theory change. J. Philos. Log. **17**(2), 157–170 (1988)
17. Hansson, S.O.: In defense of base contraction. Synthese **91**(3), 239–245 (1992)
18. Hansson, S.O.: Kernel contraction. J. Symb. Log. **59**(3), 845–859 (1994)
19. Jin, Y., Thielscher, M.: Iterated belief revision, revised. Arti. Intell. **171**(1), 1–18 (2007)
20. Levesque, H.J.: A logic of implicit and explicit belief. In: Proceedings of the Fourth National Conference on Artificial Intelligence, pp. 198–202. AAAI Press, Palo Alto, US (1984)
21. Lewis, D.: Counterfactuals. Wiley, Hoboken (2013)
22. Lindström, S., Rabinowicz, W.: DDL unlimited: dynamic doxastic logic for introspective agents. Erkenntnis **50**(2), 353–385 (1999)
23. Liu, F.: Reasoning About Preference Dynamics, vol. 354. Springer, New York (2011). https://doi.org/10.1007/978-94-007-1344-4
24. Lorini, E.: In praise of belief bases: doing epistemic logic without possible worlds. In: Thirty-Second AAAI Conference on Artificial Intelligence (2018)
25. Nayak, A.C., Pagnucco, M., Peppas, P.: Dynamic belief revision operators. Artif. Intell. **146**(2), 193–228 (2003)
26. Ramachandran, R., Nayak, A.C., Orgun, M.A.: Three approaches to iterated belief contraction. J. Philos. Log. **41**(1), 115–142 (2012)
27. Reis, M.D.L.: On the interrelation between systems of spheres and epistemic entrenchment relations. Log. J. IGPL **22**(1), 126–146 (2014)
28. Rott, H.: 'Just Because': taking belief bases seriously. In: Buss, S.R., Hájek, P., Pudlák, P. (eds.) Lecture Notes in Logic, vol. 13, pp. 387–408. Association for Symbolic Logic, Urbana, US (1998)
29. Souza, M., Moreira, Á., Vieira, R.: Dynamic preference logic as a logic of belief change. In: Madeira, A., Benevides, M. (eds.) DALI 2017. LNCS, vol. 10669, pp. 185–200. Springer, Cham (2018). https://doi.org/10.1007/978-3-319-73579-5_12
30. Souza, M., Moreira, A., Vieira, R.: Iterated belief base change: a dynamic epistemic logic approach. In: Proceedings of the Thirty-Third AAAI Conference on Artificial Intelligence. AAAI Press, Palo Alto, US (2019, to appear)
31. Souza, M., Moreira, A., Vieira, R., Meyer, J.J.C.: Preference and priorities: a study based on contraction. In: KR 2016, pp. 155–164. AAAI Press (2016)
32. Van Benthem, J.: Dynamic logic for belief revision. J. Appl. Non-Class. Log. **17**(2), 129–155 (2007)
33. Van Benthem, J., Grossi, D., Liu, F.: Priority structures in deontic logic. Theoria **80**(2), 116–152 (2014)
34. Van Riemsdijk, M.B., Dastani, M., Meyer, J.J.C.: Goals in conflict: semantic foundations of goals in agent programming. Auton. Agent. Multi-Agent Syst. **18**(3), 471–500 (2009)

Short Papers

A Dynamic Logic for QASM Programs

Carlos Tavares(✉)

High-Assurance Software Laboratory/INESC TEC, Braga, Portugal
ctavares@inesctec.pt

Abstract. We define a dynamic logic for QASM (Quantum Assembly) programming language, a language that requires the handling of quantum and probabilistic information. We provide a syntax and a model to this logic, providing a probabilistic semantics to the classical part. We exercise it with the *quantum coin toss* program.

Keywords: Quantum logic · Quantum programming · Dynamic logic

1 Introduction

The programming languages, calculi, and logics, developed in the course of the past 20 years, for quantum computing have been gaining relevance with the appearance of the first proof-of-concept quantum computers and quantum programming languages. One of such is the Quantum Assembly Language [CBSG17], the quantum circuit specification language in use in the commercially available quantum hardware supplied by IBM, the IBM Q platform [ibm18] (a small example of the language is depicted in Fig. 1).

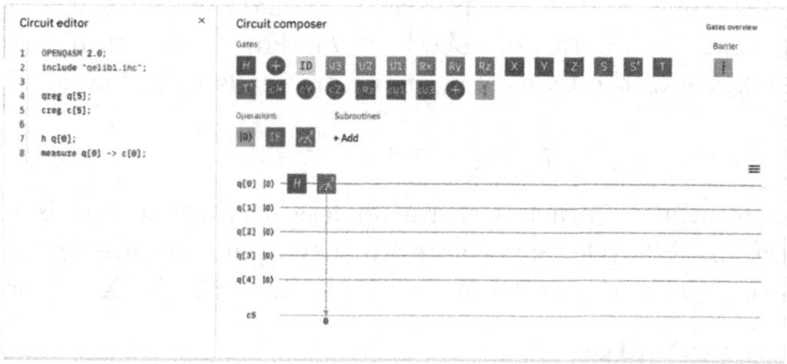

Fig. 1. Example of the definition of a circuit in the QASM language. On the right side the visual definition of the circuit and on the left side the correspondent QASM code.

Besides the description of unitary quantum circuits, the language encompasses classical control flow instructions, such as measurements, which possess a probabilistic nature, and *if statements*. We propose a dynamic logic for this language exploring two main points of interest: the direct handling of quantum and probabilistic propositions, and a possible axiomatic semantics.

L. Soares Barbosa and A. Baltag (Eds.): DaLí 2019, LNCS 12005, pp. 209–217, 2020.
https://doi.org/10.1007/978-3-030-38808-9_13

2 Quantum Computing

In this section, we introduce quantum computing from a state based perspective (i.e. by the definition of states, transitions, and acceptance states), as usually presented in the literature [Deu85]. For a more complete understanding of quantum computing, we recommend the reading of [NC02].

2.1 States

The state space of a quantum system is given by the set of unitary vectors (vectors of norm 1) definable in its respective *Hilbert space.* The qubit, the quantum version of the classical bits, consists of a *Hilbert* space of dimension 2, $\mathcal{H}^2$, with $\{|0\rangle, |1\rangle\}$ as an orthogonal basis. The correspondent state space reads as follows:

$$|\psi\rangle = \alpha|0\rangle + \beta|1\rangle ; |\alpha|^2 + |\beta|^2 = 1; \lambda|\psi\rangle \cong |\psi\rangle, \lambda \in \mathbb{C} \tag{1}$$

Quantum systems can be combined, employing the *tensor* product $\otimes$. For a n-qubit system, the set of possible states reads as follows:

$$\bigotimes_{i=0}^{n-1} \mathcal{H}_i^2 \tag{2}$$

For systems with more than one qubit, one verifies the existence of *non-separable states*, i.e. states that cannot be written as states of individual qubits, as for instance in the following *Bell* state: $|\Phi\rangle = \frac{1}{\sqrt{2}}(|00\rangle + |11\rangle)$. The latter is the mathematical expression of the so-called physical phenomenon of *entanglement.*

2.2 Transitions (programs)

In quantum mechanics, transitions preserve *unitarity* of states. Hence, programs correspond to *unitary* operators ($U.U^\dagger = I$). For a quantum system with n qubits the *signature* of the transition operators reads as follows:

$$U^{\otimes n} : \mathcal{H}^{2\otimes n} \rightarrow \mathcal{H}^{2\otimes n}$$

In quantum computation practice, a rather less *abstract* notion is used, the so-called *quantum circuits* [Deu89], where unitary operators are approximated by compositions of *primitive unitary operators*, such as the H, X, Y, or Z gates.

2.3 Acceptance States

Measurements, (mathematically $Proj_\varphi, or\,|\varphi\rangle\langle\varphi|$), can be interpreted as a method that causes the *collapse* of *superposition* states to elements of an *orthogonal basis*, (e.g. in the qubit case $|0\rangle$ and $|1\rangle$). An acceptance state is one where the correct output is obtained upon measurement, with probability[1] greater than α.

[1] The probability of obtaining φ in a measurement is $\langle s|Proj_\varphi s\rangle$ where s is a state and $\langle .|.\rangle$ is the internal product of the *Hilbert* space. In equation (1), $|\alpha|^2$ and $|\beta|^2$, are the probabilities of obtaining $|0\rangle$ and $|1\rangle$, which is 0.5 in both cases: $(\left(\frac{1}{\sqrt{2}}\right)^2 = 0.5)$.

3 A Dynamic Logic for QASM

The QASM programming language is not a *pure* quantum programming language as it involves, *measurements*, which possess a probabilistic nature, and classical flow instructions depending on those measurements, requiring the handling of probabilistic and quantum programs. Our approach to this problem is somehow inspired in the fusion of works of Baltag and Smets [BS04, BBK+14] for the quantum part and of Kozen [Koz85, Koz81] for the probabilistic part.

3.1 Syntax

As usual in dynamic logic, the syntax is divided into two layers: one of the *programs* and one of the *formulas*. The program's layer encompasses a fragment of the QASM language, which includes the classical control instructions (*if statements*, creation of *classical* and *quantum* registers, and *measurements* of quantum registers), as well as several standard unitary operations (x, z, h and cnot gates) (Fig. 2).

$\langle argument \rangle$ ::= id | id [index]

$\langle test \rangle$ ::= $\langle argument \rangle$ == $\langle natural\ number \rangle$

$\langle \pi_q \rangle$ ::= x qreg_id [index] | z qreg_id [index] | h qreg_id [index]
| cx qreg_id [index], qreg_id [index] (**unitary gates**)
| **measure** qreg_id → creg_id (**measurements**)
| $\pi_q; \pi_q$

$\langle \pi \rangle$ ::= **creg** id [size] | **qreg** id [size] (**creation of registers**)
| **if** $\langle test \rangle$ **then** π_q (**if statements**)
| $\pi;\pi$

$\langle p \rangle$ ::= $\perp \mid \underline{0} \mid \underline{1} \mid p^{register}_{index}$

$\langle \varphi \rangle$ ::= $(p, f_{\langle test \rangle} = g) \mid P^{\geq r}\varphi \mid \langle \pi \rangle \varphi \mid \neg\varphi \mid \varphi \vee \varphi \mid \varphi \wedge \varphi$

Fig. 2. Formulas layer and programs layer

On the formula side, atomic propositions are pairs $(p, f_{\langle test \rangle} = g_{\langle test \rangle})$ where p corresponds to quantum propositions over qubit states and $f_{\langle test \rangle} = g$ corresponds to equality expressions over *the probability distributions* definable on the possible tests over classical variables. On the quantum side $\underline{0}$ and $\underline{1}$ denote that 0 or 1 are true upon measurement with 1 as probability, and the $p^{register}_{index}$ *narrows* a proposition range to a specific register and qubit, as for instance $\underline{0}^q_0$, which means that qubit 0 of register q has value 0. The $P^{\geq r}\varphi$ modality establishes restrictions to the probability of propositions for instance $P^{=0.5}p$. The $\langle \pi \rangle$ has the usual meaning of "the proposition φ *may* hold upon the execution of program π" and the usual *minimal* set of Boolean connectives is included.

3.2 Semantics

The semantics of this logic is given in terms of a *Labelled transition system* [HM80], defined by a *tuple*:

$$M = (\mathcal{G}, [\![.]\!] : \mathcal{A}_p \cup \mathcal{A}_\pi \rightarrow 2^{\mathcal{G}} \cup \mathcal{G} \times \mathcal{G}) \tag{3}$$

where $\mathcal{G}$ is a set of states and $[\![.]\!]$ a *meaning* function, from the type of the *well-formed* syntactic expressions of propositions ($\mathcal{A}_p$) and programs ($\mathcal{A}_\pi$), to the *powerset*, and *Cartesian product* of the set of states, respectively.

3.3 The State Space

A state of a program in the *QASM* language is defined by its classical and quantum components. Each of such components is divided into one or many *independent* registers, each composed of a set of quantum or classical bits, resulting in the following state space:

$$\underbrace{\underbrace{\mathcal{H}^2 \otimes \ldots \otimes \mathcal{H}^2}_{\text{quantum register}} \times \ldots}_{\mathcal{S}} \times \underbrace{\underbrace{\{0,1\} \times \ldots \times \{0,1\}}_{\text{classical register}} \times \ldots}_{\mathcal{C}} \tag{4}$$

On the classic side, we work on a probabilistic setting, due to the existence of quantum measurements, which work as *random assignments*. Thus, the set of possible states corresponds to the distributions definable on the tests[2] over the classical variables. Therefore, a distribution is given by a *measure* [Koz85] from the set of *tests* to the probability interval $[0,1]$:

$$\mu_s : 2^{\mathcal{C}} \rightarrow [0,1]$$

However, the actual state in this logic is defined the equality operator over two *measures*, so an actual state is characterized as a function with *signature*:

$$\mu_s : 2^{\mathcal{C}} \times 2^{\mathcal{C}} \rightarrow \{0,1\}$$

In conclusion the state space of a QASM program is given by the Cartesian product of the possible states of the independent quantum and classical registers, denoted *Registers*, where in the former the set of states is given by the *tensor product* of quantum bits, and in the latter by the possible distributions definable over the configurations of the classical *bits*.

$$\mathcal{G} \equiv \prod_{\text{quantum register} \in Registers} \bigotimes \mathcal{H}^{2^{\otimes reg\_size}} \times \prod_{\text{classical register} \in Registers} 2^{2^{\mathcal{C}} \times 2^{\mathcal{C}}}$$

[2] Tests correspond to the σ-algebra over the valuation set $\mathcal{C}$. For valuations with a discrete domain, it corresponds to the powerset $2^{\mathcal{C}}$. Tests form a *Boolean* algebra.

3.4 Propositions

As seen in Sect. 3.1, propositions correspond to a pair of quantum and classical propositions, where quantum propositions are of type $2^{\mathcal{S}}$, the *powerset* of the quantum state space, and the probabilistic propositions of the type $2^{\mathcal{C}\times\mathcal{C}}$, the pairs of *fuzzy predicates*[3] definable on the state space $2^{\mathcal{C}\times\mathcal{C}}$. Therefore, the type of the global propositions reads as follows:

$$p : 2^{\mathcal{S}} \times \left(2^{\mathcal{C}\times\mathcal{C}}\right)$$

Definition 1. *Semantics for proposition constructors.*

We define $proj_q$ as the quantum part of a proposition, and $proj_p$ as the probabilistic part of the proposition.

i. $[[\underline{1}]] = \{s | \langle s | Proj_{\underline{1}} s\rangle = 1\}$. *Similarly for* $[[\underline{0}]]$.
$[[\bot]] - \emptyset$.
$[[p_{index}^{register}]$ - *The set where the proposition p, restricted to a register and a specific qubit index, holds.*

ii. $[\![(p, f = g)]\!] = \{s | s \in [\![p]\!] \wedge f(proj_p(s)) = g(proj_p(s))\}$ *and* $proj_p(s) \in \mathcal{C}$.

iii. $[\![P^{\geq r}\varphi]\!] = \{s | \langle s \mid Proj_{proj_q\varphi} s\rangle \geq r\}$.
The set of states where quantum proposition component φ holds with probability greater than r.

iv. $[\![\varphi_1 \wedge \varphi_2]\!] = \{s | s \in [\![proj_q(\varphi_1) \cap proj_q(\varphi_2)]\!] \wedge s \in [\![proj_p(\varphi_1) \cap proj_p(\varphi_2)]\!]\}$

v. $[\![\varphi_1 \vee \varphi_2]\!] = \{s | s \in [\![proj_q(\varphi_1) \cup proj_q(\varphi_2)]\!] \wedge s \in [\![proj_p(\varphi_1) \cup proj_p(\varphi_2)]\!]\}$

vi. $[\![\neg\varphi]\!] = \{s | s \notin [\![proj_q \varphi]\!] \wedge s \notin [\![proj_p \varphi]\!]\}$

vii. $[\![\langle\pi\rangle\,\varphi]\!] = \{s | \exists u : (s, u) \in [\![\pi]\!] \wedge u \in [\![\varphi]\!]\}$
The set of states where the proposition φ holds upon the execution of program π.

3.5 Program Semantics

Programs in this logic correspond to deterministic relations between states:

$$[\![\cdot]\!] : \mathcal{A}_\pi \to \mathcal{G} \times \mathcal{G} \tag{5}$$

This function denotes an *accessibility relation*, i.e. *directed* valid transitions between pairs of states (source to output), under the action of a given program.

---

[3] A *fuzzy predicate* corresponds to a *measurable function* [Koz85] from the set of states to the probability interval $[0, 1]$, in this case, $\mathcal{C} \to [0, 1]$. The *fuzzy predicate* is characteristic of a test.

Definition 2. *Semantics for programs (accessibility relation)*

$p \in 2^{S}$ - *any quantum proposition*
$\alpha \in 2^{C \times C}$ - *any probabilistic proposition* ($f_{\langle test \rangle} = g$).

(n) Creation of registers (upon a register is created its value is necessarily 0, both for quantum and the probabilistic parts):
$[\![creg\ reg\_id\ [size]]\!] = \{(s,u) | s \in [\![(p, \perp_{reg\_id})]\!] \wedge u \in [\![(p, f_{reg\_id=0}(u) = 1)]\!]\}$
$[\![qreg\ reg\_id\ [size]]\!] = \{(s,u) | s \in [\![(\perp_{reg\_id}, \alpha)]\!] \wedge u \in [\![\left(\underline{0}^{reg\_id}_{0..size-1}, \alpha\right)]\!]\}$.
Pairs of states where $\perp$ *holds in the source state and 0 in the output state.*
(h) Hadamard operator:

$$
\begin{aligned}
&[\![h\ reg\_id\ [index]]\!] = \\
&\quad \{(s,u) | s \in [\![\left((Pr^{=p_i} p) \wedge \underline{0}^{reg\_id}_{index}, \alpha\right)]\!] \vee s \in [\![\left((Pr^{=p_i} p) \wedge \underline{1}^{reg\_id}_{index}, \alpha\right)]\!] \\
&\quad \wedge u \in [\![\left(Pr^{=p_i*0.5}(p \wedge \underline{0}^{reg\_id}_{index}) \wedge Pr^{=p_i*0.5}(p \wedge \underline{1}^{reg\_id}_{index}), \alpha\right)]\!]\} \\
&\quad \cup \{(s,u) | s \in [\![\left(Pr^{=p_i*0.5}(p \wedge \underline{0}^{reg\_id}_{index}) \wedge Pr^{=p_i*0.5}(p \wedge \underline{1}^{reg\_id}_{index}), \alpha\right)]\!] \wedge \\
&\quad (u \in [\![\left((Pr^{=p_i} p) \wedge \underline{0}^{reg\_id}_{index}, \alpha\right)]\!] \vee u \in [\![\left((Pr^{=p_i} p) \wedge \underline{1}^{reg\_id}_{index}, \alpha\right)]\!])\}
\end{aligned}
$$

Pairs of states defined by either 0 *or* 1 *on the source state and a superposition of* 0 *and* 1 *in the output state, or* vice-versa.
(x) X operator:

$$
\begin{aligned}
&[\![x\ reg\_id\ [index]]\!] = \{(s,u) | s \in [\![\left(p \wedge \underline{1}^{reg\_id}_{index}, \alpha\right)]\!] \wedge u \in [\![\left(p \wedge \underline{0}^{reg\_id}_{index}, \alpha\right)]\!] \\
&\quad \vee s \in [\![\left(p \wedge \underline{0}^{reg\_id}_{index}, \alpha\right)]\!] \wedge u \in [\![\left(p \wedge \underline{1}^{reg\_id}_{index}, \alpha\right)]\!]\}
\end{aligned}
$$

Pairs of states where 0 *holds in the source state and* 1 *in the output state, or* vice-versa *(same effect as a classical not gate).*
(m) Measure:

$$
\begin{aligned}
&[\![measure\ qreg\_id \rightarrow\ creg\_id]\!] \\
&\quad = \{(s,u) | s \in [\![\left(\bigwedge_{i}^{2^{size}} P^{=p_i} \underline{i}, \mathcal{D}_{creg\_id}(\bigwedge_{i} f_{creg\_id==i})\right)]\!] \\
&\quad \wedge u \in [\![\left(\bigvee_{i} i, \bigwedge_{i} f_{creg\_id==i}(u) == p_i\right)]\!]\}
\end{aligned}
$$

Pairs of states where the probability distribution of the valuations of a set of qubits in the source state, is the same as the verified in a set of classical bits in the output state, where $\mathcal{D}_{creg\_id}$ *denotes a distribution* compatible upon measurement *with* $\bigwedge_{i} f_{creg\_id==i}$ ($\{d | meas \circ d = f\}$ *where* $\circ$ *is the* Lebesgue integral*)*

(;) Sequence
$[\![\pi_1; \pi_2]\!] = \{(s,u) | \exists t (s,t) \in [\![\pi_1]\!] \wedge (t,u) \in [\![\pi_2]\!]\}$

4 An Example: A Quantum Coin Tossing Program

This section, illustrates the logic through the proof of correctness of a *simple* quantum program for *quantum coin tossing* (prepare a qubit in a superposition state and measure it, obtaining 0 or 1 with equal probability), which translates into the following QASM program:

```
OPENQASM 2.0;
include "qelib1.inc";
qreg q[1];
creg c[1];
h q[0];
measure q[0] -> c[0];
```

The correctness of such program implies the following post-condition:

$$\left(\underline{0}_0^q \vee \underline{1}_0^q, f_{\langle c[0]==1\rangle}(x) = 0.5 \wedge f_{\langle c[0]==0\rangle}(x) = 0.5\right) \text{ with } x \in \mathcal{C} \quad (6)$$

where $\underline{0} \vee \underline{1}$ denotes the quantum qubit q has either, mutually exclusively, the values 0 or 1, and $\mathcal{C} = \{0, 1\}$. The fact that post-condition (6) holds upon the execution of the program qreg q[1]; creg c[1]; h q[0]; measure q[0] $\rightarrow$ c[0] is expressed through the following formula:

$$\langle \text{qreg q[1]; creg c[1]; h q[0]; measure q[0]} \rightarrow \text{c[0]}\rangle$$
$$\left(\underline{0}_0^q \vee \underline{1}_0^q, f_{\langle c[0]==1\rangle}(x) = 0.5\right) \wedge \left(\underline{0}_0^q \vee \underline{1}_0^q, f_{\langle c[0]==0\rangle}(x) = 0.5\right) \text{ with } x \in \mathcal{C}$$

This is proved by the rules of Definition 2:

Proof.

$$[\![\langle \text{qreg q[1]; creg c[1]; h q[0]; measure q[0]} \rightarrow \text{c[0]}\rangle$$
$$\left(\underline{0}_0^q \vee \underline{1}_0^q, f_{\langle c[0]==1\rangle}(x) = 0.5 \wedge f_{\langle c[0]==0\rangle}(x) = 0.5\right)]\!]$$
$$=$$
$$\{s | \exists u : (s, u) \in [\![\text{qreg q[1]; creg c[1]; h q[0]; measure q[0]} \rightarrow \text{c[0]}]\!]$$
$$\wedge\, u \in [\![\left(\underline{0}_0^q \vee \underline{1}_0^q, f_{\langle c[0]==1\rangle}(proj_p(u)) = 0.5 \wedge f_{\langle c[0]==0\rangle}(proj_p(u)) = 0.5\right)]\!]\}$$
$$\text{with } proj_p(u) \in \mathcal{C}$$
$$= \text{ (use of the (;) rule)}$$
$$\{s | \exists u : \exists t : (s, t) \in [\![\text{qreg q[1]; creg c[1]; h q[0]}]\!] \wedge (t, u) \in [\![\text{measure q[0]} \rightarrow \text{c[0]}]\!]$$
$$\wedge\, u \in [\![\left(\underline{0}_0^q \vee \underline{1}_0^q, f_{\langle c[0]==1\rangle}(proj_p(u)) == 0.5 \wedge f_{\langle c[0]==0\rangle}(proj_p(u)) = 0.5\right)]\!]\}$$
$$= \text{ (use of the (m) rule)}$$
$$\{s | \exists u : \exists t : (s, t) \in [\![\text{qreg q[1]; creg c[1]; h q[0]}]\!]$$
$$\wedge\, t \in [\![\left(P^{=0.5}\underline{0}_0^q, P^{=0.5}\underline{1}_0^q, \mathcal{D}_c(f_{\langle c[0]==0\rangle} \wedge f_{\langle c[0]==1\rangle})\right)]\!]$$

$\wedge u \in [\![(\underline{0}_0^q \vee \underline{1}_0^q, f_{\langle c[0]==1\rangle}(proj_p(u)) == 0.5 \wedge f_{\langle c[0]==0\rangle}(proj_p(u)) = 0.5)]\!]\}$

$=$ (use of (;) and (h). u can be eliminated because $u \in [\![...]\!]$ is true)

$\{s|\exists t : \exists t' : (s, t') \in [\![\text{qreg q[1]; creg c[1]}]\!]$

$\wedge \left(t' \in [\![(\underline{0}_0^q, \mathcal{D}_c(f_{\langle c[0]==0\rangle} \wedge f_{\langle c[0]==1\rangle}))]\!] \vee t' \in [\![(\underline{1}_0^q, \mathcal{D}_c(f_{\langle c[0]==0\rangle} \wedge f_{\langle c[0]==1\rangle}))]\!]\right)$

$\wedge t \in [\![(P^{=0.5}\underline{0}_0^q, P^{=0.5}\underline{1}_0^q, \mathcal{D}_c(f_{\langle c[0]==0\rangle} \wedge f_{\langle c[0]==1\rangle}))]\!]\}$

$=$ (use of (;) and (nreg) rules. t can be eliminated because $t \in [\![...]\!]$ is true)

$\{s|\exists t' : \exists t'' : (s, t'') \in [\![\text{qreg q[1]}]\!] \wedge t'' \in [\![(\underline{0}_0^q, \perp_c)]\!]$

$\wedge \left(t' \in [\![(\underline{0}_0^q, \mathcal{D}_c(f_{\langle c[0]==0\rangle} \wedge f_{\langle c[0]==1\rangle}))]\!] \vee t' \in [\![(\underline{1}_0^q, \mathcal{D}_c(f_{\langle c[0]==0\rangle} \wedge f_{\langle c[0]==1\rangle}))]\!]\right)\}$

$=$ (use of (;) and (nreg). t' can be eliminated because $t' \in [\![...]\!]$ is true)

$\{s| : \exists t'' : s \in [\![(\perp^q, \perp^c)]\!] \wedge t'' \in [\![(0_0^q, \perp^c)]\!]\}$

$=$ (t" can be eliminated because $t'' \in [\![...]\!]$ is true)

$\{s|s \in [\![(\perp^q, \perp^c)]\!]\}$ where s is valid state, finishing the proof. □

5 Conclusions

The paper defined a dynamic logic for a fragment of QASM, combining existent works on dynamic logics for quantum and probabilistic programs and we proved the correctness of a quantum coin toss. However, the logic is still work in progress, being necessary the extension to other examples.

Acknowledgements. The author wishes to thank Luís Barbosa and Leandro Gomes, for the useful discussions during the course of this work. The author was funded by an individual grant of reference SFRH/BD/116367/2016, conceded by the FCT - Fundação para a Ciência e Tecnologia under the POCH programme and MCTES national funds. This work was also supported by the KLEE project(POCI-01-0145-FEDER-030947-PTDC/CCI-COM/30947/2017), funded by ERDF by the Operational Programme for Competitiveness and Internationalisation, COMPETE2020 Programme and by National Funds through the Portuguese funding agency, FCT.

References

[BBK+14] Baltag, A., Bergfeld, J., Kishida, K., Sack, J., Smets, S., Zhong, S.: PLQP & company: decidable logics for quantum algorithms. Int. J. Theor. Phys. **53**(10), 3628–3647 (2014)

[BS04] Baltag, A., Smets, S.: The logic of quantum programs. In: Proceedings of the 2nd International Workshop on Quantum Programming Languages, pp. 39–56 (2004). https://www.mathstat.dal.ca/~selinger/qpl2004/proceedings.html

[CBSG17] Cross, A.W., Bishop, L.S., Smolin, J.A., Gambetta, J.M.: Open quantum assembly language. arXiv preprint arXiv:1707.03429 (2017)

[Deu85] Deutsch, D.: Quantum theory, the Church-Turing principle and the universal quantum computer. Proc. Roy. Soc. Lond. A. Math. Phys. Sci. **400**(1818), 97–117 (1985)

[Deu89] Deutsch, D.E.: Quantum computational networks. Proc. Roy. Soc. Lond. A. Math. Phys. Sci. **425**(1868), 73–90 (1989)

[HM80] Hennessy, M., Milner, R.: On observing nondeterminism and concurrency. In: de Bakker, J., van Leeuwen, J. (eds.) ICALP 1980. LNCS, vol. 85, pp. 299–309. Springer, Heidelberg (1980). https://doi.org/10.1007/3-540-10003-2_79

[ibm18] IBM Q - quantum computing, June 2018. https://www.research.ibm.com/ibm-q/

[Koz81] Kozen, D.: Semantics of probabilistic programs. J. Comput. Syst. Sci. **22**(3), 328–350 (1981)

[Koz85] Kozen, D.: A probabilistic PDL. J. Comput. Syst. Sci. **30**(2), 162–178 (1985)

[NC02] Nielsen, M.A., Chuang, I.: Quantum computation and quantum information (2002)

On the Construction of Multi-valued Concurrent Dynamic Logics

Leandro Gomes(✉)

HASLab INESC TEC, Univ. Minho, Braga, Portugal
leandro.r.gomes@inesctec.pt

Abstract. Dynamic logic is a powerful framework for reasoning about imperative programs. An extension with a concurrent operator, called concurrent propositional dynamic logic (CPDL) [20], was introduced to formalise programs running in parallel. In a different direction, other authors proposed a systematic method for generating multi-valued propositional dynamic logics to reason about weighted programs [15]. This paper presents the first step of combining these two frameworks to introduce uncertainty in concurrent computations. In the proposed framework, a weight is assigned to each branch of the parallel execution, resulting in a (possible) asymmetric parallelism, inherent to the fuzzy programming paradigm [2,23]. By adopting such an approach, a family of logics is obtained, called *multi-valued concurrent propositional dynamic logics* ($\mathcal{GCDL}(\mathbf{A})$), parametric on an action lattice $\mathbf{A}$ specifying a notion of "weight" assigned to program execution. Additionally, the validity of some axioms of CPDL is discussed in the new family of generated logics.

1 Introduction

Over time, the different variants of dynamic logics developed in different verification communities went hand-in-hand with the very notion of its object, the *program*. This resulted in a diverse myriad of dynamic logics tailored to specific programming paradigms. Examples include probabilistic [12], concurrent [20], quantum [1] and continuous [21] computations, and combinations thereof. An example of another non-trivial paradigm is the fuzzy one [2,23], where the execution of a program differs from both classical and probabilistic scenarios: a conditional statement is interpreted as a concurrent execution with a weight associated to each branch. The formalisation of this sort of behaviour entails the need to address both concurrency and uncertainty. An extensive research can be found in the literature on diverse formalisms to reason about programs running in parallel [10,11] and to deal with uncertainty [4,5,12,22]. However, even when

This work was founded by the ERDF—European Regional Development Fund through the Operational Programme for Competitiveness and Internationalisation - COMPETE 2020 Programme and by National Funds through the Portuguese funding agency, FCT - Fundação para a Ciência e a Tecnologia, within project POCI-01-0145-FEDER-030947.

L. Soares Barbosa and A. Baltag (Eds.): DaLí 2019, LNCS 12005, pp. 218–226, 2020.
https://doi.org/10.1007/978-3-030-38808-9_14

these two components are combined into a single framework [18], the emerging paradigm is probabilistic nondeterminism. Thus we are still missing a proper semantics to describe the behaviour of the fuzzy paradigm.

Reference [15] initiated a research agenda on the systematic development of multi-valued propositional dynamic logics, parametric on an action lattice, which defines both the computational paradigm where programs live, and the truth space where assertions are evaluated. Following another research line, an extension to propositional dynamic logic (PDL) was introduced in reference [20], called *concurrent propositional dynamic logic (CPDL)*, to reason about concurrent computations. In the models of this logic, the programs are interpreted as *binary multirelations*, to describe a parallel execution from a state to a set of states.

Combining these two research lines, this paper takes a first step on the development of a method to generate multi-valued concurrent propositional dynamic logics. As in [15], the logics are parametric on a generic action lattice, to model both the computational domain and a (possible graded) truth space where the assertions about programs are evaluated. First, the semantics of CPDL is adapted to model programs as weighted parallel executions, by introducing the concept of *fuzzy multirelations*. This means that a program is interpreted as a relation between a state and a fuzzy set of states. The intuition is that the weights of the fuzzy set describe an execution probability for each branch of the program, an asymmetric parallel flow or the energy/costs associated to each branch. Then, on a second stage, a method of generating (parametric) multi-valued CPDL is presented. The family of the resulting logics is called $\mathcal{GCDL}(\mathbf{A})$.

This paper is organised as follows. Section 2 presents a brief background overview. Then, Sect. 3 introduces fuzzy multirelations and defines some operations on them. Such an algebra is the mathematical formalism in which programs are interpreted in the generated logics. The same section ends with the study of an axiomatisation for the generated logics. Finally, Sect. 4 concludes and enumerates topics for future work.

2 Preliminaries

2.1 Semantics for Concurrency

The semantics of CPDL is based on the concept of *binary multirelation*. The relevant definition and some operators are recalled below.

Definition 1 (Binary multirelation [7]**).** *Given a set X, a binary multirelation is a subset of the cartesian product $X \times 2^X$, i.e. a set of ordered pairs (a, A), where $a \in X$ and $A \subseteq X$. The following operations over multirelations are defined:*

- *$R \cup S$ as the union of R and S;*
- *the* Peleg sequential composition

$$R \cdot S = \left\{(a, A) \mid \exists B.(a, B) \in R \wedge \exists f.(\forall b \in B.(b, f(b)) \in S) \wedge A = \bigcup f(B)\right\};$$

– *the* parallel composition $R \cap S = \{(a, A \cup B) \mid (a, A) \in R \wedge (a, B) \in S\}$.

Note that the union of binary multirelations is just the set union. The sequential composition operator is rather more complex. A pair (a, A) belongs to the sequential composition of multirelations R and S if and only if a is related with some intermediate set of states B and every $b \in B$ must be related with some subset of A such that the union of all those subsets is A. Finally, an element $(a, A) \in R \cap S$ indicates a parallel execution of a program from a state a to a set of states in A, "combining" the arriving states of R and S into A. Note that such composition is dual to $R \cup S$, where (a, B) and (a, C) correspond to distinct executions. The first kind of choice in commonly called *demonic*, while the latter is known as *angelic* [17]. Angelic nondeterminism represents achoice made by an 'angel', an thus, it occurs when the best possible choice is made. Demonic nondeterminism represents a choice made by a 'demon', i.e. the worst case scenario.

2.2 Concurrent Propositional Dynamic Logic

Concurrent propositional dynamic logic (CPDL), as introduced in [20], is an extension of PDL with a parallel operator $\cap$ added to the syntax of programs. The semantics interprets programs as binary multirelations $R \subseteq W \times 2^W$, where composed programs are interpreted according to Definition 1. Intuitively, an element (a, A) of a binary multirelation expresses that the a program executed from a state a ends in all states of A in parallel. Models of CPDL consist of tuples $(W, V, [\![-]\!])$ where W is a set of states, V is a valuation function which attributes a subset of W to each atomic formula, and $[\![-]\!]$ attributes a subset of $W \times 2^W$ to each atomic program. For instance, the formula $\langle\pi\rangle\rho$ holds in a state w if and only if $\exists U \subseteq W$ such that $(s, U) \in [\![\pi]\!]$ and $U \in V(\rho)$. For more details about the semantics of CPDL see [20]. The axiom system of CPDL is that of PDL with the additional axiom $\langle\pi_1 \cap \pi_2\rangle\rho \equiv \langle\pi_1\rangle\rho \wedge \langle\pi_2\rangle\rho$ and restricting $\langle\pi_0\rangle(\rho \vee \rho') \equiv \langle\pi_0\rangle \vee \langle\pi_0\rangle\rho'$ to atomic programs.

2.3 Parametric Construction of Multi-valued Dynamic Logics

Thus subsection provides a short review of the 'dynamisation' method introduced in [15]. Let us start by revisiting the following definition:

Definition 2 ([13]). *An* action lattice *is a tuple* $\mathbf{A} = (A, +, ;, 0, 1, *, \rightarrow, \cdot)$, *that is a residuated lattice with order* $\leq$ *induced by* $+$*:* $a \leq b$ *if and only if* $a + b = b$, *plus the axioms* $1 + a + (a^*; a^*) \leq a^*$ *and* $(x \rightarrow x)^* = x \rightarrow x$.

An action lattice is called a $\mathbb{I}$-*action lattice* when the identity of the ; operator coincides with the greatest element of the residuated lattice, i.e. $1 = \top$. Moreover, an action lattice $\mathbf{A}$ is complete when every subset of $\mathbf{A}$ has both supremum and infimum. Since operators $+$ and ; are associative and have identity, we can generalise them to n-ary operators and use the notation $\sum$ and $\prod$ to represent their iterated versions, respectively. The generation of dynamic logics illustrated in the Sect. 3 will be parametric on the class of complete action lattices, since completeness is required to ensure the existence of arbitrary suprema. The general construction of multi-valued dynamic logics is revisited bellow.

Signatures. Signatures of $\mathcal{GDL}(\mathbf{A})$ are pairs (Π, Prop) corresponding to the denotations of atomic programs and propositions, respectively.

Formulæ. The *set of programs*, denoted by $\text{Prg}(\Pi)$, contains all expressions generated by $\pi \ni \pi_0 \mid \pi;\pi \mid \pi + \pi \mid \pi^*$ for $\pi_0 \in \Pi$. Given a signature (Π, Prop), the $\mathcal{GDL}(\mathbf{A})$-formulæ for (Π, Prop) are the ones generated by the grammar $\rho \ni \top \mid \bot \mid p \mid \rho \vee \rho \mid \rho \wedge \rho \mid \rho \to \rho \mid \rho \leftrightarrow \rho \mid \langle\pi\rangle\rho \mid [\pi]\rho$ for $p \in \text{Prop}$ and $\pi \in \text{Prg}(\Pi)$.

Semantics. The space where the computations of $\mathcal{GDL}(\mathbf{A})$ are interpreted is given by the algebra $\mathbb{M}_n(\mathbf{A}) = (M_n(\mathbf{A}), +, ;, \mathbf{0}, \mathbf{1}, ^*)$ where $M_n(\mathbf{A})$ is the space of $(n \times n)$-matrices over $\mathbf{A}$, the operators $+$, ; are the usual matrix sum and multiplication, respectively, $\mathbf{0}$, $\mathbf{1}$ are the zero and the identity matrices, respectively, and * is the operator defined as in [3,14]. The matrix representation of a program expresses, for each pair of states s, s', the weight (e.g. probability, cost, uncertainty) of the program going from s to s'.

$\mathcal{GDL}(\mathbf{A})$-models for a signature (Prop, Π), denoted by $\text{Mod}^{\mathcal{GDL}(\mathbf{A})}(\Pi, \text{Prop})$, consists of tuples $\mathcal{A} = (W, V, (\mathcal{A}_\pi)_{\pi \in \Pi})$ where W is a finite set (of states), $V : \text{Prop} \times W \to A$ is a valuation function, and $\mathcal{A}_\pi \in M_n(\mathbf{A})$, with n standing for the cardinality of W.

The interpretation of a program $\pi \in \text{Prg}(\Pi)$ in a model $\mathcal{A} \in \text{Mod}^{\mathcal{GDL}(\mathbf{A})}(\Pi, \text{Prop})$ is recursively defined, from the set of atomic programs $(\mathcal{A}_\pi)_{\pi \in \Pi}$, as $\mathcal{A}_{\pi;\pi'} = \mathcal{A}_\pi \,;\, \mathcal{A}_{\pi'}$, $\mathcal{A}_{\pi+\pi'} = \mathcal{A}_\pi + \mathcal{A}_{\pi'}$ and $\mathcal{A}_{\pi^*} = \mathcal{A}_\pi^*$.

Satisfaction. The (graded) satisfaction relation, for a model $\mathcal{A} \in \text{Mod}^{\mathcal{GDL}(\mathbf{A})}(\Pi, \text{Prop})$, with $\mathbf{A}$ complete, consists of a function $\models : W \times \text{Fm}^{\Gamma(\mathbf{A})}(\Pi, \text{Prop}) \to A$ recursively defined as follows:

- $(w \models \top) = \top$
- $(w \models \bot) = \bot$
- $(w \models p) = V(p, w)$, for any $p \in \text{Prop}$
- $(w \models \rho \wedge \rho') = (w \models \rho) \cdot (w \models \rho')$
- $(w \models \rho \vee \rho') = (w \models \rho) + (w \models \rho')$
- $(w \models \rho \to \rho') = (w \models \rho) \to (w \models \rho')$
- $(w \models \rho \leftrightarrow \rho') = (w \models \rho \to \rho'); (w \models \rho' \to \rho)$
- $(w \models \langle\pi\rangle\rho) = \sum_{w' \in W} (\mathcal{A}_\pi(w, w'); (w' \models \rho))$
- $(w \models [\pi]\rho) = \prod_{w' \in W} (\mathcal{A}_\pi(w, w') \to (w' \models \rho))$

The (graded) satisfaction in a state gives the degree of certainty of a formula in such a state. For instance $M, w \models \langle\pi\rangle\rho$ is the degree of confidence on the verification of ρ on the execution of π. It is relevant to note that $\mathcal{GDL}(\mathbf{A})$ is a generalisation of PDL, for each action lattice **A**. In particular, by considering the Boolean lattice, the generated logic $\mathcal{GDL}(\mathbf{2})$ coincides with PDL.

3 Multi-valued Concurrent Dynamic Logic

Before presenting the construction of the logic, we introduce the mathematical formalism to define the model where programs will be interpreted.

3.1 Fuzzy Binary Multirelations

Definition 3 (Fuzzy set and fuzzy relation [24]**).** *Given a set X and a complete residuated lattice* **L**, *a* fuzzy subset *of X is a function $\phi : X \to L$. $\phi(x)$, defines the* membership degree of x in ϕ. *The set of all fuzzy subsets of X is denote as L^X. The support of ϕ is a fuzzy subset ψ such that $\psi(x) > 0$, $\forall x \in X$. Given sets X, Y, a* fuzzy binary relation *over X, Y is a function $\mu : X \times Y \to L$. $\mu(x, y)$ is interpreted as the truth value of how elements x, y are related by μ.*

Since an action lattice is an extension of a residuated lattice, the concepts of both fuzzy set and fuzzy relation can be defined as well for the former. Such is the case for all the remaining formalisms introduced in this paper.

Definition 4 (Fuzzy binary multirelation). *Given a set X and a complete action lattice* **A** *over carrier A, a* fuzzy binary multirelation *R over X is a set $R \subseteq X \times A^X$. The following operations for fuzzy binary multirelations are defined:*

- *$R \cup S$ as the union of R and S;*
- $R \cdot S = \Big\{(a, \phi) \mid \phi(c) = \sum_{(a,\phi_a)\in R} \Big(\prod_{(b,\phi_b)\in S} \phi_a(b); \phi_b(c)\Big)\Big\}$
- *$R \cap S = \{(a, \phi_R \cup \phi_S) \mid (a, \phi_R) \in R$ and $(a, \phi_S) \in S\}$, where $\phi_R \cup \phi_S$ is the union of fuzzy sets ϕ_R and ϕ_s, as defined in [24];*
- *$R^* = \bigcup\{R^n : n \geq 0\}$.*

We denote by $M(X)$ the set of all fuzzy binary multirelations over X.

Note, particularly, how this definition generalises the concept of binary multirelations, replacing 2 (of Definition 1) by **A**. This structure supports a set of truth values beyond the Boolean. Therefore, a program is modelled by an execution with multiple "arrows" leaving a state into a set of states in parallel, with a (possible different) fuzziness degree associated with each "arrow". Note that if **A** is the Boolean lattice **2**, any fuzzy binary multirelation $R \subseteq X \times \mathbf{2}^X$ is a binary multirelation. Since the goal is still to model programs as binary input-output relations, only the binary case is considered, and thus the remaining of this paper refers to fuzzy binary multirelations simply as fuzzy multirelations. Another aspect that is relevant for the formalisation of the logics is the restriction to fuzzy multirelations $R \subseteq X \times A^X$ where the fuzzy set ϕ in A^X is defined such that $\phi(x) > 0$, $\forall x \in X$.

The operations on fuzzy multirelations somehow mimic the classic case. Clearly operator $\cup$ corresponds to the classical set union. For the sequential composition, the expression for ϕ computes the weight of an execution that starts in a state a, arrives at a set of intermediate states ϕ_a and ends in a set of states φ_b. The parallel composition considers the union of fuzzy sets for computing the external choice, which is just a generalisation of set union used in CPDL.

3.2 Parametric Construction of Multi-valued Concurrent Dynamic Logics

Each complete action lattice $\mathbf{A}$ induces a multi-valued concurrent propositional dynamic logic $\mathcal{GCDL}(\mathbf{A})$, with weighted computations interpreted over $\mathbf{A}$. Its signature, formulæ, semantics and satisfaction relation are presented below.

Signatures. Signatures of $\mathcal{GCDL}(\mathbf{A})$ are pairs (Π, Prop) corresponding to the denotations of atomic programs and propositions, respectively.

Formulæ. The *set of programs*, denoted by $\text{Prg}(\Pi)$, consists of all expressions generated by $\pi \ni \pi_0 \,|\, \pi;\pi \,|\, \pi \cap \pi \,|\, \pi + \pi \,|\, \pi^*$, for $\pi_0 \in \Pi$. Given a signature (Π, Prop), the $\mathcal{GCDL}(\mathbf{A})$-formulæ for (Π, Prop), denoted by $\text{Fm}^{\Gamma(\mathbf{A})}(\Pi, \text{Prop})$, are the ones generated by the grammar $\rho \ni \top \,|\, \bot \,|\, p \,|\, \rho \vee \rho \,|\, \rho \wedge \rho \,|\, \rho \to \rho \,|\, \rho \leftrightarrow \rho \,|\, \langle\pi\rangle\rho$, for $p \in \text{Prop}$ and $\pi \in \text{Prg}(\Pi)$.

Semantics. The semantic domain is the set of all fuzzy multirelations over a set of states W, denoted by $M(W)$, and the operations given in Definition 4.

$\mathcal{GCDL}(\mathbf{A})$-models for a signature (Π, Prop) are tuples $M = (W, V, [\![-]\!])$ where W is a set of states, V is a valuation function $V : \text{Prop} \times W \to A$ and $[\![-]\!]$ attributes a fuzzy multirelation $R \subseteq W \times A^W$ to each atomic program.

The interpretation of a program $\pi \in Prg(\Pi)$ in a model M is recursively defined as:

$$[\![\pi;\pi']\!] = [\![\pi]\!] \cdot [\![\pi']\!],\ [\![\pi \cap \pi']\!] = [\![\pi]\!] \cap [\![\pi']\!],\ [\![\pi + \pi']\!] = [\![\pi]\!] \cup [\![\pi']\!] \text{ and } [\![\pi^*]\!] = [\![\pi]\!]^*.$$

The satisfaction relation for a model $M = (W, V, [\![-]\!])$ is given by the valuation function $\models_{\mathcal{GCDL}}: W \times \text{Fm}^{\Gamma(\mathbf{A})}(\Pi, \text{Prop}) \to A$ recursively defined as:

- $(w \models_{\mathcal{GCDL}} \top) = \bot$
- $(w \models_{\mathcal{GCDL}} \bot) = \top$
- $(w \models_{\mathcal{GCDL}} p) = V(p, w)$, for any $p \in \text{Prop}$
- $(w \models_{\mathcal{GCDL}} \rho \wedge \rho') = (w \models_{\mathcal{GCDL}} \rho) \cdot (w \models_{\mathcal{GCDL}} \rho')$
- $(w \models_{\mathcal{GCDL}} \rho \vee \rho') = (w \models_{\mathcal{GCDL}} \rho) + (w \models_{\mathcal{GCDL}} \rho')$
- $(w \models_{\mathcal{GCDL}} \rho \to \rho') = (w \models_{\mathcal{GCDL}} \rho) \to (w \models_{\mathcal{GCDL}} \rho')$
- $(w \models_{\mathcal{GCDL}} \rho \leftrightarrow \rho') = (w \models_{\mathcal{GCDL}} \rho \to \rho'); (w \models_{\mathcal{GCDL}} \rho' \to \rho)$
- $(w \models_{\mathcal{GCDL}} \langle\pi\rangle\rho) = \sum_{\phi|(w,\phi)\in[\![\pi]\!]} \left(\prod_{u \in U} (\phi(u); (u \models_{\mathcal{GCDL}} \rho)) \right)$

– $(w \models_{\mathcal{GCDL}} [\pi]\rho) = \prod_{\phi|(w,\phi)\in[\![\pi]\!]} \left(\prod_{u\in U} (\phi(u) \rightarrow (u \models_{\mathcal{GCDL}} \rho))\right)$

where $U \subseteq W$. We say that ρ is *valid* when, for any model M, and for each state $w \in W$, $(w \models_{\mathcal{GCDL}} \rho) = \top$.

The (graded) satisfaction of $(w \models_{\mathcal{GCDL}} \langle\pi\rangle\rho)$ is given by the weight of some fuzzy set ϕ which is related to state w by some fuzzy multirelation, and the weight of ρ for every state in the domain of ϕ.

As mentioned in Sect. 2, the axiomatisation of CPDL was presented as that of PDL, except for one axiom restricted to atomic programs, plus an additional axiom for concurrency. Below we study such an axiomatisation in the models of $\mathcal{GCDL}(\mathbf{A})$. First, Lemma 1 provides some auxiliary properties used to prove next lemma.

Lemma 1. *Let $\mathcal{A}$ be a complete $\mathbb{I}$-action lattice. Then*

(1.1) $(w \models_{\mathcal{GCDL}} \rho \rightarrow \rho') = \top$ *iff* $(w \models_{\mathcal{GCDL}} \rho) \leq (w \models_{\mathcal{GCDL}} \rho')$
(1.2) $(w \models_{\mathcal{GCDL}} \rho \leftrightarrow \rho') = \top$ *iff* $(w \models_{\mathcal{GCDL}} \rho) = (w \models_{\mathcal{GCDL}} \rho')$

Proof. Analogous to [15]. □

Lemma 2. *Let* **A** *be a a complete $\mathbb{I}$-action lattice. The following are valid formulæ in any $\mathcal{GCDL}(\mathbf{A})$:*

(2.1) $\langle\pi_0\rangle(\rho \vee \rho') \leftrightarrow \langle\pi_0\rangle\rho \vee \langle\pi_0\rangle\rho'$
(2.2) $\langle\pi\rangle(\rho \wedge \rho') \rightarrow \langle\pi\rangle\rho \wedge \langle\pi\rangle\rho'$
(2.3) $\langle\pi + \pi'\rangle\rho \leftrightarrow \langle\pi\rangle\rho \vee \langle\pi\rangle\rho$
(2.4) $\langle\pi\rangle\bot \leftrightarrow \bot$
(2.5) $\langle\pi \cap \pi'\rangle\rho \leftrightarrow \langle\pi\rangle\rho \wedge \langle\pi'\rangle\rho$
(2.6) $[\pi + \pi']\rho \leftrightarrow [\pi]\rho \wedge [\pi']\rho$
(2.7) $[\pi](\rho \wedge \rho') \rightarrow [\pi]\rho \wedge [\pi]\rho'$

Proof. The proof uses the definition of the satisfaction relation $\models_{\mathcal{GCDL}}$ and some axioms and properties of action lattices. The technical details are documented in the extended version of this article [8]. □

4 Conclusion

We took, in this paper, the first step in order to develop a rigorous and systematic formalism for the verification of weighted concurrent systems, motivated by the behaviour of programs in the fuzzy computational paradigm. The approach is based on the combination of some ideas from previous research [9,16,20] to characterise both the computational and logical settings on top of which a proper (axiomatic, denotational and operational) semantics for fuzzy programs will be developed, in future work.

There are numerous research lines left open and worth to pursue in the near future. The most obvious one is the study of a proper complete axiomatisation for the generated logics. In particular, the validity of the remaining axioms of CPDL, namely the ones involving operators ; and *, needs to be analysed in the models of the logic. Another prominent path to follow is the study of the relationships between PDL, CPDL and their graded variants. In one direction, we propose to investigate whether CPDL can be obtained from $\mathcal{GCDL}(\mathbf{A})$ by taking **2** as parameter. Another one would be to study if there is a way to obtain $\mathcal{GDL}(\mathbf{A})$ as special case of $\mathcal{GCDL}(\mathbf{A})$, such that there is a correspondence between the operations on fuzzy multirelations and operations on matrices. Additionally, relevant results about decidability and complexity of the logics are naturally in our agenda.

Although we based our definition of sequential composition for fuzzy multirelations in Peleg's definition [6], there are other versions of the operator in the literature. One of them corresponds to the definition introduced for giving semantics to Parikh's game logic [19]

$$R \cdot S = \left\{(a, A) \mid \exists B.(a, B) \in R \wedge (\forall b \in B.(b, A) \in S)\right\}$$

It is clearly stronger than Peleg's, since it requires that every intermediate state b must be related with the arriving set of states A. Another one, the Kleisli composition, was later studied in [6], and is motivated by the Kleisli composition of the powerset monad.

Finally, we propose to adapt the models of the generated logics in order to capture the introduction of assignments of variables to values in a given data domain. The goal is to develop (parametric) dynamic logics for the verification of programs written in a fuzzy imperative programming language, such as [23] or [2].

References

1. Baltag, A., Smets, S.: The dynamic turn in quantum logic. Synthese **186**(3), 753–773 (2012)
2. Cingolani, P., Alcalá-Fdez, J.: jFuzzylogic: a Java library to design fuzzy logic controllers according to the standard for fuzzy control programming. Int. J. Comput. Intell. Syst. **6**(sup1), 61–75 (2013)
3. Conway, J.: Regular Algebra and Finite Machines. Dover Publications, New York (1971)
4. den Hartog, J., de Vink, E.P.: Verifying probabilistic programs using a Hoare like logic. Int. J. Found. Comput. Sci. **13**(3), 315–340 (2002)
5. den Hartog, J.I.: Probabilistic extensions of semantical models. Ph.D. thesis, Vrije Universiteit, Vrije (2002)
6. Furusawa, H., Kawahara, Y., Struth, G., Tsumagari, N.: Kleisli, Parikh and Peleg compositions and liftings for multirelations. J. Log. Algebraic Methods Program. **90**, 84–101 (2017)
7. Furusawa, H., Struth, G.: Taming multirelations. ACM Trans. Comput. Log. **17**(4), 28:1–28:34 (2016)
8. Gomes, L.: On the construction of multi-valued concurrent dynamic logic. CoRR abs/1911.00462 (2019)
9. Gomes, L., Madeira, A., Barbosa, L.S.: Generalising KAT to verify weighted computations. CoRR abs/1911.01146 (2019)

10. Hoare, C.A.R.T., Möller, B., Struth, G., Wehrman, I.: Concurrent Kleene algebra. In: Bravetti, M., Zavattaro, G. (eds.) CONCUR 2009. LNCS, vol. 5710, pp. 399–414. Springer, Heidelberg (2009). https://doi.org/10.1007/978-3-642-04081-8_27
11. Jipsen, P., Moshier, M.A.: Concurrent Kleene algebra with tests and branching automata. J. Log. Algebraic Method Program. **85**(4), 637–652 (2016)
12. Kozen, D.: A probabilistic PDL. J. Comput. Syst. Sci. **30**(2), 162–178 (1985)
13. Kozen, D.: On action algebras. In: Logic and the Flow of Information, Amsterdam (1993)
14. Kozen, D.: A completeness theorem for Kleene algebras and the algebra of regular events. Inf. Comput. **110**, 366–390 (1994)
15. Madeira, A., Neves, R., Martins, M.A.: An exercise on the generation of many-valued dynamic logics. JLAMP **1**, 1–29 (2016)
16. Madeira, A., Neves, R., Martins, M.A., Barbosa, L.S.: A dynamic logic for every season. In: Braga, C., Martí-Oliet, N. (eds.) SBMF 2014. LNCS, vol. 8941, pp. 130–145. Springer, Cham (2015). https://doi.org/10.1007/978-3-319-15075-8_9
17. Martin, C.E., Curtis, S.A., Rewitzky, I.: Modelling angelic and demonic nondeterminism with multirelations. Sci. Comput. Program. **65**(2), 140–158 (2007)
18. McIver, A., Rabehaja, T., Struth, G.: An event structure model for probabilistic concurrent Kleene algebra. In: McMillan, K., Middeldorp, A., Voronkov, A. (eds.) LPAR 2013. LNCS, vol. 8312, pp. 653–667. Springer, Heidelberg (2013). https://doi.org/10.1007/978-3-642-45221-5_43
19. Parikh, R.: Propositional game logic. In: 24th Annual Symposium on Foundations of Computer Science, pp. 195–200. IEEE Computer Society (1983)
20. Peleg, D.: Concurrent dynamic logic. J. ACM **34**(2), 450–479 (1987)
21. Platzer, A.: Logical Analysis of Hybrid Systems - Proving Theorems for Complex Dynamics. Springer, Heidelberg (2010). https://doi.org/10.1007/978-3-642-14509-4
22. Qiao, R., Wu, J., Wang, Y., Gao, X.: Operational semantics of probabilistic Kleene algebra with tests. In: Proceedings - IEEE Symposium on Computers and Communications, pp. 706–713 (2008)
23. Vetterlein, T., Mandl, H., Adlassnig, K.: Fuzzy arden syntax: a fuzzy programming language for medicine. Artif. Intell. Med. **49**(1), 1–10 (2010)
24. Zadeh, L.: Fuzzy sets. Inf. Control **8**(3), 338–353 (1965)

Author Index

Printed in the United States
By Bookmasters

Printed in the United States
By Bookmasters